A PRACTICAL GERMAN REVIEW GRAMMAR

The Municipal Theater in Muenster, Germany. To the right is one wall of
the ruined Romberger Hof, left standing in memory of World War II.
Ruhnau, Deilmann, Rave, and Von Hausen, architects. (Koschinski—German
Information Center)

A PRACTICAL
GERMAN REVIEW
GRAMMAR

Emory E. Cochran, Ph.D.

Former Head of the German Department,
Tulsa University;
Former faculty member of New York University
and Fort Hamilton High School,
New York City

SECOND EDITION

ENGLEWOOD CLIFFS, N.J.
Prentice-Hall, Inc.

PRENTICE-HALL INTERNATIONAL, INC., LONDON
PRENTICE-HALL OF AUSTRALIA, PTY., LTD., SYDNEY
PRENTICE-HALL OF CANADA, LTD., TORONTO
PRENTICE-HALL OF INDIA (PRIVATE) LTD., NEW DELHI
PRENTICE-HALL OF JAPAN, INC., TOKYO

Current printing (last digit):

15   14   13   12   11   10   9   8

Library of Congress Catalog Card No.   63–7775

PRINTED IN THE UNITED STATES OF AMERICA   69070–C

PREFACE

This text is intended primarily for those students who have already studied the essentials of German grammar. The year or term in which it may be used to best advantage depends, therefore, upon the amount of grammar previously covered.

While to some teachers the first two chapters may seem rather elementary for a *review* grammar, it is the author's firm conviction that failure to understand the fundamental principles of case and tense is one of the chief stumbling blocks to students of modern languages. Failure to understand and master these points in the lower classes of language study often hampers students in the more advanced courses.

In this edition an effort has been made to meet the varying needs of class members. It is believed that the usefulness of the grammar is increased considerably by the addition of exercises making use of simple scientific terms which are rapidly becoming a part of everyday vocabulary. The book, of course, makes no claim to be a scientific-German text. The sprinkling of sentences containing technical or semi-technical terms serves merely to whet the appetite of students who are, or may become, interested in science.

This edition has been revised in other ways too. In the presentation of grammatical material some sentences have been clarified, some have been added, and a few have been omitted; the German-English and English-German vocabularies contain words that appear for the first time in this edition; the Index has been brought up to date to include the various changes; and the German poems and Lieder are supplemented with more modern selections.

The outstanding features of the book are:

(1) *A wealth of ample material making various language skills more readily attainable.*   The illustrative sentences and abundant exercises are of such a practical nature that they may even be used for *conversation*, supplemented, if possible, by films and tape recordings in German.   The book is invaluable when used intelligently in conjunction with well-graded reading texts suitable to the needs of the class.   Certain sections (notably § 49) were written expressly to enable students to develop *reading* facility. All students, but particularly those who wish to acquire a scientific vocabulary, should study Chapter 26 on word formation.   By breaking up a long German word it will be possible to grasp the meaning, usually without the aid of a dictionary.   Skill in *writing*, which gives students opportunity for self-expression, should result from the proper use of comprehensive exercises.   Writing also tends to fix expression and vocabulary encountered in reading, conversation, and audio-visual material. The author assumes that teachers will refer students to relevant sections of the grammar when the need arises, and that students themselves will soon learn to use the book independently when certain constructions are met with in the course of reading or elsewhere.   Specific application of grammatical principles will often clarify a particular construction more satisfactorily than its single occurrence in a reading lesson.

(2) *The subordination of rare to common usage.*   In line with the latest pedagogical procedure, rules are subordinated to live examples.   Illustrations are up-to-date; for example, the use of modal auxiliaries used with dependent passive forms is illustrated by:

> Das Radarsignal konnte sofort identifiziert werden.
> *The radar signal could be identified at once.*

Or, to show that the present active infinitive in German is used for the English passive:

> Er ist telefonisch nicht zu erreichen.
> *He cannot be reached by telephone.*

The author does not hesitate to state that the "future perfect tense *in its literal sense* is as rare in German as it is in English."   On the other hand, a fairly common use of this tense to denote past probability is exemplified in such a sentence as:

> Er wird wohl zu viel gegessen haben.
> *He probably ate too much.*

(3) *Concise summaries following illustrative sentences.* Students should be encouraged to formulate their own summaries of "high points" after reading the illustrative sentences.

(4) *Additional notes and cautions supplementing summaries.*

(5) *Abundant exercises at the end of each lesson.* Extensive drill enables a student to clinch points set forth in each lesson. Moreover, exercises in subsequent lessons afford him further opportunity to apply newly learned principles. The author does not expect teachers to use *all* exercises in *all* lessons but to select material appropriate to the needs of a particular class.

(6) *Successful classroom use.* The book is based on actual classroom teaching and is not a theoretical presentation of German grammar. Its point of view is that of a non-German student facing the idioms, difficulties, and pitfalls of a new language. For example, after learning that geschehen is an impersonal verb meaning *to happen,* an intellectually curious student is entitled to know that such an idea as: *He happened to be at home,* is expressed by: Er war zufällig zu Hause. This and numerous examples of a similar nature are clearly set forth in the body of the grammar.

(7) *Numerous practical idioms included in vocabularies.* Both the German-English and the English-German vocabularies—involving words of common occurrence, although not adhering slavishly to any of the various word-frequency lists—are characterized by numerous idioms of a practical nature. For example, under *make* the student will find the phrases: *to make money, to make up one's mind, to make up work (lessons, etc.), to make a speech, to make one's acquaintance,* and so forth.

(8) *A comprehensive index.* The index with references to the body of the grammar makes the book invaluable as a practical *reference grammar.*

(9) *Lists of useful idioms and classroom expressions.* These lists may be advantageously reviewed in comparatively small assignments.

(10) *The relegation of paradigms to the Appendix.* Paradigms do not clutter up the body of the grammar but appear in the Appendix. Additional sections of the Appendix that enhance the value of the book are: common proverbs; verbs similar in sound and spelling; synonyms, antonyms, and homonyms; German punctuation and capitalization; and German script.

(11) *The Supplement.* A Supplement containing selected poems and Lieder will appeal to students who are interested in German literature.

The author is deeply indebted to the following individuals and organizations for valuable suggestions, assistance, and cooperation in the preparation of this new edition: Professor Albert L. Lloyd, Department of Germanic Languages and Literature, University of Pennsylvania; Professor Frederic C. Tubach, Department of German, University of California, Berkeley; the German Information Center, New York, for the frontispiece; and to the editorial staff of Prentice-Hall, Inc.

Most of all, he is grateful to those of his students who have called attention by their intelligent questions to points of German grammar that puzzle all students of the language. The present volume is, therefore, merely an attempt to answer such questions with pertinent illustrative material.

E. E. C.

NEW YORK CITY

CONTENTS

Fundamental
CHAPTER I **Principles**
# of Case

I. CASE IN ENGLISH

Case shows the relation which a noun or pronoun bears to other words in a sentence. This relation is indicated in English by three cases: **nominative, possessive,** and **objective.**

A. The nominative case. This case has four common uses:

(1) As subject of a verb: *My friend is at home.*

(2) As predicate noun: *He is my friend.*

(3) As noun of address: *Please visit me, Mr. Smith.*

(4) As appositive referring to a noun or pronoun in the nominative case: *My friend, Mr. Smith, is in the country.*

B. The possessive case. As its name implies, this case denotes ownership. In English, but not in German, an apostrophe indicates the possessive case: *The boy's books are on the table.* Or with a plural possessive: *The boys' books are on the table.*

C. The objective case. The chief uses of this case are:

(1) As direct object of a verb: *He loves his son.*

Note: A transitive verb in the active voice requires a complement, which is called a "direct object." **Only transitive verbs take direct objects.** The complement which must follow such a verb indicates **the recipient of the action.** (In the preceding example the *son* receives his father's love.) Stated differently, a direct object denotes person or thing **acted upon:** *He threw the ball.* Here the ball was the thing acted upon. **A direct object answers the question *what?* or *whom?* after the verb.** Referring to the two examples given above: *Loves whom?* ***The son.*** *Threw what?* ***The ball.*** *Son* and *ball* are, therefore, direct objects.

(2) As indirect object of a verb.

Note: A noun or pronoun denoting the person to or for whom (or the thing to or for which) something is done is called the "indirect object." English usually supplies *to*:

> She gave **the children** the apples.

or: *She gave the apples* **to** *the children.*

In the first sentence *children* is the indirect object; *apples*, the direct object.

> She showed **me** the pictures.

or: *She showed the pictures to me.*

In the first sentence *me* is the indirect object; *pictures*, the direct object.

(3) As object of a preposition: *They ran after* **him.**

(4) As appositive referring to a noun or pronoun in the objective case: *I visited Mr. Mueller,* **our lawyer.**

2. CASE IN GERMAN

There are four cases in German: **nominative, genitive, dative,** and **accusative.** One must distinguish carefully between transitive (*cf.* § 1 **C** (1) above) and intransitive verbs. **Most** verbs that are transitive in English are also transitive in German. An intransitive verb—*e.g.*, sein, *to be*, and gehen, *to go*—is one that cannot take a direct object.

A. The nominative case. The use of the German nominative corresponds to that of the English:

(1) As subject of a verb:

> **Mein Freund** ist nicht zu Hause.
> *My friend is not at home.*

> **Das Kind** wird müde.
> *The child is getting tired.*

> **Die Frau** schreibt einen Brief.
> *The woman is writing a letter.*

> **Die Männer** arbeiten schwer.
> *The men are working hard.*

> **Der Raumflug** war erfolgreich.
> *The space flight was successful.*

(2) As predicate noun:

Er ist **mein Freund.**　　　　　Er wurde **mein Freund.**
He is my friend.　　　　　　　*He became my friend.*

(3) As noun of address:

Bitte, besuchen Sie mich, **Herr Müller!**
Please visit me, Mr. Mueller.

(4) As appositive with a noun or pronoun in the nominative case:

Mein Freund, **Herr Wagner,** ist auf dem Lande.
My friend, Mr. Wagner, is in the country.

Note: Intransitive verbs cannot be followed by an accusative object:

Er ist **mein Bruder** (nom.).
He is my brother.

B. The genitive case. The genitive corresponds to the English possessive case or to the objective case preceded by *of* to denote possession:

Die Eltern **jener Kinder** sind sehr arm.
The parents of those children are very poor.

Die Federn **des Jungen** liegen auf dem Tisch.
The boy's pens are (lying) on the table.

pl.　　Die Federn **der Jungen** liegen auf dem Tisch.
The boys' pens are (lying) on the table.

Die Kinder **der Frau** spielen Ball.
The woman's children are playing ball.

Der Bruder **des Mädchens** ist in der Schule.
The girl's brother is in school.

Note:

(1) **German does not use an apostrophe** to denote the genitive case except for words ending in an **s**-sound, in which case an **s** is not added:

Voß' Werke, *the works of Voss*
but: **Goethes** Werke, *Goethe's works*

(2) In German the genitive usually follows the noun to which it refers; the genitive of proper nouns, however, ordinarily precedes the noun (*cf.* **Note** (1) above).

Caution: Possessive adjectives and pronouns must not be confused with the possessive (*i.e.,* German genitive) case:

> **Seine** Feder liegt auf dem Tisch.
> *His pen is on the table.*

Seine is **nominative** singular to agree with the word Feder, which it modifies; it is feminine for the same reason. Students of Latin should take special note of this, since the Latin construction differs from the German.

C. The dative case. The dative is regularly used as the case of the indirect object (*cf.* § 1 **C** (2) above):

(1) Er hat **den Kindern** die Äpfel gegeben.
> *He gave the children the apples.*

or: > *He gave the apples to the children.*

> Sie zeigte **dem Manne** das Bild.
> *She showed the man the picture.*

> Ich werde **der Dame** das Buch geben.
> *I shall give the lady the book.*

> Ich werde es **ihr** geben.
> *I shall give it to her.*

Note: The last two sentences indicate that **if the direct object is a noun, the dative precedes the accusative; if the direct object is a personal pronoun, the accusative precedes the dative.**

(2) An appositive, as always, must agree in case with the noun to which it refers:

> Ich werde meinem Freunde, **dem Advokaten,** die Bücher geben.
> *I shall give the books to my friend, the lawyer.*

Note: The dative, as its name implies (Latin **dare, datus,** *to give*), is the case of **giving**—although it has many other uses. **The person to whom** a thing is given is in the dative case; **the thing** given, in the accusative.

D. The accusative case. The accusative is the case of the direct object. Remember that only transitive verbs take direct objects; (*cf.* § 1 **C** (1) above):

Er liebt **seinen Sohn.**   Ich habe **Sie** nicht gehört.
He loves his son.   *I did not hear you.*

Er wird **das Gedicht** lesen.   Wir lieben **unsere Freunde.**
He will read the poem.   *We love our friends.*

Der Sohn besucht **seine Tante.**
The son is visiting his aunt.

E. Other uses of the genitive, dative, and accusative cases.
The genitive, dative, and accusative cases have other important uses—*e.g.*,
with prepositions, adjectives, special verbs, *etc.*—which subsequent
chapters explain in detail.   Preceding examples have shown the functions
of the English "objective" case to be divided among the genitive, dative
and accusative cases in German.[1]

EXERCISE

A. Complete the following sentences:

1. Er liest d— Satz.
2. Sie ist mein— Freundin.
3. Er besuchte d— Großvater.
4. Ich werde d— Mann etwas Geld geben.
5. Wir haben d— Geschichte noch nicht gelesen.
6. D— Eltern hatten d— Kind auf der Straße gesehen.
7. Er gibt d— Frau— (*pl.*) d— Bücher.
8. Haben Sie d— Kinder gehört?
9. Sie zeigte d— Vater d— Bild.
10. Wo ist d— Mutter d— Mädchen— (*sing.*)?
11. Sie wird d— Mädchen (*pl.*) d— Blumen geben.
12. D— Arzt war gestern auf dem Lande.
13. Wer ist d— Lehrer d— Jung— (*sing.*)?
14. D— Schloß liegt am Rhein.
15. Wie heißen d— Kinder d— Frau?
16. D— Häuser sind sehr alt.
17. Wo sind d— Kleider d— Schüler?
18. Ich hatte mein— Freund, d—Zahnarzt, ein— Brief geschrieben.
19. Schreiben Sie mi— bald, — (*Mr.*) Müller!
20. Haben Sie d— Rhein gesehen?

---

[1] For the declension of articles and nouns, *cf.* §§ 93, 95, and 98 of the Appendix.

21. Die Forscher beschrieben d— Raumflug.
22. Man hat d— Flieger große Ehre erwiesen.

B.   Rewrite in the plural sentences 1, 2, 4, 10, and 13 of **A** above.

Remember:
(*a*) The English possessive becomes the German **genitive.**
(*b*) The English indirect object becomes the German **dative.**
(*c*) The English direct object becomes the German **accusative.**

C.   Translate the following sentences into German:

1. She loves her brother.
2. The children were visiting their parents.
3. He gave the woman some money.
4. Did you see the boy?
5. She showed the man the watch.
6. He will close the door.
7. The children had shown their parents the pictures.
8. The girl's flowers are beautiful.
9. He gave the horse something to eat.
10. My brother's books are on the table.
11. That village is in Germany.
12. His sister's friends are in the country.
13. He is my friend.
14. The children's parents were poor.
15. Please write me a letter, Mr. Brown.
16. He will visit his friend, the lawyer.
17. Where are your pens?
18. She had shown her brother the flowers.
19. He has given his sister the pencil.
20. The father's watch is on the table.
21. They will show the flyer great honor.
22. Modern scientists are making discoveries of great importance.

D.   Rewrite in the plural sentences 1, 4, **5,** 6, 9, 11, 13, 16, and 19 of **C** above.

CHAPTER 2 **Fundamental Principles of Tense**[1]

3. TENSE IN ENGLISH

A verb—*e.g.*, *write, wrote, written*—has six tenses. The following sentences illustrate the use of these tenses:

A. Present: *I write the letter.* *I am writing the letter.* *I do write the letter.*

Note: These three sentences all refer to the present time. The second sentence illustrates the "progressive" form; the third, the "emphatic" form.

B. Past: *I wrote the letter.* *I was writing the letter.* *I did write the letter.*

Note: There are three forms of the English past tense, just as there are three of the present; *was writing* is simply the past of *am writing*, and *did write* the past of *do write*.

C. Present Perfect: *I have written the letter.*

D. Past Perfect: *I had written the letter.*

E. Future: *I shall write the letter.*

F. Future Perfect: *I shall have written the letter.*

---

[1] Only the fundamental and nonidiomatic principles of tense are explained in this chapter. The explanation is confined to tenses of the indicative mood. (Special uses of tense, the passive voice, and the subjunctive are discussed in subsequent chapters.)

4. TENSE IN GERMAN

A German verb—*e.g.*, schreiben, schrieb, hat geschrieben, *to write*—also has six tenses. These, however, may have names different from those to which they correspond in English:

A. Present:
> **Ich schreibe** den Brief.
> *I write the letter.*
> *I am writing the letter.*
> *I do write the letter.*

B. Past (or Imperfect):
> **Ich schrieb** den Brief.
> *I wrote the letter.*
> *I was writing the letter.*
> *I did write the letter.*[1]

C. Perfect (or Present Perfect):
> **Ich habe** den Brief **geschrieben.**
> *I have written the letter.*
> *I wrote the letter.*
> *I did write the letter.*

D. Past Perfect (or Pluperfect):
> **Ich hatte** den Brief **geschrieben.**
> *I had written the letter.*

E. Future:
> **Ich werde** den Brief **schreiben.**
> *I shall write the letter.*

F. Future Perfect:
> **Ich werde** den Brief **geschrieben haben.**
> *I shall have written the letter.*

5. COMPARISON OF ENGLISH AND GERMAN TENSES

A. The following diagram shows the correspondence between German and English tenses:[2]

---

[1] The **Perfect** is more usual in this instance.
[2] For the complete conjugation of verbs, *cf.* §§ 102–110 of the Appendix.

ENGLISH	GERMAN	
I write *I am writing* *I do write*	ich schreibe	PRESENT
I wrote *I was writing*	ich schrieb	PAST
I have written *I wrote* *I did write*	ich habe geschrieben	PERFECT
I had written	ich hatte geschrieben	PAST PERFECT
I shall write	ich werde schreiben	FUTURE
I shall have written	ich werde geschrieben haben	FUTURE PERFECT

Note:

(1) In German there are no progressive forms (*i.e.*, *am, are, is, was*, and *were* followed by the present participle ending in *-ing*), nor does German have any emphatic forms with *do, does,* and *did.* The English present tense can be translated, therefore, in one way only: *he is playing, he does play,* and *he plays* are all er spielt.

(2) Since there are no progressive forms in German, *was* or *were* followed by the present participle ending in *-ing* must become the past tense: *he was writing,* er schrieb; *they were playing,* sie spielten.[1]

(3) (*a*) The English past tense—*e.g., he wrote*—is sometimes translated by the German perfect and sometimes by the German past. Figuratively expressed, the German perfect may be described as giving a **snapshot**, whereas the past gives a **motion picture** of a past action.

(*b*) In conversation the perfect is ordinarily used when referring to **a single event** that has taken place.

We saw *the children yesterday.*
Gestern **haben wir** die Kinder **gesehen.**
*When **did you see** them?*
Wann **haben Sie** sie **gesehen?**[2]

---

[1] The present participle used as adjective must not be confused with the progressive forms:

    Sie ist reizend.   Sie war reizend.
    She is charming.   *She was charming.*

[2] *Cf.* § 17 for the use of **haben** and **sein** as auxiliaries of the perfect tenses.

(*c*) The past is regularly used to express two or more acts that occurred at the same time in the past:

Er **spielte** Ball, während der Bruder einen Spaziergang **machte.**
*He **played** ball, while his brother **took** a walk.*

(*d*) In both the spoken and written language, the past is regularly used for narrating and describing past events, especially when such events are related as **a chain of facts:**

Er kam, er sah, er siegte.
He came, he saw, he conquered.

Die Mutter ging in die Stadt, kaufte sich einen neuen Hut und kam um vier Uhr nach Hause.
Mother went to the city, bought (herself) a new hat, and came home at four o'clock.

(4)   The German past perfect corresponds in use and meaning to the English past perfect:

Wir hatten ihn schon **besucht.**
*We **had** already **visited** him.*

(5)   The future tense is used chiefly as in English:

Morgen **wird** mein Freund **ankommen.**
*My friend **will arrive** tomorrow.*

(6)   The future perfect tense in its literal sense is as rare in German as it is in English:

Er wird das Buch **gelesen haben.**
*He **will have read** the book.*

Remember: **Werden** is the auxiliary of future and future perfect tenses.

B.   The exercises at the end of this chapter make use of the following verbs:

schreiben, schrieb, hat geschrieben, *to write*
lesen, las, hat gelesen, *to read*
ankommen, kam an, ist angekommen, *to arrive*
besuchen, besuchte, hat besucht, *to visit*
kommen, kam, ist gekommen, *to come*

sehen, sah, hat gesehen, *to see*
spielen, spielte, hat gespielt, *to play*
gehen, ging, ist gegangen, *to go*
sein, war, ist gewesen, *to be*
leben, lebte, hat gelebt, *to live*
machen, machte, hat gemacht, *to make*
erfahren, erfuhr, hat erfahren, *to learn*

Remember:

(1) *Am, are,* or *is* plus a verbal form ending in *-ing* is **present.**
(2) *Was* or *were* plus a verbal form ending in *-ing* is **past.**
(3) *Have* or *has* plus a past participle is **perfect.**
(4) *Had* plus a past participle is **past perfect.**
(5) *Shall* or *will* plus an infinitive is **future.**

EXERCISE

A. Complete the following sentences:

1. Mein Bruder —— das Buch —— (*has read*).
2. —— er einen Brief —— (*Will write*)?
3. Er —— (*is visiting*) den Vater.
4. Was —— er —— (*had seen*)?
5. Er —— (*was playing*) Ball auf der Straße.
6. Ich —— meinen Freund —— (*shall visit*).
7. Wann —— Sie —— (*did arrive*)?
8. Das Kind —— (*is playing*) mit dem Hund.
9. Gestern —— ich den Knaben —— (*saw*).
10. Mein Freund —— um zwei Uhr in Berlin —— (*had arrived*).
11. Ich —— (*was reading*) eine interessante Geschichte.
12. Heute —— er seine Mutter —— (*visited*).
13. Die Kinder —— (*are playing*) Ball.
14. Karl —— (*was writing*) den Satz.
15. Er —— ihn —— (*will have visited*).
16. Ich —— (*went*) in die Stadt, —— (*visited*) meinen Freund und ——(*came*) um elf Uhr nach Hause.
17. Gestern —— er seinen Freund —— (*visited*).
18. Heute —— er um acht Uhr nach Hause —— (*came*).
19. Tiere —— (*were*) in den ersten Raumkapseln.
20. Wir —— (*are living*) in dem atomischen Zeitalter.

B. Translate:

1. He had written a letter.
2. Have you read it?
3. When will your friend arrive?
4. He was visiting his father.
5. The boy is playing ball.
6. She was coming home.
7. Have you seen her?
8. They had never visited me.
9. Carl is writing the sentence.
10. When will they read the book?
11. My sister was playing the (*omit*) piano.
12. He is visiting his parents.
13. Have they arrived?
14. Had they visited him?
15. He will have read the story.
16. He was reading a poem.
17. She is arriving early.
18. He will come home late.
19. They were visiting their friends.
20. He had never read the poem.
21. He went to the country, played ball, and came home tired.
22. She went to the city, visited a friend, and came home at ten o'clock.
23. Yesterday he played ball.
24. Today she visited her uncle.
25. Many scientists will make space flights.
26. They have already learned much about world-space radiation (*or* cosmic radiation).

C. For additional practice, translate sentences 6, 7, 9–11, and 14–30 in § 43 **B.**

Uses of the Definite

CHAPTER 3 **and**

Indefinite Articles

6. USES OF THE DEFINITE ARTICLE DER AND THE INDEFINITE ARTICLE EIN

Read the following sentences carefully. Note how the German and English sentences often differ with regard to the use of the articles:[1]

A. (1) Mein Bruder ist in **der** Schweiz. Er war in **der** Türkei.
   My brother is in Switzerland.   *He was in Turkey.*

   Seine Schwester ist in **der** Tschechoslowakei.
   His sister is in Czechoslovakia.

(2) Mein Vetter ist in **den** Niederlanden.
   My cousin (masc.) *is in the Netherlands.*

   Meine Cousine ist in **den** Vereinigten Staaten.
   My cousin (fem.) *is in the United States.*

(3) Waren Sie je in Deutschland, Frankreich, Spanien oder Kanada?
   Were you ever in Germany, France, Spain, or Canada?

B. Er setzt (sich) **den** Hut auf.   Was hat sie in **der** Hand?
   *He puts **his** hat on.*   *What has she in **her** hand?*

   Was haben Sie in **der** Tasche?
   *What have you in **your** pocket?*

C. **Der** Frühling ist gekommen.
   Spring is here.

   Im Juli und **im** August haben die Schüler Ferien.
   In July and August the pupils have vacation.

---

[1] For list of contractions of the definite article with various prepositions, *cf.* § 31 **A,** *Cf.* § 93 of the Appendix for the declension of **der,** and § 95 for the declension of **ein.**

Am Samstag haben wir keine Schule.
We have no school on Saturday(s).

D. Er ist in **der** Schule.   Sie ist in **der** Kirche.
       He is in school.   *She is in church.*

       Er geht in **die** Schule.   Sie geht in **die** Kirche.
       He goes to school.   *She goes to church.*

                    Nach **der** Schule spielt er Ball.
                    After school he plays ball.

E. Ich besuche ihn zweimal **die** Woche.   Es kostet zwei Mark **das**
       *I visit him twice **a** week.*   Pfund.
                                                      *It costs two marks **a** pound.*

F. Er wohnt in **der** Friedrichstraße.
       He lives in Frederick Street.

G. **Das** Leben ist kurz.   **Der** Mensch ist sterblich.
       Life is short.   *Man is mortal.*

but:

       Not bricht Eisen.   Müßiggang ist aller Laster
       Necessity knows no law.   Anfang.
                                                      Idleness is the root of all evil.

H. **Das** Schreiben ist schwer.
       Writing is difficult.

I. Der Hund und **die** Katze sind Haustiere.
       The dog and cat are domestic animals.

       Der Vater und **die** Mutter sind nicht zu Hause.
       Father and mother are not at home.

J. (1) Sein Vetter ist Arzt.   (2) Er ist **ein guter** Arzt.
           *His cousin is **a** physician.*   *He is a good physician.*

K. Wir haben Kaffee und Brötchen zu**m** Frühstück.
       *We have coffee and rolls **for** breakfast.*

       Das Mittagessen ist fertig.
       Dinner is ready.

       Nach **dem** Abendessen haben wir die Zeitung gelesen.
       After supper we read the newspaper.

Er hat mich zu**m** Abendbrot (= Abendessen) eingeladen.
*He invited me **for** supper.*

Man hat zu**m** Frühstück geläutet.
The breakfast bell rang.
or: *They rang the bell **for** breakfast.*

Vor **dem** Frühstück machte ich einen Spaziergang.
Before breakfast I took a walk.

L.   **Die** meisten Schüler lesen Geschichten gern.
Most pupils like to read stories.

M.   In **der** Regel bleibt er vormittags zu Hause.
*As **a** rule he stays at home in the forenoon.*

Zu**r** Abwechs(e)lung gehen wir an den Strand, anstatt in die Berge.
*For **a** change we are going to the beach instead of to the mountains.*

Er wurde krank und verlor zu**r** Folge seine Stellung.
*He became ill and as **a** result lost his position.*

N.   (1) **Welch ein** Erfolg!   **Welch ein** Gebäude!
      ***What a** success!*   ***What a** building!*

                Welch eine Stadt!
                ***What a** city!*

    (2) Mit **was für einer** Feder schreiben Sie?
      *With **what kind of** (**a**) pen are you writing?*

          ⎧ **Eine solche** Hitze habe ich nie erlebt.
    (3) ⎨ **Solch eine** Hitze habe ich nie erlebt.
          ⎩ **So eine** Hitze habe ich nie erlebt.

      *I have never experienced **such** (**a**) heat.*

O.   (1) Ich habe hundert (tausend) Bücher gekauft.
      *I bought **a** hundred (thousand) books.*

    (2) Er hat Kopfweh.   Schade!
      *He has **a** headache.*   *That is (or What) **a** pity.*

P.   Man machte ihn zu**m** Führer.
He was made leader.
or: *They made him leader.*

zu**m** Beispiel (abbr. z.B.), *for example* (abbr. *e.g.*)
zu**m** Nachtisch, *for dessert*
zu**m** Schluß, *in conclusion, finally*

zum Teil, *partly, to some extent*
mit **der** Post (Luftpost) schicken, *to send by mail (airmail)*
mit **der** Eisenbahn (Straßenbahn, Untergrundbahn, Hochbahn),
   by rail (street car, subway, elevated railway)
mit **dem** Dampfer, *by steamer*
in **der** Nacht, *at night*
in **der** Tat, *in fact, in reality, indeed*
im Bett, *in bed*
bei**m** Namen nennen, *to call by name*

Q. (1) **Die** kleine Marie spielte mit ihrer Puppe.
   Little Mary was playing with her doll.

Karl **der** Große hat viele Klöster und Schulen bauen lassen.
*Charlemagne (= Charles **the** Great) built many monasteries and schools.*

(2) Voltaire lebte am Hofe Friedrichs **des** Großen.
   *Voltaire lived at the court of Frederick **the** Great.*

König Friedrichs Schloß war in Potsdam.
or: Das Schloß **des** Königs Friedrich war in Potsdam.
   King Frederick's castle was in Potsdam.

Note:

(1) (*a*) The definite article is required with feminine names of countries: die Schweiz, die Türkei, die Tschechoslowakei (*cf.* ¶ **A** (1) above).

(*b*) The definite article is required with plural names of countries: die Vereinigten Staaten, die Niederlande (*cf.* ¶ **A** (2) above).

(*c*) The definite article is not used if the name of a country is neuter. Most countries are neuter: Deutschland, Frankreich, Spanien, England, Kanada (*cf,* ¶ **A** (3) above).

Caution: Such a neuter noun, however, requires the article if it is modified:
   beautiful Germany, **das** schöne Deutschland

(2) The definite article is ordinarily used with parts of the body or articles of clothing, provided there is no doubt as to the possessor. English, however, uses the possessive instead of the article (*cf.* ¶ **B** above).

(3) The definite article is used in German when referring to the seasons, months of the year, and days of the week. In English the article is regularly omitted in such cases (*cf.* ¶ **C** above).

(4) German requires the article, but English omits it in such phrases as: *to go to school, to go to church, to be in school, to be in church,* and *after school* (*cf.* ¶ **D** above).

(5) (*a*) In expressions of price and time, the German idiom requires the definite article where English uses *a* in the sense of per (*cf.* ¶ **E** above).

(*b*) For zweimal die Woche one may also say: zweimal **in der Woche** or zweimal **wöchentlich.**

(6) Contrary to English usage, German often has the definite article with names of streets (*cf.* ¶ **F** above).

Caution: In adverbial expressions, and especially when street and number are given, the article is generally omitted:
Herrn Direktor Büchler, Rastatt, Kehlerstraße 14, Deutschland.

(7) The definite article is frequently used before nouns in general statements. In sentences of a proverbial nature, however, it is often omitted (*cf.* ¶ **G** above).

(8) German infinitives used as nouns are neuter and require the definite article (*cf.* ¶ **H** above).

(9) (*a*) German usage requires the repetition of the definite article in a series of nouns of different gender (*cf.* ¶ **I** above).

(*b*) This same rule applies to the indefinite article, to adjectives, and to possessives:
ein Mann und **eine** Frau, *a man and woman*
guter Wein und **gutes** Bier, *good wine and beer*
mein Vater und **meine** Mutter, *my father and mother*

Caution: The article should be repeated even with nouns of the same gender, if the nouns are contrasted:
der König und der Bauer, *king and peasant*
der Vater und der Sohn, *father and son*

(10) (*a*) The indefinite article is omitted before an **unmodified** predicate noun denoting vocation, rank, or station in life (*cf.* ¶ **J** (1) above):
Er ist Witwer (Soldat).
He is a widower (soldier).

(*b*) If such a noun is modified by an adjective, however, the indefinite article must be used (*cf.* ¶ **J** (2) above).

(11) The German idiom requires the definite article before names of meals (*cf.* ¶ **K** above).

(12) The superlative **meist-** must be preceded by the definite article (*cf.* ¶ **L** above).

(13) Certain phrases which have the **indefinite** article in English require the **definite** article in German.   Memorize these phrases (*cf.* ¶ **M** above).

(14) (*a*) The uninflected form of **welcher** (*i.e.,* **welch**) followed by **ein** (which must agree with the noun it precedes) is particularly common in exclamations (*cf.* ¶ **N** (1) above).

(*b*) **Für,** in the interrogative **was für ein,** lacks the force of a preposition and hence does not determine the case of the following noun (*cf.* ¶ **N** (2) above;   also § 44 **D** and **Note** 6).

(*c*) *Such a* may be translated in three ways: by **solch–** following the indefinite article and declined like an adjective; by **solch** preceding the indefinite article and undeclined; by **so** followed by the indefinite article.   In either case the article is declined regularly (*cf.* ¶ **N** (3) above).

Remember: One may also say: **Solche** Hitze habe ich nie erlebt.   Here the indefinite article disappears from both the English and the German. The plural of **solch–** is **solche**—it being inflected like **dieser** (*cf.* Appendix, § 94):

> **Solche** Menschen gibt es.
> *There are **such** people.*

(15) (*a*) The German equivalent of *a hundred* modifying a noun is simply **hundert.**   Similarly *a thousand* becomes **tausend** (*cf.* ¶ **O** (1) above).[1]

(*b*) Similarly **an** ache merely becomes –**weh** (without the article): **Kopfweh,** (*a*) *headache;* **Magenweh,** (*a*) *stomach ache;* **Halsweh,** (*a*) *sore throat;* **Zahnweh,** (*a*) *toothache;* etc. (*cf.* ¶ **O** (2) above).

(16) Observe the idiom with **machen zu** (and the definite article) and the common phrases with **der,** for which the English equivalents have no article whatever (*cf.* ¶ **P** above).

---

[1] For the use of these words as nouns, *cf.* § 18, **Note** 6.

(17) (*a*) The definite article is commonly used with names of persons, especially if a person has been already mentioned or if his name is modified by an adjective (*cf.* ¶ **Q** (1) above).

(*b*) If a proper name is preceded by a title **without** the definite article, the **name** is declined (*cf.* ¶ **Q** (2) above).

Caution: **Herr** as a title is regularly inflected even when used without the article before a proper name:

> Herr**n** Wagner**s** Hut, *Mr. Wagner's hat*
> ein Brief an Herr**n** Wagner, *a letter to Mr. Wagner*

(*c*) If the definite article is used before a title, the **title** (not the name) is declined (*cf.* ¶ **Q** (2) above).[1]

EXERCISE

A. Complete the following sentences.   In a few cases the sentences are correct without any additional words:

1. Zürich und Luzern sind Städte in —— Schweiz.
2. Letzten Sommer war ich in —— Deutschland.
3. Waren Sie jemals in —— Türkei oder in —— Tschechoslowakei?
4. Letztes Jahr war mein jüngerer Bruder in —— Frankreich.
5. Meine beiden Vettern waren nie in —— Vereinigten Staaten oder in —— Niederlanden.
6. Nächsten Sommer wird er eine Reise in (*to*) —— Schweiz machen.
7. Er ist durch —— Türkei gereist.
8. —— Kunst ist lang, —— Leben kurz.
9. —— Schreiben fällt (*is*) meinem kleinen Bruder schwerer als —— Lesen.
10. Sie setzt sich —— Hut auf.
11. Sie wird sich —— Handschuhe anziehen.
12. Was hat das kleine Mädchen in —— Hand?
13. Er wohnt in —— Kehlerstraße.
14. Dieser faule Junge kommt immer zu spät in —— Schule.
15. Sein älterer Bruder war schon in —— Schule.
16. Nach —— Schule läuft er schnell nach Hause.
17. —— Winter ist gekommen (*is here*).
18. —— (*In*) Winter laufen wir Schlittschuh (*we skate*).

---

[1] For the complete declension of proper nouns, *cf.* Appendix, § 100.

19. —— Juli ist das Wetter oft sehr heiß.
20. —— Montag werde ich ins Theater gehen.
21. Er war nie in —— Schweiz gewesen.
22. Ich besuchte ihn immer dreimal —— Woche.
23. Das Fleisch kostet eine Mark —— Pfund.
24. —— Bruder und —— Schwester waren beide zu Hause.
25. —— Hund und —— Katze sind Haustiere.
26. Ist sein Vater —— Arzt oder —— Advokat?
27. Er ist —— (*a good*) Arzt.
28. —— solch— Gewitter haben wir nie erlebt.
29. Solch —— Gewitter haben wir nie erlebt.
30. Welch— Stadt!
31. Bei— Frühstück (*at breakfast*) liest der Vater immer die Zeitung.
32. Ist —— Abendessen fertig?
33. Heute haben wir Obst —— Frühstück.
34. Nach —— Mittagessen schläft der Großvater zwei Stunden.
35. —— meisten Knaben spielen gern Ball.
36. —— (*As a*) Regel spielt Karl nach —— Schule.
37. Haben Sie —— Kopfweh?
38. Man machte ihn —— Präsidenten.
39. Der Mann war —— (*a hundred*) Jahre alt.
40. Es gibt Bäume in Kalifornien, die —— (*a thousand*) Jahre alt sind.
41. —— klein— Karl wollte seine Aufgaben nicht machen.
42. Karl d— Groß— besiegte die Sachsen (*Saxons*).
43. Als wir in Potsdam waren, sahen wir die Bibliothek Friedrich— d— Groß—.
44. König Friedrich— Schloß hieß Sanssouci.
45. Viele Bekannte d— König— Friedrich waren Künstler.
46. Der Mann ist —— (*a scientist*).
47. Er hat —— (*a*) Raumflug gemacht.

B. Translate into German.   Consider carefully the use of articles.

1. Switzerland is a republic.
2. I was never in Switzerland, but two years ago I was in Germany.
3. Last summer my younger brother was in Turkey and Czechoslovakia.
4. France is a republic but England is a monarchy.
5. Last winter my best friend was in England, France, and Spain.

6. He was never in the Netherlands but he was often in Germany
7. His older sister was never in the United States.
8. Life is short.   Art is long.   Man is mortal.
9. The old lady was putting on her gloves.
10. She had already put on her hat.
11. What has that little boy in his hand?
12. Reading is easier than writing.
13. Summer is here (*i.e.*, has come).   Winter is over (vorüber).
14. In January we usually have cold weather.
15. On Saturday he will play ball.
16. At what time do you go to school?
17. In school we must study hard.
18. After school I usually take a long walk.
19. It costs three marks a pound.
20. My old friend always visits me once a week.
21. His younger brother is a physician.
22. He is a famous physician.
23. What a man!   What a class!   What a building!
24. I never experienced such a storm.
25. Did you ever experience such (a) heat?
26. The horse and cow are domestic animals.
27. " Is he a teacher or a dentist? "   " He is a good dentist."
28. Put on your new hat.
29. Why were those little boys not in school today?
30. Spring is here (*i.e.*, has come) and they are very lazy.
31. Before breakfast I always take a short walk.
32. After supper I read the paper.
33. Is dinner ready?
34. My best friend invited me for supper.
35. As a rule I study in the evening.
36. Most girls like to dance.
37. They (**man**) made him king.
38. Have you a headache?
39. Charlemagne (= Charles the Great) was a famous emperor.
40. The woman is a hundred years old.
41. That tree is a thousand years old.
42. Little Fred is already in bed.
43. What did you have for breakfast this morning?
44. Many artists lived at the court of Frederick the Great.

45. Voltaire was King Frederick's guest.
46. The orator did not speak about cosmic radiation.
47. He was one of the first space travelers.

7. THE POSITION OF NICHT

Read the following sentences carefully and note the position of **nicht**.
Note also how to say *not a, not at all,* and *nothing at all:*

A. Er hat das Buch.   Er hat das Buch **nicht**.
He has the book.   *He does not have the book.*

Er hatte den Bleistift **nicht**.
He did not have the pencil.

B. Sie sieht ihn **nicht** an.   Sie sah ihn **nicht** an.
She does not look at him.   *She did not look at him.*

Sehen Sie ihn **nicht** an !
Do not look at him.

C. Wir werden es ihm **nicht** geben. Wir werden es **nicht** ansehen.
We shall not give it to him.   *We shall not look at it.*

D. Ich habe es ihm **nicht** gegeben. Ich habe es **nicht** angesehen.
I have not given it to him.   *I have not looked at it.*

E. Er ist **nicht** schläfrig.
He is not sleepy.

F. Sie ist **nicht** zu Hause.   Das Kind spielt **nicht** auf der Straße.
She is not at home.   *The child is not playing on the street.*

G. Er ist **nicht** hier.
He is not here.

H. Er ist **nicht** Arzt.
He is not a physician.

I. Sie hat **nicht** die Feder sondern den Bleistift.
She does not have the pen but the pencil.

J. Er versteht es **gar nicht**.   Er hat **gar nichts**.
*He does **not** understand it **at all**.*   *He has **nothing at all**.*

CHAPTER 4

Adjective Declension

8. THE WEAK ADJECTIVE DECLENSION

Read the following sentences very carefully. Note the bold-faced forms:

A. Singular number.

(1) The nominative case:

Der deutsche Rhein entspringt in der Schweiz.
The German Rhine has its source in Switzerland.

Die alte Stadt Heidelberg liegt am Neckar.
The old city of Heidelberg is situated on the Neckar.

Das ganze Land ist kleiner als der Staat Texas.
The whole country is smaller than the state of Texas.

(2) The genitive case:

Der Vater **des** kleinen Jungen ist zu Hause.
The little boy's father is at home.

Die Straßen **der** alten Stadt sind sehr eng.
The streets of the old city are very narrow.

Die Eltern **des** kleinen Kindes sind auf dem Lande.
The little child's parents are in the country.

(3) The dative case:[1]

Er gab **dem** alten Mann ein Buch.
He gave the old man a book.

Ich zeigte **der** guten Frau das Bild.
I showed the good woman the picture.

Sie folgte **dem** kleinen Kinde.
She followed the little child.

---

[1] For a detailed explanation of verbs governing the dative case, *cf.* § 34.

(4) The accusative case:

Sie aß **den** roten Apfel.   Er besuchte **die** alte Dame.
She ate the red apple.   *He visited the old lady.*

Wir kauften **das** große Haus.
We bought the large house.

B. Plural number.

(1) The nominative case:

Die kleinen Bleistifte (Federn, Bücher) liegen auf dem Tisch.
The small pencils (pens, books) are (lying) on the table.

(2) The genitive case:

Die Eltern **der** fleißigen Schüler (Schülerinnen, Kinder) sind
zufrieden.
*The parents of the diligent boy pupils (girl pupils, children) are
satisfied.*

(3) The dative case:

Er wird **den** armen Männern (Frauen, Kindern) helfen.
He will help the poor men (women, children).

(4) The accusative case:

Ich habe **die** alten Bäume (Burgen, Dörfer) gesehen.
I have seen the old trees (castles, villages).

Summary: The above sentences indicate that adjectives after the definite article (**der**) have the ending –**en** in all cases except the nominative singular (all genders) and the accusative singular (feminine and neuter genders). These are the so-called " weak " endings. In the paradigm below, **dieser** stands for **any** " **der**-word " and the ending after the dash, for that of **any** adjective:[1]

	SINGULAR			PLURAL
	MASC.	FEM.	NEUT.	MASC., FEM., NEUT.
Nom.	dieser –**e**	diese –**e**	dieses –**e**	diese –en
Gen.	dieses –en	dieser –en	dieses –en	dieser –en
Dat.	diesem –en	dieser –en	diesem –en	diesen –en
Acc.	diesen –en	diese –**e**	dieses –**e**	diese –en

[1] For further details and illustrations of the weak adjective declension, *cf.* § 99 **B** of the Appendix.

C. The weak adjective declension with other der-words. The following **der**-words are also followed by adjectives with weak endings: **dieser** (*this*), **jener** (*that*), **jeder** (*each* or *every*), **mancher** [*many (a)*], **solcher** [*such (a)*], and **welcher** (*which* or *what*):[1]

Dieses deutsche Buch gefällt mir.
I like this German book.

Welchen alten Mann haben Sie gesehen?
What old man did you see?

Er wohnt in **jenem** neuen Haus.
He lives in that new house.

Lernen Sie **diese** kurzen Sätze!
Learn these short sentences.

9. THE STRONG ADJECTIVE DECLENSION

Read the following sentences very carefully. Note the endings which an adjective takes when used alone with its corresponding noun (*i.e.*, without any **der-** or **ein-**word):

A. Singular number.

(1) The nominative case:

Arm**er** Mann, was fehlt Ihnen?
Poor man, what is the matter with you?

Lieb**e** Frau, wo sind Ihre Kinder?
Dear woman, where are your children?

Lieb**es** Kind, wo ist deine Mutter?
Dear child, where is your mother?

(2) The genitive case:

Er bestellte ein Glas rot**en** Wein**es** (or rot**en** Wein).
He ordered a glass of red wine.

Er trank ein Glas erfrischend**er** (or erfrischend**e**) Limonade.
He drank a glass of refreshing lemonade.

Er gab mir ein Glas kalt**en** Wasser**s** (or kalt**es** Wasser).
He gave me a glass of cold water.

Er hatte nur ein Stück trock(e)n**en** Brot**es** (or trocken**es** Brot).
He had only a piece of dry bread.

---

[1] For descriptive adjectives after **alle**, *cf.* § 12.

Note:

(*a*) Ordinary conversation employs the optional forms in parentheses; these are not genitives but accusatives in apposition with preceding nouns.

(*b*) Choice speech, however, tends to employ the genitive case after a noun of measurement or quantity (*e.g.*, Glas or Stück), when the thing to be measured or counted is modified by an adjective (*cf.* § 33, **F**, **Note** 3).

(3) The dative case:

Er ist ein alter Mann mit lang**em** Bart.
He is an old man with a long beard.

Er schreibt mit rot**er** Tinte.
He writes with red ink.

Sie ist eine alte Frau mit weiß**em** Haar.
She is an old woman with white hair.

(4) The accusative case:

Gut**en** Morgen![1]   Gut**e** Nacht![1]
Good morning.   *Good night.*

Kaufen Sie frisch**es** Brot!
Buy fresh bread.

B. Plural number.

(1) The nominative case:

Alt**e** Freunde sind gut**e** Freunde.
Old friends are good friends.

(2) The genitive case:

Sie kaufte sich vier Paar feinst**er** Handschuhe.
She bought (herself) four pairs of the finest gloves.

(3) The dative case:

Die schweren Wagen wurden von kräftig**en** Pferden gezogen.
The heavy wagons were drawn by strong horses.

(4) The accusative case:

Kurz**e** Geschichten liest er am liebsten.
He likes best to read short stories.

---

[1] *Cf.* § 35, **G**.

Sie hat drei kluge Kinder.
She has three bright children.

Summary: The preceding sentences indicate that an adjective used alone with its noun takes the endings of **dieser.** These are known as the "strong" endings.[1] Cardinals other than **ein** require the following adjective to have the strong endings (see last sentence under (4) above).

Note: In the genitive singular of the masculine and neuter, however, the ending **–en** replaces **–es** in modern German (*cf.* ¶ **A** (2) above).

10. THE MIXED ADJECTIVE DECLENSION

Read the following sentences very carefully.   Note the endings which an adjective takes when used after an **ein**-word:

A. Singular number.

(1) The nominative case:

Ein fleißig**er** Schüler fällt selten durch.
A diligent pupil rarely fails.

München ist **eine** schöne Stadt.
Munich is a beautiful city.

Ein deutsch**es** Buch liegt auf dem Tisch.
A German book is (lying) on the table.

(2) The genitive case:

Das ist der Rat **eines** guten Arztes.
That is the advice of a good physician.

Er ist der Sohn **einer** berühmten Sängerin.
He is the son of a famous singer (fem.).

Sie ist die Mutter **eines** klugen Kindes.
She is the mother of a bright child.

(3) The dative case:

Er machte einen Spaziergang mit **einem** alten Freund.
He took a walk with an old friend.

---

[1] For further details of the strong adjective declension, *cf.* § 99 **A** of the Appendix.

Er gab **einer** alten Frau etwas Geld.
He gave an old woman some money.

Er hatte **einem** armen Kind geholfen.
He had helped a poor child.

(4)   The accusative case:

Ich werde **einen** kleinen Hund kaufen.
I shall buy a little dog.

Sie hat **eine** interessante Geschichte erzählt.
She told an interesting story.

Haben Sie je **ein** deutsches Buch gelesen?
Did you ever read a German book?

B.   Plural number.

(1)   The nominative case:

Meine kleinen Bleistifte (Federn, Bücher) liegen auf dem Tisch.
My small pencils (pens, books) are (lying) on the table.

(2)   The genitive case:

Die Bücher **meiner** fleißigen Schüler (Schülerinnen, Kinder) sind interessant.
The books of my diligent boy pupils (girl pupils, children) are interesting.

(3)   The dative case:

Er wird **meinen** armen Freunden (Freundinnen, Kindern) helfen.
He will help my poor friends (masc.) [*friends* (fem.), *children*].

(4)   The accusative case:

Haben Sie **meine** schönen Vögel (Blumen, Bilder) gesehen?
Have you seen my beautiful birds (flowers, pictures)?

Summary: The above sentences indicate that the **ein**-words are: **ein** (*one* or *a*), **kein** (*no* or *not a*), and the possessives **mein** (*my*), **dein** [*your* (sing. fam.)], **sein** (*his* or *its*), **ihr** (*her* or *their*), **unser** (*our*), **euer** [*your* (pl. fam.)], and **Ihr** [*your* (sing. or pl. of formal address)].

Note:
(1) An adjective following an **ein**-word has the same endings as one following a **der**-word except in the nominative singular (masculine and

neuter genders) and in the accusative singular (neuter gender). In these three places the adjective has the endings of **dieser** (*i.e.*, strong endings). Adjective endings after **ein**-words are often called " mixed " endings, since they are partly weak and partly strong.

(2) **Either the der-word, the ein-word, or the adjective preceding a noun must be distinctive**—*i.e.*, it must show the gender, case, and number of that noun: **der gute Mann, ein** guter Mann. Since **ein** is not distinctive, the adjective **gut** takes the ending –**er** to show the gender, case, and number of **Mann. Der,** however, has a distinctive ending; hence the following adjective (**gute**) has a weak ending.

(3) **Unser** and **euer** are not to be confused with **der**-words because they happen to end in –**er:**

unser lieb**er** Freund, *our dear friend*

but: dieser lieb**e** Freund, *this dear friend*

euer gut**er** Vater, *your good father*

but: der gut**e** Vater, *the good father*

(4) In the following summary of adjective endings used after **ein**-words, **mein** stands for **any ein**-word; and the ending after a dash, for that of **any** adjective:[1]

	SINGULAR					PLURAL
	MASC.		FEM.		NEUT.	MASC., FEM., NEUT.
Nom.	mein	–**er**	meine	–e	mein –**es**	meine –en
Gen.	meines	–en	meiner	–en	meines –en	meiner –en
Dat.	meinem	–en	meiner	–en	meinem –en	meinen –en
Acc.	meinen	–en	meine	–e	mein –**es**	meine –en

11. ADJECTIVES IN A SERIES; DERIVED FROM NAMES OF TOWNS; USED AS NOUNS

A. Adjectives in a series. Two or more descriptive adjectives modifying the same noun have the same endings:

ein gut**er** alt**er** Mann, *a good, old man*

der gut**e** alt**e** Mann, *the good, old man.*

---

[1] For further details of the mixed adjective declension, *cf.* § 99 **C** of the Appendix.

B.   Adjectives derived from names of towns. Adjectives are formed from names of towns by adding **–er.**   Such adjectives are capitalized and are indeclinable:

> eine Hamburg**er** Zeitung, *a Hamburg newspaper*
> das Heidelberg**er** Schloß, *Heidelberg Castle*

C.   Adjectives used as nouns. Adjectives used as nouns are capitalized but keep their adjective endings:

> die Reich**en** und die Arm**en,** *the rich and the poor*
> der Reich**e,** *the rich man*
> ein Arm**er,** *a poor man*
> die Arm**e,** *the poor woman*
> Er besuchte Reich**e** und Arm**e.**
> *He visited rich and poor.*

EXERCISE

Substitute other appropriate adjectives and also other nouns of the same gender for those used in the illustrative sentences in this chapter.   If a noun is of the same gender as one used here, **any** German adjective will have the same ending as that in the original sentence.

12.   DESCRIPTIVE ADJECTIVES AFTER ALLE; **ADJECTIVES AFTER:** VIELE, WENIGE, ANDERE, EINIGE, **AND** MEHRERE

A.   Descriptive adjectives after alle. Observe the adjective ending after **alle** in the following sentences:

> **Alle** gut**en** Menschen liebten ihn.
> *All good people loved him.*
> **Aller** gut**en** Dinge sind drei.
> *All good things come in threes.*
> lit.:   *There are three* **of all** (gen. pl.) *good things.*
> In **allen** deutsch**en** Städten hatte er Bekannte.
> *He had acquaintances in all German cities.*
> Er liest **alle** deutsch**en** Zeitschriften gern.
> *He likes to read all (the) German magazines.*

Summary: The above sentences indicate that the **descriptive** adjective after **alle** (*all*) has weak endings (*i.e.,* in **–en**).

Note: Limiting words such as **diese** and **seine** are not descriptive adjectives:

>alle diese Bücher, *all these books*
>alle seine Freunde, *all his friends*

B. **Adjectives after:** viele, wenige, andere, einige, and mehrere. Observe the adjective ending after the various boldfaced words:

>Er hat **viele** liebe Freunde.
>*He has **many** dear friends.*
>
>**Wenige** ehrliche Männer würden das billigen.
>***Few** honest men would approve of that.*
>
>**Andere** gute Gründe hat er mir gegeben.
>*He gave me **other** good reasons.*
>
>Wir haben **einige** alte Damen getroffen.
>*We met **some** old ladies.*
>
>**Mehrere** wichtige Dinge haben Sie vergessen.
>*You forgot **several** important things.*

Summary: The above sentences indicate that adjectives following **viele** (*many*), **wenige** (*few*), **andere** (*other*), **einige** (*some*), and **mehrere** (*several*) end in –e in the nominative and accusative plural (*i.e.*, they have strong endings).

Note: **Manch–** is used chiefly in the singular; one may say either:

>mancher liebe Freund ⎫
>or: **manch** lieber Freund ⎭ ***many** a dear friend*

Similarly:

>welches schöne Haus ⎫
>or: **welch** schönes Haus ⎭ *what a beautiful house*
>
>solches gute Wetter ⎫
>or: **solch** gutes Wetter ⎭ *such good weather*

EXERCISE

A. Complete the following sentences:

1. Haben Sie d— deutsch— Zeitung gelesen?
2. Hat er weiß— oder gelb— Papier gekauft?
3. Das ist ein schön— Buch.
4. Trinkt er kalt— oder warm— Milch?

5. Der Wolf ist ein wild— Tier.
6. Gut— Morgen! Gut— Nacht!
7. Das ist ein gut— Witz.
8. Er gibt mir immer gut— Rat.
9. Heute haben wir wunderschön— Wetter.
10. Lieb— Junge, wie geht es dir?
11. D— arm— Frau hatte kein Geld.
12. Lieb— Kind, was fehlt dir?
13. Ihr gut— Freund war nicht zu Hause.
14. Warum schreiben Sie mit grün— Tinte?
15. Im Klassenzimmer hängt ein—groß— Wandkarte von Deutschland.
16. Er ist ein Mann von hoh— Gestalt.
17. Sagen Sie mir d— ganz— Wahrheit!
18. Geben Sie mir ein Glas kalt— Wassers!
19. D— klein— Kinder spielen auf der Straße.
20. Er hatte nur ein Stück trocken— Brotes.
21. Der Adler ist ein groß— Vogel.
22. Dieser gut— alt— Mann ist mein best— Freund.
23. Ich habe ein deutsch— Buch. Ich lerne Deutsch.
24. Er besitzt ein groß— Vermögen.
25. D— alt— Mann ist plötzlich verschwunden.
26. Unser reich— Freund wird uns bald besuchen.
27. Er hat d— erst— Zug verpaßt.
28. Wie heißt der Sohn d— alt— Mannes?
29. Wo war die Mutter d— klein— Mädchens?
30. Wo liegt die Vaterstadt d— beid— Freunde?
31. Was hat er d— arm— Leut— gegeben?
32. Das Buch gehört mein— klein— Bruder.[1]
33. Gehören Sie zu d— deutsch— Verein?[2]
34. Er hat ein— gut— Vater und ein— gut— Mutter.
35. Das war ein groß— Unglück.
36. Er trägt ein— schwer— Überrock.
37. Das Buch liegt auf d— klein— Tisch.
38. Was haben Sie in d— link— Tasche?

---

[1] The preposition **zu** is not used with the verb **gehören,** when the latter denotes ownership.

[2] The preposition **zu** is required with the verb **gehören** when the latter means *belong to,* in the sense of *to be a part* (or *a member*) *of.*

39. Er ist ein gut— Schüler.
40. Haben Sie kein— gut— Stuhl?
41. Bei d— groß— Städten (= in d— Vorstädten) haben viele Deutsch— klein— Gärten.
42. Jeder Deutsch— hat sein— klein— Garten gern.
43. Sie ist ein gut— klein— Mädchen.
44. Haben Sie d— Leipzig— Messe besucht?
45. Er hat all— deutsch— Zeitungen gelesen.
46. Ich lasse all— gut— Freunde grüßen.
47. Der Lehrer hat viel— gut— Schüler.
48. Manch tapfer— Soldat ist gefallen.   (Rewrite with mancher.)
49. Welcher klug— Mann!   (Rewrite with welch.)
50. Er hat viel— treu— Freunde.
51. Das Buch gehört d— klein— Jungen (sing.).
52. Er gehört zu d— deutsch— Gesangverein.
53. Wir werden d— alt— Stadt Rothenburg besuchen.
54. Unser alt— Freund war letzten Sommer da.
55. Die Eltern d— klein— Jungen (sing.) sind auf dem Lande.
56. Lieb— Mädchen, was fehlt dir?
57. Sie ist ein— schön— Frau mit kurz— Haar.
58. Haben Sie frisch— Brot gekauft?
59. Er hat mehrere wichtig— Dinge vergessen.
60. Unser freundlich— Arzt hatte ein— München— Zeitung gekauft.
61. Andere gut— Gründe werde ich Ihnen geben.
62. Der Reich— hat d— Arm— (masc. sing.) geholfen.
63. Wenig— ehrlich— Leute würden das tun.
64. Das ist ein klein— alt— Haus.
65. Alle deutsch— Bücher habe ich zu Hause.
66. Kinder, wo ist euer lieb— Onkel?
67. Ich habe viele gut— Freunde.
68. Unser reich— Onkel ist nicht zu Hause.
69. Der Rhein ist ein berühmt— deutsch— Strom.
70. Er hat alles, was zu ein— bequem— Leben gehört.
71. Mit bloß— Auge kann man ein— klein— Satelliten nicht sehen.
72. Die groß— Raumforschungsrakete stieg in die höheren Luftschichten.

B.   Translate:

1. Our dear friend (*masc.*) is in the country this week.

2. The little child was eating a large piece of cake.
3. The Rhine is a beautiful stream.
4. Children, where is your dear father?
5. His rich uncle is in Switzerland this year.
6. Yesterday I visited my best friend.
7. That is an old proverb.
8. Berlin is the largest city in (of) Germany.
9. He is carrying a long cane.
10. The lady has a beautiful voice.
11. She sat down after the first dance.
12. Those boys go to the same school.
13. The old men were in the same school, when they were boys.
14. The first snow fell (*perf.*) today.
15. I finally found (*perf.*) a good tailor.
16. Have you seen the beautiful castles on the Rhine?
17. Write the second sentence on the board.
18. He is a famous German singer.
19. He is wearing a new coat.
20. She will take a long trip.
21. He was sitting in the third row.
22. He had always given me good advice.
23. Have you ever seen a German city hall?
24. We shall pass (bestehen) this easy examination.
25. Konrad Adenauer was the first chancellor of the Federal Republic of Germany.
26. Have you a sharp knife in your (the) pocket?
27. I shall tell (erzählen) you an interesting story.
28. He gave the old men some money.
29. She was showing the little boy a beautiful picture.
30. The lion is a wild animal.
31. The dog is a domesticated animal.
32. She was singing a beautiful song.
33. He is reading a German book.
34. I gave him many good reasons.
35. Our old friend is a good physician.
36. On (An) that evening she wore a beautiful dress.
37. When did you see that little boy?
38. He had bought a new house.
39. The girl's parents were both in the country.

40. He had given his little sister a beautiful book.
41. The boy's books were on the little table.
42. She was showing her older brother an interesting picture.
43. Where did you buy your new hat?
44. Write these short sentences in (*w. acc.*) your notebook.
45. If you don't understand, raise your (the) right hand.
46. Last month I visited my old grandmother.
47. She has a beautiful face.
48. I have learned one German poem by heart.
49. That is a very high building.
50. We have a large classroom.
51. He has many good friends.
52. She will sing a well-known German folksong.
53. Have you read that interesting story?
54. That is a beautiful old village.
55. The little girl's books were on the table.
56. All diligent pupils have written the short sentences.
57. I have learned many German poems by heart.
58. He gave the old lady the beautiful flowers.
59. Give me other important reasons.
60. Did you help the little children?
61. He has several valuable books in his library.
62. I bought a Berlin newspaper.
63. Few poor people wear such clothes.
64. He will attend (besuchen) the Leipzig fair.
65. Our dear father is not at home.
66. My rich uncle lives in a suburb.
67. Write with black ink.
68. She has red hair.
69. Good morning.   Good evening.   Good night.
70. Today we are having beautiful weather.
71. Poor people are not always unhappy.
72. Help the poor (*use adj. as noun*).
73. To whom do these German books belong?
74. Do you belong to the German glee club?
75. We sing many beautiful folksongs.
76. There were several large space-research rockets in the stratosphere.
77. With (the) naked eye one cannot see small satellites.

CHAPTER 5 **Nouns**

13. STRONG, WEAK, MIXED, AND IRREGULAR NOUNS

Read the following sentences very carefully. Note the forms of the various cases:

A. Strong nouns:

    (1) Mein Onkel besucht mich.
        My uncle is visiting me.

        Das Haus meines Onkel**s** liegt an einem schönen Fluß.
        My uncle's house is situated on a beautiful river.

        Meine Onkel wohnen auf dem Lande.
        My uncles live in the country.

    (2) Mein Freund ist nicht zu Hause.
        My friend is not at home.

        Die Mutter meines Freund**es** ist in Deutschland.
        My friend's mother is in Germany.

        Meine Freund**e** werden ihm helfen.
        My friends will help him.

    (3) Das Kind spielt mit dem Hund(e).
        The child is playing with the dog.

        Die Eltern des Kind**es** sind arm.
        The child's parents are poor.

        Die Kind**er** gehen jetzt nach Hause.
        The children are going home now.

B. Weak nouns:

    (1) Der Junge heißt Fritz.
        The boy's name is Fred.

        Der Vater des Jung**en** ist Advokat.
        The boy's father is a lawyer.

Er hat dem Jung**en** ein deutsches Buch gegeben.
He gave the boy a German book.

Ich habe den Jung**en** auf der Straße getroffen.
I met the boy on the street.

Die Jung**en** gehen in die Schule.
The boys go to school.

Die Bücher der Jung**en** liegen auf dem Tisch.
The boys' books are (lying) on the table.

Er hat den Jung**en** die deutschen Bücher gegeben.
He gave the boys the German books.

Ich habe die Jung**en** auf der Straße getroffen.
I met the boys on the street.

(2) Die Frau ist meine Freundin.
The woman is my friend.

Der Vater der Frau ist in Europa.
The woman's father is in Europe.

Die Frau**en** machen einen Spaziergang.
The women are taking a walk.

Die Kleider der Frau**en** sind schön.
The women's dresses are beautiful.

C. Mixed nouns:

Mein Vetter ist Lehrer.
My cousin (masc.) is a teacher.

Der Freund meines Vetter**s** ist Arzt.
My cousin's friend is a physician.

Meine beiden Vetter**n** besuchen mich.
My two cousins are visiting me.

D. Irregular nouns:

Er hat ein gutes Herz.
He has a good heart.

Er sprach aus dem Grunde des Herz**ens**.
He spoke from the depths of his heart.

Ich tue es von Herz**en** (sing.) gern.
I (will) do it with all my heart.

Sie sind zwei Herz**en** und ein Schlag.
They are bosom friends.

lit.:   *They are two hearts and one beat.*

E.   Weak feminine nouns in –in:

Sie war meine Lehrer**in**.
She was my teacher.

Kennen Sie diese Lehrer**innen**?
Do you know these teachers (fem.)?

F.   Nouns in –nis:

Das war ein interessantes Erleb**nis**.
That was an interesting experience.

Er schrieb über seine Erleb**nisse** in Deutschland.
He wrote about his experiences in Germany.

G.   Plural noun forms:

(1) Er hat den Männer**n** (den Frau**en**, den Kinder**n**) geholfen.
He helped the men (the women, the children).

(2) Die Männ**er** (Frau**en**, Kind**er**) arbeiten schwer.
The men (women, children) are working hard.

Die Kleider der Männ**er** (der Frau**en**, der Kind**er**) sind zerrissen.
The men's (women's, children's) clothes are torn.

Er besuchte die Männ**er** (die Frau**en**, die Kind**er**).
He visited the men (the women, the children).

H.   The dative singular of masculine and neuter monosyllabics:

Er half dem Mann**e** (**or** dem Mann).
He helped the man.

Sie folgte dem Kind**e** (**or** dem Kind).
She followed the child.

Note:

(1) German nouns whose genitive singular ends in –**s** or –**es** form their plural:

(*a*) With no additional ending: der Onk**el**, des Onk**els**, die Onk**el**[1] (*cf.* ¶ **A** (1) above)—the so-called first class of strong nouns.

(*b*) By adding the ending –**e**: der Freund, des Freund**es**, die Freund**e** (*cf.* ¶ **A** (2) above)—the second class of strong nouns.

(*c*) By adding the ending –**er**: das Kind, des Kind**es**, die Kind**er** (*cf.* ¶ **A** (3) above)—the third class of strong nouns.[2]

(2) (*a*) Masculine nouns of the weak declension take –**n** or –**en** in all cases except the nominative singular: der Junge, des Jung**en**, die Jung**en** (*cf.* ¶ **B** (1) above).[3]

(*b*) Feminine nouns (except proper names) **never** take endings in the singular. Weak feminine nouns have the ending –**n** or –**en** in all cases of the plural: die Frau, der Frau, die Frau**en** (*cf.* ¶ **B** (2) above).

(3) The mixed declension consists of nouns that have the strong declension in the singular (always –**s** or –**es** in the genitive) but the weak declension in the plural (–**n** or –**en** in all cases): der Vetter, des Vetter**s**, die Vetter**n** (*cf.* ¶ **C** above).[4]

(4) There are also a few irregular nouns that do not fit into any of the above classifications: *e.g.*, das Herz, des Herz**ens**, dem Herz**en**, das Herz, die Herz**en**, der Herz**en**, den Herz**en**, die Herz**en** (*cf.* ¶ **D** above).[4]

(5) Feminine nouns in –**in** have –**innen** throughout the plural. The plural of die Lehrer**in** is, therefore: die Lehrer**innen**, der Lehrer**innen**, den Lehrer**innen**, die Lehrer**innen** (*cf.* ¶ **E** above).

(6) Nouns ending in –**nis** double the **s** when it is followed by an ending: das Erleb**nis**, des Erleb**nisses**, die Erleb**nisse** (*cf.* ¶ **F** above).

(7) **General rules for all nouns:**

(*a*) The dative plural always ends in –**n** (*cf.* ¶ **G** (1) above): den Männer**n**, den Frau**en**, den Kinder**n**.

(*b*) The nominative, genitive, and accusative plurals always have the same form (*cf.* ¶ **G** (2) above): die Männer, der Männer, die Männer; die Frauen, der Frauen, die Frauen; die Kinder, der Kinder, die Kinder.

---

[1] These three key forms, or principal parts—*viz.*, the nominative and genitive singular, and the nominative plural—should be learned together with each new noun.

[2] For the few exceptions to these rules, *cf.* **Note** (3) following; for further details (including umlaut), *cf.* Appendix, § 98 **A.**

[3] For further details, *cf.* Appendix, § 98 **B.**

[4] For further details, *cf.* Appendix, § 98 **C.**

(8) The dative singular ending –e for strong masculine and neuter nouns of one syllable may be omitted (*cf.* ¶ H above): dem Manne (or dem Mann), dem Kinde (or dem Kind).

EXERCISE

A. Learn, together with its definite article, the nominative and genitive singular, and nominative plural of each new noun. Make it a rule to use new words in sentences. The following lists comprise some of the more common nouns. These are arranged according to strong and weak classification and are contained in sentences at the end of this chapter.

(1) Strong nouns:

(*a*) *Class I:*

das **Abendessen,** –s, —, supper
der **Apfel,** –s, ¨, apple
der **Bäcker,** –s, —, baker
der **Boden,** –s, ¨ (*or* —), floor, ground
der **Bruder,** –s, ¨, brother
der **Dampfer,** –s, —, steamer
der **Dichter,** –s, —, poet
der **Diener,** –s, —, servant
das **Dienstmädchen,** –s, —, servant girl
der **Einwohner,** –s, —, inhabitant
der **Esel,** –s, —, donkey
der **Fehler,** –s, —, mistake
das **Fenster,** –s, —, window
das **Feuer,** –s, —, fire
der **Finger,** –s, —, finger
der **Flieger,** –s, —, flyer
der **Forscher,** –s, —, scientist, scientific researcher
das **Fräulein,** –s, —, young lady, Miss
der **Garten,** –s, ¨, garden
das **Gebäude,** –s, —, building
der **Hügel,** –s, —, hill
der **Kellner,** –s, —, waiter
der **Koffer,** –s, —, trunk

der **Lehrer,** –s, —, teacher
der **Löffel,** –s, —, spoon
das **Mädchen,** –s, —, girl
das **Messer,** –s, —, knife
die **Mutter,** —, ¨, mother
der **Ofen,** –s, ¨, stove
der **Onkel,** –s, —, uncle
der **Rücken,** –s, —, back
der **Schatten,** –s, —, shadow, shade
der **Schlüssel,** –s, —, key
der **Schüler,** –s, —, pupil
der **Sommer,** –s, —, summer
der **Teller,** –s, —, plate
das **Theater,** –s, —, theater
die **Tochter,** —, ¨, daughter
das **Ufer,** –s, —, shore
der **Vater,** –s, ¨, father
der **Vogel,** –s, ¨, bird
das **Wasser,** –s, —, water
das **Wetter,** –s, —, weather
der **Winter,** –s, —, winter
das **Wunder,** –s, —, wonder, miracle
das **Zeichen,** –s, —, sign
das **Zimmer,** –s, —, room
der **Zweifel,** –s, —, doubt

(b) Class II:

der **Abend,** –s, –e, evening
der **Arm,** –(e)s, –e, arm
der **Arzt,** –es, ⁔e, physician
der **Aufsatz,** –es, ⁔e, composition
der **Augenblick,** –(e)s, –e, moment
der **Ausdruck,** –(e)s, ⁔e, expression
der **Bahnhof,** (–e)s, ⁔e, railroad station
der **Ball,** –(e)s, ⁔e, (game of) ball
der **Bart,** –(e)s, ⁔e, beard
der **Baum,** –(e)s, ⁔e, tree
das **Bein,** (e)s, –e, leg
der **Berg,** –(e)s, –e, mountain
der **Besuch,** –(e)s, –e, visit
der **Bleistift,** –(e)s, –e, pencil
der **Brief,** –(e)s, –e, letter
das **Brot,** –(e)s, –e, bread
der **Dieb,** –(e)s, –e, thief
der **Flug,** –(e)s, ⁔e, flight
der **Fluß,** Flusses, Flüsse, river
der **Freund,** –(e)s, –e, friend
das **Frühstück,** –(e)s, –e, breakfast
der **Fuß,** –es, ⁔e, foot
der **Gast,** –es, ⁔e, guest
das **Gedicht,** –(e)s, –e, poem
das **Gepäck,** –(e)s, –e, baggage
das **Geschäft,** –(e)s, –e, business
das **Gespräch,** –(e)s, –e, conversation
das **Haar,** –(e)s, –e, hair
der **Hals,** Halses, Hälse, throat, neck
die **Hand,** —, ⁔e, hand
das **Hindernis,** –nisses, –nisse, hindrance, obstacle
der **Hof,** –(e)s, ⁔e, court, yard, estate
der **Hund,** –(e)s, –e, dog

der **Hut,** –(e)s, ⁔e, hat
das **Jahr,** –(e)s, –e, year
der **Kopf,** –(e)s, ⁔e, head
der **Krieg,** –(e)s, –e, war
die **Kuh,** —, ⁔e, cow
der **Markt,** –(e)s, ⁔e, market
die **Maus,** —, Mäuse, mouse
der **Monat,** –(e)s, –e, month
die **Nacht,** —, ⁔e, night
das **Paar,** –(e)s, –e, pair
das **Pferd,** –(e)s, –e, horse
der **Platz,** –es, ⁔e, place, seat
der **Raum,** –(e)s, ⁔e, space, room, place
der **Raumflug,** –(e)s, ⁔e, space flight
der **Rock,** –(e)s, ⁔e, coat
der **Satz,** –es, ⁔e, sentence
der **Schuh,** –(e)s, –e, shoe
der **Sohn,** –(e)s, ⁔e, son
der **Spaziergang,** –(e)s, ⁔e, walk
das **Spiel,** –(e)s, –e, game, play
die **Stadt,** —, ⁔e, city
das **Stück,** –(e)s, –e, piece
der **Stuhl,** –(e)s, ⁔e, chair
der **Tag,** –(e)s, –e, day
das **Tier,** –(e)s, –e, animal
der **Tisch,** –es, –e, table
der **Vorort,** –(e)s, –e, suburb
die **Vorstadt,** —, ⁔e, suburb
die **Wand,** —, ⁔e, wall
der **Weg,** –(e)s, –e, way, road
der **Wirt,** –(e)s, –e, host, landlord, hotelkeeper
der **Zahn,** –(e)s, ⁔e, tooth
der **Zug,** –(e)s, ⁔e, train
der **Zustand,** (–e)s, ⁔e, condition

(c) Class III:

das **Bild,** –(e)s, –er, picture
das **Blatt,** –(e)s, ⁔er, leaf
das **Buch,** –(e)s, ⁔er, book
das **Dach,** –(e)s, ⁔er, roof
das **Dorf,** –(e)s, ⁔er, village

das **Ei,** –(e)s, –er, egg
das **Fach,** –(e)s, ⁔er, line of work, special subject (*studied in school*)
das **Feld,** –(e)s, –er, field
der **Geist,** –es, –er, spirit

das **Geld,** –(e)s, –er, money
das **Gesicht,** –(e)s, –er, face
das **Haus,** Hauses, Häuser, house
das **Huhn,** –(e)s, ⸚er, chicken
das **Kind,** –(e)s, –er, child
das **Kleid,** –(e)s, –er, dress; (*pl.*)
    dresses (*or* clothes)
das **Kraut,** –(e)s, ⸚er, herb, vege-
    table; (= das Unkraut) weed
das **Land,** –(e)s, ⸚er, land, country
das **Licht,** –(e)s, –er, light
das **Lied,** –(e)s, –er, song

der **Mann,** –(e)s, ⸚er, man
das **Schloß,** Schlosses, Schlösser,
    castle
das **Tal,** –(e)s, ⸚er, valley
das **Volk,** –(e)s, ⸚er, people
der **Wald,** –(e)s, ⸚er, forest
das **Wort,** –(e)s, –e (*or* ⸚er), word;
    –e, words (*in connected discourse*);
    ⸚er, words (*single and discon-
    nected*)
das **Wörterbuch,** –(e)s, ⸚er, dic-
    tionary

(2) Weak nouns:

die **Antwort,** —, –en, answer
die **Arbeit,** —, –en, work
die **Aufgabe,** —, –n, lesson, task
die **Bahn,** —, –en, road, track
die **Blume,** —, –n, flower
die **Burg,** —, –en, castle
die **Dame,** —, –n, lady
die **Decke,** —, –n, cover, ceiling
die **Fahrt,** —, –en, ride, drive, trip,
    journey
die **Feder,** —, –n, pen, feather
die **Forschung,** —, –en, investiga-
    tion, inquiry, research
die **Frage,** —, –n, question
die **Frau,** —, –en, woman
der **Fürst,** –en, –en, prince
die **Geschichte,** —, –n, story,
    history
die **Gesellschaft,** —, –en, society,
    company
der **Herr,** –n, –en,[1] gentleman, Mr.
der **Junge,** –n, –n, boy
die **Karte,** —, –n, card, map
die **Katze,** —, –n, cat
die **Klasse,** —, –n, class
der **Knabe,** –n, –n, boy
die **Küche,** —, –n, kitchen
der **Mensch,** –en, –en, human
    being, man
die **Minute,** —, –n, minute

die **Nadel,** —, –n, needle
der **Narr,** –en, –en, fool
der **Präsident,** –en, –en, president
die **Prüfung,** —, –en, examination
die **Rede,** —, –n, speech, discourse
die **Reise,** —, –n, trip
der **Satellit,** –en, –en, satellite
die **Scheune,** —, –n, barn
die **Schule,** —, –n, school
die **Schwester,** —, –n, sister
die **See,** —, –n, sea
die **Seite,** —, –n, side, page
der **Soldat,** –en, –en, soldier
die **Sonne,** —, –n, sun
die **Sprache,** —, –n, language
die **Stimme,** —, –n, voice
die **Straße,** —, –n, street
die **Stunde,** —, –n, hour, class,
    period
die **Tante,** —, –n, aunt
die **Tasche,** —, –n, pocket
die **Tasse,** —, –n, cup
die **Tinte,** —, –n, ink
die **Tür,** —, –en, door
die **Uhr,** —, –en, watch, clock
die **Universität,** —, –en, univer-
    sity
die **Wahrheit,** —, –en, truth
die **Witwe,** —, –n, widow
die **Woche,** —, –n, week

---

[1] Note that this noun has the ending **-en** in the **plural** only.

(3) Mixed and irregular nouns:

das **Auge,** –s, –n, eye
das **Auto,** –s, –s, auto
der **Bauer,** –s, –n (*sometimes w. wk. sing.*), peasant, farmer
das **Bett,** –(e)s, –en, bed
der **Doktor,** –s, –en, doctor
das **Ende,** –s, –n, end
der **Felsen,** –s, —, cliff, rock
der **Gedanke,** –ns, –n, thought
der **Glaube(n),** –ns –n, belief
das **Gymnasium,** –s, Gymnasien, gymnasium (*the German school that prepares students for the Universität*)
der **Haufe(n),** –ns, –n, heap, pile; (*colloq.*) a lot of
das **Hemd,** –(e)s, –en, shirt

das **Herz,** –ens, –en (*dat. sing.* –en), heart
das **Hotel,** –s, –s, hotel
der **Nachbar,** –s, –n (*sometimes w. wk. sing.*), neighbor
das **Ohr,** –(e)s, –en, ear
der **Professor,** –s, –en, professor
das **Radio,** –s, –s, radio
der **Schmerz,** –es, –en, pain
der **See,** –s, –n, lake (*not to be confused with* die **See,** —, –n, sea)
der **Staat,** –es, –en, state (*not to be confused with* die **Stadt,** —, ¨e, city)
der **Vetter,** –s, –n, cousin (*the corresponding feminine noun is* die Cousine, —, –n)

B. Rewrite the following sentences in the plural:

1. Das Dienstmädchen wird das große Zimmer reinigen.
2. Der Schüler hat das deutsche Buch verloren.
3. Der Kellner hat das gute Trinkgeld gern.
4. Das Kind hatte das schöne Lied gesungen.
5. Der Dieb schwimmt über den breiten Fluß.
6. Das Mädchen spitzte den stumpfen Bleistift.
7. Der kluge Junge antwortet auf jede Frage.
8. In diesem kleinen Dorf habe ich eine Uhr gekauft.
9. Hast du das hohe Gebäude in der Stadt gesehen?
10. Der bekannte Dichter wird das neue Haus kaufen.
11. Siehst du den schönen Baum in jenem tiefen Tal?
12. Ich bewundere das alte Schloß auf dem hohen Berg.
13. Der Junge hat diesen großen Fehler gemacht.
14. Mein Onkel hat mir das scharfe Messer gegeben.
15. Die kurze Geschichte gefällt der Tochter.
16. Dieser kleine Vogel ist durch das offene Fenster geflogen.
17. Mein Bruder wird den alten Mann besuchen.
18. Die Mutter ist mit der kleinen Tochter fortgegangen.
19. Er hat das schöne Pferd in dem deutschen Dorf gekauft.
20. Der Soldat dachte an seinen lieben Sohn.
21. Der berühmte Arzt hat dem Mann sehr geholfen.
22. Mein Freund hatte mir diesen langen Brief geschrieben.

23. Die Katze fängt die graue Maus.
24. Wo hat die Dame diesen kostbaren Hut gekauft?
25. Wie heißt deine Nachbarin?
26. Der freundliche Herr wird mir das Buch geben.
27. Der kürzeste Weg ist nicht immer der beste.
28. Der Lehrer hatte den langen Satz geschrieben.
29. Lerne diesen idiomatischen Ausdruck auswendig!
30. Dieser Herr ist mein bester Freund.
31. Er hat den allerschönsten Hof.
32. Das neue Kleid gefällt dem Mädchen nicht.
33. Ich habe meine gute Freundin besucht.
34. Das ist die kürzeste Aufgabe, die ich je gehabt habe.
35. Die gute Frau wird die alte Burg bewundern.
36. Die Schwester hatte ihrem Bruder diese interessante Geschichte erzählt.
37. Mein reicher Vetter hat das große Auto gekauft.
38. Ich warte schon lange auf den alten Doktor.
39. Verstehst du das neue Wort nicht?
40. Das Bild an der Wand ist sehr schön.
41. Der Professor **an** dieser Universität hat das große Buch geschrieben.
42. Mein Vetter ist Student **auf** der Münchner Universität. (Do not rewrite the auf-phrase in the plural.)
43. Mein älterer Bruder besucht das Gymnasium.
44. Die Sängerin wird das alte Volkslied singen.
45. Er mußte jedes Hindernis überwinden.
46. Der Flieger hat einen langen Raumflug gemacht.
47. Der Forscher entdeckte einen Satelliten.

C. Translate:
1. The Germans are very proud of (stolz auf *w. acc.*) their beautiful forests.
2. Our country consists of fifty states, of which Alaska is the largest.
3. Did you visit the beautiful city of Munich?
4. The porter will carry my heavy suitcase through the railroad station.
5. My dear friend had seen the old castles on the Rhine.
6. That little girl has a beautiful face.
7. I gave the tall (lang) waiter a good tip.
8. That little boy always gives good answers to (auf *w. acc.*) my questions.
9. The old lady likes beautiful flowers.

10. Is your older brother a professor at the university?
11. My younger brother is a student at the same university.
12. I was thinking of that old gentleman.   (*Rewrite in the plural.*)
13. He had written me that long letter.
14. She will give them those German books.
15. He was showing the men the beautiful pictures.
16. Did she sing that well-known folksong?
17. She entered the large room and sat down on the sofa.
18. The servant girl had broken (zerbrechen) many good plates.
19. The fastest German steamers were formerly the (die) Europa and the (die) Bremen.
20. The flyers were hoping for favorable weather.
21. I have been waiting an hour and a half for my dear mother.
22. Did you see the President when you were in the capital?
23. Our English teacher will give us a very easy examination.
24. Our old physician had taken a long trip.
25. Wait a moment.   I shall give you a better book.
26. That little bird flew through an open window.
27. Those rich women live in a beautiful suburb.
28. How long have you been waiting for that train?
29. How many idiomatic expressions did you learn by heart?
30. During the war many soldiers died for their native land.
31. The President delivered (halten) a short speech.
32. At what time will you go to school tomorrow?
33. My best friend attends (besuchen) a " gymnasium."
34. His rich uncle had given him a new car (*i.e.*, auto).
35. The dog sees its own shadow in the water.
36. Last summer I often went to the theater.
37. I like the German language.
38. With what kind of (a) pen are you writing?
39. Yesterday the little children took a long walk.
40. In the fall the trees have beautiful leaves.
41. Last month the old man visited his youngest daughter.
42. The waiter will bring you another cup of coffee.
43. Tell me the whole truth.
44. The singers (*fem.*) do not earn so much money this year.
45. That man will easily overcome all obstacles.
46. The scientists had not expected to discover so many satellites.
47. The flyers have already made many long space flights.

CHAPTER 6   # Weak, Strong, and Irregular Weak Verbs

14. WEAK VERBS

German weak verbs correspond to English " regular " verbs:

PRESENT INFINITIVE	PAST (IMPERFECT)	PAST PARTICIPLE
hören	**hörte**	**gehört**
to hear	*heard*	*heard*

Read the following sentences very carefully. Note the form of the verb in each:

A.   Sie liebt ihn.
She loves him.

Sie liebte ihn.
She loved him.

Sie hat ihn geliebt.
She (has) loved him.

Sie hatte ihn geliebt.
She had loved him.

Sie wird ihn lieben.
She will love him.

Sie wird ihn geliebt haben.
She will have loved him.

B.   Er wartet auf mich.
He is waiting for me.

Er wartete auf mich.
He was waiting for me.

Er hat auf mich gewartet.
He (has) waited for me.

Er hatte auf mich gewartet.
He had waited for me.

Er wird auf mich warten.
He will wait for me.

Er wird auf mich gewartet haben.
He will have waited for me.

C.   Ich studiere die Aufgabe.
I am studying the lesson.

Ich studierte die Aufgabe.
I was studying the lesson.

Ich hatte die Aufgabe studiert.
I had studied the lesson.

Ich werde die Aufgabe studieren.
I shall study the lesson.

Ich habe die Aufgabe studiert.
I (have) studied the lesson.

Ich werde die Aufgabe studiert haben.
I shall have studied the lesson.

D. Er beantwortet die Frage.
He answers the question.

Er hatte die Frage beantwortet.
He had answered the question.

Er beantwortete die Frage.
He answered the question.

Er wird die Frage beantworten.
He will answer the question.

Er hat die Frage beantwortet.
He (has) answered the question.

Er wird die Frage beantwortet haben.
He will have answered the question.

E. Ich mache die Tür zu.
I am closing (or close) the door.

Ich hatte die Tür zugemacht.
I had closed the door.

Ich machte die Tür zu.
I was closing (or closed) the door.

Ich werde die Tür zumachen.
I shall close the door.

Ich habe die Tür zugemacht.
I (have) closed the door.

Ich werde die Tür zugemacht haben.
I shall have closed the door.

Summary: The above sentences indicate that the characteristics of weak verbs are: the past tense ending **–(e)te,** and the past participle ending **–(e)t.**[1]

Note:

(1) The past tense ending **–te** is added to verb stems. The stem is found by dropping final **–en** from the present infinitive of a verb (*cf.* ¶¶ **A, C,** and **E** above).

(2) The past tense ending **–ete** is added if the stem of a verb ends in **–d** (*e.g.,* reden, redete, *to speak*) or **–t** (*cf.* ¶¶ **B** and **D** above), or if it ends in **–m** or **–n** preceded by a consonant other than **l** or **r** (*e.g.,* atmen, atmete, *to breathe;* but warnen, warnte, *to warn*).

(3) The past participle ending of weak verbs whose past tense ends in **–ete** is **–et** instead of **–t:** gewartet, beantwortet, geatmet.

(4) Verbs ending in **–ieren**[2] are weak and do not take the participial

---

[1] For the conjugation of weak verbs, *cf.* §§ 103 and 107 of the Appendix.
[2] Such verbs regularly accent the **-ie-.**

prefix **ge–** (*cf.* ¶ **C** above).   A few of the more common verbs in –**ieren** (usually of foreign origin) are: regieren (*to govern*), probieren (*to try*), buchstabieren (*to spell*), telefonieren (or telephonieren) (*to telephone*), telegrafieren (or telegraphieren) (*to telegraph*), operieren (*to operate*), sich amüsieren (*to have a good time*), spazieren (*to walk*), studieren (*to study*), and sich interessieren für (*to be interested in*).

(5) Verbs (both weak and strong) with the inseparable prefixes **be–**, **emp–**, **ent–**, **er–**, **ge–**, **ver–**, **zer–**, and sometimes **miß–** take no prefix in the past participle (*cf.* ¶ **D** above).[1]

(6) Verbs (both weak and strong) with separable prefixes have the participial prefix **ge–** between prefix and verb: **zu**ge**macht** (*cf.* ¶ **E** above).[1]

————————————

Learn the conjugation of the auxiliary verbs **haben, sein,** and **werden** and the weak verb **lernen** (*cf.* Appendix, §§ 102 and 103).

15. STRONG VERBS

German strong verbs correspond to English " irregular " verbs:

PRESENT INFINITIVE	PAST (IMPERFECT)	PAST PARTICIPLE
singen	**sang**	**gesungen**
to sing	*sang*	*sung*

Read the following sentences very carefully.   Note the form of the verb in each:

A. (1) Wir bl**ei**ben zu Hause.   Wir waren zu Hause gebl**ie**ben.
We stay at home.   *We had stayed at home.*

Wir bl**ie**ben zu Hause.   Wir werden zu Hause bl**ei**ben.
We stayed at home.   *We shall stay at home.*

Wir sind zu Hause gebl**ie**ben.   Wir werden zu Hause gebl**ie**ben
We (have) stayed at home.   sein.
                                     We shall have stayed at home.

(2) Er g**ie**ßt das Wasser ins Glas.
He pours the water into the glass.

————————————

[1] For further details consult Chapter 20 on Separable and Inseparable Prefixes.

Er goß das Wasser ins Glas.
He poured the water into the glass.

Er hat das Wasser ins Glas geg**ossen.**
He (has) poured the water into the glass.

Er hatte das Wasser ins Glas geg**ossen.**
He had poured the water into the glass.

Er wird das Wasser ins Glas gi**eß**en.
He will pour the water into the glass.

Er wird das Wasser ins Glas geg**ossen** haben.
He will have poured the water into the glass.

(3) Sie s**i**ngt das Lied.
She sings the song.

Sie s**a**ng das Lied.
She sang the song.

Sie hat das Lied ges**u**ngen.
She has sung the song.

(4) Er spr**i**cht zu schnell.
He speaks too rapidly.

Er spr**a**ch zu schnell.
He spoke too rapidly.

Er hat zu schnell gespr**o**chen.
He has spoken too rapidly.

(5) Sie l**ie**st das Buch.
She is reading the book.

Sie l**a**s das Buch.
She was reading the book.

Sie hat das Buch gel**e**sen.
She (has) read the book.

(6) Er schl**ä**gt den Hund.
He strikes the dog.

Er schl**u**g den Hund.
He struck the dog.

Er hat den Hund geschl**a**gen.
He (has) struck the dog.

(7) Er l**äu**ft nach Hause.
He runs home.

Er l**ie**f nach Hause.
He ran home.

Er ist nach Hause gel**au**fen.
He has run home.

B. Karl, spr**i**ch nicht zu schnell! L**ie**s das Buch!
Carl, do not talk too rapidly.   Read the book.

Schl**a**ge den Hund nicht! L**au**fe nach Hause!
Do not strike the dog.   Run home.

C. Er steht schnell auf.
He gets up quickly.

Er st**a**nd schnell auf.
He got up quickly.

D. Ich verstehe den Satz.
I understand the sentence.

Ich verst**a**nd den Satz.
I understood the sentence.

Er ist schnell aufgestan**den.**   Ich habe den Satz verstan**den.**
He got up quickly.   *I (have) understood the sentence.*

Summary: The above examples indicate that the characteristics of strong verbs are: a change in the stem vowel of the present infinitive in the past and usually in the past participle, and the past participle ending **–en.**[1]

Note:

(1) The best way to learn a verb is to know its principal parts and **use it in the various tenses.** Form **sentences** with principal parts. Since many strong verbs change their stem vowels in the second and third persons singular of the present indicative, as well as in the past and often in the past participle, the present indicative should be learned together with the principal parts of a verb.

(2) Grammarians have divided strong verbs into seven classes (*i.e.,* the ablaut series), according to the vowel changes which characterize each group. [The examples under ¶ **A** above correspond to these seven classes (from ¶ **A** (1)–(7) inclusive) and the following subdivisions (from (*a*)–(*g*) inclusive) in turn refer to these examples.]

(*a*) Class I: **ei—ie—ie** or **ei—i—i:** bleiben, blieb, geblieben; schneiden, schnitt, geschnitten.

(*b*) Class II: **ie—o—o.** The **o** may be short or long: gießen, goß, gegossen; ziehen, zog, gezogen.

(*c*) Class III: **i—a—u.** These vowels are short: singen, sang, gesungen.

(*d*) Class IV: **e—a—o.** The **e** and **o** of this class are sometimes long and sometimes short; short **e** becomes **i** and long **e, ie** in the second and third persons singular of the present indicative and in the singular familiar imperative:

sprechen, sprach, hat gesprochen, er spricht, sprich!
stehlen, stahl, hat gestohlen, er stiehlt, stiehl!

(*e*) Class V: **e—a—e.** The **a** is regularly long but the **e** varies both in the infinitive and in the participle; vowel changes in the present indicative and singular familiar imperative are the same as for Class IV:

---

[1] For the complete conjugation of strong verbs, *cf.* §§ 104–106 of the Appendix.

lesen, las, hat gelesen, er liest, lies!
essen, aß, hat gegessen, er ißt, iß!

(*f*) Class VI: **a—u—a.** The **u** is regularly long but the **a** varies in both cases; in the second and third persons singular of the present indicative the latter becomes **ä,** but not in the singular imperative:

schlagen, schlug, hat geschlagen, er schlägt, schlag(e)!
wachsen, wuchs, ist gewachsen, er wächst, wachs (wachse)!

(*g*) Class VII: All verbs of this class have **ie** or **i** in the past; the vowel of the past participle is always the same as that of the present infinitive; **a** changes to **ä** in the present indicative, but not in the singular familiar imperative (just as in Class VI):

laufen, lief, ist gelaufen, **er läuft, lauf(e)!**
fangen, fing, hat gefangen, **er fängt, fang(e)!**

Caution:

(*a*) **Rufen** (*to call*) is the only verb in this class with **u** as the stem vowel. The vowel is not modified.

rufen, rief, hat gerufen, **er ruft, ruf(e)!**

(*b*) **Heißen** [(tr.), *to bid, call;* (intr.) *to be called*] is the only verb with **ei** in the present infinitive which does not belong to Class I:

heißen, hieß, hat geheißen, er heißt, heiß(e)!

(3) (*a*) **The singular familiar imperative of strong verbs** has no vowel ending, if **e** is the stem vowel of an infinitive: **sprich!**, **lies!** (*cf.* ¶ **B** above).

Caution: A few verbs, however, such as **gehen, stehen,** and **heben,** which **do not change the stem vowel in the present indicative,** may have singular familiar imperative forms in –**e : geh(e)!, steh(e)!, heb(e)!**

(*b*) All other strong verbs, including those with the stem vowel **a** (which becomes **ä** in the present indicative but not in the singular familiar imperative) **may** have a final **e** in the imperative.[1]

Caution: In conversation, however, this **e** is usually omitted: **fall!** for **falle!, komm!** for **komme!**

---

[1] For strong verbs with the stem vowels **au, o,** and **u,** *cf.* **Note** (2) (*g*) above.

(4) (a) The **present infinitive** is often used as an imperative, particularly in giving commands to children and directions to the general public:

Mund **halten**!   *Hold your tongue.*
Schweigen!   *Be quiet.*
Umsteigen!   *Change cars.*

(b) The **past participle** is used with the force of an imperative in giving sharp commands and warnings:

Vorgesehen!   *Look out.*
Aufgestanden!   *Get up.*
Aufgepaßt!   *Pay attention.*

(5) For separable verbs, both strong and weak, *cf.* § 14, **Note** (6).

(6) For inseparable verbs, both strong and weak, *cf.* § 14, **Note** (5) above.

Learn the conjugation of the strong verbs **sehen** and **kommen** from § 104 of the Appendix.

16. IRREGULAR WEAK VERBS

Read the following sentences very carefully. Note the vowel changes and the endings of verb forms in each:

A. Kennen Sie ihn?
Do you know him?

Das Feuer brennt.
The fire is burning.

Ich **kannte** ihn.
I knew him.

Es **brannte**.
It was burning.

Ich habe ihn ge**kannt**.
I knew him.

Es hat ge**brannt**.
It (has) burned.

Sie denkt an mich.
She is thinking of me.

Sie **dachte** an mich.
She was thinking of me.

Sie hat an mich ge**dacht**.
She (has) thought of me.

B. (1) (*a*) **Kennen** Sie den Mann?
*Do you **know** the man?*

(*b*) Er **kennt** Goethes Werke.
*He **knows** (i.e., is familiar with) Goethe's works.*

(2) (*a*) Ich **weiß,** daß er recht hat.   (*b*) Ich **weiß** es.
*I **know** that he is right.*   *I **know** it.*

(3) (*a*) Er **kann** Deutsch.   (*b*) Sie **kann** ihre Aufgabe nicht.
*He **knows** German.*   *She does not **know** her lesson.*

(*c*) Wir **können** das Gedicht.
*We **know** (i.e., have learned) the poem.*

Summary:

(1) The sentences under ¶ **A** above indicate that certain verbs have weak tense endings (*i.e.,* –**te** in the past) and weak participial forms (*i.e.,* ending in –**t**), but that, on the other hand, these same verbs resemble strong verbs because their stem vowels change. [The modal auxiliaries and the verb **wissen** (*cf.* §§ 109 and 110 **B**) show similar changes, but have a different historical origin and are therefore not listed here.]

Note: Such verbs are known as irregular weak verbs and the most common of them are:

PRESENT INFINITIVE	PAST	PERFECT	PAST SUBJUNCTIVE	
brennen	brannte	hat gebrannt	brennte	*to burn*
kennen	kannte	hat gekannt	kennte	*to know*
nennen	nannte	hat genannt	nennte	*to name*
rennen	rannte	ist gerannt	rennte	*to run*
senden	sandte (sometimes sendete)	hat gesandt (sometimes gesendet)	sendete	*to send*
wenden	wandte (sometimes wendete)	hat gewandt (sometimes gewendet)	wendete	*to turn*
bringen	brachte	hat gebracht	brächte	*to bring*
denken	dachte	hat gedacht	dächte	*to think*

Caution: Do not confuse **brachte** (from bringen) with **brach** (from brechen). **Note particularly that the past subjunctive of the first six verbs listed above keeps the stem vowel of the present infinitive.**[1]

(2) The sentences under ¶ **B** above indicate that there are three common ways of translating the English *know :*

(*a*) **Kennen** means *to know* in the sense of **to be acquainted with,** and may refer either to persons (*cf.* ¶ **B** (1) (*a*) above) or to things (*cf.* ¶ **B** (1) (*b*) above).

(*b*) **Wissen** means **to know a fact** (*cf.* ¶ **B** (2) (*a*) and (*b*) above).

Note: **Es** in ¶ **B** (2) (*b*) refers, of course, to some fact.

(*c*) **Können** (which usually means *to be able, can, etc.*) may mean *to know* in the sense of **having acquired knowledge by study** (*cf.* ¶ **B** (3) (*a*), (*b*), and (*c*) above).

17. THE AUXILIARIES HABEN AND SEIN

Read the following sentences very carefully. Note particularly the auxiliary, whether **haben** or **sein,** which is used with each verb:

A. Er **hat** den Brief geschrieben.
He has written (or *wrote*) *the letter.*

Er **hatte** den Brief geschrieben.
He had written the letter.

Sie **hat** das Lied gesungen.
She has sung (or *sang*) *the song.*

Sie **hatte** das Lied gesungen.
She had sung the song.

Er **hat** die Tür zugemacht.
He (has) closed the door.

Ich **hatte** eine Geschichte erzählt.
I had told a story.

B. Er **ist** aufgestanden.
He (a)rose [or *has (a)risen*].

Sie **waren** gekommen.
They had come.

Er **ist** nach Hause gegangen.
He has gone (or *went*) *home.*

Sie **war** nach Hause gegangen.
She had gone home.

Er **ist** gekommen.
He has come (or *came*).

Er **war** aufgestanden.
He had (a)risen.

---

[1] *Cf.* also § 110 of the Appendix.

C.   Sie **ist** eingeschlafen.
She has fallen (or fell) asleep.

Sie **war** eingeschlafen.
She had fallen asleep.

Es **ist** kalt geworden.
It has become (or became) cold.

Es **war** kalt geworden.
It had become cold.

D.   Hier **hat** er gestanden.
Here he (has) stood.

Er **hatte** gestanden.
He had stood.

Er **hat** nicht geschlafen.
He has not slept (or did not sleep).

Er **hatte** nicht geschlafen.
He had not slept.

Summary:

(1) The sentences under ¶ **A** above indicate that **all transitive[1] verbs require the auxiliary haben, to form their perfect tenses.**[2]

Note: The same holds true for the rare future perfect:

Er wird den Brief geschrieben **haben.**
He will have written the letter.

(2) The sentences under ¶ **B** above indicate that **intransitive verbs require the auxiliary sein, to form their perfect tenses, provided they denote a change of place.**

Note: The same holds true for the rare future perfect:

Er wird gekommen **sein.**
He will have come.

Caution: **Haben** is used as an auxiliary when **the action itself is emphasized** and **not the goal** toward which the action is directed:

Haben Sie lange geschwommen?
Did you swim long?

Here the **action** of swimming is referred to.

but: Ich **bin** über den Fluß geschwommen.
I swam across the river.

In this sentence the **goal**—the other side of the river—is implied.

---

[1] For the definition of a transitive verb, *cf.* § 1 **C** (1).
[2] For the complete conjugation of verbs with **haben** and **sein** *cf.* §§ 102–110 of the Appendix.

(3) The sentences under ¶ **C** above indicate that **intransitive verbs require the auxiliary** sein, **provided they denote a change of condition.**

(4) The sentences under ¶ **D** above indicate that **intransitive verbs are conjugated with** haben, **provided they do** *not* **denote a change of place or condition.**

Remember: An intransitive verb is one which cannot take a direct object.

E.   Other verbs conjugated with sein. The following verbs are also conjugated with **sein:**

bleiben	blieb	ist geblieben	*to remain*
geschehen	geschah	ist geschehen	*to happen*
sein	war	ist gewesen	*to be*
gelingen	gelang	ist gelungen	*to succeed*
glücken	glückte	ist geglückt	*to succeed*

Note: **Geschehen, gelingen,** and **glücken** are impersonal verbs:

Es ist ihm noch nicht gelungen, den Bleistift zu finden.
He has not yet succeeded in finding his pencil.

EXERCISE

A.   Rewrite the following sentences in the past, perfect, past perfect, and future tenses (nos. 1–12 relate to § 14; nos. 13–34 to § 15; nos. 35–44, to § 16; and nos. 45–55, to § 17):

1. Ich warte auf meinen lieben Freund.
2. Er studiert zu Hause.
3. Fritz liebt die Mutter sehr.
4. Ich beantworte die erste Frage.
5. Sie macht die Tür auf.
6. Marie buchstabiert das lange Wort.
7. Ich amüsiere mich.
8. Er redet nicht gern.
9. Sie sagt nichts Gutes über ihn.
10. Heinrich macht seine Aufgabe.
11. Das Kind gehorcht der Mutter.

12. Ich vermisse dich sehr.
13. Mein reicher Vetter fährt um zehn Uhr ab.
14. Er geht nach Hause.
15. Wir kommen um halb neun in die Schule.
16. Frau Schmidt trägt einen neuen Hut.
17. Sie sieht müde aus.
18. Er gibt mir immer guten Rat.
19. Sie liest nicht gern.
20. Es wird heiß.
21. Klara schneidet das Brot.
22. Wir stehen um sechs Uhr auf.
23. Er kommt immer zu spät an.
24. Sie nimmt das deutsche Buch in die Hand.
25. Die Mutter ruft das kleine Mädchen.
26. Ich schreibe den kurzen Satz.
27. Er nimmt den Hut ab.
28. Das wilde Tier läuft in den Wald.
29. Wir singen ein altes Volkslied.
30. Sie (*You*) sprechen immer zu schnell.
31. Er schlägt den Mann.
32. Ich verstehe das Gedicht nicht.
33. Er ißt langsam.
34. Der Baum wächst schnell.
35. Ich denke an dich.
36. Er brennt vor (*with*) Ungeduld.
37. Er kennt meinen besten Freund.
38. Ich weiß es.
39. Sie kann Französisch.
40. Das bringt Glück.
41. Das Kind rennt schnell zu der Mutter.
42. Ich nenne ihn Fritz.
43. Er sendet ihn zu mir.
44. Warum wendest du ihm den Rücken zu?
45. Er schläft nicht.
46. Er schläft schnell ein.
47. Er steht an der Tafel.
48. Er steht langsam auf.
49. Der kleine Junge fällt ins Wasser.
50. Das Wasser gefällt ihm nicht.

51. Der Vogel fliegt auf das Dach.
52. Wir gehen aufs Land.
53. Wir kommen bald zurück.
54. Es gelingt mir nicht, das zu tun.
55. Meine Eltern bleiben auf dem Lande.
56. Es gelingt dem Flieger, einen Weltraumflug zu machen.
57. Er bleibt mehrere Stunden in den höheren Luftschichten.

B.   Translate into German [nos. 1–12 relate to § 14;   nos. 13–34, to § 15;   nos. 35–44, to § 16; nos. 45–55, to § 17;   and nos. 56–65, to § 15, **Note** (3)].   Nos. 66–67 involve scientific vocabulary.

1. He did not hear me.
2. She is answering the second question.   (*Translate first with* antworten, *then with* beantworten.)
3. My older brother was traveling through Switzerland.
4. He visited (*perf.*) many old friends.
5. My younger brother was studying his lesson.
6. She had never loved him.
7. When did you telephone me?
8. They were having a good time.
9. Why did you not open the door?
10. He asked me what that long word meant (bedeutete).
11. When did you buy that large house?
12. He was sitting down on the sofa.
13. How long did you stay in the country?
14. Those little boys looked very tired.
15. He had written a long letter to his old parents.
16. She was taking off her hat.
17. When does school begin?
18. They always arrived late.
19. Were they singing a German folksong?
20. After school Fred ran (*perf.*) home.
21. He had given the old men some money.
22. Have you read those German books?
23. He was eating too fast.   (*Rewrite in the perfect tense.*)
24. She will help the poor.   (*Rewrite in the past perfect tense.*)
25. He speaks too rapidly.   (*Rewrite in the perfect tense.*)
26. The little dog was lying under a chair.
27. When did that famous man die?

28. He drank (*perf.*) too much.
29. Why did you strike that animal?
30. Who came (*perf.*) today?
31. They were going home. (*Rewrite in the past perfect tense.*)
32. She is wearing a beautiful dress. (*Rewrite in the past perfect tense.*)
33. He enters (*i.e.*, steps into) the room. (*Rewrite in the perfect tense.*)
34. He has not yet found his German book.
35. I was burning with impatience. (*Compare with German sentence no. 36 of this lesson.*)
36. We call the little boy Fred.
37. He knows German.
38. She knows Schiller's works.
39. Do you know where he lives?
40. He was thinking of you. (*Rewrite in the perfect tense.*)
41. The child ran quickly to its father.
42. That always brings me good luck. (*Rewrite in the perfect tense.*)
43. Why did he turn his back on me?
44. I do not know that old man.
45. Why did you stay in the city this summer?
46. Have you succeeded in translating these short sentences?
47. My best friends had gone to the country.
48. They have not yet returned.
49. How long did you sleep?
50. When did you fall asleep?
51. When did you get up this morning?
52. I was standing at the blackboard. (*Rewrite in the perfect tense.*)
53. He had fallen into the water.
54. A bird flew (*perf.*) through the open window.
55. What has happened?
56. Carl, give me your book.
57. Fred, read more slowly.
58. Marie, take the chalk in your hand.
59. Henry, tell the truth.
60. Children, help your mother.
61. William, take off your hat.
62. Children, go to sleep.

63. Carl, go to sleep.
64. Marie, do not eat so fast.
65. Fred, don't fall into the water.
66. The flyers who were carrying out space-flight experiments remained in the air several hours.
67. They learned much about cosmic radiation.

CHAPTER 7 **Numerals**

18. CARDINAL NUMERALS

Read the following sentences carefully. Note the use of the numerals in each:

A. Zählen Sie von **eins** bis **ein**undzwanzig!
Count from 1 to 21.

B. (1) **Ein** Bleistift liegt auf dem Tisch.
A [or one (said emphatically)] pencil is on the table.

(2) „Wie viele Bleistifte liegen darauf?"   „**Einer.**"
"How many pencils are on it?"   *"One."*

(3) **Ein** Buch gehört mir.   **Ein(e)s** gehört mir nicht.
One book belongs to me.   *One does not belong to me.*

(4) „Haben Sie **ein** Buch?"   „Ja, ich habe **ein(e)s.**"
"Have you a book?"   *"Yes, I have one."*

C. **Der eine** Sohn war in der Stadt, der andere war auf dem Lande.
(The) one son was in the city, the other was in the country.

D. **Sein einer** Sohn war in der Schule.
His one son was in school.

E. Die Stadt Berlin hat über vier **Millionen** Einwohner.
The city of Berlin has more than four million inhabitants.

F. (1) Es waren **hundert** Menschen da.
*There were **a hundred** people there.*

Ich habe viele **Hunderte** gesehen.
I saw many hundreds.

(2) Es waren **tausend** Menschen da.
*There were **a thousand** people there.*

Ich habe viele **T**ausend**e** gesehen.
*I saw many thousand**s**.*

G. Das ist **eine Fünf.**   Er ist **eine Null.**
That is a (figure) five.   *He is a nobody* (lit. *a zero*).

H. Es ist **ein** Uhr.
or: Es ist **eins.**
It is one o'clock.

„Was ist das?" „Es ist ein**e** Uhr."
"What is that?" "It is a watch."

I. Das Kind kroch auf allen vier**en.**
The child crept on all fours.

J. (1) Ihre **beiden** Brüder spielen Schach.
*Her **two** (or both her) brothers are playing chess.*

(2) Keiner von den **beiden** interessiert sich für die Musik.
*Neither of the **two** is interested in music.*

(3) Welches von den **beiden** Häusern haben Sie verkauft?
*Which (one) of the **two** houses did you sell?*

(4) Meine **beiden** Schwestern sind musikalisch.
*My **two** (or both my) sisters are musical.*

Note:

(1) The form **eins** is used in counting, except where **und** follows (*cf.* ¶ **A** above).

(2) (*a*) When followed by a noun, the numeral **ein** is declined like the indefinite article (*cf.* ¶ **B** (1), (3), and (4) above).

(*b*) If **ein** stands alone (*i.e.*, as a pronoun), it has the endings of a **der**-word (*cf.* ¶ **B** (2), (3), and (4) above).

(3) After a **der**-word **ein** has the weak endings (*cf.* ¶ **C** above).

(4) After an **ein**-word (*e.g.*, **sein** in ¶ **D** above), **ein** takes the customary endings of a descriptive adjective.

(5) (*a*) **Million** is a weak feminine noun and, therefore, takes the ending –**en** in the plural (*cf.* ¶ **E** above).

(*b*) **Milliarde** is also a weak feminine noun.

(6) *A hundred* and *a thousand* are rendered by **hundert** and **tausend,** which are capitalized when used as nouns: Hundert, Tausend. Observe the plurals Hunderte and Tausende (*cf.* ¶ **F** above).

(7) Cardinals are feminine when used as nouns (*cf.* ¶ **G** above).

(8) **Ein** takes no ending in the phrase **ein Uhr,** *one o'clock* (*cf.* ¶ **H** above).

(9) (*a*) It is rather rare in modern German for any other numerals than the above-mentioned to take endings. Occasionally, however, the cardinals from two to twelve do:

durch **zweier** (*gen. pl.*) Zeugen Mund, *by the mouth of two witnesses*

(*b*) Observe also the common phrase auf allen vier**en,** *on all fours* (*cf.* ¶ **I** above).

(10) (*a*) When referring to but two of a kind, English *two* is usually translated by German **beide** (with adjective inflection) (*cf.* ¶ **J** above).

(*b*) Instead of **die beiden** Männer, one may also say **beide** Männer without change of meaning.

K. The cardinals. Cardinals are listed below; forms requiring particular attention appear in boldface:

0 = Null	11 = elf	30 = **dreißig**
1 = ein(s)	12 = zwölf	31 = einunddreißig
2 = zwei	13 = dreizehn	40 = vierzig
3 = drei	14 = vierzehn	50 = fünfzig
4 = vier	15 = fünfzehn	60 = **sechzig**
5 = fünf	16 = **sechzehn**	70 = **siebzig**
6 = **sechs**	17 = **siebzehn**	80 = achtzig
7 = **sieben**	18 = achtzehn	90 = neunzig
8 = acht	19 = neunzehn	100 = hundert
9 = neun	20 = zwanzig	101 = hundert(und)eins
10 = zehn	21 = einundzwanzig	200 = zweihundert

1000 = tausend   1,000,000 = eine Million

100,000 = hunderttausend   1,000,000,000 = eine Milliarde

1934 = neunzehnhundertvierunddreißig

Note: All multiples of ten, except dreißig, end in –**zig.**

19. ORDINAL NUMERALS

Read the following sentences carefully. Note the form of bold-faced words:

A.   Das ist der **zweite** Fehler.
That is the second mistake.

Heute fehlt der **fünfte** Schüler in der **vierten** Reihe.
The fifth pupil in the fourth row is absent today.

Mein Geburtstag ist am **sechsten** Oktober.
also: Der **sechste** Oktober ist mein Geburtstag.
October 6 is my birthday.

Mein Freund wird am **achtzehnten** (18ten or 18.) oder am **neunzehnten** (19ten or 19.) dieses Monats abreisen.
My friend will leave on the 18th or 19th of this month.

B.   Heute ist der **erste** Schnee gefallen.
The first snow fell today.

Das ist das **dritte** Buch, das er verloren hat.
That is the third book (that) he has lost.

Haben Sie das **achte** Kapitel gelesen?
Did you read the eighth chapter?

C.   Heute ist der **zwanzigste** Juni.
or: Heute haben wir den **zwanzigsten** Juni.
Today is June 20.

Goethe wurde am **achtundzwanzigsten** August siebzehnhundert-neunundvierzig geboren.
Goethe was born August 28, 1749.

Er starb in Weimar am **zweiundzwanzigsten** März achtzehn-hundertzweiunddreißig.
He died in Weimar March 22, 1832.

Was ist der Inhalt des **dreiunddreißigsten** Kapitels?
What are the contents of the thirty-third chapter?

Summary: The above sentences indicate that ordinals are declined like adjectives.

Note:

(1) Ordinals up to *nineteenth* (except *first, third, eighth,* and sometimes *seventh*) are formed by adding the suffix –t to the corresponding cardinals (*cf.* ¶ **A** above).

(2) The ordinals *first, third,* and *eighth* are irregular (*cf.* ¶ **B** above).

(3) Ordinals from *twentieth* upward are formed by adding –st to the corresponding cardinals (*cf.* ¶ **C** above).

(4) (*a*) When used in dates, ordinals are usually abbreviated:

Heute ist der 20. Juni.   Goethe wurde am 28. August 1749 geboren.
Today is June 20.   *Goethe was born August 28, 1749.*

(*b*) Similarly:

die 3. Ausgabe, *the third edition*
Wilhelm I. (read der Erste), *William I* (or *the First*)

Caution: If the ordinal ending [*e.g.*, –**te(n)** or –**ste(n)**] is omitted after figures, **a period must take its place.**

D. The Ordinals.   Some ordinals are listed below and their irregular forms are in boldface:

   1. = der (die, das) **erste,** *first*
   2. = der (die, das) zweite, *second*
   3. = der (die, das) **dritte,** *third*
   4. = der (die, das) vierte, *fourth*
   5. = der (die, das) fünfte, *fifth*
   7. = der (die, das) siebente or **siebte,** *seventh*
   8. = der (die, das) **achte,** *eighth*
   9. = der (die, das) neunte, *ninth*
  19. = der (die, das) neunzehnte, *nineteenth*
  20. = der (die, das) zwanzigste, *twentieth*
  21. = der (die, das) einundzwanzigste, *twenty-first*
  30. = der (die, das) dreißigste, *thirtieth*
 100. = der (die, das) hundertste, *hundredth*
1000. = der (die, das) tausendste, *thousandth*

20. DERIVATIVES FROM NUMERALS

A. Forms in –mal.   The indeclinable forms **einmal** (*once*), **zwei-mal** (*twice*), **dreimal** (*three times*), *etc.* are formed regularly by adding –**mal** to the corresponding cardinals:

Wir haben Deutsch **fünfmal** die Woche.
We have German five times a week.

B. Forms in –erlei. The indeclinable forms **einerlei** (*one kind of*), **zweierlei** (*two kinds of*), **dreierlei** (*three kinds of*), **wievielerlei** (*how many kinds of*), *etc.* are formed regularly by adding **–erlei** to the corresponding cardinals:

> „**Wievielerlei** Farben hat der Schmetterling?" „**Dreierlei:** gelb, schwarz und weiß."
> *"How many (different) colors has the butterfly?"   "Three kinds: yellow, black and white."*

C. Forms in –ens. The adverbial forms **erstens** (*first, in the first place*), **zweitens** (*secondly, in the second place*), **drittens** (*thirdly, in the third place*), *etc.* are formed by adding **–ens** to the stem of the corresponding ordinals:

> Sie konnte mich nicht besuchen: **erstens** war sie beschäftigt, **zweitens** hatte sie kein Reisegeld.
> *She could not visit me:* **in the first place,** *she was busy;* **in the second place,** *she had no money for traveling.*

D. Forms in –fach. The adjectives **dreifach** (*threefold*), **vierfach** (*fourfold*), *etc.* are formed by adding **–fach** to the corresponding cardinals:

> Er trägt eine **dreifache** Krone.
> *He wears a triple crown.*

Similarly with forms in **–stufig**, *e.g.*, **dreistufig** (with three steps; three-stage, *ref.* to space rockets).

Note: For *double* or *twofold* one may say **doppelt, zweifach,** or **zwiefach.**

E. Fractions. The fractions **ein Drittel** (*a third*), **ein Viertel** (*a fourth*), **ein Zwanzigstel** (*a twentieth*), *etc.* are neuter nouns formed by adding **–el** to the stem of the corresponding ordinals:[1]

> **Zwei Drittel** von einundzwanzig ist vierzehn.
> *Two thirds of twenty-one is fourteen.*

---

[1] The fraction *half* is an exception (*cf.* ¶ **F** below).

Note: The preceding explanation is a simple and practical one for the formation of fractions. What actually happens, however, is that the suffix **–tel** (from Teil, *part*) is added to the stem of an ordinal, which drops the final **t**; thus dritt– plus –tel (literally *third part*) becomes **Drittel.**

F. Halb and combinations with halb.

(1) **Halb** is the adjective for *half:*

Er hat einen **halben** Apfel gegessen.
He ate half an apple.

(2) Die **Hälfte** is the noun for *half:*

Die andere **Hälfte** hat er der Schwester gegeben.
He gave his sister the other half.

Note:

(1) The form **anderthalb,** *one and a half,* takes no ending and is followed by a plural noun:

Ich wartete **anderthalb** Stunden.
I waited an hour and a half.

(2) The same applies to the forms **zwei(und)einhalb,** *two and a half;* **sechs(und)einhalb,** *six and a half; etc.:*

In **acht(und)einhalb** Jahren kehrt er zurück.
In eight and a half years he will return.

EXERCISE

A. Complete the following sentences:

1. Zwei Bleistifte liegen auf dem Tisch. —— (*One*) gehört mir.
2. Ich habe zwei Bücher gelesen. —— (*One*) war sehr interessant.
3. —— (*A or One*) Bleistift und —— (*a or one*) Buch liegen auf dem Tisch.
4. —— (*One*) Tisch ist in diesem Zimmer, —— (*one*) ist im Nebenzimmer.
5. „Wie viele Tische sind hier?" „Nur —— (*one*)."
6. —— (*One*) Zimmer ist groß, —— (*one*) ist klein.
7. „Wie viele Zimmer hat der Student?" „—— (*One*)."
8. D— ein— Stuhl gefällt mir.
9. Er hat —— (*a hundred*) Briefmarken gekauft.

10. Er hat viele —— (*hundreds*) in seiner Briefmarkensammlung (*stamp collection*).
11. Es waren —— (*a thousand*) Menschen da.
12. Viele —— (*thousands*) klatschten in die Hände.
13. Wie viele —— (*million*) Einwohner hat die Stadt?
14. Ist das —— (*an eight*) oder —— (*a zero*)?
15. Er hat —— (*sixteen*) Bücher, aber nur —— (*six*) davon hat er gelesen.
16. Das kleine Kind kann noch nicht gehen. Es kriecht auf allen —— (*fours*).
17. Mein Geburtstag ist am —— (*30th*) April.
18. Heute haben wir d—— (*17th*) Dezember. Heute ist d— —— (*17th*) Dezember.
19. Meine Schwester ist am —— (*20th*) Mai geboren.
20. Schiller wurde am —— (*10th*) November —— (*1759*) geboren.
21. Er starb in Weimar am —— (*9th*) Mai —— (*1805*).
22. Karl ist d— —— (*16th*) Schüler in der Klasse.
23. Fritz sitzt in d— —— (*6th*) Reihe.
24. Heinrich, lies d— —— (*20th*) Satz!
25. Aus zweierlei Gründen bin ich nicht nach Europa gereist: —— (*in the first place*) war ich krank, —— (*in the second place*) hatte ich kein Geld.
26. Wir mußten d— —— (*30th*) Satz —— (*ten times*) schreiben.
27. Der Satz hatte eine —— (*threefold*) Bedeutung.
28. Nach —— (*an hour and a half*) erschien er.
29. Bitte, geben Sie mir —— (*half a cup of*) Kaffee.
30. Hat der Mann —— (*a third*) oder —— (*a fourth*) seines Vermögens verloren?
31. Welches von den —— (*two*) Mädchen ist deine Freundin?
32. —— (*One*) der ersten Weltraumfahrer war ein Hund.
33. —— (*Hundreds*) von Männern sind untersucht worden. Man wollte wissen, ob sie zum Fliegen taugten.

B.   Translate:

1. Today is the 30th of January. (*Translate in two ways.*)
2. Washington was (wurde) born on the 22nd of February 1732.
3. The 22nd of February is Washington's birthday.
4. He died on the 14th of December 1799.
5. The 16th of June is my birthday.

6. Today the sixth pupil in the first row is absent.
7. Is that a seven or a nine?
8. I saw a hundred autos this morning.
9. Hundreds of (von) people were looking at them.
10. It cost a thousand dollars.
11. Thousands of (von) people are unemployed (arbeitslos).
12. The city has about eight million inhabitants.
13. One son will go to the country, one will remain in the city.
14. His one son does not yet go to school.
15. "How many boys are absent today?"   "One."
16. "How many books did you buy?"   "One."
17. One boy had forgotten a book.
18. I cannot take a walk today: in the first place, I am too tired; in the second place, it is raining.
19. He had read that interesting book three times.
20. Give me half a pound of tea.
21. The dress has four colors (*i.e.*, four kinds of color): red, blue, white, and yellow.
22. It is a quarter after twelve.
23. He had eaten half an orange.
24. Those goods (Waren) have a fourfold value.
25. After an hour and a half he came.
26. Which one of the two sisters was interested in music?
27. Hundreds of three-stage research rockets have risen into (the) world space.
28. Many millions of dollars are being spent for such research.

The Comparison
CHAPTER 8 of Adjectives
and Adverbs

21. USES OF THE COMPARATIVE AND SUPERLATIVE

In German as in English, the adjective has three degrees of comparison:[1] **positive, comparative,** and **superlative:**

gut, besser, der beste (or am besten), *good, better, best*

Study the following sentences very carefully. Note the umlauted vowels and **bold-faced** endings which show the degree of comparison:

A. (1) Das Eisen ist schwer.
Iron is heavy.

Das Blei ist schwer**er.**
Lead is heavier.

Welches Metall ist am schwer**sten?**
Which metal is heaviest?

(2) Karl ist stark.
Carl is strong.

Fritz ist stärk**er.**
Fred is stronger.

Johann ist am stärk**sten.**
John is strongest.

(3) Der Mond ist groß.
The moon is large.

Die Erde ist größ**er.**
The earth is larger.

Die Sonne ist am größ**ten.**
The sun is largest.

B. (1) Karl ist ein starker Junge.
Carl is a strong boy.

Fritz ist ein stärk**erer** Junge.
Fred is a stronger boy.

Johann ist der stärk**ste** Junge.
John is the strongest boy.

Er ist der stärk**ste.**
He is the strongest.[2]

---

[1] Certain adjectives, of course, cannot be compared because of their meaning: **tot** (*dead*), **halb** (*half*), **mündlich** (*oral*), **neunfach** (*ninefold*), **etc.**

[2] Here the noun (Junge) is understood.

(2) Marie ist eine gute Köchin.   Luise ist die **beste** Köchin.
Mary is a good cook.   *Louise is the best cook.*

Klara ist eine bess**ere** Köchin.   Sie ist die **beste.**
Clara is a better cook.   *She is the best.*

(3) Er schreibt einen kurzen Satz.
He writes a short sentence.

Er schreibt einen kürz**eren** Satz.
He writes a shorter sentence.

Er schreibt den kürz**esten** Satz.
He writes the shortest sentence.

C. Es war eine dunkle Nacht.   Es war eine dunkl**ere** Nacht.
   It was a dark night.   *It was a darker night.*

Es war die dunkel**ste** Nacht.
It was the darkest night.

D. Es wird immer heiß**er.**   Es wurde immer schlimmer.
   It is getting hotter and hotter.   *It was getting worse and worse.*

E. Er geht langsam.   Er geht langsam**er.**
   He walks slowly.   *He walks more slowly.*

Er geht am langsam**sten.**
He walks most slowly.

F. (1) Sie sang aufs schön**ste.**
    She sang most (or very) beautifully.

Das Rauchen ist aufs streng**ste** (or frequently streng**stens**) verboten.
Smoking is most strictly forbidden.

(2) Das ist höch**st** interessant.
That is very (or extremely) interesting.

Die Reise war äußer**st** gefährlich.
The trip was very (or exceedingly) dangerous.

G. (1) Sie ist die allerschön**ste.**
or: Sie ist die schön**ste** von allen.
    She is the most beautiful of all.

Das ist das allerbe**ste.**
That is the best of all.

(2) Sie tanzt am allerbe**sten.**
She dances best of all.

Sie schreibt am allerschön**sten.**
She writes most beautifully of all.

Summary: The above sentences indicate that the comparative is formed by adding **–er** to the stem (*i.e.*, the uninflected form) of an adjective; the superlative, by adding **–(e)st.** (Compare this with the procedure in English: *faster, fastest;* but note that German does not use **more** and **most** in comparison: *more interesting,* interessant**er**; *most interesting,* **am** interessant**esten.**[1])

Note:

(1) Adjectives of one syllable with the vowels **a, o,** or **u** usually take umlaut in the comparative and superlative degrees (*cf.* ¶ **A** (2) and (3) and ¶ **B** (1) and (3) above).

(2) (*a*) The superlative form with **am,** known as the "adverbial superlative," is used either as a predicate adjective (*cf.* ¶ **A** (1), (2), and (3) above) or as an adverb (*cf.* last sentence under ¶ **E** above).

(*b*) The English equivalent of the adverbial superlative does not have the definite article, wherein it differs from the "relative superlative" (explained in **Note** (3) following).

(3) The superlative with the definite article, known as the "relative superlative," is used both when a noun is expressed (*cf.* third sentences in ¶ **B** (1), (2), and (3) and ¶ **C** above) and when it is understood (*cf.* last sentences in ¶ **B** (1) and (2) above).

(4) Adjectives and adverbs of more than one syllable do not take umlaut (*cf.* ¶¶ **C** and **E** above).

(5) **Immer** followed immediately by the comparative is often used instead of two comparatives connected by **und** (*cf.* ¶ **D** above).

---

[1] **Mehr** followed by the positive degree is used when two qualities in the same individual (or thing) are compared:

Er war mehr verdrießlich als zornig.
He was more vexed than angry.

Die Reise war mehr anstrengend als interessant.
The trip was more strenuous than interesting.

(6) (*a*) Many German adjectives may, without change of form, be used as adverbs (*cf.* **langsam,** in ¶ **E** above). Similarly:

Sie ist **gut.**   Sie schreibt **gut.**
She is good.   *She writes well.*

(*b*) The comparative of adverbs must always end in –**er** and the superlative (unless used absolutely, as explained in **Note** (7) following) must use the invariable **am**-form.

(7) (*a*) The superlative adverb in **aufs,** known as the " absolute superlative," denotes merely a very high degree without any idea of comparison (*cf.* ¶ **F** (1) above).

(*b*) Another form of the absolute superlative is **höchst** or **äußerst** —or some similar word in the sense of *very*—followed by the positive degree (*cf.* ¶ **F** (2) above).

Caution: Both the adverbial superlative (*cf.* **Note** (2) above) and the relative superlative (*cf.* **Note** (3) above) express real comparison. The absolute superlative, however, is not used for purposes of comparison.

(8) The comparative degree may also be used absolutely without any idea of comparison:

eine **ältere** Dame, *an elderly lady*
seit **längerer** Zeit, *for some time*

(9) **Aller** (gen. pl. *of all*) may be used to strengthen the superlative adjective (*cf.* ¶ **G** (1) above) or the superlative adverb (*cf.* ¶ **G** (2) above). It is then invariable and serves for all cases and genders.

Caution: Endings are added to the **stem** of the comparative and superlative, just as they are to the uninflected form of an adjective in the positive degree:

(1) Comparative: ein **ärmerer** Mann (*a poorer man*), eines **ärmeren** Mannes, einem **ärmeren** Manne, *etc.* (here the comparative stem is **ärmer–**).

(2) Superlative: der **ärmste** Mann (*the poorest man*), des **ärmsten** Mannes, dem **ärmsten** Manne, *etc.* (here the superlative stem is **ärmst–**).

22. SPECIAL AND IRREGULAR FORMATIONS OF THE COMPARATIVE AND SUPERLATIVE

A. Adjectives ending in –d, –t, or an –s-sound; in –e; in –el, –en, and in –er.

(1) Adjectives ending in **–d, –t,** or an **–s**-sound add **–est** to form the superlative: kurz, kürzer, der kürzeste, am kürzesten.

Note: Present participles used as adjectives do not insert this e; thus the superlative of **reizend** (*charming*) is der reizend**ste.**

(2) Adjectives drop final –e before a comparative ending: **weise** (*wise*), **weiser** (*wiser*).

(3) Adjectives ending in **–el, –en,** and **–er** usually drop the **e** before a comparative ending: **dunkel, dunkler, der dunkelste, am dunkelsten** (*dark*).

Note: The **e** is also frequently dropped before an ending in the positive degree:

eine **dunkle** Nacht, *a dark night*

B. Adjectives that take umlaut and their exceptions.

(1) The following are the most common adjectives that take umlaut in forming the comparative and superlative degrees:[1] alt, arm, dumm, fromm, grob, groß, hart, hoch, jung, kalt, klug, krank, kurz, lang, nah(e), scharf, schwach, schwarz, stark, warm.

Note: The comparative of **rot** may be either **röter** or **roter.**

(2) The following are exceptions to the rule that adjectives of one syllable take umlaut in the comparative and superlative degrees:

(*a*) Adjectives that never take umlaut: klar, rasch, voll, froh, lahm, rund, starr, schlank, and all **au**-stems (*e.g.,* laut, blau, schlau, *etc.*).

(*b*) Adjectives that sometimes take umlaut, although occurring also without it: blaß, glatt, karg, naß, schmal.

---

[1] Remember that monosyllabic adjectives **only** may take umlaut.

C. The irregular comparison of adjectives and adverbs.

(1) The following adjectives are irregular in their comparison:

groß (*large*)	größer	der größte	am größten
gut (*good*)	besser	der beste	am besten
hoch (*high*)	höher	der höchste	am höchsten
nah (*near*)	näher	der nächste	am nächsten
viel (*much*)	mehr	der meiste	am meisten

Note:

(*a*) If the positive **hoch** takes an ending, the –c– is dropped:

ein **hoher** Berg, *a high mountain*

(*b*) Contrary to English usage, the definite article must be used with **meist–**:

die meisten Frauen, *most women*
die meisten Schüler, *most pupils*

(2) The following adverbs are irregular in their comparison:

bald (*soon*)	eher	am ehesten
gern (*gladly*)	lieber	am liebsten

Note:

(1) **Früher** (*sooner*) is quite frequently used instead of **eher**; it is also very often used in the sense of *formerly*.

(2) (*a*) **Gern** is used idiomatically with **haben** to translate the English verb *to like*, provided what is liked is the direct object of the verb:

Ich **habe** Englisch **gern**.   Ich **habe** Französisch **lieber**.
I like English.   *I prefer French.*

Ich **habe** Deutsch **am liebsten**.
I like German best.

(*b*) If the action of the subject of a sentence is the point of comparison, merely add **gern**:

Er spricht **gern**.   Er spricht **lieber**.
He likes to talk.   *He prefers to talk.*

Er spricht **am liebsten**.
He likes best to talk.

Here the act of talking is the point of comparison.

D. The use of als **and** wie **in comparison.**

(1) **Als** is used **after the comparative degree:**

Sie ist **fleißiger als** ihr Bruder.
She is more industrious than her brother.

(2) **Wie** is used after the positive degree (affirmative or negative):

Sie ist ebenso **fleißig wie** ihr Bruder.
She is just as industrious as her brother.

Sie ist nicht so **fleißig wie** ihr Bruder.
She is not as industrious as her brother.

EXERCISE

A. Form sentences according to the following model:

Die Mutter, der Vater, der Großvater, alt sein.
Die Mutter ist alt.   Der Vater ist **älter.**   Der Großvater ist **am
ältesten.**

1. Das Dienstmädchen, die Tochter, die Mutter, fleißig sein.
2. Die Stunde, die Minute, die Sekunde, kurz sein.
3. Das Haus, die Kirche, der Berg, hoch sein.
4. Das Silber, das Gold, das Platin, teuer sein.
5. Afrika, Amerika, Asien, groß sein.
6. Das Auto, der Schnellzug, das Flugzeug, schnell fahren.
7. Marie, Klara, Luise, jung sein.
8. Herr Schmidt, sein Vetter, sein Nachbar, arm sein.
9. Frau Werner, ihre Freundin, die Großmutter, langsam gehen.
10. Dieses Jahr, letztes Jahr, vorletztes Jahr, warm sein.
11. Karl, Fritz, Johann, gern lesen.
12. Eine Taschenuhr, ein Fernsehapparat, ein künstlicher Erdsatellit, kostspielig sein.

B. Supply comparative and superlative forms according to the model:
Er ist ein kluger Junge.   Sein Bruder ist ein **klügerer** Junge.
Fritz ist der **klügste** Junge.

1. Heute ist ein kalter Tag.   Gestern war ein —— Tag.   Vorgestern war der —— Tag des ganzen Winters.
2. Das war ein harter Schlag.   Das war ein —— Schlag.   Das war der —— Schlag, den er dem Weltmeister gegeben hat.

3. Ein langer Weg liegt vor mir. Ein —— Weg liegt vor mir. Der —— Weg liegt vor mir.

4. Das ist ein scharfes Messer. Das ist ein —— Messer. Das ist das —— Messer, das ich je gekauft habe.

5. Er war ein starker Mann. Sein Bruder war ein —— Mann. Simson war der —— Mann, von dem ich je gelesen habe.

6. Versicherungsgesellschaft ist ein langes Wort. Feuerversicherungsgesellschaft ist ein —— Wort. Fliegertauglichkeitsuntersuchungen ist das —— Wort, das in diesem Buche vorkommt.

C. Complete:

1. Sie wurde —— (*weaker and weaker*).
2. Die Nacht wird —— (*darker and darker*).
3. Wir kamen —— (*nearer and nearer*).
4. Das Buch wurde —— (*easier and easier*).
5. Sie sang —— [*most (i.e., very) beautifully*].
6. Sie sang —— [*most beautifully* (as compared with others)].
7. Sie war —— (*the most beautiful of all*).
8. —— [*The most beautiful* (as compared with others)] Dame sang das Lied.
9. Die Forschungsrakete steigt —— (*higher and higher*).

D. Translate:

1. That is a good book, but this is a better book.
2. He works most diligently when he is alone.
3. She likes to read. She prefers to talk. She likes best to dance.
4. She is a charming woman. Her sister is more charming. Her friend (*fem.*) is most charming.
5. He likes the English book. (*Use* gern.) He prefers the French book. He likes the German book best.
6. February is usually a colder month than March.
7. January was the coldest month in the whole year.
8. Which month was coldest?
9. Have you ever seen a more beautiful village?
10. He will visit the most famous cities in Germany.
11. Most students like to talk German.
12. That is most (*use proper form of* hoch) interesting.
13. That building is high, but this one is higher. Which one is highest?

14. Formerly the Woolworth Building was the highest building in New York.
15. The Rhine is one of the most beautiful rivers of Europe.
16. This week we are having warmer weather.
17. Please give me a longer pencil.
18. That is the longest lesson we ever had.
19. In what season are the days shortest?
20. He is just as poor as his brother.
21. She always speaks more clearly than her sister.
22. He usually speaks as clearly as she.
23. Next summer we shall buy a larger house.
24. Last winter he saw the largest cities in Germany.
25. The weather is becoming colder and colder.
26. He works most diligently (*as compared with others*).
27. The most diligent boy in the class was reading the sentence.
28. He was the most diligent of all.
29. Most boys like to play ball.
30. My younger brother was not in school today.
31. Last month my older brother was in the country.
32. My youngest brother does not yet go to school.
33. He writes better than his sister.
34. She does not write as well as her brother.
35. My old friend likes to travel.
36. German grammar (*supply def. art.*) is becoming clearer and clearer.
37. That is very (*i.e.*, exceedingly) dangerous.
38. The number of technical terms is becoming greater and greater.
39. The scientists were shown the greatest honor, because they had made important discoveries in (the) world space.

Various Expressions
CHAPTER 9 **of Time and
Date**

23. THE DAYS, MONTHS, AND SEASONS

Read the following sentences carefully:

A. The days of the week.

(1) Es war **am** Dienstag, dem 21. Juni.
It was on Tuesday, June 21.

(2) **Letzten** Donnerstag war ich bei meinem Freund.
Last Thursday I was at my friend's house.

Nächsten Sonntag wird er mich besuchen.
He will visit me next Sunday.

Jeden Freitag gehe ich ins Theater.
Every Friday I go to the theater.

(3) **Eines** Sonntags war ich auf dem Lande.
One Sunday I was in the country.

B. The months.

(1) Es war **im** März (Dezember).
It was in March (December).

Sein Geburtstag ist **am** 17. Oktober.
His birthday is on October 17.

(2) As the heading of a letter:
den 22. Mai, *May 22nd.*

C. The seasons.

(1) **Im** Frühling singen die Vögel.
The birds sing in spring.

(2) **Jeden** Sommer macht er eine Reise.
He takes a trip every summer.

Letzten Herbst war sie in der Schweiz.
She was in Switzerland last fall.

Nächsten Winter werden wir zu Hause bleiben.
We shall stay at home next winter.

Note:

(1) (*a*) In phrases such as *on Monday(s)*, *on Tuesday(s)*, *etc.*, English omits, but German requires, the definite article after the preposition *on*— *i.e.*, German **an** becomes **am** (*cf.* ¶ **A** (1) above). The preposition, however, may be omitted both in English and German:

Montag (acc.) war ich beschäftigt.
I was busy (on) Monday.

(*b*) The use of *last, next*, and *every* in ¶¶ **A** (2) and **C** (2) above illustrates the use of the accusative to denote **definite** time.

(*c*) Instead of **jeden Freitag** (*every Friday*) one may also say: **Freitags, des Freitags,** or **alle Freitage**. This applies also to other days of the week.

(*d*) The genitive case is used to denote **indefinite** time (*cf.* ¶ **A** (3) above).

(*e*) The days of the week are all masculine:

(der) Sonntag, *Sunday*	(der) Mittwoch, *Wednesday*
(der) Montag, *Monday*	(der) Donnerstag, *Thursday*
(der) Dienstag, *Tuesday*	(der) Freitag, *Friday*
(der) Samstag (or Sonnabend), *Saturday*	

(2) (*a*) The months are preceded by the definite article when they are used with a preposition (*cf.* in ¶ **B** (1) above); *in* becomes **im,** and *on* (before days of the month) becomes **am.**

(*b*) The date in the heading of a letter is in the accusative case (*cf.* ¶ **B** (2) above).

(c) The months are all masculine:

(der) Januar, *January*	(der) Juli, *July*
(der) Februar, *February*	(der) Augúst, *August*[1]
(der) März, *March*	(der) September, *September*
(der) Apríl, *April*	(der) Oktober, *October*
(der) Mai, *May*	(der) November, *November*
(der) Juni, *June*	(der) Dezember, *December*

Note: Observe the spelling of März, Oktober, and Dezember.

(3) The seasons are regularly preceded by the definite article; *in*, therefore, becomes **im** (*cf.* ¶ **C** (1) above).

24. HOURS, MINUTES, AND IDIOMATIC TIME EXPRESSIONS

A. Hours:

Wieviel Uhr ist es?

or: Wie spät ist es?
What time is it?

Es ist ein Uhr.

or: Es ist eins.
It is one o'clock.

Es ist halb vier.
It is half past three.

Es ist ein Viertel nach zwölf.

or: Es ist ein Viertel (auf) eins.
It is a quarter after twelve.

Es ist ein Viertel vor elf.

or: Es ist drei Viertel elf.
It is a quarter to eleven.

B. Minutes:

Es ist zehn Minuten nach acht.
It is ten minutes after eight.

Es ist sieben Minuten vor zwei.
It is seven minutes to two.

---

[1] **August** as a boy's name has the accent on the first syllable.

C. Idiomatic time expressions:

Er wird **um** sieben Uhr kommen.
*He will come **at** seven o'clock.*

Er wird **ungefähr um** sieben Uhr kommen.
or: Er wird **gegen** sieben Uhr kommen.
*He will come (at) **about** seven o'clock.*

Der wievielte ist heute?
or: Den wievielten haben wir heute?
What is today's date?
or: *What day of the month is it?*

Heute ist der 25. Januar.
or: Heute haben wir den 25. Januar.
Today is the 25th of January.

Der wievielte ist morgen?
What is tomorrow's date?

Morgen ist der 26. Januar.
Tomorrow is (or will be) the 26th of January.

Vor zwei Stunden
Vor acht Tagen
Vor einem Monat } erhielt ich das Telegramm.
Vor drei Jahren

I received the telegram { *two hours ago.*
a week ago.
a month ago.
three years ago.

Heute über acht Tage wird er abreisen.
He will leave a week from today.

Sie geht **auf** einen Monat aufs Land.
*She is going to the country **for** a month.*

25. PERIODS OF THE DAY IN TIME EXPRESSIONS

A. Adverbial phrases denoting time:

(1) am Morgen (morgens *or* des Morgens), *in the morning*
am Vormittag (vormittags *or* des Vormittags), *in the forenoon*

am Mittag (mittags *or* des Mittags), *at noon*
Wir essen zu Mittag.   *We eat dinner.*
am Nachmittag (nachmittags *or* des Nachmittags), *in the afternoon*
am Abend (abends *or* des Abends), *in the evening*
Wir essen zu Abend.   *We eat supper.*
am Tage, *in the daytime*

(2) in der Nacht, *at night*

(3) gegen Abend, *toward evening*
gegen Morgen, *toward morning*

Note: The forms in parentheses are particularly common when denoting some customary or habitual action:[1]

Vormittags bin ich immer zu Hause.
I am always at home in the forenoon.

Nachmittags macht der Großvater ein Schläfchen.
In the afternoon grandfather takes a nap.

B. The accusative to denote definite time. The **accusative** case is used to denote definite time (*cf.* § 23, **Note** (1) (*b*) above):

Jeden Morgen stehe ich früh auf.
I get up early every morning.

Jeden Abend mache ich einen Spaziergang.[2]
I take a walk every evening.

C. The accusative to denote duration of time. Duration of time is expressed by the **accusative** case:

Er arbeitete **den ganzen** Morgen (**die ganze** Nacht).
He worked all morning (all night).

D. Combinations with heute, morgen, gestern. Combinations with **heute, morgen,** and **gestern,** and such words as **morgen, vormittag, mittag,** *etc.* are not capitalized, since they function as adverbs:

heute morgen, *this morning*
heute vormittag, *this forenoon*

---

[1] *Cf.* § 23, **Note** (1) (*d*).
[2] This construction applies also to other periods of the day.

heute mittag, *this noon*
heute nachmittag, *this afternoon*
heute abend, *this evening, tonight*
heute nacht, *tonight*
gestern morgen, *yesterday morning*
gestern vormittag, *yesterday forenoon*
gestern mittag, *yesterday noon*
gestern nachmittag, *yesterday afternoon*
gestern abend, *yesterday evening, last night*
gestern nacht, *last night*
but: vorige **N**acht, *last night*
vorgestern, *day before yesterday*
morgen früh, *tomorrow morning*
frühmorgens, *early in the morning*
morgen vormittag, *tomorrow forenoon*
morgen mittag, *tomorrow noon*
morgen nachmittag, *tomorrow afternoon*
morgen abend, *tomorrow evening* (or *night*)
morgen nacht, *tomorrow night*
übermorgen, *day after tomorrow*

EXERCISE

A.   Complete:

1. Letzt— Jahr war ich in Deutschland.
2. Nächst— Sommer werde ich nach Europa reisen.
3. Jed— Winter geht mein Freund nach Florida.
4. Vorig— Woche war ich im Theater.
5. Herr Weiß besuchte mich a— Sonntag.
6. Er ist a— 15. Mai 1905 geboren.
7. Ein— Morgen— erhielt ich einen langen Brief von ihm.
8. „D— 18. Juni" stand oben auf der ersten Seite des Briefes.
9. Nächst— Montag muß ich diesen Brief beantworten.
10. D— wie— ist heute?
11. D— wie— haben wir heute?
12. Es ist—— (*half past twelve*).
13. Es ist—— (*a quarter to nine*).
14. Es ist —— (*a quarter after three*).

15. Der Vater wird —— (*at*) zwei Uhr kommen.
16. D— wie— war gestern?
17. D— wie— hatten wir gestern?
18. —— (*Tomorrow morning*) werde ich aufs Land gehen.
19. —— (*Yesterday evening*) war ich in der Oper.
20. —— (*This morning*) habe ich einen Spaziergang gemacht.
21. —— (*This evening*) werde ich zu Hause bleiben.
22. —— (*In*) Frühling blühen die Obstbäume.
23. Nächst— Winter werden meine Freunde mich besuchen.
24. —— (*In*) Winter fällt der Schnee.
25. —— (*In*) Sommer schwimme ich gern.
26. D— ganz— Sommer habe ich mich herrlich amüsiert.
27. —— (*In*) Herbst fallen die Blätter von den Bäumen.
28. Jed— Herbst bewundere ich die schönen Farben der Blätter.
29. —— Tage arbeiten wir.   Arbeiten Sie d— ganz— Tag?
30. —— (*At*) Nacht scheint der Mond.
31. —— Frühling ist die schönste Jahreszeit.
32. Ein— Tag— beantwortete ich den langen Brief.
33. Ein— Morgen— regnete es.   Es regnete d— ganz— Morgen.
34. Mein Freund ist —— 10. März geboren.
35. Der Arzt besuchte mich jed— Tag.
36. Ein— Tag— begegnete ich meinem alten Freund auf der Straße.
37. Letzt— Woche habe ich viel gelernt.
38. —— (*On the*) 11. September fängt die Schule an.
39. —— (*On the*) 30. Juni schließt sie.
40. Dies— Sommer werde ich auf dem Lande sein.
41. Der Sturm war am heftigsten —— (*toward*) Morgen.
42. Wir gehen —— zwei Monat— in die Berge.
43. Heute —— acht Tag— wird der Flieger in Berlin ankommen.
44. —— acht Tag— (*A week ago*) war ich bei meinem Vetter.
45. Wir frühstücken —— (*about*) halb acht.
46. —— (*At nine minutes after six*) begann die Sonnenfinsternis. Sie endete —— (*at half past ten*).

B. Translate:

1. Every Saturday I go to the theater.
2. Last Saturday my dear friend was in the movies.
3. Next week I shall see him.

4. Last Friday he forgot (*perf.*) to give[1] me my German book.
5. Next year she will go to Germany.
6. At the top of (oben auf) the first page of the letter I wrote: " June 16."
7. She was born on the 13th of December.[2]
8. Goethe was born on the 28th of August 1749.
9. Goethe died on the 22nd of March 1832.
10. This morning I wrote my parents a long letter.
11. Next week I shall receive an answer.
12. At (In) night the stars shine.
13. In the daytime we go to school.
14. Tomorrow morning he will visit me.
15. Yesterday morning I was not at home.
16. Tomorrow afternoon we shall go to the country.
17. Yesterday afternoon we were at my friend's house.
18. Last night I did not sleep well (gut).
19. On Sundays I always read the German newspaper.
20. Did you see him day before yesterday?
21. Day after tomorrow we shall read those German stories.
22. Winter begins in December.
23. Spring begins in March.
24. He likes to swim in summer.
25. School begins in the fall.
26. One summer I visited my rich uncle.
27. What is today's date?
28. What is tomorrow's date?
29. It is half past one.
30. It is a quarter after two.
31. It is a quarter to three.
32. It is ten minutes after four.
33. It is twelve minutes to five.
34. My older brother will come at half past six.
35. His younger sister usually studies in the forenoon.
36. In the afternoon I always take a long walk.
37. Last Thursday we played ball.
38. Some (*i.e.*, One) day we shall have a good team (die Mannschaft).

---

[1] The infinitive **zu geben** stands at the end of the sentence.

[2] **Note:** Use **ist** geboren, if the person is still living; **wurde** geboren, if he is dead (*cf.* § 74 **B**).

39. Next month we shall win (siegen).
40. Every day we must work hard.
41. The performance (Die Vorstellung) begins at about eight o'clock.
42. I saw my old friend a week ago.
43. A week from today I shall go to the beach.
44. The storm was most violent toward evening.
45. We are going to the country for a month.
46. The eclipse of the moon began at midnight and ended about five hours later.

26. PREPOSITIONS WITH THE ACCUSATIVE

Read the following sentences very carefully:

A. Bis:

Er hat **bis** zehn Uhr gewartet. *He waited until ten o'clock.*
Er hat mich **bis** München begleitet.
He accompanied me to (i.e., as far as) Munich.

Note: In the three sentences below, the preposition that follows **bis** determines the case of the noun (*cf.* **Note** (1) on p. 91):

Er ging **bis an** die Tür.
He went up to (i.e., as far as) the door.

Er hat mich **bis auf** den Tod gequält.
He worried (lit. *tortured*) *me almost to death.*

Er war **bis vor** wenigen Jahren gesund.
Until a few years ago, he was well.

B. Durch:

Er ging **durch das** Zimmer.
He went through the room.

Der Löwe wurde **durch einen** Schuß getötet.
The lion was killed by a shot.

C. Für:

Die Mutter kaufte ein Geschenk **für die** Tochter.
The mother bought a gift for her daughter.

Wir lernen nicht **für die** Schule, sondern **fürs** Leben.
We do not learn for school but for life.

D. Gegen:

Was haben Sie **gegen ihn?**
*What have you **against him?***

Es war **gegen den** Wunsch seines Vaters.
*It was **contrary to** his father's wish(es).*

Gegen Morgen sind sie weggefahren.
*They left **toward morning.***

E. Ohne:

Ohne dich kann ich nicht leben.
*I cannot live **without you.***

Ohne Freunde ist das Leben traurig.
*Life is dreary **without friends.***

F. Um:

Der Gärtner baute einen Zaun **um den** Garten.
*The gardener built a fence **around the** garden.*

Kümmern Sie sich nicht **um mich!**
*Don't worry **about me.***

G. Wider:

Er tat es **wider seinen** Willen.
*He did it **contrary to his** wishes* (lit. *against his will*).[1]

Summary: The above sentences indicate that the following prepositions govern the accusative case: **bis** (*to, until, as far as*), **durch** (*through*), **für** (*for*), **gegen** (*against*), **ohne** (*without*), **um** (*around*), and **wider** (*against*).

Note:

(1) **Bis** is usually followed by another preposition which determines the case of the following noun.   If the noun is preceded by an article, a second preposition **must** be used with **bis.**

(2) *By* usually becomes **von** with a passive verb to denote the **personal agent** (*cf.* § 28 G).   **Durch,** however, is often used to denote the means or instrument (*cf.* second sentence under ¶ **B** above).

(3) Do not confuse the adverb wieder, *again*, with the preposition **wider,** *against.*

---

[1] *Cf.* § **D** above.

27. THE USE OF OHNE, UM, AND ANSTATT WITH INFINITIVES

Read the following sentences very carefully:

A. Ohne:

Er sprach **ohne aufzustehen.**
*He spoke **without getting up.***

B. Um:

Um zu verstehen, muß man aufpassen.
In order to understand, one must pay attention.

C. Anstatt:

(An)statt zu kommen, spielte er Ball.
Instead of coming, he played ball.

Summary: The above sentences indicate that **ohne** (*without*), **um** (*in order to*), and **(an)statt** (*instead of*) require the infinitive with **zu.**

Note:

(1) The English equivalent of such an infinitive is frequently the participial form in -*ing*.

(2) **Ohne** and **um** govern the accusative case (*cf.* § 26 **E** and **F**) when followed by nouns or pronouns.

(3) **Anstatt** governs the genitive case when followed by a noun or pronoun (*cf.* § 32).

28. PREPOSITIONS WITH THE DATIVE

Read the following sentences very carefully:

A. Aus:

Er kommt **aus dem** Hause.
*He comes **out of the** house.*

Was ist **aus ihm** geworden?
*What has become **of him?***

Der Tisch ist **aus** Holz.
*The table is (made) **of** wood.*

B. Außer:

> **Außer meinem** Bruder war niemand da.
> *Nobody was there **but** (or **except**) my brother.*

> Ich war **außer mir** vor Freude.
> *I was **beside myself** with joy.*

Note: When *beside* means *next to*, use **neben.**

C. Bei:

> Das Haus steht **bei der** Kirche.
> *The house is **near the** church.*

> **Bei wem** wohnt er?
> ***With whom** (or **At whose house**) does he live?*

> Ich habe kein Geld **bei mir.**
> *I have no money **with me.***

D. Mit:

> Sie reiste **mit der** Mutter.   Man ißt Suppe **mit einem** Löffel.
> *She traveled **with her** mother.*   *One eats soup **with a** spoon.*

E. Nach:

> **Nach dem** Frühstück geht er in die Schule.
> ***After** breakfast he goes to school.*

> Morgen fährt er **nach** Berlin.
> *Tomorrow he will go (lit. goes) **to** Berlin.*

> In der Klasse sitzen die Schüler **nach dem Alphabet.**
> *In class the pupils are seated alphabetically (lit. sit **according to the**
>   **alphabet**).*

> **Nach der** Schule gehen sie **nach Hause.**
> *After school they go **home.***

> **Der Sage nach** ist Rübezahl Herrscher über das Riesengebirge.
> ***According to the legend,** Ruebezahl is ruler of (lit. over) the
>   Riesengebirge (i.e., Giants' Mountains).*

F. Seit:

Seit dem Krieg habe ich ihn nicht gesehen.
*I have not seen him **since the war.***

Seit vier Monaten wohne ich in diesem Haus.
*I have been living in this house **for four months.***

Seit wann sind Sie hier?
***How long** have you been here?*

G. Von:

Der Zug kommt **von** Hamburg.
*The train comes **from** Hamburg.*

Das ist ein Gedicht **von** Goethe.
*That is a poem **by** Goethe.*

Was will er **von mir?**
*What does he want **of me?***

Der Löwe wurde **von dem** Jäger getötet.
*The lion was killed **by the** hunter.*[1]

H. Zu:

Ich gehe **zu meinem** Bruder.
*I am going **to my** brother's (house).*

Er sagte **zu mir:** „Ich werde Sie **zu Weihnachten** besuchen."
*He said **to me:** " I shall visit you **at Christmas.**"*

Er war nicht **zu Hause.**
*He was not **at home.***

I. Gegenüber:

Er saß **mir gegenüber.**   Unser Haus liegt **dem Park gegenüber.**
*He sat **opposite me.**   Our house is **opposite the park.***

Summary: The above sentences indicate that the following prepositions govern the dative case: **aus** (*out of, of, from*), **außer** (*except, besides*), **bei** (*near, with, at, at the house of*), **mit** (*with*), **nach** (*to, toward, after, according to*), **seit** (*since*), **von** (*of, from, by*), **zu** (*to*), and **gegenüber** (*opposite*).

---

[1] *Cf.* **Note** (2) of § 26.

Note:

(1) Observe particularly the common use of **bei,** meaning *at the house of* (compare the French preposition *chez*):

> bei mir, *at my house*
> bei meinem Onkel, *at my uncle's (house)*

Caution: For German equivalents of English **by,** see § 26 **B** and § 28 **G.**

(2) In the sense of *according to,* **nach** frequently follows its noun (*cf.* last example under ¶ **E** above).

(3) The second sentence under ¶ **F** above illustrates the use of the present tense for an action begun in the past and continued in the present: *Four months **ago** I moved into this house and I am **still** living in it.* Similarly the last sentence in this group implies that the person addressed came some time **ago** and is **still** present.

(4) Observe especially that **von** is the preposition regularly used to denote the personal agent with a passive verb (*cf.* fourth example under ¶ **G** above).

(5) (*a*) After a verb of going (*e.g.,* **gehen**) *to* becomes **zu,** provided the action is directed toward a person: **zu meinem Bruder.**

Note, however, the use of **zu** in such phrases as **zur** (*or* in die) Kirche, *to church*; **zur** (*or* in die) Schule, *to school.*

Caution: Before names of cities or countries, however, *to* becomes **nach:**

> Er reist **nach Deutschland (Berlin).**
> *He is traveling **to Germany (Berlin).***

(*b*) The preposition **zu** is required after the verb **sagen,** provided the quotation is **direct** (*cf.* second sentence under ¶ **H** above).

Caution: In an **indirect** quotation, however, **zu** must be omitted:

> Er sagte mir, er würde mich zu Weihnachten besuchen.
> *He told me that he would visit me at Christmas.*

(6) **Gegenüber** often follows the word it governs (*cf.* ¶ **I** above).

29. PREPOSITIONS WITH THE DATIVE OR ACCUSATIVE

Read the following sentences very carefully:

A. An:

Er steht **an der** Tafel.   Er geht **an die** Tafel.
*He is standing **at the** board.*   *He is going **to the** board.*

Am Sonntag brauchen wir nicht in die Schule zu gehen.
***On** Sundays we do not have* (lit. *need*) *to go to school.*

B. Auf:

Das Buch liegt **auf dem** Tisch.   Er legt das Buch **auf den** Tisch.
*The book lies **on the** table.*   *He puts the book **on the** table.*

Sie ist **auf dem** Lande.   Sie geht **aufs** (= **auf das**) Land.
*She is **in the** country.*   *She goes* (or *is going*) ***to the*** *country.*

C. Hinter:

Der Hund liegt **hinter der** Tür.   Der Hund läuft **hinter die** Tür.
*The dog lies **behind the** door.*   *The dog runs **behind the** door.*

D. In:

Sie ist **im** (= **in dem**) Zimmer.
*She is **in the** room.*

Sie kommt **ins** (= **in das**) Zimmer.
*She enters **the** room.*

Im Winter sind die Nächte lang.
***In** winter the nights are long.*

Er geht **im** Zimmer auf und ab.
*He is walking up and down **in the** room.*

E. Neben:

Ich saß **neben ihm.**   Ich setzte mich **neben ihn.**
*I sat **beside him.***   *I sat down **beside him.***

F. Über:

Eine Lampe hängt **über dem** Tisch.
*A lamp hangs **over the** table.*

Hängen Sie die Lampe **über den** Tisch!
*Hang the lamp **over the** table.*

Er sprach **über den** Krieg.
*He spoke **about** (or **of**) **the** war.*

Er wundert sich **über die** Schnelligkeit des Flugzeugs.
*He marvels **at the** speed of the airplane.*

G. Unter:

Er schlief **unter dem** Baum.   Er lief **unter den** Baum.
*He was sleeping **under the** tree.*   *He ran **under the** tree.*

Unter meinen Papieren habe ich diesen Brief gefunden.
*I found this letter **among my** papers.*

Er hält es **unter seiner** Würde.
*He considers it **beneath his** dignity.*

Das bleibt **unter uns.**
*That is **between ourselves.***

H. Vor:

Er steht **vor der** Klasse.   Er tritt **vor die** Klasse.
*He stands **before the** class.*   *He steps **before the** class.*

Vor kurzer Zeit überquerten die ersten Flieger den Ozean.
A short time ago *the first flyers crossed the ocean.*

I. Zwischen:

Er saß **zwischen mir** und **meinem** Bruder.
*He was sitting **between me** and **my** brother.*

Er setzte sich **zwischen mich** und **meinen** Bruder.
*He sat down **between me** and **my** brother.*

Summary: The above sentences indicate that the following prepositions may govern either the dative or accusative: **an** (*at, on, to*), **auf** (*on, upon*), **hinter** (*behind*), **in** (*in, into*), **neben** (*beside, next to*), **über** (*over, about, across*), **unter** (*under, beneath, below, among*), **vor** (*before, in front of, ago*), and **zwischen** (*between*).

Note:

(1)   The dative case is used in answer to the question *where?* or *when?* — *i.e.*, when the verb is one of **rest**; the accusative, in answer to the ques-

tion *whither?*—*i.e.*, when the verb denotes **motion toward some goal.**
Expressed in German this is:

| wo? oder wann? | Ruhe: | Dativ |
| wohin? | Bewegung: | Akkusativ |

(2) Motion **within** a place requires the dative (*cf.* last sentence under
¶ **D** above).

(3) (*a*) **Über** meaning *about* or *concerning* requires the accusative.

(*b*) The idiom **sich wundern über** also takes the accusative at all
times (*cf.* last two sentences under ¶ **F** above).

(4) **Vor** meaning *ago* requires the dative and, contrary to English
usage, must precede the noun it governs (*cf.* last sentence under ¶ **H** above;
compare with the French and Spanish idioms).

30. WO- **AND** DA- **FORMS**

Instead of prepositions followed by the dative or accusative cases,[1]
wo- and **da-** forms are used as follows:

A.   Womit, wodurch, woraus, wovon, woran, etc.

(1) These **wo-**forms must be used in questions **when a thing is
referred to** (*cf.* § 44, **Note** (4) for exceptions):

| **Womit** schreibt er? | **Wovon** spricht sie? |
| *With what* is he writing? | *Of what* is she speaking? |

Note: If the preposition begins with a vowel, **wor-** instead of **wo-**
forms are used: wor**i**n, wor**a**uf, wor**a**us, *etc.*

(2) These **wo-**forms **may** also be used as relatives **when things are
referred to:**

> Die Feder, **womit** [= mit der (*or* welcher)] ich schreibe, gehört
> meiner Schwester.
> *The pen **with which** I am writing belongs to my sister.*

> Die Bücher, **wovon** [= von denen (*or* welchen)] er sprach, gefallen
> mir.
> *I like the books **of which** he was speaking.*

---

[1] Certain prepositions, however—*e.g.*, **ohne, seit** and **außer**—cannot take **da-** or
wo-forms.

B. Damit, dadurch, daraus, davon, daran, etc. These **da**-forms are used instead of prepositions with the dative or accusative of the personal pronouns **when things are referred to:**

Er schreibt **damit.**	Sie spricht **davon** (or **darüber**).
*He is writing **with it.***	*She is talking **about it.***
Das Kind hat viele Spielsachen.	Es spielt **damit.**
The child has many playthings.	*It is playing **with them.***

Note:

(1) **Wo**- and **da**-forms are invariable and may refer to a singular **or plural noun** (*cf.* last sentences under ¶ **A** (2) and ¶ **B** of this section).

(2) **Wo**- and **da**-forms cannot be used when referring to **people:**

Ich denke **daran.**	but: Ich denke **an ihn.**
*I think **of it.***	*I think **of him.***
Woran denken Sie?	but: **An wen** denken Sie?
*Of **what** are you thinking?*	*Of **whom** are you thinking?*

31. CONTRACTIONS

A. The most common contractions. The following are the most common contractions of prepositions with the definite article:

am	(= an dem)		**im**	(= in dem)
ans	(= an das)		**ins**	(= in das)
aufs	(= auf das)		**vom**	(=von dem)
beim	(= bei dem)		**zum**	(= zu dem)
fürs	(= für das)		**zur**	(= zu der)

Note: **Zur** is the only feminine contraction.

B. Other contractions. Contractions other than those just listed are always intelligible, provided one remembers that final –m stands for **dem** and final –s for **das: durchs** (= durch das), **ums** (= um das), **hinterm** (= hinter dem).

Note: Contractions in –n, which stands for **den,** are quite rare: **übern** (= über den).

32. PREPOSITIONS WITH THE GENITIVE

Read the following sentences very carefully:

A. Während:

Während der Nacht regnete es. **Während des Tages** arbeiten wir.

During the night it rained. *During the day we work.*

B. Wegen:

Wegen des schlechten Wetters blieb er zu Hause.

or: **Des schlechten Wetters wegen** blieb er zu Hause.

He stayed at home on account of the bad weather.

Tun Sie es nicht **meinetwegen!** **Meinetwegen** darf er das tun.

Do not do it on my account. *He may do that for all I care.*

C. Trotz:

Trotz des kalten Wetters machte er einen Spaziergang.

He took a walk in spite of the cold weather.

D. (An)statt:

(An)statt des Vaters kam die Mutter.

Mother came instead of father.

(An)statt des baren Geldes gab ich ihm einen Scheck.

I gave him a check instead of cash.

E. Diesseits:

Der Dom ist **diesseits des Flusses.**

The cathedral is on this side of the river.

F. Jenseits:

Das Rathaus ist **jenseits des Flusses.**

The town hall is on that side of the river.

G. Oberhalb:

Oberhalb des Dorfes ist eine kleine Kirche.

Above the village there is a small church.

H. Unterhalb:

Unterhalb der Kirche ist eine schöne Wiese.

There is a beautiful meadow below the church.

I. Außerhalb:

Er wohnt **außerhalb der Stadt.**
*He lives **outside of the city.***

J. Innerhalb:

Innerhalb einer Stunde muß ich fertig sein.
*I must be ready **within an hour.***

K. Um ... willen:

Um Gottes (or **Himmels**) **willen!**
For heaven's sake!

Tun Sie es **um meinetwillen!**
Do it for my sake.

Summary: The above sentences indicate that the following prepositions govern the genitive case: **während** (*during*), **wegen** (*on account of*), **trotz** (*in spite of*), **(an)statt** (*instead of*), **diesseits** (*on this side of*), **jenseits** (*on that side of*), **oberhalb** (*above*), **unterhalb** (*below*), **außerhalb** (*outside of*), **innerhalb** (*inside of* or *within*), and **um ... willen** (*for the sake of*).

Note:

(1) **Wegen** may precede or follow the noun it governs (*cf.* first example under ¶ **B** above).

(2) **Wegen** must follow when used with personal pronouns, which assume a form in –t: meinetwegen (*on my account*), deinetwegen [*on your* (sing. fam.) *account*], seinetwegen (*on his account*), ihretwegen [*on her* (*its* or *their*) *account*], unsertwegen (*on our account*), euretwegen [*on your* (pl. fam.) *account*], Ihretwegen (*on your account*).

(3) **Meinetwegen** may also mean *for all I care* (*cf.* last example under ¶ **B** above).

Other uses and meanings of common prepositions. Only the most common prepositions have been included in this chapter. There are many others—chiefly with the genitive and dative—which occur, for the most part, in the written language. The common prepositions have many other uses and meanings than those given above, particularly in idiomatic expressions (*cf.* Chapter XXV) and with certain reflexive verbs (*cf.* Chapter XVII). The simplest conversation is apt to involve idioms with prepositions—*e.g.*, the common phrase *in other words* must become **mit**

anderen Worten. The following sentences, which might be multiplied indefinitely, show that the same English preposition may have numerous German equivalents:

I thank you for the book.
Ich danke Ihnen **für** das Buch.

I ask you for the book.
Ich bitte Sie **um** das Buch.

He hopes for good weather.
Er hofft **auf** gutes Wetter.

She longs for her friends.
Sie sehnt sich **nach** ihren Freundinnen.

For what reason did he do that?
Aus welchem Grunde hat er das getan?

For what price?
Zu welchem Preise?

She has been here for two months.
Sie ist **seit** zwei Monaten hier.

Cologne is famous for its cathedral.
Köln ist **durch** den Dom (or **wegen** des Domes) berühmt.

He is looking for me.
Er sucht mich.[1]

EXERCISE

A.   Complete the following sentences:

1. Ein kleiner Vogel ist auf d— hoh— Baum geflogen.
2. Er geht an d— Fenster.
3. Er sitzt an d— Fenster.
4. Während d— Sommer— war ich auf dem Lande.
5. Er wohnt bei sein— älter— Schwester.
6. Er bereitet sich auf sein— nächst— Prüfung vor.
7. Sie sehnte sich nach d— alt— Heimat.
8. Tun Sie es mein— Sohn— wegen!
9. —wegen (*On your account*) werde ich es tun.
10. Das Kind hat mit d— Ball gespielt.
11. Kümmern Sie sich nicht um ih—!
12. Der Junge war dreimal um d— Haus gelaufen.
13. Der Flieger wartet auf günstig— Wetter.
14. Trotz d— Hitze arbeitete er auf d— Feld.
15. Berlin liegt an d— Spree.
16. Er war nach—— (*him*) gelaufen.

---

[1] German omits the preposition here.

17. Der Boxer kämpfte gegen d— Weltmeister.
18. Man trinkt Kaffee aus ein— Kaffeetasse.
19. Der Apfelbaum steht neben d— Haus.
20. Außer d— Mutter war niemand da.
21. Anstatt ein— König— hat das Land jetzt einen Präsidenten.
22. Mein Freund ist seit ein— Woche krank.
23. Der Bleistift liegt auf d— Tisch.
24. Ich lege den Bleistift auf d— Tisch.
25. Er begleitete mich bis an d— Tür.
26. Was haben Sie gegen mi—?
27. Bayern liegt diesseits d— Alpen.
28. Jenseits d— Gebirg— liegt die Schweiz.
29. Gehen Sie hinter mi—!
30. Sie stand hinter mi—.
31. Er bleibt bis zu— nächst— Monat in Bonn.
32. Ich habe an mein— alt— Freund gedacht.
33. Sie hatte einen Brief von ihr— best— Freundin erhalten.
34. Innerhalb ein— Jahr— hat mein Freund viele Länder besucht.
35. Früher hat er außerhalb d— Stadt gewohnt.
36. Ich setzte mich neben d— klein— Jung— (sing.).
37. Ich saß neben d— klein— Jung— (sing.).
38. Das ist gegen d— Wunsch seiner Mutter.
39. Der Vater hat ein Geschenk für sein— jüngst— Sohn gekauft.
40. Meine Schwester wohnt in d— Stadt.
41. Gestern sind meine Freunde in d— Stadt gekommen.
42. Er sagt zu d— Mädchen: „Du solltest nach Europa reisen."
43. Sie wohnt d— alt— Kirche gegenüber.
44. Das Luftschiff schwebt über unser— Haus.
45. Gestern ist das Luftschiff über uns— Haus geflogen.
46. Ich halte ihn für ein— ehrlich— Mann.
47. Man darf nicht gegen d— Strom schwimmen.
48. —— (*In*) Sommer sind die Tage heiß.
49. Er wird über ei— interessant— Buch sprechen.
50. Um Gott— willen!
51. D— Sage nach kommen die Hexen in d— Walpurgisnacht nach d— Brocken.
52. Wohnen Sie bei Ihr— Eltern?
53. Er hatte sich zwischen d— beid— Brüder geworfen.
54. Er stand zwischen d— beid— Brüder—.

55. Nach d— Regen schien die Sonne.
56. Der Dom ist jenseits d— Strom—.
57. Während welch— Monate haben Sie Ferien?
58. Die deutschen Kinder gehen durch d— schön— Wald spazieren.
59. Viele Leute standen um d— jung— Mann.
60. Die Kinder traten vor d— groß— Haustür.
61. Vor d— groß— Haustür stand die Mutter.
62. Was ist aus Ihr— alt— Freund geworden?
63. Seit d— groß— Krieg hat er mich nicht besucht.
64. Er wird es um sein—willen tun.
65. Stecken Sie das Taschentuch in d— link— Tasche!
66. Das Taschentuch ist schon in d— link— Tasche.
67. Ohne Ihr— Hilfe bin ich verloren.
68. Das ist unter mein— Würde.
69. Er tauchte unter d— Wasser.
70. Nach d— Abendessen liest er die deutsche Zeitung.
71. Er winkte mir mit d— Hand.
72. Ein Wasserfall ist oberhalb d— klein— Gasthaus—.
73. Unterhalb d— schön— Wasserfall— ist ein großer Wald.
74. Das Buch wird von d— Schüler gelesen werden.
75. Früher wohnte sie d— deutsch— Theater gegenüber.
76. Bayreuth ist durch d— Vorstellungen der Wagneropern berühmt.
77. Er sagte zu d— klein— Kinder—: „Seid fleißig!"
78. Wir setzten uns unter d— schön— Lindenbaum.
79. Köln liegt an d— (or a—) Rhein.
80. Das Haus wird von d— alt— Zimmermann gebaut.
81. Deutschland liegt zwischen d— Meer und d— Alpen.
82. Ist das für —— (him) oder für —— (her)?
83. Er setzte sich —— (without saying anything).
84. Er geht in die Schule —— (in order to learn German).
85. —— (Instead of working), spielte er immer.
86. „—— [From (i.e., out of) what] trinkt er?" „Aus d—Tasse."
87. Er trinkt —— [from (i.e., out of) it].
88. „—— (With what) schreibt er?" „Mit d— Feder."
89. Er schreibt —— (with it).
90. „—— (Of what) spricht er?" „Von d— Wetter."
91. Ich spreche —— (of it). Er spricht —— (of him).
92. Gehen Sie —— Hause? Mein Bruder ist schon —— Hause.
93. Das Pult ist —— Holz.

94. Das Gedicht ist —— Goethe.
95. Der wesentlichste Unterschied zwischen —— (*the*) Erde und
—— (*the*) Planeten Venus findet sich in —— (*the*) chemischen
Zusammensetzungen der Atmosphären und in —— (*the*) grö-
ßeren Sonnennähe der Venus.

B. Rewrite the following sentences:

(1) As questions with the proper **wo**-form.
(2) As declarative sentences with the proper **da**-form.

MODEL: Man sieht **mit** den Augen.
     Wo-form: W**omit** sieht man?
     Da-form: Man sieht da**mit**.

1. Er denkt **an** die Vergangenheit.
2. Die Bücher lagen **auf** dem Tisch.
3. Er wird **über** die Geschichte sprechen.
4. Er hat sich **nach** der Heimat gesehnt.
5. Die Kinder waren **durch** das Zimmer gelaufen.
6. Sie hat dem Mann **für** das Buch gedankt.

C. Translate:

1. The little children had run through the large house.
2. Instead of a pencil he had a pen in his hand.
3. The brown dog was lying under the table.
4. It (*i.e.*, the dog) ran under a small chair.
5. With whom will he travel this summer?
6. Did he put (legen) the German books on the round table?
7. The German newspaper was (liegen) already on the table.
8. In spite of the bad weather, she had come to school.
9. That is contrary to the wishes of my dear parents.
10. What have you against them?
11. He will come out of the house at half past nine.
12. My old friend was standing by (German **an**) the window.
13. I walked up to (German **an**) the window.
14. On what days do you not go to school?
15. Formerly he lived on this side of the bridge.
16. Now he lives on that side of the river.
17. He accompanied me as far as Berlin.
18. Have you any money with you?

19. At whose house do you live now?
20. One never sees him without a (*omit*) hat.
21. He will buy a gift for his best friend.
22. He entered the room; then he sat down.
23. His older brother was already in the room.
24. We are beside ourselves with joy.
25. He sat down beside her.
26. He was sitting beside her.
27. The dog is lying under the small table.
28. The dog runs under the small table.
29. During the night it had rained hard (stark).
30. During the vacation I read many German books.
31. " Shall (Soll) I open the window? "   " Yes, for all I care."
32. After breakfast he will take a long walk.
33. For two hours she has been reading that French book.
34. The house had been built by the old carpenter.
35. In most classes the pupils sit according to the alphabet.
36. I have not seen him since day before yesterday.
37. What did he want of me?
38. That is a poem by Schiller.
39. After school I must go home quickly.
40. According to the legend, Siegfried killed the dragon.
41. She never worries about him.
42. Many people are standing around her.
43. He will jump over the small table.
44. Over the table (there) was a beautiful picture.
45. It happened a week ago.
46. He was talking about (über) his interesting experiences.
47. She is standing before the pupils.
48. She steps in front of the pupils.
49. Two years ago I visited my old parents.
50. He never does anything contrary to her wishes.
51. I sat down between him and his brother.
52. I was sitting between him and his brother.
53. Above (Oberhalb) the village is an old inn.
54. Below (Unterhalb) the inn is a cool spring.
55. She said to me: " You must visit me next summer."
56. She told me that I should visit her next summer.
57. We now live opposite the beautiful park.

58. Yesterday I received a long letter from my old grandmother.
59. When will you go to Germany?
60. Today I am going to my brother('s house).
61. He passed me without saying a word.
62. We eat in order to live.   We do not live in order to eat.
63. Instead of going away at once, he remained five weeks.
64. For heaven's sake!
65. Within (Innerhalb) an hour I shall have written the letter.
66. Does he now live outside of the city?
67. " Of what are you thinking? "   " I was thinking of you."   " I was thinking of it."
68. " Of whom are you thinking? "   " I was thinking of my dear friend."
69. " With what was he writing? "   " He was writing with a pen." " He was writing with it."
70. The pen with which I am writing belongs to my older brother.
71. By whom was the house built?
72. " For what is Cologne famous? "   " It is famous for its (*i.e.*, the) cathedral (*or* for it)."
73. For whom were you working?
74. There can be (Es besteht) no doubt about the high temperature of the surface of the planet Venus.   This was confirmed (wurde bestätigt) by scientific investigations.

CHAPTER 11

Special Uses of Case

33. USES OF THE GENITIVE CASE

A. The genitive to denote indefinite time. The genitive case is frequently used to denote **indefinite** time:

Eines Tages (eines Morgens, eines Abends) besuchte er mich.
One day (one morning, one evening) he visited me.

Similarly with the adverbial forms **morgens** (*in the morning*), **abends** (*in the evening*), **etc.**[1]

B.   The genitive with certain verbs.

(1)   A few verbs may take a genitive as sole object.   These verbs should be noted in order to develop reading facility.   In modern German, however, many such verbs are felt to be poetic, choice, pedantic or archaic.   It is generally advisable to use other constructions in writing and conversation.   Such alternative constructions are given in the examples that follow:

(*a*) **Bedürfen:**

Ich bedarf **Ihrer Hilfe.**

also: Ich brauche Ihre Hilfe.

I need your help.

(*b*) **Denken:**

Ich denke **seiner.**

also: Ich denke an ihn.

I think (or *am thinking*) *of him.*

(*c*) **Gedenken:**

Gedenke **deines Eides!**

Remember your oath.

(2)   A number of reflexive verbs may govern the genitive case, although other constructions are often possible:

---

[1] For additional examples, *cf.* § 23 **A** (3), and ¶ **A** and **Note** of § 25.

(a) **Sich erbarmen:**

        Erbarmen Sie sich **meiner!**

also: Erbarmen Sie sich über mich!

or: Haben Sie Mitleid mit **mir!**

        (*Have*) *pity* (*on*) *me.*

(b) **Sich bedienen:**

        Ich bediente mich **seiner Güte.**

also: Ich machte von seiner Güte Gebrauch.

        I availed myself (or *made use*) *of his kindness.*

(c) **Sich bemächtigen:**

        Er hat sich **unseres Eigentums** bemächtigt.

also: Er hat unser Eigentum in Besitz genommen.

        He took possession of our property.

(d) **Sich erinnern:**

        Er erinnert sich **des Vorfalls.**

also: Er erinnert sich an den Vorfall.

        He remembers the incident.

(e) **Sich rühmen:**

        Er rühmt sich **seines Erfolgs.**

also: Er prahlt mit seinem Erfolg.

        He boasts of his success.

(f) **Sich schämen:**

        Schämt er sich **seiner Armut?**

also: Schämt er sich über seine Armut?

        Is he ashamed of his poverty?

(3) Verbs of " judicial action " (*e.g.*, **anklagen** and **beschuldigen,** *to accuse*) and certain verbs of separation or deprivation (*e.g.*, **berauben,** *to rob*) take the genitive of the **thing** (that of which one is accused or from which one is separated) but the accusative of the **person:**

(a) **Anklagen:**[1]

        Man hat **ihn des Diebstahls** angeklagt.

or: Er wurde **des Diebstahls** angeklagt.

        He was accused of theft.

---

[1] The preposition **wegen** is often used with verbs of accusing:
Er wurde **wegen** Mordes angeklagt.
He was charged with murder.

(*b*) **Beschuldigen:**[1]

Hast du **ihn der Unehrlichkeit** beschuldigt?
*Did you accuse **him of dishonesty**?*

(*c*) **Berauben:**

Er hat **mich meines ganzen Geldes** beraubt.
*He robbed **me of all my money**.*

Note: **Rauben,** however, takes the dative of the person and the accusative of the thing:

Man hat **ihm alles** geraubt.
*They robbed **him of everything**.*

C. The genitive with certain adjectives. Certain adjectives govern the genitive case. A few of the more common ones (usually followed by *of* in English) are:

(1) **Bedürftig** (*in need of*):[2]

Sie ist **meines Trostes** bedürftig.
She is in need of (or *needs*) **my consolation**.

(2) **Bewußt** (*conscious*):

Ich bin mir **keines Unrechts** bewußt.
*I am **not** conscious **of any injustice**.*

(3) **Fähig** (*capable*):

Er ist **einer solchen Tat** fähig.
*He is capable **of such a deed**.*

(4) **Froh** (*happy*):

Sie wird **ihrer hohen Stellung** nicht froh.
*She does not enjoy **her high position**.*

Er wird **seines Lebens** nicht mehr froh.
*He doesn't enjoy **life** any more.*

Note: The adjective **froh** with the genitive usually means *happy in.* To be *happy about* is froh sein **über,** which, like the verbal idiom **sich freuen über,** is followed by the accusative.

---

[1] The preposition **wegen** is often used with this verb; *cf.* footnote on preceding page.

[2] *Cf.* the verb **bedürfen** followed by the genitive, ¶ **B** (1) (*a*) of this section.

(5) **Gewahr werden** (*become conscious of, perceive*):

Er wurde **seines Irrtums** gewahr.
He perceived (or *became conscious of*) **his mistake.**

Note:
(1) **Gewahr** is used only with **werden.**
(2) **Gewahr** sometimes takes the accusative.

(6) **Gewiß** (*certain*):

Er ist **seiner Sache** gewiß.
He knows what he is about.
lit.: *He is sure **of his case.***

(7) **Mächtig** (*master* or *in control of*):

Er war **seiner Sinne** nicht mächtig.
He was not in (*control of*) **his senses.**

(8) **Müde** (*tired*):

Ich bin **dieses Treibens** müde.
*I am tired **of this activity.***

Note: **Müde** (*tired*) and **los** (*free, rid of*) very often govern the accusative in modern German:

Ich bin **es** müde.   Ich bin **es** los.
*I am tired **of it.***   *I am rid **of it.***

This is due to the fact that this **es** was genitive in the older language but came to be felt as accusative—a use of the accusative which spread to forms other than **es:**

Ich bin **ihn** los.
*I am rid **of him.***

(9) **Sicher** (*sure*):

Sie sind **meines Beistands** sicher.
*You are sure **of my assistance.***

(10) **Wert** (*worth*): In modern German this adjective usually governs the accusative (*cf.* § 35 **H**) but in a few idiomatic expressions it governs the genitive:

Es ist nicht **der Mühe** wert.   Es ist nicht **der Rede** wert.
It is not worth while.   *It is not worth talking about.*
or: *It is not worth the trouble.*

(11) **Würdig** (*worthy*):

Die Angelegenheit ist **Ihrer Unterstützung** würdig.
The affair deserves your support.
lit: *The affair is worthy **of your support**.*

Summary: The above sentences indicate that **adjectives governing the genitive usually** *follow* **the word they govern.**

D.   **The genitive in idiomatic expressions:**

Ich fahre **zweiter Klasse.**   Er ist **derselben Meinung.**
I travel ***second class.***   *He is **of the same opinion.***

Leichten (schweren) Herzens ging er an die Arbeit.
With a light (heavy) heart *he went to work.*

Sie ist **guter Laune** [or **guten Mut(e)s**].
She is in (a) good humor.

Meines Wissens verhalten sich die Tatsachen anders.
As far as I know, *the facts are different.*

Laß ihn **seines Weges** ziehen!
*Let him go **his way**.*

Note: Many adverbs preserve traces of the genitive (*cf.* also ¶ **A** above): **meinerseits,** *on my part;* **glücklicherweise,** *fortunately;* **jedenfalls,** *in any event* (or *case*); **keineswegs,** *by no means;* **gewissermaßen,** *in a certain sense;* **links (rechts),** *on* (*at* or *to*) *the left* (*right*); **unverrichteterdinge,** *unsuccessfully; etc.*

E.   **Other uses of the genitive.** For the use of the genitive **to denote possession,** *cf.* § 2 **B**; for the genitive **of personal pronouns,** *cf.* § 42; for the genitive **with certain prepositions,** *cf.* § 32.

F.   **When the genitive is not used.**

(1) **Proper names** used in apposition after, and **names of months** preceded by *of* are **not** in the genitive but in the same case as nouns preceding them:

die Stadt **München,** *the city **of Munich***
im Monat **Mai,** *in the month **of May***
den 25. **Juni,** *the 25th **of June*** (as the heading of a letter)

Note: Observe the difference between the German and English idioms in the above phrases.

(2) Nouns of **number, weight, measure,** and **kind** are **not** followed by the genitive:

> drei Pfund **Butter,** *three pounds of butter*
> zwei Glas **Bier,** *two glasses of beer*
> eine neue Art **Teppich,** *a new kind of carpet*

Note:

(1) Masculine and neuter nouns denoting measurement are usually in the singular, provided they follow a numeral: **drei** Pfund, **zwei** Glas, *etc.* Feminine nouns ending in –**e,** however, require the plural form:

> drei Tassen Tee, *three cups of tea*

(2) **Die Mark** [*mark* (German coin)] always has the singular form:

> zwanzig **Mark,** *twenty marks*

(3) (*a*) If the thing weighed or measured is modified by an adjective, the genitive **may** be used:

> ein Glas kalten Wassers, *a glass of cold water*
> drei Pfund frischen Fleisches, *three pounds of fresh meat*

(*b*) In ordinary speech, however, the thing measured is in the same case as the preceding noun: ein Glas kaltes Wasser, drei Pfund frisches Fleisch, *etc.*

EXERCISE

A. Complete the following sentences, **if necessary.** (Nos. 1–18 illustrate the most common uses of the genitive; nos. 19–37 are for more advanced students.) Some of them do **not** involve the genitive:

1. Ein— Morgen— begegnete ich ihm auf der Straße.
2. Die Hafenstadt —— Hamburg liegt an der Elbe.
3. Ein— Tag— wird er mich besuchen.
4. Er war sich sein— Schuld bewußt.
5. Sind Sie d— Leben— müde?
6. Sie ist ihr— Sache gewiß.
7. Ich hatte sechs Pfund frisch— Fleisch— gekauft.
8. Er bestellte zehn Glas —— Bier für die Gesellschaft.
9. Zwei Pfund —— Butter haben wir noch zu Hause.
10. Ein Gast wollte ein Glas hell— Bier—.
11. Ist das eine neue Art —— Telefon?

12. Jetzt bin ich —— (*it*) los. Ich war —— (*it*) müde.
13. Es ist nicht d— Mühe wert, die Geschichte zu lesen.
14. Ein— Abend— werde ich einen langen Spaziergang machen.
15. Fahren Sie gewöhnlich erst— oder zweit— Klasse?
16. Sind Sie —— (*of the same*) Meinung?
17. Ist er ein— solch— Tat fähig?
18. Er ist Ihr— Hilfe würdig.
19. Er beraubte ih— sein— Vermögen—.
20. Sie wird nie ihr— Leben— froh.
21. Er wurde d— Verrat— (*treason*) angeklagt.
22. Erst jetzt werde ich mein— Irrtum— gewahr.
23. Er schämt sich sein— arm— Eltern nicht.
24. Ich war mein— Sinn— (pl.) nicht mächtig.
25. Er rühmt sich sein— Glück—.
26. Sind Sie d— Geld— bedürftig?
27. Erinnern Sie sich —— unser Versprechen?
28. Haben Sie ihn d— Lüge beschuldigt?
29. Bedürfen Sie ein— Arzt—?
30. Gedenke dein— Versprechen—!
31. Leicht— Herz— (sing.) liefen die Kinder nach Hause.
32. Heute ist er gut— Laune.
33. Mein— Wissen— ist er heute nicht hier.
34. Sie wohnt link— vom Walde.
35. Laß mich mein— Weg— ziehen!
36. Kein—weg— (*By no means*).
37. Die ersten Männer, die in den Weltraum stiegen, hießen Astronauten. Die Mäuse, die in den ersten Forschungsraketen waren, hat man humoristisch—weise „Astromäuse" genannt.

B. Translate the following sentences. (Nos. 1–18 illustrate the most common uses of the genitive; nos. 19–37 are for more advanced students.) A few of them do **not** involve the genitive:

1. Please give me three pounds of meat.
2. He is not ashamed of his friends.
3. Is that a new kind of hat?
4. I often think of him.
5. Some (*i.e.*, One) day I shall visit him.
6. My old friend had arrived in the city of Dresden in the month of August.

7. One evening the little children took a long walk.
8. Do you remember that young lady?
9. One morning I did not get up until half past eight. (*Translate* " not until " *by* erst.)
10. Do you know what you are about? (*Use the idiom with* gewiß).
11. She is not capable of such a deed.
12. He is rid of it.   He was tired of it.
13. He wanted a cup of hot coffee.
14. The city of Munich is the capital of (von) Bavaria.
15. He never travels third class.
16. She is of the same opinion.
17. That is not worth while.
18. Remember your promise!
19. She noticed (*or* perceived) her mistake.
20. He needs a doctor.
21. He was not conscious of any injustice.
22. Avail yourself (*or* make use) of his advice.
23. He always boasts of his success.
24. They were not in (control of) their senses.
25. He was accused of theft.
26. Fear seized (*or* took possession of) the whole company.
27. They robbed him of all his money.
28. She is worthy of your help.
29. He was charged with (*or* accused of) the lie.
30. (Have) pity (on) them!
31. Are you in good humor today?
32. With a heavy heart she went to work.
33. As far as I know, nobody is absent today.
34. They live to the right of (von) the church.
35. Let her go her way.
36. In any case, I am sure of his help.
37. Fortunately, the animals which were in the first artificial earth satellites landed safely on (**auf** *w. dat.*) the surface of the earth.

34. USES OF THE DATIVE CASE

A. The dative with certain verbs. The following are a few of the more common verbs that govern the dative case:

(1) **Antworten** (*to answer*):

Antworten Sie **mir**!
Answer **me.**

Note:

(*a*) **Antworten** takes the dative **of the person.**   Observe, however, its idiomatic use with **auf** and the accusative:

Antworten Sie **auf die Frage**!
Answer **the question.**

(*b*) **Beantworten,** on the other hand, takes a direct object:

Beantworten Sie die Frage!
Answer the question.

(2) **Befehlen** (*to command, order*):

Der Herr befahl **dem Diener,** bald zurückzukommen.
The master ordered **the servant** *to return soon.*

(3) **Begegnen** (*to meet*):

Er ist **mir** auf der Straße begegnet.
He met **me** *on the street.*

(4) **Danken** (*to thank*):

Er wird **ihnen** danken.
He will thank **them.**

(5) **Dienen** (*to serve*):

Er hat **seinem König** treu gedient.
He has served **his king** *faithfully.*

(6) **Drohen** (*to threaten*):

Er drohte **ihm** mit Schlägen.
He threatened **him** *with blows.*

(7) **Einfallen** (*to occur, come to one's mind*):

Das war **mir** nie eingefallen.
That had never occurred **to me.**

Was fällt **Ihnen** denn ein?
What (*in the world*) *do you* **mean** (said in a tone of critical disagreement)?

(8) **Fehlen** (*to be the matter with, lack*):

    Was fehlt **Ihnen?**   **Mir** fehlen zwei Bücher.

    *What is the matter **with you?***   *I am short two books.*

(9) **Folgen** (*to follow*):

    Er wird **den Männern** folgen.

    *He will follow **the men.***

Note:

    (1) In the sense of *follow*, **folgen** must be conjugated with **sein:**

        Er war **mir** gefolgt.

        *He had followed **me.***

    (2) In the sense of *obey*, **folgen** is conjugated with **haben:**

        Er hat **mir** gefolgt.

        *He obeyed **me.***

(10) **Gefallen** (*to please*):

    Wie gefällt **Ihnen** das neue Buch?

    *How do **you** like the new book?*

Note: **What** one likes is the subject of the verb.

(11) **Gehorchen** (*to obey*):

    Das Kind gehorcht **der Mutter.**

    *The child obeys **its mother.***

(12) **Gehören** (*to belong*):

    Es gehört **mir.**

    *It belongs **to me.***

Note: The preposition **zu** is not used with gehören if the verb denotes ownership; it is required if the verb is used in the sense of *to be a part of:*

    Das Haus gehört **zum** (= **zu dem**) Gut.

    The house belongs to (i.e., is a part of) the estate.

(13) **Gelingen** and **glücken** (*to succeed*):

    Es ist **ihm** nicht gelungen (*or* geglückt), das zu tun.

    He has not succeeded in doing that.

Note: Both of these verbs are conjugated with **sein,** and both are impersonal. **A thing** may be the subject:

> **Dieser Plan** ist mir nicht gelungen.
> *This plan did not turn out well for me.*

(14) **Genügen** (*to suffice, satisfy*):

> Es genügt **ihm** nicht ganz.
> *He is not quite satisfied with it.*
> or: *It isn't quite enough for him.*

(15) **Geschehen:**

> Es geschieht **ihm** recht.
> *It serves him right.*

Note: This verb is used only impersonally.

(16) **Gleichen** (*to resemble*):

> Er gleicht **der Mutter.**
> *He resembles his mother.*

(17) **Glauben** (*to believe*):

> Ich glaube **Ihnen.**
> *I believe you.*
> but: Ich glaube es nicht.
> *I do not believe it.*

Note: **Glauben** takes the dative of the **person** but the accusative of the **thing.**

(18) **Gratulieren** (*to congratulate*):

> Ich gratuliere **Ihnen** zu Ihrem Erfolg.
> *I congratulate you on your success.*

(19) **Helfen** (*to help*):

> Helfen Sie **dem armen Manne!**
> *Help the poor man.*

(20) **Sich nähern** (**nahen** or less commonly **sich nahen**) (*to approach*):

> Ich näherte mich **der Stadt.**
> *I approached the city.*

(21) **Nützen** (*to be of use, benefit*):
Was nützt **ihm** das?
Of what use is that to him?

(22) **Passen** (*to fit, be convenient, suit*):
Der Rock paßt **mir** nicht.
The coat does not fit me.
Es paßte **mir** nicht, heute aufs Land zu gehen.
It was not convenient for me to go to the country today.

(23) **Raten** (*to advise*):
Wozu raten Sie **mir**?
What do you advise me to do?

Note: **Raten,** *to guess* (*at*) and **erraten,** *to guess* (in the sense of *to succeed in guessing* or *guess correctly*) both take the accusative:
Er kann raten, aber er wird es niemals erraten.
He can guess at it, but he will never succeed in guessing it.

(24) **Schaden** (*to harm, hurt*):
Das wird **Ihrer Gesundheit** schaden.
That will harm (or *hurt*) *your health.*

(25) **Schmeicheln** (*to flatter*):
Der Maler hat **dem Mädchen** in diesem Bild geschmeichelt.
The artist flattered the girl in this picture.

Note: **Schmeicheln** is often used with the dative **reflexive:**
Schmeich(e)le **dir** nicht!
Don't flatter yourself.

(26) **Trauen** (*to trust, believe in*):
Ich traue **ihm** nicht.
I don't trust him.

(27) **Vergeben** (*to forgive*):
Vergeben Sie **ihnen**!
Forgive them.

(28) **Widersprechen** (*to contradict*):
Widersprechen Sie **mir** nicht!
Don't contradict me.

B. Verbs governing both dative and accusative. Many verbs such as **geben** (*to give*), **zeigen** (*to show*), and **sagen** (*to tell*) take an accusative of the **direct object** and a dative of the **indirect object**:

Ich werde es ihm geben.   Er wird mir das Bild zeigen.
I shall give it to him.   *He will show me the picture.*

Sagen Sie mir die ganze Wahrheit!
Tell me the whole truth.

C. Verbs of *taking* and *stealing*. Most verbs of **taking** and **stealing** have the thing stolen in the accusative but the person from whom it was taken in the dative:[1]

Der Dieb hat **mir** die Uhr gestohlen.
The thief stole my watch.

lit.:   *The thief has stolen the watch **from me**.*

D. The dative with certain adjectives. Some of the more common adjectives governing the dative case are:

(1) **Ähnlich** (*similar, resembling*):

Der Sohn ist **der Mutter** ähnlich.
*The son resembles **his mother**.*

(2) **Angenehm** (*pleasant, agreeable*):

Das warme Wetter ist **mir** sehr angenehm.
I find the warm weather very agreeable.

(3) **Bekannt** (*known*):

Das Gedicht war **ihm** nicht bekannt.

also: Er kannte das Gedicht nicht.
He did not know (or was not familiar with) the poem.

(4) **Bequem** (*comfortable*):

Mache es **dir** bequem!
Make yourself at home.

(5) **Böse** (*angry*):

Seien Sie **mir** nicht böse!

or: Seien Sie nicht böse auf mich!
*Don't be angry **with me**.*

---

[1] *Cf.* also § 33 **B** (3) for other constructions.

(6) **Dankbar** (*grateful*):

Er war **seinen Eltern** stets dankbar.
*He was always grateful **to his parents**.*

(7) **Feindlich (gesinnt)** (*hostile*):

Ich bin **Ihnen** nicht feindlich gesinnt.
*I am not hostile **to you**.*

(8) **Fremd** (*strange*):

Er ist **mir** fremd.
*He is a stranger **to me**.*

(9) **Freundlich** (*friendly*):

Seien Sie **ihm** freundlich!
or: Seien Sie freundlich gegen ihn!
Be friendly to (or toward) him.

(10) **Gelegen** (*opportune*):

Das kommt **mir** recht gelegen.
*That comes quite opportunely **for me**.*

(11) **Gleich** (*like, the same*):

Die Gestalten gingen **Gespenstern** gleich an uns vorüber.
***Like ghosts** the figures passed us.*

Es ist **mir** ganz gleich.
*It is all the same **to me**.*

(12) **Leicht** (*easy*):

Es war **dem Schüler** leicht, die Prüfung zu bestehen.
*It was easy **for the pupil** to pass the examination.*

(13) **Lieb** (*dear, charming*):

Es ist **ihm** sehr lieb.
***He likes** it very much.*

Note: **Lieb** is often followed by a **daß**-clause:

Es ist **mir** lieb, daß Sie das sagen.
I am pleased to hear you say that.

(14) **Nah(e)** (*near*):[1]

Das Dorf liegt **unserer Stadt** nahe.
The village is near our city.

(15) **Nützlich** (*useful*):

Der Staatsmann ist **dem Lande** nützlich.
The statesman is useful to the country.

(16) **Schwer** (*difficult*):

Diese Arbeit ist (*or* fällt) **den kleinen Kindern** schwer.
This work is hard for the little children.

(17) **Treu** (*true, faithful*):

Werden Sie **mir** treu bleiben?
Will you be (or remain) true to me?

(18) **Willkommen** (*welcome*):

Seien Sie **mir** herzlich willkommen!
You are heartily welcome.

Note: **Mir** may be left untranslated (*cf.* ¶ F of this section) or it may be brought out in the translation: *I wish you a hearty welcome.*

Summary: The above sentences indicate that **adjectives governing the dative case** *follow* **the word they govern.**

E.   **The dative of possession.** The English construction to denote possession with reference to parts of the body or to articles of clothing is the **possessive adjective;** the German idiom, however—usually with the dative—ordinarily uses the **definite article,** provided there is no doubt as to the possessor.

Ich wasche **mir die** Hände.	Ich wasche **dem Kinde die** Hände.
I wash my hands.	*I wash the child's hands.*
Er setzt **(sich) den** Hut auf.	Er setzt **dem Jungen den** Hut auf.
He puts on his hat.	*He puts the hat on the boy's head.*

---

[1] *Near* is more frequently rendered by **in der Nähe:**
He lives near me (her, you, us).
Er wohnt in meiner (ihrer, Ihrer, unserer) Nähe.

F. The dative of reference. The dative is often used to denote the person concerned in a statement, or the person with reference to whom the statement holds good:

Schreiben Sie **mir** diese Aufgabe ab!	Es war **ihm** ein Rätsel.
Copy this exercise for me.	*It was a riddle to him.*

Note: It is sometimes advisable not to translate such a dative:[1]

Zu Hause nahm ich **mir** nur Zeit, mich anzuziehen und zu frühstücken.
At home I merely took time to dress and to (have) breakfast.

G. The dative as indirect object, with certain prepositions, and with reflexive and impersonal verbs. For the use of the dative as indirect object, *cf.* § 2 **C**; with certain prepositions, *cf.* §§ 28 and 29. Reflexive and impersonal verbs with the dative are explained in §§ 61 **F** and 62 **B** respectively.

EXERCISE

A. Complete the following sentences:

1. Antworten Sie d— alt— Mann!
2. Antworten Sie ⸺ dies— Frage!
3. D— jünger— Tochter ist d— Vater ähnlich.
4. Dies— kurz— Geschichte ist mi— gar nicht bekannt.
5. We— sind Sie auf d— Straße begegnet?
6. Haben Sie d— gut— Frau geholfen?
7. Ich werde es mi— bequem machen.
8. Mein tapfer— Bruder hatte sein— Vaterland treu gedient.
9. Was fehlt d— klein— Jung— (sing.)?
10. D— jung— Männer sind uns all— fremd.
11. Seien Sie ⸺ (*them*) freundlich!
12. We— gehören dies— deutsch— Bücher?
13. Er gehorchte mi— immer.
14. Die Ferien kommen d— klein— Kind— (pl.) gelegen.
15. Das Heer ist jen— neutral— Land nicht feindlich gesinnt.
16. Ihr Besuch ist mein— älter— Bruder stets angenehm.
17. Das geschieht d— unehrlich— Mann recht!

---

[1] *Cf.* also ¶ **D** (18).

18. D— jüngst— Kind gleicht d— Mutter.
19. Glauben Sie —— (them)? Glauben Sie —— (it)?
20. D— klein— Hund ist sein— Herr— treu.
21. Das war —— (her) nie eingefallen.
22. Vergeben Sie d— arm— Leut—!
23. Fällt (or ist) dies— kurz— Prüfung d— Schüler— (pl.) schwer?
24. Ich gratuliere —— (you) zum Geburtstag.
25. Der berühmte Mann wird sein— Vaterland nützlich sein.
26. Es ist —— (us) all— sehr lieb, daß Sie das sagen.
27. Langsam näherte er sich d— alt— Dorf.
28. Er befahl mi—, bald zurückzukehren.
29. Das war —— (them) ein Rätsel.
30. Er hatte —— (his) Hände gewaschen.
31. Sie setzte —— (her) Hut auf.
32. Wir haben —— (ourselves) nicht geschmeichelt. Schmeicheln Sie —— (yourself) nicht!
33. Diese Speise wird dein— Gesundheit nicht schaden.
34. Wie gefällt —— (you) dies— lang— Geschichte?
35. Der Polizist (or colloq. Schupo) ist d— Dieb gefolgt.
36. Es ist mi— ganz gleich, was er sagt. Ich glaube —— (it) nicht.
37. Widersprich d— Eltern nicht!
38. Ihr Wort genügt mi—.
39. Er hat d— arm— Frau viel Geld gegeben.
40. Sie war ihr— Vater stets dankbar.
41. Das Dorf liegt mein— Vaterstadt nahe.
42. Seien Sie —— (him) nicht böse!
43. Wozu haben Sie —— (her) geraten?
44. Zeigen Sie d— klein— Mädchen (sing.) d— schön— Bild!
45. Es ist mi— noch nicht gelungen, diesen Plan auszuführen.
46. Ohne Zweifel wird man bald in Raumfahrzeugen an —— (the) Planeten Venus vorbeifliegen und viel Neues erfahren. Eines der wichtigsten Ergebnisse dieser wissenschaftlichen Experimente könnte —— (the) Klärung der Frage nach —— (the) Entstehung des organischen Lebens auf der Erde dienen.

B. Translate:

1. How do you like this new book?
2. The policeman had followed the thieves.

3. That will not hurt her health.
4. It was all the same to me what he said. I saw it myself.
5. She had given the poor children some apples.
6. Show those little boys the interesting pictures.
7. That was a riddle to her.
8. Carl, have you washed your hands? (*Rewrite with* children and Mr. Werner *instead of* Carl.)
9. He is putting on his hat.
10. Don't flatter yourself.
11. Don't contradict that old man.
12. Finally it occurred to me.
13. This short examination was easy for them.
14. Is writing difficult for you?
15. They are slowly approaching the city of Berlin.
16. Formerly we lived near them (*i.e.*, in their vicinity).
17. We were helping our dear friends.
18. Those little dogs are faithful to their master.
19. " Did you answer him? "   " No, I did not answer his questions."
20. Do you believe him?   Do you believe it?
21. The older brother resembles his mother.
22. The youngest child resembles its father.
23. That serves you right!
24. I met that famous man on the street today.
25. Many happy returns of the day [*i.e.*, I congratulate you, *etc.* (*cf.* sentence no. 24 of ¶ **A**)].
26. Make yourself (*formal address*) at home.
27. She will obey her mother.
28. To whom do these interesting pictures belong?
29. Be friendly to her.
30. They are all strangers (*use adj.* fremd) to me.
31. What is the matter with those young men?
32. He will serve his native land faithfully.
33. I shall always be grateful to him.
34. What (in the world) do you mean?
35. Of what use is that to you?
36. With regard to (hinsichtlich *w. gen.*) (*the*) size, the planet Venus is very much like the earth.

35. USES OF THE ACCUSATIVE CASE

A. The accusative to denote definite time. The accusative case is used to denote **definite** time:

Letzten Monat war ich bei ihm.
Last month I was at his house.

Nächsten Sommer wird er mich besuchen.[1]
*He will visit me **next summer**.*

Caution: The genitive is used to denote **indefinite** time (*cf.* § 33 **A**).

B. The accusative to denote duration of time. The accusative case is used to express **duration** of time:

Wir arbeiteten **den ganzen Tag.**   **Den ganzen Morgen** spielte er Ball.
*We worked **all day**.*   *He played ball **all morning**.*

C. The accusative to denote extent. The accusative case is used to denote **extent,** especially with such adjectives as **breit, dick, hoch, lang,** and **tief:**

einen Zoll **breit,** *an inch wide*   eine Meile **lang,** *a mile long*
einen Fuß **hoch,** *a foot high*   einen Ton **tiefer,** *a tone lower*
einen Fuß **dick,** *a foot thick*   einen Kopf **größer,** *a head taller*

D. The double accusative. Certain verbs such as **lehren** (*to teach*), **nennen** and **heißen** (*to call*), and **schelten** and **schimpfen** (*to call names*) take **two accusative objects:**

Sie lehrte **ihn das Lied.**   Er nannte (*or* hieß) **mich seinen Freund.**
*She taught **him the song**.*   *He called **me his friend**.*

Er hat **ihn einen Narren** geschimpft (*or* gescholten).
*He called **him a fool**.*

Note: The verb **kosten** (*to cost*) may take either the accusative or dative of the person, but always the accusative of the thing:

Es kostete **ihn** (*or* ihm) ein**en** Dollar.
It cost him a dollar.

Das Buch kostete **mich** (*or* mir) zehn Mark.
The book cost me ten marks.

---

[1] For additional examples, *cf.* § 23 **A** (2) and **C** (2), and § 25 **B**.

E. The cognate accusative. The **cognate accusative** repeats the idea contained in a verb:

> Gar schöne **Spiele** spiel' ich mit dir.   (Goethe)
> *I shall play very beautiful games with you.*
>
> Er starb **einen sanften Tod** (*or* eines sanften Todes).
> *He passed away peacefully.*

lit.:   *He died an easy death.*

Note: The second optional form indicates that **sterben** is sometimes followed by the genitive.

F. The absolute accusative. The accusative case is often used **absolutely** with some such word as *having* understood:

> **Den Stock** unter dem Arm, ging er in den Wald.
> **With** (*i.e., having*) **his cane** *under his arm, he went into the forest.*

G. The accusative in salutations. Such expressions as **guten Morgen!, guten Abend!, guten Tag!, etc.,** are in the accusative case because they imply a verb of wishing: *I wish you a good morning (evening, day, etc.)*.

H. The accusative with gewohnt, wert, and entlang. The accusative is used with **gewohnt** (*accustomed*), **wert** (*worth*), and **entlang** (*along*):

>   Er ist schwere Arbeit gewohnt.
> or: Er ist **an** schwere Arbeit gewöhnt.
>   *He is used to hard work.*

> Es ist einen Dollar wert.   Er ging **das Ufer** entlang.
> *It is worth a dollar.*   *He walked along the shore.*

Note:

(1) For **müde** and **los,** *cf.* § 33 **C** (8).

(2) For the use of **wert** in certain phrases with the genitive, *cf.* § 33 **C** (10).

(3) **Entlang** governs the dative occasionally and the genitive still less frequently. It sometimes precedes the noun it governs.

I. Compounds from intransitive verbs. Many intransitive verbs become transitive when compounded:[1]

(1)

Er folgte mir.   but:
He followed me.

{ Er **be**folgte meinen Rat.
He followed my advice.
Er **ver**folgte **mich.**
He pursued me.

Er steigt auf den Berg.   Ich wohne in diesem Haus.
but: Er **be**steigt **den** Berg.   but: Ich **be**wohne dieses Haus.
He climbs the mountain.   *I live in this house.*

Note: **Be–** is the most common transitive prefix.

(2) Similarly:

Er redete **mich an.**   Sie haben **den** alten Mann fast **über**fahren.
He addressed me.   *You almost ran over the old man.*

J. Causatives. Causative verbs, which require a direct object, must not be confused with intransitive verbs of similar spelling:

(1) Die Bäume **fallen** (intr.) im Sturm.
The trees fall in the storm.

Die Holzhacker **fällen** die Bäume.
The woodcutters fell (i.e., **cause** *to fall or cut down) the trees.*

Die Männer **ertrinken** (intr.).
The men are drowning.

Sie **ertränken** die Katze.
They are drowning the cat (i.e., **cause** *it to drown).*

(2) Similarly: **liegen** (intr. *to lie*), **legen** (tr. *to lay*); **sitzen** (intr. *to sit*), **setzen** (tr. *to set*); **versinken** (intr. *to sink*), **versenken** (tr. *to sink*); **erschrecken** (intr. str. *to be frightened*), **erschrecken** (tr. wk. *to frighten*); **verschwinden** (intr. *to disappear*), **verschwenden** [tr. *to squander (i.e., cause to disappear)*].

Summary: The above examples indicate that **causative** verbs derive their name from the element of **causation** which inheres in them.

Note: Causative verbs are regularly **weak.**

---

[1] Attention has already been called to **antworten** and **beantworten** (*cf.* § 34 **A** (1)) and to **rauben** and **berauben** (*cf.* § 33 **B** (3) (*c*)). For additional examples, *cf.* § 91 **B** (2) and Chapter 20 on Separable and Inseparable Prefixes.

K. Other uses of the accusative. For the use of the accusative **as direct object,** *cf.* § 2 **D**; **with certain prepositions,** *cf.* §§ 26 and 29; **with reflexive verbs,** *cf.* Note (3) following § 61 **B**; **with impersonal verbs,** *cf.* § 62 **B.**

EXERCISE

A. Complete the following sentences:

1. Wir werden d— ganz— Sommer in Europa sein.
2. Er hatte mi— sein— best— Freund genannt.
3. —— Hut in d— Hand, trat er in d— Zimmer.
4. Jed— Samstag gehe ich in— Theater.
5. Nächst— Sommer werde ich —— Hause bleiben.
6. Gut— Morgen! Gut— Abend! Gut— Tag! Gut— Nacht.
7. D— ganz— Monat war ich auf dem Lande.
8. Ein— Tag— wurde ich krank.
9. Das Band war ein— Finger breit.
10. Sie lehrte mi— d— schön— Lied.
11. Die Wand war ein— Fuß dick.
12. Er hatte —— (*him*) ein— Narren gescholten.
13. Das Buch kostete —— (*her*) ein— Dollar.
14. Ich bin d— Frühaufstehen nicht gewohnt.
15. Langsam ging er d— Straße entlang.
16. Das Brett ist nur ein— Fuß lang.
17. Endlich bin ich d— Sache los.
18. Fritz ist ein— Kopf größer als sein jüngerer Bruder.
19. Beantworten Sie mein— erst— Frage!
20. Antworten Sie —— mein— erst— Frage!
21. Ein— ganz— Tag verfolgte er mi—.
22. Jedermann nannte —— (*him*) ein— ehrlich— Mann.
23. Ich träumte ein— schön— Traum.
24. Er starb ein— edl— Tod. (Edl- comes from edel.)
25. Jed— Winter bleibe ich in d— Stadt.
26. Ein— Morgen— hatten wir viel Schnee.
27. Es ist kein— Dollar wert.
28. Die Arbeit kostete mi— viel Mühe.
29. Letzt— Woche beschrieb der Forscher einen künstlichen Erdsatelliten.
30. Nächst— Monat wird er einen Raumflug machen.

B.   Translate:

1. Next winter my best friend will visit me.
2. Every Sunday I take a long walk.
3. We shall be in Germany the whole summer.
4. With his cane in his hand, he walked through the village.
5. I had called him my friend.
6. He is going along the street.
7. It is worth a dollar.
8. They were not used to hard work.
9. He taught her the German songs.
10. Good morning!   Good evening!   Good night!
11. Were you working all morning?
12. Last summer I visited my best friend.
13. The handkerchief cost (me) a mark.
14. She had called him a fool.
15. The board was a foot wide.
16. One winter my parents took a trip to Florida.
17. Last winter they stayed at home.
18. My little brother played ball all afternoon.
19. The thief followed me through the dark street.
20. He pursued me for a whole hour.
21. Why didn't you answer my question?
22. The water is a foot deep.
23. I am tired of it.   At last I am rid of it.
24. The box was a foot high.
25. He walked slowly along the river.
26. The ribbon was an inch wide.
27. The brave flyers died a noble death.
28. The work cost me much trouble.
29. I was frightened.   I frightened him.
30. They were sinking.   They were sinking the ship.
31. The tall trees were falling.   They were felling the tall trees.
32. He was drowning.   He was drowning the cat.
33. She disappears.   She never squanders her money.
34. Several flyers have described the space flights they made last May.
35. Last year we learned much about artificial earth satellites.

CHAPTER 12

Special Uses of Tense

36. THE IDIOMATIC USE OF THE PRESENT FOR THE ENGLISH PRESENT PERFECT

Read the following sentences very carefully:

A. Er **ist** schon zwei Monate hier.

*He **has been** here for two months.*
i.e.: *He came here two months **ago** and is **still** here.*

Wie lange **lernen Sie** schon Deutsch?
*How long **have you been studying** German?*
i.e.: The person addressed began the study of German some time **ago** and is **still** studying it.

Wir **arbeiten** schon einen Monat.
*We **have been** working for a month.*
i.e.: *We began to work a month **ago** and are **still** working.*

B. Sie ist (schon) **seit drei Jahren** in dieser Stadt.
or: Sie ist **schon drei Jahre** in dieser Stadt.
*She has been in this city **for three years**.*
i.e.: *She came three years **ago** and is **still** in the city.*

Seit wann wohnen Sie in dieser Stadt?
***Since when** have you been living in this city?*
i.e.: The person addressed is **still** living in the city.

Ich wohne **erst** seit zwei Monaten hier.
*I have been living here for **only** two months.*

Summary: The above sentences indicate that German uses the present tense to denote an action begun in the past and still continuing in the present, whereas English requires the present perfect.   (French, Spanish, and Latin use the present tense as does German.)

Note:

(1) **Schon** often accompanies the present tense in this idiomatic use (*cf.* sentences under ¶ **A** above).

(2) **Seit** (lit. *since*) with the dative case may be used in this same construction (*cf.* sentences under ¶ **B** above).

Caution: If **seit** is **not** used, the noun denoting time must be in the accusative (*cf.* first and third sentences under ¶ **A** above and § 35 **A** for uses of the accusative).

(3) **Erst** (*only*) is often used in idiomatic sentences of this type (*cf.* last sentence under ¶ **B** above).

37. THE USE OF THE PRESENT FOR THE FUTURE

Read the following sentences very carefully:

Bald sind wir da.	Morgen reist mein Freund ab.
We shall soon be there.	*My friend will leave tomorrow.*

Wenn Sie sich beeilen, so werden Sie ihn noch einholen.
If you (will) hurry, you will still catch (up with) him.

Summary: The above sentences indicate that the present tense is often used instead of the future, particularly when accompanying adverbs of time—such as **bald** and **morgen**—clearly show futurity. If the future indicative occurs in the main clause of a conditional sentence, the present indicative is ordinarily employed in the **wenn**-clause (just as in English).

Note: The present tense is also used for the future in other types of sentences, where there can be no chronological ambiguity.

38. IDIOMATIC USES OF THE PAST

A.   The use of the past for the English past perfect.
Read the following sentence very carefully:

Er **wartete** schon anderthalb Stunden auf mich, als ich kam.
*He **had been waiting** an hour and a half for me when I came.*
i.e.: *He began to wait for me at some time in the past and was **still** waiting for me when I came.*

Summary: The above sentence indicates that the German past is used to denote an action begun at some previous time and still continuing up to the time referred to in the past. (Compare this with the use of the present tense, as explained in § 36 above.)

Note: **Seit** and **schon** are commonly used with the past in sentences of the following type:

Er **kannte** mich schon seit vielen Jahren.
*He **had known** me for many years.*

Wir **waren** schon lange Freunde.
*We **had been** friends for a long time.*

B. **The use of the past to denote a customary occurrence in the past.** Read the following sentences very carefully:

Früher **rauchte** er viel.
*Formerly he **used to smoke** (or he smoked) a great deal.*

Er **stand gewöhnlich** um sieben Uhr auf.
*He **used to get up** (or he usually got up) at seven o'clock.*

Wenn er bei mir war, **sprach** er immer über seine Zukunftspläne.
*Whenever he was at my house, he **would** always **talk** (or he always talked) about his plans for the future.*

Summary: The above sentences indicate that a recurring or habitual past action—which may be expressed in English by *used to* or *would* (not with conditional force, as in present contrary-to-fact conditions) with a dependent infinitive—is expressed in German by the **past,** frequently reënforced by such adverbs as **früher, gewöhnlich,** and **immer.**

Note: **Pflegen** [*to be accustomed* (or *used*) *to*] with a dependent infinitive is a common equivalent of the above construction: Er pflegte viel zu rauchen.   Er pflegte um sieben Uhr aufzustehen.   Er pflegte über seine Zukunftspläne zu sprechen.

39. THE IDIOMATIC USE OF THE FUTURE AND FUTURE PERFECT WITH WOHL

Read the following sentences very carefully:

A. Er wird es wohl verstehen.
He doubtless understands it.
Sie wird wohl wissen, was das bedeutet.
She doubtless knows what that means.

Summary: The above sentences indicate that the German future, usually with **wohl,** may be used to denote a **present probability.**

B. Mein Freund wird wohl krank gewesen sein.
My friend was probably sick.
Er wird wohl zu viel gegessen haben.
He probably ate too much.

Summary: The above sentences indicate that the German future perfect, usually with **wohl,** is often used to denote a **past probability.**

Note: The above is the chief use of this tense, which is **rarely** used to refer to the future.   (Cf. also **Note** (4) of § 87 **F.**)

EXERCISE

A.   Translate into idiomatic English:
1. Wie lange ist Herr Schmidt schon in Amerika?
2. Wir waren schon eine Viertelstunde im Hotel, als er kam.
3. Sie wartet schon eine Stunde auf mich.
4. Sie wird wohl wissen, warum ich zu spät komme.
5. Seit wann ist Ihr alter Freund auf dem Lande?
6. Er wird wohl gewußt haben, warum ich ihn letzten Sommer nicht besuchen konnte.
7. Ich wohne erst seit zwei Tagen in diesem Haus.
8. Der Winter ist bald da (*here*).
9. Wenn Sie sich nicht warm anziehen, so werden Sie sich erkälten.
10. Wie lange ist der Mann schon da?

11. Die alte Dame ist schon dreißig Jahre in den Vereinigten Staaten, aber sie spricht noch nicht fließend Englisch.
12. Der Mann wird wohl zu viel getrunken haben.
13. Wir waren schon lange Freunde.
14. Seit drei Tagen suche ich mein deutsches Buch.
15. Ich werde es wohl verlegt haben.
16. Er pflegte früh aufzustehen.
17. Schon seit dem Jahre 1957 konstruiert man künstliche Satelliten, die der Wissenschaft wichtige Forschungsergebnisse liefern.

B. Translate into German.   Consider the tense very carefully.

1. Since when has your rich uncle been living in this small village?
2. He doubtless knows why I am here.
3. I have been waiting an hour and a half for him.
4. She had been there half an hour when I came.
5. How long has your dear friend been in the country?
6. I have been here since half past eight.
7. Her little brother is probably in school.
8. Our old German doctor has been in the United States for forty years, but he does not yet speak English fluently.
9. For four days I have been looking for my fountain pen.
10. I probably misplaced it.
11. Spring will soon be here (da).
12. She has been living in this city for only one month.
13. I had known her for many years.
14. She probably has a headache.
15. She probably studied too hard.
16. He used to speak about his experiences.
17. Scientific firms will doubtless construct many artificial earth satellites.   With these satellites many important investigations will be carried out (durchführen).

CHAPTER 13 **Personal Pronouns**

40. THE FORM AND USE OF PERSONAL PRONOUNS

Read the following sentences very carefully. Note the form and use of the personal pronouns which are boldfaced:

A. The nominative case:

(1) „Wo ist der Bleistift?"   „**Er** ist auf dem Tisch."
"Where is the pencil?"   *"**It** is on the table."*

(2) „Wo ist die Feder?"   „**Sie** ist auf dem Tisch."
"Where is the pen?"   *"**It** is on the table."*

(3) „Wo ist das Buch?"   „**Es** ist auf dem Tisch."
"Where is the book?"   *"**It** is on the table."*

(4) Karl, was schreibst **du?**
*Carl, what are **you** writing?*

(5) Kinder, was schreibt **ihr?**
*Children, what are **you** writing?*

(6) Herr Schmidt, was schreiben **Sie?**
*Mr. Smith, what are **you** writing?*

(7) Meine Herren, was wollen **Sie?**
*Gentlemen, what do **you** wish?*

(8) „Wo ist Marie?"   „Jetzt ist **sie** zu Hause."
"Where is Mary?"   *"**She** is at home now."*

(9) „Wo waren ihre Schwestern?"   „Gestern waren **sie** auf dem Lande."
"Where were her sisters?"   *"Yesterday **they** were in the country."*

(10) „Wo ist Wilhelm?"   „**Er** ist in Deutschland."
"Where is William?"   *"**He** is in Germany."*

(11) **Ich** freue mich, daß **wir** endlich schönes Wetter haben.
I am glad that at last we are having beautiful weather.

B. The dative case:

(1) Er gibt **mir** das Buch.
He gives me the book.

(2) Karl, ich werde **dir** das Bild zeigen.
Carl, I shall show you the picture.

(3) Kinder, ich werde **euch** die Bilder zeigen.
Children, I shall show you the pictures.

(4) Ich sagte **ihm** die Wahrheit.
I told him the truth.

(5) Wo ist das Kind? Ich wollte **ihm** etwas geben.
Where is the child? I wanted to give it something.

(6) Sie erzählte **ihr** eine Geschichte.
She told her a story.

(7) Was fehlt **Ihnen,** Herr Schmidt?
What is the matter with you, Mr. Smith?

(8) Meine Herren, was fehlt **Ihnen?**
Gentlemen, what is the matter with you?

(9) Er hatte **uns** das Geld gegeben.
He had given us the money.

(10) Wir haben **ihnen** geholfen.
We have helped them.

C. The accusative case:

(1) Er hat **mich** gesehen.
He saw me.

(2) Karl, ich werde **dich** besuchen.
Carl, I shall visit you.

(3) Kinder, wir werden **euch** bald besuchen.
Children, we shall visit you soon.

(4) Wir haben **ihn** nicht gehört.
We did not hear him.

(5) Wo ist das Kind? Ich sehe **es** nicht.
Where is the child? I do not see it.

(6) Was sagte Luise? Ich habe **sie** nicht verstanden.
*What did Louise say? I did not understand **her**.*

(7) Wo ist meine Füllfeder? Ich kann **sie** nicht finden.
*Where is my fountain pen? I cannot find **it**.*

(8) Was sagten ihre Schwestern? Ich habe **sie** nicht verstanden.
*What did her sisters say? I did not understand **them**.*

(9) Die Männer haben **uns** besucht.
*The men visited **us**.*

(10) Herr Schmidt, ich muß **Sie** loben.
*Mr. Smith, I must praise **you**.*

(11) Meine Herren, ich muß **Sie** loben.
*Gentlemen, I must praise **you**.*

Note:

(1) *It* is translated by **er, sie,** or **es**—depending upon the gender of the noun to which it refers (*cf.* ¶ **A** (1), (2), and (3) above).

(2) There are three personal pronouns for *you*:

(*a*) **Du** is the singular familiar pronoun (*cf.* ¶¶ **A** (4), **B** (2), and **C** (2) above). It is used when addressing a child, parent, close friend, or an animal, and the Deity.

(*b*) **Ihr** is the plural familiar pronoun (*cf.* ¶¶ **A** (5), **B** (3), and **C** (3) above). It is used when addressing children, parents, close friends, and animals.

(*c*) **Sie** (always capitalized) is the pronoun of formal address and is used when addressing single persons (*cf.* ¶¶ **A** (6), **B** (7), and **C** (10) above) or a group of persons (*cf.* ¶¶ **A** (7), **B** (8), and **C** (11) above).

(3) **Es, sie,** and **Sie** serve both as nominative (*cf.* ¶ **A** (2), (3), (6), (7), (8), and (9) above) and accusative (*cf.* ¶ **C** (5), (6), (7), (8), (10), and (11) above).

(4) **Uns** and **euch** serve both as dative (*cf.* ¶ **B** (3) and (9) above) and accusative (*cf.* ¶ **C** (3) and (9) above).

(5) **Ihm** may mean either *to him* (*cf.* ¶ **B** (4) above) or *to it* (*cf.* ¶ **B** (5) above). (*Cf.* also § 30 **B** for **da**-forms, when *to it* refers to **things.**)

(6) **Sie** (not capitalized unless it heads a sentence) may mean either *she* (*cf.* ¶ **A** (8) above), *her* (*cf.* ¶ **C** (6) above), *they* (*cf.* ¶ **A** (9) above), or

them (*cf.* ¶ **C** (8) above).   When referring to a feminine inanimate object, it may also mean *it*—either nominative (*cf.* ¶ **A** (2) above) or accusative (*cf.* ¶ **C** (7) above).

(7) The only difference between the various forms of **sie** (*they*) and **Sie** (*you*) is that the latter is capitalized (*cf.* ¶¶ **A** (6), (7), (9); **B** (7), (8), (10); and **C** (8), (10), and (11) above).

Caution: **Es,** in initial position when the grammatical subject follows a verb, must not be confused with **es** (*it*), the personal pronoun:

> Es sind dreißig Schüler in dieser Klasse.
> *There are thirty pupils in this class.*

Note also:

Es waren meine Freunde.	Ich bin es.	Ist er es?
They were my friends.	*It is I.*	*Is it he?*

41. THE PERSONAL PRONOUNS

The personal pronouns, singular and plural, for all cases are listed below:

SINGULAR

NOM.	ich (*I*)	du (*you*)	er (*he*)	sie (*she*)	es (*it*)	Sie (*you*)
GEN.	(meiner)[1]	(deiner)	(seiner)	(ihrer)	(seiner)	(Ihrer)
DAT.	mir	dir	ihm	ihr	ihm	Ihnen
ACC.	mich	dich	ihn	sie	es	Sie

PLURAL

NOM.	wir (*we*)	ihr (*you*)	sie [*they* (all genders)]	Sie (*you*)
GEN.	(unser)	(euer)	(ihrer)	(Ihrer)
DAT.	uns	euch	ihnen	Ihnen
ACC.	uns	euch	sie	Sie

42. USES OF THE GENITIVE OF PERSONAL PRONOUNS

A. The genitive of personal pronouns with certain verbs, adjectives, and numerals. The genitive form of the personal pro-

---

[1] The short genitive forms **mein** (*of me*), **dein** (*of you*), **sein** (*of him*), **ihr** (*of her*) are found chiefly in poetry, set phrases, and a few isolated words such as das Vergiß**mein**nicht (*forget-me-not*).

nouns is rare in modern German and, therefore, appeared in parentheses in the preceding section.   It is found with certain verbs, adjectives, and numerals:

> Schone **meiner!**   Erbarmen Sie sich **meiner!**
> *Spare me.*   *Pity me.*
>
> Gedenke **seiner!**   Erinnere dich **seiner!**
> or: Erinnere dich **an ihn!**   *Remember him.*
>
> Er wurde **seiner** gewahr.   Wir waren **unser** drei.
> *He perceived him.*   *There were three of us.*

B.   The genitive of personal pronouns with certain prepositions.
The genitive of the personal pronouns is also found with prepositions governing the genitive case, particularly in combinations with **wegen** (*on account of*), **um** . . . **willen** (*for the sake of*), and **halb(en)** (*on account of*).   As explained in **Note** (2) of § 32, pronouns thus used assume a form in –t instead of –r:

> meinetwegen, *on my account*   um meinetwillen, *for my sake*
> seinetwegen, *on his account*   Ihrethalben, *on your account*

43.   PRONOUNS OF DIRECT ADDRESS IN LETTERS

In letters all pronouns of **direct address** are capitalized.   This applies also to the corresponding possessive forms:

Mein lieber Karl!

Lange habe ich nichts von **D**ir gehört.   Vielleicht ist **D**ein letzter Brief verlorengegangen.

> Dein **D**ich liebender Fritz.

EXERCISE

A.   Complete the following sentences (review first ¶¶ **A** and **B** of § 34):

1. Bitte, geben Sie —— (*me*) das Buch!
2. Wird er —— [*you* (fam. sing.)] heute besuchen?
3. Sie hat —— (*me*) heute auf der Straße gesehen.
4. Das wird —— [*you* (fam. sing.)] nicht schaden.

5. Ich hatte —— (*him*) nicht verstanden.
6. Kinder, hat die Mutter —— (*you*) geholfen?
7. Ich gab —— (*him*) die Feder.
8. Wir werden —— (*her*) nächsten Monat besuchen.
9. Sie hat —— (*us*) nicht erkannt.
10. Gefällt di— das Buch?
11. Gefällt ih— die Geschichte?   (*Complete in three ways.*)
12. Er folgte —— (*us*).
13. Was fehlt —— [*you* (formal address)]?
14. Er kannte —— (*them*).
15. Er begegnete —— (*me*) in der Stadt.
16. Er hat —— (*me*) auf dem Lande getroffen.
17. Gehört das Buch —— (*her*) oder —— (*him*)?
18. Er hatte —— (*her*) nicht gehört.
19. Er hat —— (*me*) befohlen aufzustehen.
20. Der Hund wird —— (*him*) nicht beißen.
21. Bitte, tun Sie das —— (*on my account*)!
22. Ich werde —— [*you* (formal address)] die Bücher geben.
23. Nächste Woche werde ich —— [*you* (formal address)] besuchen.
24. Frau Schmidt, man muß —— [*you* (formal address)] loben.
25. Meine Damen, man muß —— [*you* (formal address)] loben.
26. Der Stuhl ist schön.   —— (*It*) gehört —— (*her*).
27. Die Prüfung ist nicht schwer.   —— (*It*) ist leicht.
28. Das Kleid ist schön.   —— (*It*) gefällt mi—.
29. Zeigen Sie es —— (*them*)!
30. Ich werde es —— [*you* (formal address)] zeigen.
31. Astronomen beobachten den Planeten Mars. Ist es —— gelungen zu erfahren, was die „Kanäle" auf diesem Planeten in Wirklichkeit sind?

B. Translate:

1. "Where is my trunk?"   "It is in the station."
2. I have lost my key.   Where is it?
3. Please give me the ink.   Is it black or red?
4. "Have you a pen?"   "It is on the table."
5. He has a large room.   He likes it.
6. My old friend was visiting me.
7. He will help me.
8. Do it for my sake.

9. My older brother lives with (bei) me.
10. I have not forgotten him.
11. I shall write him a long letter.
12. How are you? (*Translate in three ways.*)
13. Do you like the books? (*Translate in three ways, using the verb* gefallen *in each sentence.*)
14. Our old physician had not believed them.
15. My younger sister did not understand them.
16. Children, did your (*i.e.,* the) mother call you?
17. Carl, your father was calling you.
18. Did you not hear me?
19. Why have you forgotten her?
20. I shall thank her for the letter.
21. When did you see him?
22. He did not recognize me.
23. Tell me what he said.
24. He always loved her.
25. What is the matter with him?
26. A large dog bit him.
27. When will you visit me?
28. I did not understand him.
29. We had not heard them.
30. He will praise you. (*Translate in three ways.*)
31. In 1877 an astronomer observed a network of straight lines on the planet Mars. However, he did not succeed in solving the riddle of these so-called "canals."

CHAPTER 14 Interrogatives

44. WER, WAS, WELCHER, WAS FÜR EIN, AND WO-FORMS

Read the following sentences very carefully. Note the bold-faced forms.

A. Wer:

(1) The nominative case:

    (*a*) **Wer** ist die Dame?
        Who is the lady?

    (*b*) **Wer** sind die Damen?
        Who are the ladies?

(2) The genitive case:

    (*a*) **Wessen** Buch ist das?
        Whose book is that?

    (*b*) **Wessen** Bücher sind das?
        Whose books are those?

(3) The dative case:

    (*a*) **Wem** haben Sie die Briefe gegeben?
        To whom did you give the letters?

    (*b*) Mit **wem** hat er einen Spaziergang gemacht?
        With whom did he take a walk?

(4) The accusative case:

    (*a*) **Wen** haben Sie heute gesehen?
        Whom did you see today?

    (*b*) An **wen** denken Sie?
        Of whom are you thinking?

B. Was:

(1) The nominative case:

    Was ist das?
    What is that?

(2) The genitive case:

Weshalb (*or* **wes**wegen) haben Sie die Stadt verlassen?
Why did you leave the city?

(3) The accusative case:

(*a*) **Was** hat er gefunden?   *What did he find?*
(*b*) Er wußte nicht, **was** er tun sollte.[1]
He didn't know what to do.

C. Welcher:

(1) **Welcher** Mann ist zu Hause?   *Which* (adj.) *man is at home?*

(2) **Welcher** ist zu Hause, der Professor oder sein Sohn?
Which one (pron.) *is at home, the professor or his son?*

D. Was für ein:

(1) Mit **was für einem** Bleistift schreiben Sie?
With what kind of (*a*) (used as adj.) *pencil are you writing?*

(2) **Was für einen** haben Sie gekauft?
What kind (*of one*) (used as pron.) *did you buy?*

(3) **Was für** Bücher haben Sie?
What kind (used as adj.) *of books do you have?*

[**Was für ein** (plural **was für**) in exclamations has no interrogative force.
Was für ein Unglück!   *What a misfortune!*
Was für Leute!   *What people!*]

E.   Womit, worauf, *etc.*:

(1) **Worauf** warten Sie?   but: Auf wen warten Sie?
For what are you waiting?   *For whom are you waiting?*

(2) **Womit** schreiben Sie?   but: Mit wem sprechen Sie?
With what are you writing?   *With whom are you speaking?*

---

[1] The last part of this sentence is an **indirect question**. The original (direct) question was:

Was soll ich tun?
What shall I (or *am I to*) *do?*

The indirect form of ¶ **B** (1) would be: Ich weiß nicht, **was das ist.** For further details, *cf.* last part of **Note** (7) following.

Note:

(1) **Wer** and **was,** the most common interrogative pronouns, have no plural forms but may be followed by a plural form of the verb *to be* (*cf.* also ¶ **A** (1) (*b*) above):

> Was **sind** die Dinge da?
> *What **are** those things?*

(2) The declension of **wer** and **was** follows:

Masculine and Feminine		Neuter
NOM.	wer	was
GEN.	wessen	(wessen, wes) (rare)
DAT.	wem	————
ACC.	wen	was

(3) **Was** is found almost exclusively in the nominative (*cf.* ¶ **B** (1) above) and in the accusative (*cf.* ¶ **B** (3) above). The genitive is extremely rare and is confined chiefly to such adverbial combinations as **wes**halb and **wes**wegen, both meaning *why* (*cf.* ¶ **B** (2) above).

(4) The missing dative of **was** is supplied by **wo-** in such combinations as **womit, worauf,** *etc.* The accusative **was** is quite rare after prepositions and is also usually replaced by these **wo**-forms (*cf.* § 30). **Um was** instead of **worum,** however, is quite common in such a sentence as:

> Um was handelt es sich?
> *What is it (all) about?*

(5) **Welcher** [**welche** (*fem.*), **welches** (*neut.*)] may be used either as an interrogative adjective (*cf.* ¶ **C** (1) above) or as an interrogative pronoun (*cf.* ¶ **C** (2) above).

(6) (*a*) **Was für (ein)** may be used either as an interrogative adjective (*cf.* ¶ **D** (1) and (3) above) or as an interrogative pronoun (*cf.* ¶ **D** (2) above).

(*b*) **Für,** in the interrogative **was für ein,** is not a preposition and does not, therefore, determine the case of a following noun (*cf.* ¶ **D** (1) above).

(*c*) The plural of **was für ein** is simply **was für** (*cf.* ¶ **D** (3) above).

(7) (*a*) When an interrogative is not the subject of a verb, the inverted word order is used, just as in English:

> An wen denken Sie?
> *Of whom are you thinking?*

(*b*) An interrogative pronoun may introduce an indirect question;[1] it is then necessary for the verb to come at the end of a clause:

> Er fragte mich, wer gekommen **wäre** (or **sei**).
> *He asked me who had come.*

Caution:

(1) Do not confuse **was** and **welcher**. **Was** cannot modify a noun:

> **Welcher** Bleistift?   **Welche** Feder?
> *What pencil?*   *What pen?*
>
> **Welches** Buch?   but : **Was** ist das?
> *What book?*   *What is that?*

(2) Do not confuse **wessen** and **dessen**.   Both are translated by *whose* but **wessen is used in questions**, whereas **dessen** is the genitive (masculine and neuter singular) of the relative pronoun (*cf.* § 45):

> **Wessen** Buch haben Sie?
> *Whose book have you?*
>
> Der Mann, **dessen** Buch ich habe, ist in Deutschland.
> *The man **whose** book I have is in Germany.*

EXERCISE

A.   Complete the following sentences:

1. —— (*Whom*) haben Sie heute besucht?
2. —— (*To whom*) hat er die Bilder gezeigt?
3. —— (*What*) hat er in der Hand?
4. —— (*With what*) wird er den Brief schreiben?
5. Mit —— [*what kind of (a)*] Feder schreibt er?
6. —— (*What*) Bücher lagen auf dem Tisch?
7. —— (*What*) Junge ist heute nicht hier?
8. —— (*Which one*) fehlt heute?

---

[1] For the use of other interrogatives introducing indirect questions, *cf.* § 77, **Note** (4).

9. —— (*Whom*) haben Sie auf der Straße gesehen?
10. —— (*Whom*) sind Sie auf dem Lande begegnet?
11. —— (*To whom*) hatte er das Geld gegeben?
12. —— (*Whom*) hat er gestern getroffen?
13. —— (*Whose*) Arbeit ist das?
14. Er fragte mich, —— (*who*) gekommen wäre.
15. —— (*On what*) sitzen Sie?
16. —— (*With what*) hört man?
17. —— (*Whom*) hat er geschlagen?
18. —— (*To whom*) sagte er das?
19. In —— [*what kind of* (*a*)] Buch haben Sie das gelesen?
20. —— (*Of what*) denken Sie?
21. —— (*Of whom*) denken Sie?
22. —— (*Why*) haben Sie mich verlassen?
23. „Ich habe ein Buch vergessen." „—— (*Which one*) haben Sie vergessen?"
24. —— (*For what*) warten Sie?
25. —— (*For whom*) warten Sie?
26. —— (*What kind of*) wissenschaftliche Bücher haben Sie neulich gelesen?
27. Das Ballon-Teleskop, —— (*with which*) man Aufnahmen der Sonnenoberfläche machte, erreichte eine Höhe von 24,350 Metern.

B. Translate:

1. With whom are the little children playing?
2. With what were they playing?
3. Who is that old gentleman? Which one is ill?
4. Who are those old gentlemen?
5. Which friend did you see today?
6. Which one (*i.e.*, friend) did you see?
7. Whose pens are those?
8. Whom did you visit yesterday?
9. For what are you waiting?
10. For whom was he waiting?
11. With what kind of (a) pen had he written the letter?
12. What book did your little brother bring along today?
13. Which one did the lazy boy forget?
14. Which story do you like?

15. What kind of (a) woman is she?
16. Of whom are you thinking?
17. Of what were you thinking?
18. On what is that little boy sitting?
19. On what kind of (a) chair was his older brother sitting?
20. Whom had his younger brother followed?
21. Whom did the old lady meet? (*Translate first with* treffen *and then with* begegnen.)
22. Whose book is that?
23. Why will he leave this beautiful city?
24. Whom did he see yesterday?
25. To whom did you give those interesting German books?
26. The gigantic balloon which reached an altitude of about 25,000 meters in (a) relatively short time remained (verbleiben) at this height for several hours. With what is such a balloon usually filled?
27. The man whose name is generally associated with the law of the conservation of energy was a German physicist. Do you know who he was?

45. THE RELATIVES DER **AND** WELCHER

Read the following sentences very carefully. Note the bold-faced forms:

A. Singular number.

(1) The nominative case:

    (*a*) Der reiche Mann, **der** (or **welcher**) sein Geld verloren hatte, war unehrlich.

    The rich man who had lost his money was dishonest.

    (*b*) München ist eine Stadt, **die** (or **welche**) durch ihre Schönheit berühmt ist.

    Munich is a city which is famous for its beauty.

    (*c*) Das deutsche Buch, **das** (or **welches**) auf dem Tische liegt, gehört meinem Bruder.

    The German book which is lying on the table belongs to my brother.

(2) The genitive case:

    (*a*) Ein Witwer ist ein Mann, **dessen** Frau gestorben ist.

    A widower is a man whose wife is dead.

    (*b*) Eine Witwe ist eine Frau, **deren** Mann gestorben ist.

    A widow is a woman whose husband is dead.

    (*c*) Eine Waise ist ein Kind, **dessen** Eltern gestorben sind.

    An orphan is a child whose parents are dead.

(3) The dative case:

    (*a*) Der Herr, **dem** (or **welchem**) ich das Buch gegeben habe, ist mein bester Freund.

    The gentleman to whom I gave the book is my best friend.

(b) Leipzig ist eine Handelsstadt, **in der** (or **welcher**) jährliche Messen stattfinden.
*Leipzig is a commercial city **in which** annual fairs are held.*

(c) Das Haus, **in dem** (**in welchem** or **worin**) wir jetzt wohnen, gefällt mir nicht.
*I do not like the house **in which** we now live.*

(4) The accusative case:

(a) Er ist der Mann, **den** (or **welchen**) ich gestern besucht habe.
*He is the man **whom** I visited yesterday.*

(b) Wo ist die Feder, **die** (or **welche**) ich heute gekauft habe?
*Where is the pen (**that**) I bought today?*

(c) Das ist das Buch, **das** (or **welches**) ich gestern gelesen habe.
*That is the book (**that**) I read yesterday.*

B. Plural number.

(1) The nominative case:

Das sind die Männer (die Frauen, die Kinder), **die** (or **welche**) uns gegenüber wohnen.
*Those are the men (the women, the children) **who** live opposite us.*

(2) The genitive case:

Das sind die Männer (die Frauen, die Kinder), **deren** Bücher wir jetzt lesen.
*Those are the men (the women, the children) **whose** books we are now reading.*

(3) The dative case:

Das sind die Männer (die Frauen, die Kinder), **denen** (or **welchen**) wir das Geld gegeben haben.
*Those are the men (the women, the children) **to whom** we gave the money.*

(4) The accusative case:

Das sind die Männer (die Frauen, die Kinder), **die** (or **welche**) wir letztes Jahr besucht haben.
*Those are the men (the women, the children) **whom** we visited last year.*

Summary: The above sentences indicate that there are two common relative pronouns, **der** and **welcher**. **Welcher** has no genitive forms in the singular or in the plural.

Note:

(1) The declension of **der** and **welcher** follows. Observe that the declension of the relative **der** is the same as that of the definite article, except for the five forms in boldface:

	SINGULAR			PLURAL
	MASC.	FEM.	NEUT.	MASC. FEM. NEUT.
Nom.	der (welcher)	die (welche)	das (welches)	die (welche)
Gen.	**dessen**	**deren**	**dessen**	**deren**
Dat.	dem (welchem)	der (welcher)	dem (welchem)	**denen** (welchen)
Acc.	den (welchen)	die (welche)	das (welches)	die (welche)

(2) The relative **der** is used much more frequently than **welcher,** especially in conversation. **Welcher,** however, is often used to avoid a repetition of some form of **der.** In the following sentence **der** would occur successively in three forms—the demonstrative, the relative, and the definite article—if **welcher** were not used:

Die Freude war groß, denn der, **welcher** der Familie am liebsten war, war heimgekehrt.
*The joy was great, for the one **who** was dearest to the family had returned home.*

(3) (*a*) **The relative pronoun agrees in gender and number with its antecedent.** *Whose* is always genitive, but particular care must be taken to have it agree with its antecedent and **not** with the noun following:

Er ist der Mann, **dessen** Frau krank ist.
*He is the man **whose** wife is ill.*

Here **dessen** is masculine singular to agree with **Mann.**

(*b*) **The case of a relative is determined by its use in the relative clause**—not by its antecedent (*cf.* sentences above).

(4) Since all relative clauses are dependent, the verb must come at the end of a clause (*cf.* sentences above).

(5) Contrary to English usage, **the relative pronoun is never omitted in German** (*cf.* ¶ **A** (4) (*b*) and (*c*) above).

(6) Relative clauses in German **must be set off by commas** (*cf.* sentences above).

(7) A **wo**-form (*cf.* § 30) is frequently used instead of a preposition and a relative, provided the antecedent is a **thing** (*cf.* ¶ **A** (3) (*c*) above).

46. THE RELATIVE WAS

Read the following sentences very carefully.   Note the bold-faced forms:

A.   **Alles, was** er sagt, ist wahr.
    *All (**that**) he says is true.*

B.   **Nichts, was** sie tat, ist ihr gelungen.
    *Nothing (**that**) she did turned out well for her.*

C.   Es gibt **vieles, was** mir fehlt.
    *There is **much that** I lack.*

D.   Das ist **etwas, was** sie noch nicht weiß.
    *That is **something** (**that**) she does not yet know.*

E.   Er hat **manches** vergessen, **was** er in der Schule gelernt hat.
    *He has forgotten **much** (or **many a thing**) **that** he learned in school.*

F.   **Das Beste, was** ich habe, gebe ich dir.
    *I am giving you **the best** (**that**) I have.*

G.   Er sagte, **es gehe ihm gut, was** mich sehr freute.
    *He said **he was well, which** made me very happy.*

H.   Das ist **das Buch, das** (or **welches**) ich zweimal gelesen habe.
    *That is **the book** (**that**) I read twice.*

Note:

(1) **Was** must be used instead of **das** or **welches**, if indefinite neuter forms such as **alles, nichts, vieles, etwas, manches,** or **a neuter super-lative** are the antecedent of the relative (*cf.* ¶¶ **A–F** above).

(2)₀ **Was** may also refer to **the thought of a preceding clause** (*cf.* ¶ **G** above).

(3) **If the antecedent is a noun,** was **cannot be used** (*cf.* ¶ **H** above).

47. THE RELATIVE WO

Wo as a relative equivalent to *in which*, but often translated by *where*, requires the verb at the end of the clause:

> Das ist **der Ort, wo** meine Wiege stand.
> *That is **the place where** I was born.*
> lit.:   *That is the place where my cradle stood.*

Note:

(1) Relative **wo** is not to be confused with interrogative **wo,** which requires the inverted word order:

> Wo stand Ihre Wiege?
> *Where were you born?*

(2) *At the time **when*** is often rendered by zur Zeit, **als** (da *or* wo) with the dependent word order:

> Zur Zeit, **als** (da *or* wo) er im Lande war, gab es keine Eisenbahnen.
> *There were no railroads (at the time) **when** he was in the country.*

48. THE GENERAL (OR INDEFINITE) RELATIVES WER AND WAS

Read the following sentences very carefully:

A. **Wer** nicht für mich ist, (der) ist gegen mich.
Whoever *is not for me is against me.*

B. **Was** nicht gut ist, (das) ist schlecht.
Whatever *is not good is bad.*

Summary: The above sentences indicate that the general (or indefinite) relatives **wer** (*whoever*) and **was** (*whatever*) **never have an antecedent.**

Note:

(1) The general relatives **wer** and **was** are not to be confused with the interrogatives **wer** and **was** (*cf.* preceding chapter).

(2) Remember that the verb must always come at the end of a relative clause.

49. A SUBSTITUTE CONSTRUCTION FOR A RELATIVE CLAUSE

In the **written** language, a noun may be modified by a **preceding article and participle with modifiers** instead of by a following relative clause:

> **A.** **Ein** von allen Zeitungen gelobt**er Sänger** ist heute angekommen.
>
> *i.e.:* Ein Sänger, den alle Zeitungen gelobt haben, ist heute angekommen.
> *A singer whom all the newspapers have praised arrived today.*

> **B.** **Ein** alt**es** ursprünglich nicht zu Schulzwecken bestimmt**es Gebäude** stand an der Ecke.
>
> *i.e.:* Ein altes Gebäude, das ursprünglich nicht zu Schulzwecken bestimmt war, stand an der Ecke.
> *An old building, which was not originally intended for school purposes, stood on the corner.*

> **C.** Das Dach **des** schon seit dem Dreißigjährigen Kriege von der Familie Wagner bewohnt**en Hauses** ist neulich umgebaut worden.
>
> *i.e.:* Das Dach des Hauses, das die Familie Wagner schon seit dem Dreißigjährigen Kriege bewohnt, ist neulich umgebaut worden.
> *The roof of the house that the Wagner family has occupied since the Thirty Years' War, has recently been rebuilt.*

Note:

(1) Although this construction is now condemned by German stylists, it should nevertheless be mastered by the student **who wishes to develop his ability to read German rapidly.** It is a usage to which recognized literary writers were formerly inclined, and one to which many modern journalists, business men, and writers of technical and scientific works

still adhere. **The student, however, should avoid this use of the participle—both in conversation and in written work;** rather, he should imitate the equivalent relative constructions following each of the above sentences (indicated by *i.e.*).

(2) (*a*) Occasionally an adjective capable of being expanded into a relative clause is used instead of a participle in this construction:

> Die Zunge ist **ein** für die Sprache so **wichtiges** Organ, daß viele Völker das Wort „Zunge" benutzen, um die ganze Sprache zu bezeichnen.
> *The tongue is such an important organ of speech that many peoples use the word " tongue " to designate the whole language.*

lit.:   *The tongue is an organ (which is) so important for speech that many peoples use the word " tongue " to designate the whole language.*

(*b*) To master this construction (*i.e.*, recognize it in reading and get the meaning without loss of time), the student must, first of all, have a keen sense for adjective endings. If an adjective does not immediately follow the article (*cf.* ¶ **A** above), he should not pause, but read right ahead until the necessary participial adjective and noun appear. If an adjective does immediately follow the article, but the noun is some distance ahead (*cf.* ¶ **B** above), he should likewise continue reading until participle and noun appear to complete the thought unit. The **ending** of an adjective immediately following the article often indicates the gender of the noun to follow. While reading the complete subject (ein . . . Gebäude) **as a unit,** the student should **sense**—even before reaching the end—that **some** neuter noun will complete the thought. Similarly in ¶ **C** above, des . . . Hauses should be felt as a **genitive unit** modifying the subject.

(3) A simple variation of this use of the participle is to be found at the end of letters, where the possessive replaces the article:

> Dein Dich liebender Vater, *your loving father*
> Deine Dich liebende Mutter, *your loving mother*

50. PERSONAL PRONOUNS FOLLOWED BY A RELATIVE

Read the following sentences very carefully:

A. Ich, der ich selber krank war, konnte nicht mitgehen.
     *I, **who** was ill myself, could not go along.*

Wir, die wir selber krank waren, konnten nicht mitgehen.
We, who were ill ourselves, could not go along.

Similarly:

Du, der du selber krank warst, konntest nicht mitgehen.
You (fam. sing.), *who were ill yourself, could not go along.*

Ihr, die ihr selber krank wart, konntet nicht mitgehen.
You (fam. pl.), *who were ill yourselves, could not go along.*

B.   Ich, der schon so viel gelitten hat, verlor noch mein Vermögen.
I, who have suffered so much already, lost my fortune besides (or *in addition to that*).

Summary: The above sentences indicate that the relative **der**—not **welcher**—follows a personal pronoun.

Note:

(1) If the antecedent is a personal pronoun of the first or second person, it is usually repeated after the relative (*cf.* ¶ **A** above).

(2) If the pronoun is not repeated, the verb is in the third person (*cf.* ¶ **B** above).

51.   CONCESSIVE CLAUSES WITH WER AUCH, WAS AUCH, WO AUCH, **ETC.**

A.   Wer auch (*whoever*):

Wer er **auch** sein mag, ich werde ihm helfen.
Whoever he may be, I will help him.

B.   Was auch (*whatever*):

Was sie **auch** tun mag, er wird sie lieben.
Whatever she may do, he will love her.

C.   Wo auch (*wherever*):

Wo er **auch** sein mag, man wird ihn finden.
Wherever he may be, he will be found.

Summary: The above sentences indicate that the normal word order is used in a clause following one of concessive force introduced by **wer**

auch (*whoever*), **was auch** (*whatever*), **wo auch** (*wherever*), *etc.* The combinations with **auch** are used if *nevertheless* may be supplied as introducing the second clause.

Note: Such sentences were originally independent, hence the normal word order where one would expect inversion. For example, ¶ **C** originally read: *It doesn't matter where he may be. They will find him.*

EXERCISE

A. Complete the following sentences:

1. Der alte Mann, —— er das Geld gab, war sehr arm.
2. Der Reiche, —— der Richter bestrafte, war unehrlich.
3. Der Stuhl, —— in der Ecke steht, gefällt mir.
4. Der Lehrer, —— Buch ich jetzt habe, ist heute zu Hause.
5. Die schöne Stadt, —— an der Isar liegt, heißt München.
6. Die Stadt, —— Dom weltbekannt ist, heißt Köln.
7. Die Frau, —— ich die Bücher gegeben habe, wohnt in der Stadt.
8. Die Feder, —— ich in der Hand habe, gehört meinem Freund.
9. Ein Löschblatt ist ein Blatt, —— man Tinte löscht.
10. Das Haus, —— wir gekauft haben, besteht aus zehn Zimmern.
11. Das Kind, —— Eltern arm sind, heißt Karl.
12. Der Bleistift, —— ich jetzt schreibe, ist gelb.
13. Die Bücher, —— er die Geschichten gelesen hat, sind interessant.
14. Die Freunde, —— wir besuchen wollten, waren nicht zu Hause.
15. Die Kinder, —— auf der Straße spielen, amüsieren sich.
16. Die Jungen, —— ich helfen wollte, arbeiten fleißig.
17. Die Schüler, —— Eltern reich sind, arbeiten nicht.
18. —— reich ist, (der) ist nicht immer glücklich.
19. —— sie verspricht, (das) vergißt sie immer.
20. —— blind ist, kann nicht sehen.
21. Sie sagte, es gehe ihr gut, —— mich sehr freute.
22. Das war etwas, —— ich noch nicht wußte.
23. Alles, —— ich hatte, ist jetzt verloren.
24. Ich gab ihm das Geld, —— ich bei mir hatte.

25. Nichts, —— sie sagt, ist wahr.
26. Zur Zeit, —— mein Urgroßvater lebte, waren Indianer noch im Lande.
27. Ist das der Ort, —— seine Wiege stand?
28. Die Herren, mit —— ich gesprochen habe, waren Ausländer.
29. Die Künstlerin, —— Werke ich bewundert habe, ist heute abgefahren.
30. Ein Raumfahrzeug ist ein Fahrzeug, —— man benutzt, wenn man durch den Weltraum fliegt.
31. Luftverkehrsgesetze sind Gesetze, —— den Luftverkehr regulieren sollen.

B.   Translate:

1. The people in whose house (bei) I lived have moved (umziehen).
2. The German books which I read last month were very interesting.
3. My old friends who live in the country will visit me next week.
4. The pupils whose sentences I have corrected worked very hard.
5. Those (Das) are the boys whom I helped.
6. The beautiful village which I visited last year is (situated) on the Rhine.
7. Germany is a land which has many beautiful rivers and castles.
8. The little girl to whom I shall give the books is at home today.
9. The child whose parents are poor has gone to the country.
10. That is the door at which he was knocking.
11. Where is the pen with which you wrote the long letter?
12. The letter which is (liegen) on the table consists of four pages.
13. The woman whose son was in my class is very rich.
14. I like the story which my little brother is reading.
15. The rich man, whose children are in school now, lives in a small village.
16. The gentleman whom I met (begegnen) yesterday is my best friend.
17. I don't like (gefallen) the chair I bought yesterday.
18. Whoever is deaf cannot hear.
19. He gave me everything he had.
20. At the time when I visited him he was ill.
21. That is something he will not understand.
22. I told him that I was very well—which made him very happy.

23. He gave his wife the money he had earned.
24. Whoever she may be, I will help her.
25. The old men, to whom he had given the money, thanked him.
26. My grandfather, whom I visited last summer, is eighty years old.
27. Nothing I have is safe.
28. Did you find the beautiful umbrella you lost yesterday?
29. The old village in which he is now living has many beautiful castle ruins.
30. That is the city I like best.
31. Whatever he says, I don't believe it.
32. Nothing he says is true.
33. The German poem that I learned by heart is very beautiful.
34. We, who are ill ourselves, cannot help the others.
35. The lady whose beautiful voice I admired left (abfahren) today.
36. A coffee cup is a cup from (*i.e.*, out of) which one drinks coffee.
37. Hamburg, Bremen, and Lübeck are German cities that were formerly Hanseatic states (Hansestaaten).
38. Heidelberg is a German city which is famous for its university.
39. That is the most beautiful thing (*use neut. adj. as noun*) that I have ever (je) seen.
40. That is the best that we have.
41. Last month we met a scientist whose accomplishments are of great importance.
42. Much that we read in good magazines nowadays has scientific value.

CHAPTER 16

Possessives, Demonstratives, and Indefinite Pronouns and Adjectives

52. POSSESSIVE ADJECTIVES

Read the following sentences very carefully. Note the bold-faced forms:

A. (1) **Mein** lieber Bruder ist zu Hause.
My dear brother is at home.

(2) **Dein** alter Vater hat eine lange Reise gemacht.
Your old father took a long trip.

(3) **Sein** jüngster Sohn ist aufs Land gegangen.
His youngest son has gone to the country.

(4) **Ihr** reicher Onkel ist auf dem Lande.
Her rich uncle is in the country.

(5) **Unser** bester Freund hatte ihn gesehen.
Our best friend had seen him.

(6) Kinder, wo ist **euer** kleiner Hund?
*Children, where is **your** little dog?*

(7) Wo ist **ihr** lieber Vater?
*Where is **their** dear father?*

(8) Wo ist **Ihr** neues Buch?
*Where is **your** new book?*

B. (1) Ich habe **meinen** Bleistift verloren.
*I have lost **my** pencil.*

(2) Du hast **deinen** Bleistift verloren.
*You have lost **your** pencil.*

(3) Er hat **seinen** Bleistift verloren.
*He has lost **his** pencil.*

(4) Sie hat **ihren** Bleistift verloren.
*She has lost **her** pencil.*

(5) Es (*e.g.*, das Kind) hat **seinen** Bleistift verloren.
*It has lost **its** pencil.*

(6) Wir haben **unsere** Freunde besucht.
*We have visited **our** friends.*

(7) Ihr habt **eure** Freunde besucht.
*You have visited **your** friends.*

(8) Sie haben **ihre** Freunde besucht.
*They have visited **their** friends.*

(9) Sie haben **Ihre** Freunde besucht.
*You have visited **your** friends.*

Summary:

(1) The sentences under ¶ **A** above indicate that the possessive adjectives are: **mein, dein, sein, ihr, unser, euer,** and **Ihr.**[1]

(2) The sentences under ¶ **B** above indicate that the personal pronouns with their corresponding possessive adjectives are:

PERSONAL PRONOUN	POSSESSIVE ADJECTIVE	PERSONAL PRONOUN	POSSESSIVE ADJECTIVE
ich	mein (*my*)	wir	unser (*our*)
du	dein (*your*)	ihr	euer (*your*)
er	sein (*his*)		
sie	ihr (*her*)	sie	ihr [*their* (all genders)]
es	sein (*its*)		
		Sie	Ihr (*your*)

Note:

(1) **Ihr** (not capitalized unless it heads a sentence) may mean either *her* (*cf.* ¶ **A** (4) and ¶ **B** (4) above) or *their* (*cf.* ¶ **A** (7) and ¶ **B** (8) above).

---

[1] For the declension of possessives, *cf.* § 96 of the Appendix.

When it refers to an inanimate object or to an abstract noun which is feminine in German, it must be translated by *its*:

> **Die Sache** hat **ihre** gute Seite.
> *The affair has its good* (or *bright*) *side.*

(2) **Sein** may mean either *his* (*cf.* ¶ **A** (3) above) or *its* (*cf.* ¶ **B** (5) above), depending upon whether it refers to a masculine or to a neuter noun. In a few instances it must be translated by *her*, if the noun is feminine in English:

> **Das Mädchen** hat **sein** Buch.
> *The girl has her book.*

(3) The German equivalent of *its* (as parts (1) and (2) of this **Note** indicate) may be either **sein** (if the reference is to a masculine or neuter noun) or **ihr** (if the reference is to a feminine noun):

> **Jeder Staat** hat **seine** Vorzüge.
> *Each state has its advantages.*

> **Die Stadt** ist durch **ihre** Museen berühmt.
> *The city is famous for its museums.*

> **Das Kind** liebt **seinen** Vater.
> *The child loves its father.*

(4) English *your* becomes **dein** when addressing one person with the familiar pronoun (*cf.* ¶ **A** (2) and ¶ **B** (2) above); **euer,** when addressing two or more persons with the familiar pronoun (*cf.* ¶ **A** (6) and ¶ **B** (7) above); and **Ihr** (always capitalized), when addressing one or any number of persons with the pronoun of formal address (*cf.* ¶ **A** (8) and ¶ **B** (9) above).

(5) For the use of **der** as possessive adjective, *cf.* § 34 **E**.

EXERCISE

A.   Review § 10 (**ein**-words) and substitute nouns of different gender for those in the sentences of this section: (pp. 160 — 161).

B.   Change the sentences to the plural or vice versa: Meine liebe Schwester ist zu Hause.   Meine lieben Schwestern sind zu Hause.

53. AGREEMENT OF THE POSSESSIVE ADJECTIVE

Read the following sentences very carefully:

A. **Ihr** kleiner Bruder liest das Buch.
Her little brother is reading the book.

B. **Seine** kleine Schwester lernt Deutsch.
His little sister is studying German.

C. Er hat **seine** Bücher.
He has his books.

Note:

(1) The gender of a possessive is determined by that of the noun it modifies and **not** by that of the possessor. In ¶ **A** above, **ihr** (*her*) is masculine to agree with *brother;* in ¶ **B, seine** (*his*) is feminine to agree with *sister.*

(2) The case and number of a possessive adjective is the same as that of the noun it modifies (*cf.* ¶ **C** above).

54. POSSESSIVE PRONOUNS

Read the following sentences very carefully:

A. Mein Buch ist auf dem Tisch.   Wo ist **Ihres?**
My book is on the table.   Where is yours?

B. Mein Vater ist in der Stadt.   **Seiner** ist in Deutschland.
My father is in the city.   His is in Germany.

Summary: The above sentences indicate that a possessive not followed by a noun becomes a pronoun and takes the endings of **dieser:** the nominative singular masculine takes the ending **–er** (*cf.* ¶ **B** above); the nominative and accusative singular neuter, the ending **–es** (*cf.* ¶ **A** above)[1].

Note:

(1) The gender of a possessive pronoun—like that of a possessive adjective (*cf.* § 53)—is determined by the gender of the noun **to which it refers.**

---

[1] Possessive **adjectives,** being **ein**-words, have no endings in these three places.

(2) If the subject of a sentence is a **noun,** the possessive pronoun does not take an ending in the predicate:

Das Buch ist mein.   Der Bleistift ist dein.
The book is mine.   *The pencil is yours.*

Caution: The forms **ihr** (*her* or *their*) and **Ihr** (*your*), however, require an ending in the predicate:

Das Buch ist ihr**es.**   Der Bleistift ist Ihr**er.**
The book is hers (or *theirs*).   *The pencil is yours.*

(3) If the subject of a sentence is indefinite **es** or **das,** the possessive pronoun requires the proper ending:

„Wessen Bleistift ist das?"   „Es ist mein**er.**"
" *Whose pencil is that?* "   " *It is mine.*"

„Wessen Buch ist das?"   „Es ist mein**es.**"
" *Whose book is that?* "   " *It is mine.*"

(4) **Gehören** without **zu** is commonly used instead of the verb *to be* followed by a possessive (*cf.* **Note** under ¶ A (12) of § 34):

Das Buch gehört mir.
The book is mine (lit. *belongs to me*).

55. POSSESSIVES WITH VARIOUS FORMS OF THE IMPERATIVE

Read the following sentences very carefully:

Karl, lies **deine** Aufgabe!   **Kinder,** lest **eure** Aufgabe!
Carl, read your lesson.   *Children, read your lesson.*

Bitte, **lesen Sie Ihre** Aufgabe!
Please read your lesson.

Summary: The above sentences indicate that **dein** is used with the singular familiar imperative; **euer,** with the plural familiar; and **Ihr,** with the formal imperative.[1] Observe that the plural familiar imperative has the same form as the second person plural of the present indicative (but without the personal pronoun).

Note: The pronouns **du** and **ihr** are omitted in the imperative.

---

[1] This is merely an application of **Note** (4), § 52.

56. OTHER FORMS OF THE POSSESSIVE PRONOUN

Other forms of the possessive pronoun are:

	MASCULINE	FEMININE	NEUTER
NOM.	der meine	die meine	das meine
GEN.	des meinen, *etc.*	der meinen, *etc.*	des meinen, *etc.*
or			
NOM.	der meinige	die meinige	das meinige
GEN.	des meinigen, *etc.*	der meinigen, *etc.*	des meinigen, *etc.*

Note: These long forms are met with chiefly in books and are to be avoided in conversation and composition. They cannot be used with nouns. The following, therefore, are the three possible translations of the question: *Where is mine* (referring to some masculine noun such as der Bleistift)?

Wo ist **meiner**?
Wo ist **der meine**?
Wo ist **der meinige**?

EXERCISE

A. Complete the following sentences with the correct possessive form:

1. Die Mutter liebt ——— (*her*) Kind. Das Kind liebt ——— (*its*) Mutter.
2. Ist das Kind ——— (*hers*)?
3. Der Vater suchte ——— (*his*) Sohn.
4. Mein Sohn ist in der Schule. Wo ist ——— (*his*)?
5. Geben Sie mir ——— (*my*) Buch!
6. Mein Buch ist auf dem Tisch. Wo ist ——— (*yours*)?

(Rewrite sentences 1–6 in the plural.)

7. Er hat ——— (*his*) Freunden viel Geld gegeben.
8. Sie hat ——— (*her*) Bruder das Bild gezeigt.
9. Er wird ——— (*his*) Schwester die Geschichte erzählen.
10. Karl, wo ist ——— (*your*) Mutter?
11. Kinder, was tut ——— (*your*) Vater?
12. Bitte, zeigen Sie mir ——— (*your*) Buch!
13. Wir sollten ——— (*our*) Feinde lieben.
14. Die Schüler hatten ——— (*their*) Bücher vergessen.

15. Das Mädchen hatte —— (*her*) Buch verloren.
16. Die Stadt ist durch —— (*its*) Dom berühmt.
17. Heidelberg[1] ist durch —— (*its*) Universität berühmt.
18. Ich sehne mich nach —— (*my*) Vater, —— (*my*) Mutter und —— (*my*) alt— Freunden.
19. Dieser Stuhl ist —— (*mine*). Wo ist —— (*his*)?
20. Das Buch ist —— (*his*). Wo ist —— (*yours*)?
21. —— (*Her*) Bruder ist Physiker.
22. —— (*His*) Schwester heiratete einen Chemiker. Sie interessiert sich auch für die Chemie.

B. Complete the following sentences with the proper imperative and possessive forms (*cf.* § 55).

1. Karl, —— (*eat*) —— (*your*) Suppe!
   Kinder, —— (*eat*) —— (*your*) Suppe!
   Bitte, —— (*eat*) —— (*your*) Suppe!
2. Karl, —— (*read*) —— (*your*) Aufsatz!
   Kinder, —— (*read*) —— (*your*) Aufsatz!
   Bitte, —— (*read*) —— (*your*) Aufsatz!
3. Fritz, —— (*break*) —— (*your*) Stock nicht!
   Meine lieben Kinder, —— (*break*) —— (*your*) Stöcke nicht!
   Herr Schmidt, bitte, —— (*break*) —— (*your*) Stock nicht!
4. Marie, —— (*give*) mir —— (*your*) Buch!
   Marie und Luise, —— (*give*) mir —— (*your*) Bücher!
   Herr Werner, bitte, —— (*give*) mir —— (*your*) Buch!
5. Johann, —— (*help*) —— (*your*) Freund!
   Johann und Wilhelm, —— (*help*) —— (*your*) Freund!
   Bitte, —— (*help*) —— (*your*) Freund!
6. Karl, —— (*take*) —— (*your*) Feder in die Hand!
   Kinder, —— (*take*) —— (*your*) Feder in die Hand!
   Frau Weiß, bitte, —— (*take*) —— (*your*) Feder in die Hand!
7. Friedrich, —— (*forget*) —— (*your*) Aufgabe nicht!
   Kinder, —— (*forget*) —— (*your*) Aufgabe nicht!
   Bitte, —— (*forget*) —— (*your*) Aufgabe nicht!
8. Karl, —— (*strike*) —— (*your*) Hund nicht!
   Kinder, —— (*strike*) —— (*your*) Hund nicht!
   Bitte, —— (*strike*) —— (*your*) Hund nicht!

---

[1] **Note: Names** of cities are neuter:
das schöne Berlin, *beautiful Berlin.*

9. Herr Krause, Sie fahren zu schnell. —— (*Look at*) —— (*your*) Geschwindigkeitsmesser (masc.)! Er zeigt eine Geschwindigkeit von 100 Meilen die Stunde.

C. Supply a suitable adjective for each of the direct objects in the above sentences.

D. Translate:

1. That is my old coat. Where is yours?
2. He has lost his new hat. Where is mine?
3. That German book is mine. Where is hers?
4. Have you seen my black fountain pen? Where is his?
5. I have not yet found my good pencil.
6. That is mine, his, hers, yours, theirs, ours. (*Assume that these forms all refer to a masculine singular noun such as* Bleistift.)
7. Carl, do not strike the little dog. (*Rewrite with* children *and* Mr. Schmidt *instead of* Carl.)
8. John, read your new story. Children, read your new story. Please read your new story.
9. The father is praising his youngest daughter.
10. The mother was calling her eldest son.
11. Her younger son is not in school today.
12. Tomorrow he will give me his German book.
13. She had put (legen) her books on the little round table.
14. For two months we have been looking for our old friend.
15. Cologne is famous for its beautiful cathedral.
16. We shall show them our new radio.
17. They sold theirs, because they had no money. Have you one (*i.e.,* radio)?
18. They were preparing (themselves) for [sich vorbereiten auf (*w. acc.*)] their examination.
19. His house is larger than mine but not as large as yours.
20. " Whose book is that? Yours? " " No, not mine."

57. THE DEMONSTRATIVES DIESER, JENER, DERSELBE, AND DERJENIGE

A demonstrative is a word that points out, *e.g., this* or *that.* A demonstrative may be an adjective: ***This** man is my friend;* or it may be a pronoun: ***This** is mine.*

Read the following sentences very carefully and note the bold-faced words:

A. Dieser (*this*):

(1) **Dieser** Junge ist mein Bruder, **jener** (*or* der andere da) ist mein Vetter.
  *This boy is my brother, **that one** is my cousin.*

(2) **Dieses** Buch gefällt mir.   **Diese** Bücher gefallen mir.
  *I like **this** book.*   *I like **these** books.*

B. Jener (*that*):

(1) **Jener** Berg (*or* der Berg da) ist der Brocken.
  ***That** mountain is the Brocken.*

(2) **Jene** Häuser (*or* die Häuser da) wurden im Mittelalter gebaut.
  ***Those** houses were built in the Middle Ages.*

C. Derselbe (*the same*):

(1) Er ist **derselbe** Mann, den ich gestern gesehen habe.
  *He is **the same** man whom I saw yesterday.*

(2) Die beiden Schwestern sind an **demselben** Tag geboren.
  *The two (or Both) sisters were born on **the same** day.*

(3) Ich hatte **denselben** Lehrer, wie mein Bruder.
  *I had the **same** teacher as my brother.*

D. Derjenige (*that, the one*):

(1) Das ist nicht mein Buch, sondern **dasjenige** meiner Schwester.
  *That is not my book but **my sister's**.*
  lit.: *That is not my book but **that** of my sister.*

(2) **Dasjenige** im roten Einband habe ich schon gelesen.
  *I have already read **the one** with a red cover.*

(3) **Diejenigen,** die das nicht verstehen, sollen Fragen stellen.
  ***Those** who do not understand that are to ask questions.*

Summary:

(1) The sentences under ¶¶ **A** and **B** above indicate that **jener** is declined like **dieser** (*cf.* Appendix, § 94 for declension).   **Jener** is frequently replaced by the definite article with **da** or **dort** following the noun. In modern German **jener** is generally restricted in use to a specific con-

trast with **dieser.** It may also be noted that **dieser** is often translated by *the latter* and **jener** by *the former.*

(2) The sentences under ¶¶ **C** and **D** above indicate that **derselbe** and **derjenige** (*cf.* Appendix, § 97 for complete declension) are each written as one word, but that the second component of each is declined like a weak adjective:

NOM.	Sing.:	**der**selbe	**der**jenige
GEN.	Sing.:	**des**selben, *etc.*	**des**jenigen, *etc.*
NOM.	Pl.:	**die**selben, *etc.*	**die**jenigen, *etc.*

Note:

(1) (*a*) The determinative **derjenige** is followed either by a genitive (*cf.* ¶ **D** (1) above), a prepositional phrase (*cf.* ¶ **D** (2) above), or a relative clause (*cf.* ¶ **D** (3) above).

(*b*) **Derjenige** is frequently used instead of **der** to avoid a repetition of **der**-words:

> **Derjenige,** der das gesagt hat, ist nicht mein Freund.
> *The one who said that is not my friend.*

Here the construction der, der ... *etc.* has been avoided, as similarly that of die, die ... *etc.* was in ¶ **D** (3) above.

(*c*) The German equivalent of *my brother's, my sister's, etc.* (the noun being understood) is *that* (or *the one*) *of my brother, that* (or *the one*) *of my sister, etc.* (*cf.* ¶ **D** (1) above). In modern German the demonstrative **der** (*cf.* ¶ 58) usually replaces **derjenige** in this usage.

(2) **Derselbe** (weakly accented) is often used—particularly in the written language—instead of a personal pronoun:

> Er hat viele Schulden aber er will **dieselben** nicht bezahlen.
> *He has many debts but he does not want to pay **them**.*

Caution: In the above sentence **diesélben Schulden,** accented on the second syllable, would mean *the same debts.*

58. THE DEMONSTRATIVE DER

Read the following sentences very carefully. Note the bold-faced forms:

A. (1) **Der** (accented) Mann ist klug.
   That man is clever.

(2) **Der** (accented) ist immer auf dem Lande.
He is always in the country.

B. Tut Gutes **denen,** die euch hassen!
Do good to those who hate you.

C. (1) Nimm diese Äpfel, es gibt **deren** genug.
Take these apples; there are plenty of them.

(2) Das ist die Schuld **derer,** die nicht mitgeholfen haben.
That is the fault of those who did not help.

D. Es war einmal eine wunderschöne Prinzessin, **die** hatte jedermann lieb.

Once upon a time there was an exceedingly beautiful princess whom (lit. *that one*) *everybody loved.*

Summary: The sentences under ¶ **A** indicate that demonstrative **der** may be used either as adjective (1) or as pronoun (2).

Note:

(1) As adjective, **der** is declined like the definite article.

(2) As demonstrative pronoun, **der** is declined like the relative pronoun (*cf.* Appendix, § 101 **D**).   In addition to **deren,** however, the genitive plural has also the form **derer.**   If used for persons, the latter immediately precedes a relative clause (*cf.* ¶ **C** (2) above).   **Deren** is the usual form when the pronoun precedes the word on which it depends (*cf.* ¶ **C** (1) above).

(3) Demonstrative **der** is accented and, when printed, is sometimes letterspaced (*i.e.,* **d e r**) to indicate the stress (*cf.* ¶ **A** (1) and (2) above).   If **der** in ¶ **A** (1) above were not accented, it would mean: *The man is clever.*

(4) Demonstrative **der** is much more common in conversation than **jener.**

(5) Demonstrative **der** is used in fairy tales where we should expect the relative.   The word order shows the form to be demonstrative (*cf.* ¶ **D** above).

(6) Demonstrative **der** cannot be used in such a sentence as:

I was thinking of that.
Ich dachte **daran.**[1]

---

[1] For the use of **daran, darüber,** *etc. cf.* § 30, **B.**

(7) Note the following combinations with the genitive of the demonstrative:

> **infolgedessen,** *in consequence of that, consequently*
> **währenddessen** (= inzwischen), *in the meantime*
> **dessenungeachtet** (= trotzdem), *in spite of that*

59. THE USE OF SOLCHER

Read the following sentences very carefully:

A.   **Solch schönes** Wetter haben wir nicht im Winter.
or: **Solches schöne** Wetter haben wir nicht im Winter.
We do not have such beautiful weather in winter.

B.   Er ist **kein solcher** Narr.
*He is **no such** fool.*

Summary:

(1) The first sentence under ¶ **A** above indicates that if **solch** is uninflected, the following adjective takes strong endings; the second, that if **solch** takes strong endings, the following adjective is weak.

(2) The sentence under ¶ **B** above indicates that *no such* is **kein solch–**.

Note: For a detailed explanation of the various ways of translating *such a, cf.* § 6, **Note** (14) (*c*).

EXERCISE

A.   Complete the following sentences:

1. Diese kurze Geschichte gefällt mir. —— (*That one*) gefällt mir nicht.
2. Dieser reiche Mann ist mein Vetter. —— (*That one*) ist mein Onkel.
3. Dieses neue Haus ist viel schöner als —— (*that one*).
4. —— (*This*) Gebäude ist nicht so hoch wie —— (*that one*).
5. —— (*This*) Hund ist viel älter als —— (*that one*).
6. —— (*This*) Insel ist ebenso groß wie —— (*that one*).
7. Das ist —— (*the same*) Junge, den ich gestern gesehen habe.
8. Es ist —— (*the same*) Krawatte, die ich immer getragen habe.

9. Das ist —— (*the same*) Kleid, das sie gestern getragen hat.
10. Ich habe —— (*the same*) Mann oft geholfen.
11. —— (*The same one*) hat mich heute besucht.
12. Er hatte —— (*the same*) Kindern viele schöne Geschenke gegeben.
13. Im Herbst —— (*of the same*) Jahres sind die beiden Brüder nach Amerika gekommen.
14. —— (*Those*), die den Satz nicht verstehen, sollen Fragen stellen.
15. Das sind die Namen —— [*of those* (dem.)], die mitgeholfen haben.
16. Treue Freunde halte fest! Es gibt —— [*of them* (dem.)] nicht viele.
17. Groß war die Freude, denn —— (*the one*), der dem Vater am liebsten war, hatte den ersten Preis gewonnen.
18. —— (*That*) Junge ist klug.
19. —— [*He* (emphatic dem.)] arbeitet immer fleißig.
20. Hilf —— (*those*), die dir geholfen haben!
21. Das ist der Erfolg —— [*of those* (dem.)], die tüchtig arbeiten.
22. Karl hatte —— (*no such*) Erfolg.
23. Ich denke —— (*of that*).
24. Er wird —— (*for that*) warten.
25. Er hatte —— (*about that*) gesprochen.
26. —— (*Such a*) Hitze haben wir nie in dieser Stadt erlebt.
27. —— (*Such*) Fragen wie —— (*these*) hat er nie beantwortet.
28. Sie sprachen von —— (*this*) Jungen und von —— (*that*) Mädchen.
29. —— (*Those*) sind unsere Bücher. Fritz hat —— (*no such*) Buch.
30. —— (*Those*) sind die Männer, denen ich die Bücher gegeben habe.
31. Vorige Nacht hat es stark geregnet. —— (*Consequently*) sind die Straßen jetzt sehr naß.
32. —— (*In the meantime*) müssen wir zu Hause bleiben.
33. —— (*In spite of that*) werden wir später einen kurzen Spaziergang machen.
34. Die Astronauten sprachen über —— (*this*) und —— (*that*).
35. Ich begegnete Herrn Braun und Herrn Fischer auf der Straße.
    —— (*The former*) ist Mathematiker; —— (*the latter*) ist Arzt.

36. Die ersten Raumflugexperimente mit Mäusen, Ratten, Hunden und Schimpansen waren zufriedenstellend. —— (*Consequently*, or *in consequence of that*) waren viele der darauffolgenden Weltraumflüge bemannt.

B. Translate:

1. This large trunk is heavier than that one.
2. This beautiful country is warmer than that one.
3. This narrow street is longer than that one.
4. That German book belongs to my sister. This one belongs to my brother.
5. She sang that beautiful song twice. Why did she not sing this one?
6. I met the same men last summer in the country.
7. He always tells the same stories.
8. That little boy was helping his brother. This one was playing ball.
9. The two (Die beiden) sisters had gone to America in the spring of the same year.
10. The two men have moved (ziehen) into the same house.
11. Last winter they were in the same German village.
12. Those who have made mistakes must correct them.
13. That man is my best friend. (*Translate in two ways.*)
14. That woman is never at home. (*Translate in two ways.*)
15. Take these interesting German books. There are (es gibt) few of them (*dem.*).
16. That is the fault of those who have not paid attention.
17. The clever pupils will think of that.
18. My dear friend had waited for that.
19. He always speaks of that.
20. I have never read such a book.
21. Have you ever read such books?
22. He never writes with such a pen.
23. Did you ever see such a crowd?
24. Give me another knife. This one does not cut well.
25. Bring me another (*i.e.*, an additional) pencil. I like this one.
26. The two brothers went to the same school.
27. One day we took a long walk. As a result of that (*i.e.*, consequently) we both became very tired.

28. My father has gone to Germany.   In the meantime I must stay
    at home.
29. Nevertheless (*i.e.*, in spite of that), I shall have a good time.
30. A friend of mine (von mir) visited me last month.
31. The average speed of these cars (autos) is fifty miles an hour.
32. Two members of our club are Mr. Trautmann and Mr.
    Schneider.   The former is a physicist; the latter is a technician.
33. The same men who made a space flight last month would now
    like to fly to the moon.

60.   INDEFINITE PRONOUNS AND ADJECTIVES

Read the following sentences very carefully:

A.   Man tut das nicht.
     That is not done.
lit.: *One does not do that.*

B.   (1) Jemand hat das gesagt.
         Somebody (or *someone*) *said that.*

   (2) Hat **irgend jemand** das Buch gefunden?
       Did anyone find the book?

   (3) Haben Sie **jemand anders** besucht?
       Did you visit someone else?

C.   (1) Jedermann (or **jeder**) weiß das.
         Everybody knows that.

   (2) **Alle** geben es zu.
       All admit it.

D.   (1) Niemand (or **keiner**) war zu Hause.
         Nobody (or *no one*) *was at home.*

   (2) **Niemand anders** glaubt ihm.
       No one else believes him.

E.   (1) Hat er **etwas** gesagt?
       Did he say something?

   (2) Haben Sie **etwas** Interessant**es** gefunden?
       Did you find something interesting?

(3) Sie hat **etwas** Brot gekauft.
*She bought **some** bread.*

(4) Ich vermisse **irgend etwas.**
*I miss **something** (**or other**).*

(5) Er hat **einige** Bücher mitgebracht.
*He brought **some** books along.*

F. (1) Vor **ein paar** Tagen war er bei mir.
*A **few** (or **several**) days ago he was at my house.*

(2) **Mehrere** Studenten fehlen heute.
***Several** students are absent today.*

G. (1) Er hat **nichts** gegessen.
*He ate (or has eaten) **nothing.***

(2) Es gibt **nichts N**eues.
There is no news.

lit.:   *There is **nothing** new.*

H. (1) Er hat **wenig** Geld bei sich.
He hasn't much money with him.

lit.:   *He has **little** money with him.*

(2) Er hat **wenige** Freunde.
*He has **few** friends.*

(3) Ich weiß **wenig G**utes über ihn zu erzählen.
*I know **little** good to relate about him.*

I. (1) Haben Sie **viel** Geld verloren?
*Did you lose **much** money?*

(2) Sie hat **viel G**utes getan.
*She has done **much** good.*

(3) Ich habe **viele** Schulden.
*I have **many** debts.*

(4) Man kann **vieles** lernen und doch nicht viel wissen.
*One can learn **many things** and still not know much.*

J. Er hat **allerlei D**ummes gesagt.
*He said **all sorts of** stupid things.*

Note:

(1) The indefinite pronouns **man** (*one, they, people, you*), **jemand** (*somebody, someone*), **jedermann** (*everybody*), **niemand** (*nobody, no one*), **etwas** (*something, some*), and **nichts** (*nothing*) occur only in the singular.

(2) (*a*) **Man**[1] is used only in the nominative. The other cases are supplied by the forms **eines, einem,** and **einen:**

> Es tut **einem** weh.
> *It hurts one.*

(*b*) **Man** always governs a singular verb in the third person. Therefore, when used with reflexive verbs (*cf.* § 61), **sich** serves both as dative and accusative reflexive pronoun:

> Damals konnte **man sich** (dat.) so etwas nicht leisten.
> *At that time one couldn't afford such a thing.*

> **Man** gewöhnt **sich** (acc.) endlich an alles.
> *One finally gets used to everything.*

(*c*) The nominative **einer** is sometimes used instead of **man.**

(*d*) **Man** and **er** cannot be used interchangeably; if **man** is used, it must be retained throughout the sentence:

> Wenn **man** etwas nicht weiß, soll **man** (not **er**) nichts sagen.

(3) (*a*) **Jemand** and **niemand** have a genitive in –(e)s. In modern German the dative and accusative of these pronouns usually occur without endings:

> Er hat **niemand** gesehen.
> *He saw **no one**.*

Datives in –**em** and accusatives in –**en,** however, are also found.

(*b*) **Sonst jemand** may be used for **jemand anders,** and **sonst niemand** for **niemand anders** (*cf.* ¶¶ **B** (3) and **D** (2) above).

(4) (*a*) **Jedermann** has a genitive ending in –**s** but its dative and accusative are like the nominative.

(*b*) **Alle** is used as the plural of **jedermann** (*cf.* ¶ **C** (2) above).

(5) **Jeder** is often used for **jedermann** (*cf.* ¶ **C** (1) above), and **keiner** for **niemand** (*cf.* ¶ **D** (1) above).

---

[1] *Cf.* § 75 **A,** and ¶ **D** and **Note** (1) of § 62 for constructions involving **man.**

(6) **Nichts, etwas, allerlei,** and **ein paar** are indeclinable.

(7) (*a*) Neuter adjectives are capitalized when used as nouns following **etwas, nichts, viel, wenig,** and **allerlei** (*cf.* ¶¶ **E** (2), **G** (2), **H** (3), **I** (2), **J** above). The adjective has the strong ending **–es.**

Caution: The word **anderes,** however, is not capitalized:
> **etwas anderes,** *something else*
> **nichts anderes,** *nothing else*

(*b*) **Alles** usually requires the following adjective to be capitalized. The adjective has the weak ending **–e.**
> **alles Gute,** *everything good, all good things*
> but: **alles mögliche,** *everything possible*
> **alles übrige,** *all the rest*
> **alles andere,** *all else*

(8) *Some* is ordinarily rendered by **etwas** when followed by a singular noun (*cf.* ¶ **E** (3) above); by **einige,** when followed by a plural noun (*cf.* ¶ **E** (5) above).

(9) (*a*) **Irgend** [*any, some* (*or other*)] is rarely used alone, but appears in various combinations:
> **irgend jemand,** *anyone* [emphatic (*cf.* ¶ **B** (2) above)]
> **irgend etwas,** *something or other* (*cf.* ¶ **E** (4) above)
> **irgendein** (adj.), *some* (*or other*)
> **irgendeiner,** *someone* (emphatic)
> **irgendwie,** *somehow, anyhow*
> **irgendwo,** *somewhere, anywhere*

(*b*) **Nirgend(s)** is the negative of **irgend:**
> **nirgendwo,** *nowhere, not anywhere*

(10) (*a*) **Viel(e)**[1] and **wenig(e)** have both singular and plural forms (*cf.* ¶¶ **H** (1)–(3) and **I** (1)–(4) above).

(*b*) The form **vieles** is very often equivalent to the English *many things* (*cf.* ¶ **I** (4) above).

(11) Strong adjective endings are used in the nominative and accusative after **manche, viele, einige, etliche, wenige, andere, mehrere,** and **verschiedene** (*cf.* § 12 **B**).

---

[1] For additional notes on **viel** and **viele,** *cf.* §§ 12 **B** and 22 **C.**

(12) Distinguish between **klein,** *little* (in size), and **wenig,** *little* (in quantity):

       ein **kleines** Geldstück, *a small coin*

but: **wenig** Geld, *little (i.e., not much) money*

(13) For the use of **mancher,** *cf.* Note of § 12 **B.**

EXERCISE

A. Complete the following sentences:

1. —— (*Everybody*) sagt es.
2. —— (*No one*) ist im Zimmer.
3. Ich höre —— (*someone*) kommen.
4. —— [People (indef.)] glaubt ihm.
5. Sie hat —— (*some*) Butter gekauft.
6. —— (*Some*) Häuser in dieser Stadt sind sehr hoch.
7. Haben Sie etwas —— (*new*) gehört?
8. Ich habe nichts —— (*interesting*) gelesen.
9. Er hat wenig —— (*good*) getan.
10. Sie hat viel —— (*beautiful*) geschrieben.
11. —— (*Something*) gefällt ihm nicht.
12. Außer seiner Schwester war —— (*no one else*) da.
13. Hat —— (*anybody*) Karl gesehen?
14. Fehlt —— (*any one else*) heute?
15. Haben Sie —— (*nothing*) getan?
16. Er hat —— (*little*) Geduld.
17. Mit —— (*few*) Worten hat er alles erklärt.
18. Haben Sie —— (*many*) Freunde?
19. Er wird —— (*much*) Geld verdienen.
20. Er hat —— (*no one*) geholfen.
21. Haben Sie —— (*everything possible*) getan?
22. Er hatte —— (*everything else*) vergessen.
23. Mein alter Freund wohnt —— (*somewhere*) in dieser Stadt.
24. Ich konnte ihn —— (*nowhere*) finden.
25. Das macht —— (*one*) Freude.
26. Er hat —— (*many things*) vergessen.
27. —— (*Some*) bekannt— Wissenschaftler meinen, daß die „Kanäle" auf dem Planeten Mars Spalten in großen Eis-Ozeanen sind.

28. —— (*Others*) sind der Meinung, daß das erste Reiseziel im Weltraum nach dem Mond nicht Mars, sondern der geheimnisvolle Planet Venus sein wird.

B. Translate:

1. Please give me some money.
2. Have you some German books?
3. Tell me something interesting.
4. No one believes that.
5. People (*indef.*) had never believed him.
6. Someone will sing a German song.
7. She was reading something else.
8. Everybody knows that.
9. He will do much good.
10. There is something she does not like. (*Translate:* Something does not please her.)
11. Nobody was in that large room.
12. My dear friends had seen no one.
13. Did you visit anyone this summer?
14. No one else understood the first sentence.
15. My little brother has little patience.
16. That old man had many enemies.
17. Formerly he earned much money.
18. That gives one pleasure.
19. Here they (*indef.*) speak German.
20. My best friend lives somewhere in this old village.
21. That is something different.
22. Have you forgotten everything else?
23. I did everything possible.
24. Nowhere are there better streets than in this city.
25. He will help somebody.
26. When I was in Europe, I saw many things.
27. He read the story in some book or other.
28. Some scientists believe that the planet Mars is covered with ice.
29. Others are of the opinion that within the next two hundred years one will travel from the earth to the planet Venus.

61. REFLEXIVE VERBS

Read the following sentences very carefully.   Compare the sentences that are opposite each other:

A. (1) Ich wasche das Kind.	**B.** (1) Ich wasche **mich.**
I wash the child.	*I wash myself.*
(2) Du wäsch(e)st das Kleid.	(2) Du wäsch(e)st **dich.**
You wash the dress.	*You wash yourself.*
(3) Sie wäscht das Handtuch.	(3) Sie wäscht **sich.**
She washes the towel.	*She washes herself.*
(4) Wir waschen die Strümpfe.	(4) Wir waschen **uns.**
We wash the stockings.	*We wash ourselves.*
(5) Ihr wascht die Kleider.	(5) Ihr wascht **euch.**
You wash the clothes.	*You wash yourselves.*
(6) Sie waschen die Taschentücher.	(6) Sie waschen **sich.**
They wash the handkerchiefs.	*They wash themselves.*
(7) Haben Sie die Tischtücher gewaschen?	(7) Haben Sie **sich** gewaschen?
Did you wash the tablecloths?	*Did you wash yourself?*

Note:

(1) The direct objects of the verb in ¶ **A** above do **not** refer to the subject.

(2) The direct objects of the verb in ¶ **B** above are **pronouns referring to the subject.**   Such pronouns are known as **reflexive pronouns;** such verbs, as **reflexive verbs.**

(3) Reflexive pronouns, if used as direct objects (*cf.* ¶ **F** below for reflexives with dative objects), have the same form as the accusative of

personal pronouns, except that **sich replaces personal pronouns of the third person** (singular and plural). **Mich, dich, uns,** and **euch,** therefore, serve both as personal and reflexive pronouns (*cf.* ¶ **B** (1), (2), (4), and (5) above), but **ihn, sie** (*her*), **es, sie** (*them*), and **Sie** become **sich** (*cf.* ¶ **B** (3), (6), and (7) above).

(4) Reflexive verbs[1] are conjugated with the auxiliary **haben** (*cf.* ¶ **B** (7) above).

(5) (*a*) The same verb (*e.g.*, **waschen** above) may be reflexive (*cf.* ¶ **B** above) or nonreflexive (*cf.* ¶ **A** above), according to its use in a sentence:

Sie sieht sich (refl.) im Spiegel.   Sie sieht (nonrefl.) den Mann.
She sees herself in the mirror.   *She sees the man.*

Sie zieht sich (refl.) an.   Sie zieht (nonrefl.) das Kind an.
She dresses herself.   *She dresses the child.*

(*b*) In English the reflexive pronoun is frequently omitted if the meaning is clear without it: ***She dresses herself*** or simply ***she dresses.***

(6) For reflexive verbs governing the genitive, *cf.* § 33 **B** (2).

C. Idiomatic expressions with reflexive verbs. Certain verbs are reflexive in German but not in English. They must, therefore, be considered as idiomatic expressions and mastered thoroughly. Many reflexives require a special preposition which must also be noted carefully as part of the idiom:

Er interessiert sich **für** die Musik.
*He is interested **in** music.*

Sie fürchtet sich **vor** Mäusen.
*She is afraid **of** mice.*

Ich werde mich **um** die Stellung bewerben.
*I shall apply **for** the position.*

Wir freuten uns **auf** die Ferien.
*We were looking forward with pleasure **to** the vacation.*

Ich muß mich dar**an** gewöhnen.
*I must get used **to** it.*

Kümmern Sie sich nicht dar**um**!
*Don't bother **about** it.*

---

[1] For the complete conjugation of reflexive verbs, *cf.* § 107 of the Appendix.

D. Common reflexives.   Some of the more common reflexive verbs are:

sich **amüsieren,** to have a good time

sich **ánkleiden** (*or* **ánziehen**), to dress (oneself)

sich **ärgern über** (*w. acc.*), to be provoked (*or* vexed) at

sich **aúsruhen,** to rest

sich **aúsziehen,** to undress (oneself)

sich **bedanken bei** (einer Person) **für** (etwas), to thank (a person) for (something)

sich **beeilen,** to hurry

sich **befinden,** to be, feel

sich **benehmen** (*or* **betragen**), to behave (oneself)

sich **bewegen,** to move (oneself)

sich **bewerben um,** to apply for

sich **bücken,** to stoop

sich (*dat.*) **denken** (**eínbilden** *or* **vórstellen**), to imagine

sich **empfehlen,** to take (one's) leave

sich **entschließen,** to decide

sich **erbarmen** (*w. gen. or* **über** *and acc.*), to pity

sich **erholen von,** to recover (*or* recuperate) from

sich **erinnern** (*w.* **an** *and acc.*), to remember

sich **erkälten,** to catch cold

sich **erkundigen nach,** to make inquiries about

sich **freuen,** to be glad

sich **freuen auf** (*w. acc.*), to look forward with pleasure to

sich **freuen über** (*w. acc.*), to be happy about, rejoice at

sich **fürchten vor** (*w. dat.*), to be afraid of

sich **gewöhnen an** (*w. acc.*), to get used to

sich **grämen über** (*w. acc.*), to grieve over

sich **hüten vor** (*w. dat.*), to guard against

sich **interessieren für,** to be interested in

sich **irren,** to be mistaken

sich **kümmern um,** to trouble (*or* concern) oneself about, worry (*or* bother) about

sich **legen,** to lie down

sich (*dat.*) **leisten,** to afford

sich **nähern** (*w. dat.*), to approach

sich **rächen an** (*w. dat.*), to take revenge on

sich **rühren,** to stir, move; bestir oneself

sich **schämen** (*w. gen. or* **über** *and acc.*), to be ashamed of

sich (*dat.*) **schmeicheln,** to flatter oneself

sich **sehnen nach,** to long for

sich **setzen,** to sit down, seat oneself

sich (*dat.*) **Sorgen machen um,** to worry (*or* be anxious) about

sich **üben,** to practice

sich **verbeugen vor** (*w. dat.*), to bow to

sich **verirren,** to get lost

sich **verlassen auf** (*w. acc.*), to rely (*or* depend) on

sich **waschen,** to wash (oneself)

sich (*dat.*) **weh tun,** to hurt oneself

sich **wundern über** (*w. acc.*), to be surprised at

E.   Reflexives instead of the passive.   German frequently employs a reflexive verb instead of the passive voice:

Das macht sich leicht.	Das läßt sich nicht tun.
That is easily done.	*That can't be done.*
Es wird sich bald zeigen.	Alles hat sich aufgeklärt.
It will soon be seen.	*Everything has been cleared up.*
Es versteht sich.	So etwas lernt sich bald.
It is understood.	*Such things are soon learned.*

F. Dative reflexives. Certain reflexive verbs—*e.g.*, sich einbilden, sich vorstellen, sich denken, sich Sorgen machen um, sich leisten, sich schmeicheln, and sich weh tun (*cf.* ¶ **D** above)—take a dative instead of an accusative reflexive object:

So etwas hätte ich **mir** nie vorgestellt (*or* eingebildet).
I should never have imagined such a thing.

Ich mache **mir** Sorgen um meine Geschwister.
I am worrying about my brothers and sisters.

Kannst du **dir** das leisten?	Schmeich(e)le **dir** nicht!
Can you afford that?	*Don't flatter yourself.*

Ich habe **mir** weh getan.
I hurt myself.

Note: **Sich, uns,** and **euch** serve both as accusative and dative reflexive pronouns, but **mich** and **dich** become **mir** and **dir** with dative reflexive verbs.

G. The intensives selbst **and** selber. In translating *myself, himself, etc.*, one must distinguish carefully between reflexives and intensives. **Selbst** and **selber,** when used as intensives, follow (but not always immediately) the personal pronoun, reflexive pronoun, or noun which they emphasize:

(1)   Ich setzte **mich** (refl.).   Ich **selbst** (or **selber**) habe es gesehen.
       I sat down.   or: Ich habe es **selbst** (intens.) gesehen.
lit.:   *I seated **myself.***   *I saw it **myself.***

(2)   Sie lobt **sich selbst** (or **selber**).
      *She praises **herself.***

Here **selbst** strengthens the reflexive. The reflexive, however, cannot be omitted.

(3) Sie ist die Freundlichkeit **selbst.**
    She is friendliness personified.
lit.:   *She is friendliness **itself.***

Here **selbst** emphasizes the noun.

Note:

(1) **Selbst** and **selber** never change their forms.

(2) **Selbst** in the sense of *even* precedes a noun or pronoun:

    Selbst er hat das verstanden.
    ***Even** he understood that.*

(3) **Selbst** occurs in a number of compounds: selbstverständlich, *that is understood (as a matter of course);* selbstgebackenes Brot, *home-made bread;* das Selbstgespräch, *monologue, soliloquy;* die Selbststeuerung, *automatic control; etc.*

H. The reciprocal pronoun einander. The reciprocal pronoun **einander** is often used for the dative and accusative plural of the reflexive pronouns—*i.e.,* instead of **uns, euch,** and **sich.**

(1) Wir sehen **einander** (*or* uns) bald wieder.
    We shall soon see each other again.

(2) Sie loben **einander** (*or* sich).
    They praise each other.

Note:

(1) **Einander** never changes its form.

(2) (*a*) **Einander** occurs in combinations with prepositions: **an**einander, **auf**einander, **aus**einander, **bei**einander, **durch**einander, **mit**einander, **nach**einander, **neben**einander, **von**einander, and **zu**einander:

    Sie kümmern sich nicht **um**einander.
    They aren't concerned about each other.

(*b*) These forms, whose meaning varies with that of the preposition, are in turn combined with numerous verbs: aneinander**binden,** *to tie together* (lit. *to tie to each other);* aufeinander**folgen,** *to follow each other; etc.*

EXERCISE

A. Complete the following sentences:

1. Erkundigen Sie sich —— d— Herrn!
2. Freuen Sie sich —— (*look forward with pleasure to*) d— Reise?
3. Haben Sie sich —— d— Besuch Ihres Freundes gefreut (*be happy about*)?
4. Kann ich mich —— dies— Jungen (sing.) verlassen?
5. Er verbeugte sich —— d— König.
6. Er hat sich —— sein— Feind— (pl.) gerächt.
7. Hüten Sie sich —— jen— Mann!
8. Haben Sie sich —— all— (*everything*) gewöhnt?
9. Warum ärgern Sie sich —— dies— Frau?
10. Haben Sie sich —— —— (*him*) gewundert?
11. Kümmern Sie sich nicht —— mi—!
12. Er bewirbt sich —— d— Stellung.
13. Fürchten Sie sich —— d— Tier?
14. Erinnern Sie sich —— Ihr— Kindheit?
15. Schämen Sie sich —— Ihr— Armut (fem.)?
16. Grämt er sich —— d— verloren— Kind?
17. Ich sehne —— —— mein— Heimat.
18. Ich kümmere —— nicht —— —— (*him*).
19. Erinnerst du —— —— (*it*)?
20. Er verläßt sich —— —— (*her*).
21. Wir machen —— Sorgen —— —— (*him*).
22. Kinder, freut ihr ——, daß der Vater wieder zu Hause ist?
23. Er hat sich —— ein— schwer— Krankheit erholt.
24. (*a*) Ich habe —— entschlossen, eine lange Reise zu machen.
    (*b*) Ich habe —— zu einer langen Reise entschlossen.
25. Ich interessiere —— —— d— Chemie [*chemistry* (fem.)].
26. Karl, hast du —— weh getan?
27. Diesen Sommer werden wir —— herrlich amüsieren.
28. Fritz, ziehe —— schnell an! Kinder, zieht —— schnell an!
29. Ich muß —— beeilen, sonst komme ich zu spät an.
30. Letzte Woche habe ich —— stark erkältet.
31. Marie, benimm —— anständig!
32. So etwas kann ich —— gar nicht vorstellen.
33. Er wunderte sich sehr —— d— Größe der Stadt.
34. Ich bedankte —— —— —— (*him*) —— d— schön— Buch.

35. Schmeich(e)le —— (*yourself*) nicht!
36. Es wird —— bald zeigen, wer recht hat.
37. Astronomische Untersuchungen in hohen Schichten der Atmosphäre lassen —— am günstigsten mit Hilfe eines bemannten und unbemannten Ballons durchführen.
38. Viele Forscher haben —— für die Verwendung eines solchen Ballons —— (sich entscheiden). Ein automatisches „Observatorium" (eine automatische „Sternwarte") —— (sich lösen) vom Riesenballon und sinkt an einem Fallschirm langsam zur Erde.

B. Translate:

1. Did you have a good time?
2. He took leave (*i.e.*, said goodbye) suddenly.
3. I shall always rely on you.
4. Do you remember those interesting people we met last month?
5. I am looking forward with pleasure to your visit.
6. Don't trouble (*i.e.*, concern yourself) about my little brother.
7. He will apply for the first prize.
8. His little sister was behaving badly.
9. They will never get used to it.
10. When did you catch cold? (*Translate in three ways.*)
11. She had dressed quickly.
12. Be ashamed (of yourself)! (*Translate in three ways.*)
13. I am rejoicing at his great success.
14. He is always provoked at me.
15. Even a physician is sometimes mistaken.
16. They love each other.
17. It can't be done. (*Cf.* ¶ **E** above.)
18. She did that herself.
19. He is honesty personified (*i.e.*, itself).
20. Even I understand that.
21. That is understood.
22. He will long for his old friends.
23. Have a good time. (*Translate in three ways.*)
24. What are you interested in?
25. I have decided to take a long walk.
26. We can't imagine such a thing.
27. You must hurry; otherwise you will arrive late.

28. Fred, sit down on the bench.
29. He is not afraid of that large dog.
30. You must get used to hard work.
31. I thanked (bedanken) her for the beautiful books.
32. Many people are interested in scientific investigations.
33. Such investigators are not afraid of difficulties which must be overcome.

62. IMPERSONAL VERBS

Verbs that require impersonal **es** as their subject are known as **impersonal verbs.** They are used **only** in the third person singular and have neither passive nor imperative. Except for the type of verbs explained in ¶¶ **A** and **B** following, there are comparatively few German verbs that are **always** impersonal. Quite common, however, is the verb **geschehen** (*to happen*), which can only be used impersonally—*i.e.*, it cannot have as subject a noun or pronoun referring to a person. It cannot, therefore, be used in such a sentence as:

> *He **happened to be** at home.*
> Er **war zufällig** zu Hause.

or: **Zufälligerweise war** er zu Hause.

A.   Impersonal verbs denoting operations of nature.   Verbs denoting phenomena of nature are regularly impersonal. They are as follows:

(1) Es schneit.	*It is snowing.*	(5) Es hagelt.	*It hails.*
(2) Es regnet.	*It is raining.*	(6) Es friert.	*It freezes.*
(3) Es blitzt.	*It lightens.*	(7) Es tagt.	*It is dawning.*
(4) Es donnert.	*It thunders.*	(8) Es dämmert.	*It is getting dark* (or *light*) (depending upon the time of day)

B.   Impersonal verbs denoting mental or physical states.   Verbs denoting mental or physical states that are impersonal follow:

(1) **Ihn** schläfert.   (2) **Mir** schwindelt.
or: Er ist schläfrig.   · or: Mir ist schwind(e)lig.
      He is sleepy.   *I am dizzy.*

(3) **Mir** graut.
I shudder.

Note:

(1) Some impersonal verbs denoting mental or physical states take the dative (*cf.* (2) and (3) above); others govern the accusative (*cf.* (1) above).

(2) Impersonal **es** is the **understood** subject of verbs in the above examples.   Such verbs often omit the **es** in **inverted word order: Mir graut** for **Mir graut es** (or less commonly **Es graut mir**).

C.   Es gibt and **es ist** (pl. **es sind**).   Read the following sentences very carefully:

(1) **Es gibt** weiße Mäuse.
 *There **are** white mice.*
i.e.:   *It is a fact that there are white mice.*

(2) **Es sind** zwei weiße Mäuse in diesem Zimmer.
 *There **are** (not pointing) two white mice in this room.*

(3) **Da sind** zwei weiße Mäuse.
 *There (pointing) **are** two white mice.*

(4) **Es gibt keinen** Winter in jenem Lande.
 *There **is** no winter in that country.*

Note:

(1) **Es gibt** is used in a general sense (*cf.* (1) above).   It is always singular and must be followed by the **accusative** case (*cf.* (4) above).

(2) **Es ist** (pl. **sind**) is more specific and definite (*cf.* (2) above).

(3) **Da** serves as a demonstrative (*cf.* (3) above).

D.   The Impersonal use of intransitive verbs in the passive. Compare the following active and passive forms:

(1) Active voice: (2) Passive voice:

(*a*) Man tanzt viel.   (*a*) Es wird viel getanzt.
 There is much dancing.   *There is much dancing.*

(*b*) Er hilft mir.   (*b*) Mir wird von ihm geholfen.
 He helps me.   *I am helped by him.*

(*c*) Man folgte ihnen nicht.   (*c*) Ihnen wurde nicht gefolgt.
 They (lit. *one*) *did not follow them.*   *They were not followed.*

(*d*) Der Arzt riet mir, in die Berge zu gehen.	(*d*) Mir wurde von dem Arzt geraten, in die Berge zu gehen.
The physician advised me to go to the mountains.	*I was advised by the physician to go to the mountains.*

Note:

(1) **Man**—or rather the dative **einem** (*cf.* **Note** (2) (*a*) of § 60)—is omitted in the passive (*cf.* 1 (*a*) and 2 (*a*), and 1 (*c*) and 2 (*c*) above).

(2) Intransitive verbs that take the dative—*e.g.*, **helfen, folgen, raten, glauben, etc.**—**keep the dative in the passive voice** and are used impersonally with **es,** expressed or understood. If the inverted word order is used in this construction, **es** must be omitted (*cf.* (2) (*b*), (*c*), and (*d*) above). If **es** is expressed, it comes at the head of a sentence: **Es** wurde mir von dem Arzt geraten, in die Berge zu gehen.

EXERCISE

A. Study carefully the following sentences; impersonal verbs predominate:

1. Es hat stark gefroren.
2. Es gibt dreibeinige Stühle. Es sind zwei dreibeinige Stühle in diesem Zimmer. Da ist ein dreibeiniger Stuhl.
3. Es hat lange geregnet.
4. Im achtzehnten Jahrhundert gab es noch viele Indianer in den Vereinigten Staaten.
5. Wird es morgen schneien?
6. Ihm graut, wenn er daran denkt.
7. Mich schläfert (*or* Ich bin schläfrig).
8. Es ist so schnell geschehen, daß er nicht wußte, um was es sich handelte.
9. Sein Vater war zufällig (*or* Zufälligerweise war sein Vater) auch da.
10. Ihm wurde von dem Arzt geraten (for the customary Der Arzt riet ihm), an den Strand zu gehen.
11. Es wurde viel getrunken.
12. Da liegt mein deutsches Buch. Es gibt nicht viele Bücher dieser Art. Es sind verschiedene deutsche Zeitschriften im Nebenzimmer.

13. Wer dies nicht versteht, dem ist nicht zu helfen.
14. Es blitzt schon seit einer Stunde.
15. Vorigen Monat hat es stark gehagelt.
16. Es gibt zahllose Himmelskörper, die man noch nicht entdeckt hat.
17. Der Ballon wird erst später in die Stratosphäre aufsteigen, weil es heute stark regnet.

B. Translate:

1. It was thundering.
2. I think (that) it will rain tomorrow.
3. I shudder when I think of that.
4. Did it snow yesterday?
5. He is not believed.
6. They were not helped.
7. There are three-legged chairs. There are ten chairs in the next (*or* adjoining) room. There (*pointing*) is a chair.
8. It has been raining for three hours.
9. She is dizzy.
10. There are many students who like to read German books.
11. She was advised by the physician to go to the mountains.
12. There was much dancing.
13. There (*pointing*) are the notebooks.
14. There is much laughter. (*Use the verb* lachen.)
15. It happened so quickly that I didn't know what it was all about.
16. My mother happened to be there too.
17. Last month it froze hard.
18. It has been snowing for an hour and a half.
19. The men will not be able to fly until later, because it is snowing today.
20. There are countless celestial bodies which can be seen only with a telescope.

63. NORMAL WORD ORDER

The sequence in **normal word order** is: (1) subject and modifiers; (2) verb; and (3) verbal modifiers.
Read the following sentences very carefully:

A. Die Sonne geht um sechs Uhr auf.
The sun rises at six o'clock.

B. Der Apfel ist reif.
The apple is ripe.

C. Mein Freund ist müde geworden.
My friend has become tired.

D. Die Dame, die mich jetzt besucht, ist meine Freundin.
The lady who is visiting me now is my friend.

E. Er arbeitet nie.   Sie spielt immer.
He never works.   *She always plays.*

Note:

(1) If the subject comes first, the verb follows it (*cf.* ¶¶ **A–E** above).

(2) In a main clause containing a compound tense (*cf.* ¶ **C** above), the auxiliary (here **ist**) follows the subject and the infinitive or participle (here **geworden**) stands at the end of the sentence.

(3) The complete subject may contain modifiers—*e.g.*, a relative clause (*cf.* ¶ **D** above). In this event, the main verb (here **ist**) follows the **complete** subject.

(4) Contrary to English usage, an adverb cannot come between subject and verb (*cf.* ¶ **E** above).

F.   Coördinating conjunctions requiring normal word order.
The most common **coördinating conjunctions**[1] which require the normal word order are: **und** (*and*), **aber** (*but*), **sondern** (*but*), **denn** (*for*), and **oder** (*or*).

Note: **Denn** is a weak causal conjunction and is to be noted particularly, since it must not be confused with **dann** (*then*), which requires the inverted word order:

> Er ist nicht hier, **denn er ist** krank.
> *He is not here, for he is sick.*

64. INVERTED WORD ORDER

The sequence in **inverted word order** is: (1) any word (except a conjunction) other than the subject; (2) verb;[2] (3) subject; and (4) other modifiers.

Read the following sentences very carefully. Note the bold-faced verbs and their subjects:

A.   Wann **geht die Sonne** auf?
When does the sun rise?

B.   **Ist der Apfel** reif?
Is the apple ripe?

C.   Heute morgen **machte ich** einen Spaziergang.
This morning I took a walk.

D.   Nach dem Spaziergang **ging ich** nach Hause.
After the walk, I went home.

E.   Den Hut **hatte ich** vergessen.
I had forgotten my hat.

F.   Dem alten Manne **hatte er** die Bücher gegeben.
He had given the old man the books.

G.   Schön **ist sie** nicht.
She is not beautiful.

---

[1] For details relative to the meaning and use of coördinating conjunctions, *cf.* Chapter 19. For use of **allein,** see footnote 1 § 67.

[2] *Cf.* **Note** (2) below.

H. „Ich werde mitkommen,'' **sagte er.**
" I shall come along,'' he said.

I. Er war krank, darum **ging er** zum Arzt.
He was ill; therefore he went to a doctor.

Dann **ging er** nach Hause.
Then he went home.

J. Als ich in die Schule ging, **regnete es.**
As I was going to school, it was raining.

Weil er gestern nicht gearbeitet hat, **wird er** heute doppelt fleißig sein.
Since he didn't work yesterday, he will be twice as industrious today.

Note:

(1) If a sentence begins with any word, or **single** group of related words—*e.g.*, a phrase (*cf.* ¶ **D** above) or a clause (*cf.* ¶ **J** above)—other than the subject, **the verb follows immediately as second element in the sentence. (Not more than one element**—*i.e.*, a word or single group of related words—should stand at the head of a sentence.) **The subject must follow the verb.**

(2) The verb ordinarily comes **first** in direct questions, as in English (*cf.* ¶ **B** above).

(3) If the verb in a main clause (having inverted word order) is a compound tense (*cf.* ¶¶ **E** and **F** above), the **auxiliary** must be the second element in the sentence (except in a direct question, when it comes first). The infinitive or participle comes at the end of the sentence.

(4) (*a*) The introductory element in a sentence with inverted order may be an interrogative (*cf.* ¶ **A** above), the verb (*cf.* ¶ **B** above), an adverb (*cf.* ¶ **C** above), a conjunctive adverb (*cf.* ¶ **I** above), a phrase (*cf.* ¶ **D** above), the direct object (*cf.* ¶ **E** above), the indirect object (*cf.* ¶ **F** above), an adjective (*cf.* ¶ **G** above), a direct quotation (*cf* ¶ **H** above), a dependent clause (*cf.* ¶ **J** above), or even an infinitive or a participle:

Arbeiten will er nicht.   **Gearbeitet** hat er nie.
He does not want to work.   *He has never worked.*

(*b*) A word is frequently put at the head of a clause for special emphasis (*cf.* ¶¶ **E** and **G** above), thus causing inversion.

(5) Particular attention should be paid to sentences of the type of those under ¶ **J** above. **If a dependent clause comes first in a sentence, the main clause following has the inverted word order.** This is because the dependent clause is equivalent to an adverb (or some other part of speech)—*e.g.,* **dann** and **darum** may be substituted for dependent clauses in ¶ **J** (*cf.* also ¶ **I** above):

> **Dann** regnete es.
> *Then it was raining.*

> **Darum** wird er heute doppelt fleißig sein.
> *Therefore he will be twice as industrious today.*

(6) (*a*) The insertion of a comma after ordinal conjunctions derived from numerals, can change inverted to normal word order:

> Zweitens, er bespricht alles sehr genau.
> *In the second place, he discusses everything in great detail.*

(*b*) When a comma is inserted after the word **nun,**[1] the meaning also changes:

> **Nun,** wir werden doch durchkommen.
> *Well, we shall nevertheless (manage to) get along.*

but: **Nun** werden wir fortfahren.
> *Now we shall continue.*

65. DEPENDENT (OR TRANSPOSED) WORD ORDER

The sequence in **dependent** (or **transposed**) **word order** is: (1) subordinating conjunction or words functioning as subordinating conjunctions (*e.g.,* relative or interrogative pronouns, relative or interrogative adverbs); (2) subject; (3) modifiers; and (4) verb.

Read the following sentences very carefully:

A. Als ich in Deutschland **war,** besuchte ich meine Freunde.
When I was in Germany, I visited my friends.

B. Hunde, die viel **bellen,** beißen nicht.
Dogs that bark a great deal do not bite.

---

[1] Observe that both **jetzt** and **nun** may be translated as *now;* **jetzt** refers specifically to present time, whereas **nun** has consecutive force—*i.e.,* there is an implied connection between what follows and what has preceded it.

C. Wenn er die Tür **aufmacht,** wird es zu kühl im Zimmer sein.
If he opens the door, it will be too cool in the room.

D. Wenn ich Zeit gehabt **hätte,** so hätte ich ihn besucht.
If I had had time, I would have visited him.

E. Das ist ein Rätsel, das er nicht **hat** lösen können.
That is a riddle which he has been unable to solve.

F. Je mehr ich Goethe **lese,** desto mehr bewundere ich ihn.
The more I read Goethe, the more I admire him.

Je reicher er **wird,** desto unverschämter benimmt er sich.
The richer he becomes, the more insolently he behaves.

G. Er fragte mich, ob ich ihn verstanden **hätte.**
He asked me whether I had understood him.

H. Ich fragte ihn, wer das gesagt **hätte.**
I asked him who had said that.

I. Er fragte mich, wo ich gewesen **wäre.**
He asked me where I had been.

Note:

(1) Dependent (or transposed) word order is required in dependent clauses. **The verb must stand at the end of a clause.**

(2) All relative clauses are dependent. The verb must therefore come at the end of a clause (*cf.* ¶ **B** above).

(3) Separable verbs are not separated in dependent clauses (*cf.* ¶ **C** above).

(4) **The auxiliary** in compound tenses must come at the end of a dependent clause (*cf.* ¶¶ **D, G, H,** and **I** above).

(5) In a dependent clause having the double infinitive construction (*cf.* **Note** (4) of § 83 and **Note** (2) of § 84), **the auxiliary precedes both infinitive forms** (*cf.* ¶ **E** above).

(6) (*a*) Clauses with a **je** and **desto,** both followed by comparative, take dependent word order in the first clause and inverted word order in the second (*cf.* ¶ **F** above).

(*b*) **Um so** (less frequently **je** in modern German) may be used instead of **desto**:

Je mehr er hat, um so mehr will er haben.
The more he has, the more he wants.

(7) (*a*) Indirect questions are dependent clauses and therefore have the verb at the end of a clause (*cf.* ¶¶ **G, H,** and **I** above).

(*b*) The introductory word of the dependent clause in ¶ **G** is a conjunction.   Paragraphs **H** and **I** show how interrogative pronouns and adverbs introduce subordinate clauses in indirect questions (*cf.* also **Note** (4) of § 77).

J.   Subordinating conjunctions.   The most common **subordinating conjunctions**[1]—*i.e.*, those which introduce subordinate (or dependent) clauses—are: **als, als ob, bis, da, damit, daß, ehe** (or **bevor**), **falls, indem, nachdem, ob, obgleich, obwohl, obschon, seitdem, sobald, solange, sooft, während, weil,** and **wenn.**

Note: The only exception to the rule that a subordinating conjunction must introduce a dependent clause, is that **a preposition** may precede a relative or interrogative pronoun (functioning as a subordinating conjunction):

Das ist das Haus, **in dem** er früher **wohnte.**
That is the house in which he formerly lived.

Ich fragte ihn, **von wem** er das gehört **hätte.**
I asked him from whom he had heard that.

66. SPECIAL POINTS ABOUT WORD ORDER

A.   The omission of daß.   If **daß** is omitted, the normal word order is required:

Er sagte, **er hätte** ihn gesehen.
but: Er sagte, daß er ihn gesehen hätte.
He said that he had seen him.

---

[1] For details relative to the meaning and use of subordinating conjunctions, *cf.* Chapter 19.

B. The omission of wenn. If **wenn** is omitted, the inverted word order is required:

Hätte ich Geld, so würde ich reisen.

but: Wenn ich Geld hätte, so würde ich reisen.

If I had money, I would travel.

or: *Had I money, I would travel.*

C. The position of unemphatic pronoun objects. Unemphatic —*i.e.,* unstressed—pronoun objects often come between verb and subject, contrary to the rule for inverted word order:

Heute **hat mich niemand** besucht.

Nobody called on me today.

D. The position of adverbs of time, manner, and place. Adverbs (or adverbial phrases) of time and manner precede those of place:

Er geht jetzt nach Hause.   Er fährt mit dem Zug nach Hause.

He is going home now.   *He goes home by train.*

E. The position of direct and indirect object. Unless the direct object is a personal or reflexive pronoun, the indirect object precedes it:

Er zeigte dem Freunde das Bild.   Er zeigte es dem Freunde.

He showed his friend the picture.   *He showed it to his friend.*

Er zeigte ihm das Bild.   Er zeigte es ihm.

He showed him the picture.   *He showed it to him.*

Der König zeigte sich dem Volke.

The king showed himself to the people.

F. The position of pronoun objects. These precede adverbs:

Er hatte es gestern nicht.

He did not have it yesterday.

G. The position of nicht **and** nie. For a detailed explanation of the position of **nicht** and **nie,** *cf.* § 7.

EXERCISE

A. Rewrite the following sentences. Introduce **the second** sentence of each pair by the words in parentheses:

1. Sie war nicht hier. Sie war krank. (denn)
2. Wir kamen ins Zimmer. Wir setzten uns. (dann)

3. Man setzt sich. Man ist müde. (wenn)
4. Ich besuchte ihn. Er war auf dem Lande. (als)
5. Er arbeitet jetzt. Er ist schläfrig. (obgleich)
6. Der Mann ist zu Hause. Seine Frau ist in der Stadt. (aber)
7. Ich war gestern im Bett. Es regnete stark. (als)
8. Die Leute fliehen. Sie sind in Gefahr. (denn)
9. Er schreibt den Satz nicht. Er versteht ihn nicht. (weil)
10. Antworten Sie nicht! Er fragt Sie. (ehe or bevor)
11. Er antwortete. Er schrieb den Satz an die Tafel. (dann)
12. Er ging aufs Land. Ich hatte ihn besucht. (nachdem)
13. Der Schimpanse machte die Reise in einer Raumkapsel. Man hatte ihn monatelang auf seinen Raumflug vorbereitet. (nachdem)
14. Man wählte einen Schimpansen. In bezug auf Körperbau, physiologische Merkmale und sogar Temperament ist er dem Menschen sehr ähnlich. (weil)

B. Rewrite the following sentences **with the dependent clause first:**

1. Es regnete stark, als er in der Schule war.
2. Ich habe nichts gegessen, weil ich nicht hungrig war.
3. Er wird reisen, sobald er Geld hat.
4. Sie antwortete nicht, obgleich ich sie zweimal fragte.
5. Sie arbeitete schwer, obwohl sie müde war.
6. Die Männer reisten nach Deutschland, nachdem ich sie besucht hatte.
7. Ich reise gern, wenn ich Geld habe.
8. Er sagte nichts, ehe (or bevor) ich ihn fragte.
9. Er reist nicht, weil er kein Geld hat.
10. Er wird das Buch lesen, wenn es nicht zu schwer ist.
11. Eine direkte Beobachtung der Venus-Oberfläche ist unmöglich, weil die dichte, wolkenerfüllte Atmosphäre des Planeten die eigentliche Planetenoberfläche vollständig und dauernd verbirgt.
12. In einigen Ländern wurden Fliegertauglichkeitsuntersuchungen durch Nicht-Mediziner abgeschafft, weil sie als zu einseitig angesehen wurden.

C. Translate the following sentences after having studied the illustrative sentences in §§ 63–66:

1. The sun sets at half past seven.
2. Her little brother is not in school, for he is ill.
3. She is not happy, although she is very rich.
4. The old men had become tired.
5. The more I study these short German sentences, the more I know.
6. My dear friends who are at my house today, live in a beautiful suburb.
7. If he closes (zumachen) the door, it will not be so cool in the room.
8. She always stays at home.
9. He never visits me.
10. This evening he will take a long walk.
11. When will you read that German book?
12. As I was reading it (*i.e.*, the book) this morning, my little sister entered the room.
13. He always speaks German.
14. The books that are lying on the small table belong to my older brother.
15. After he had read the first sentence, he wrote it on the blackboard.
16. Although he wrote the sentences, he made many mistakes.
17. While I was in the country last summer, I met my old friends.
18. He had given the old men some money.
19. They were never at home when I visited them.
20. When will you take (machen) the examination?
21. I know that I shall pass (bestehen) it.
22. I cannot fail (durchfallen), for I have studied very hard.
23. If I close the door, it will be too warm in the room.
24. I shall see the sunrise if I get up early.
25. The more money he makes (verdienen), the more he wants.
26. I shall come along as soon as I have written these short sentences.
27. He is not going along, for he is too tired.
28. When will you visit her?
29. He is not going to Germany, because he has no money.
30. Some scientists believe that the planet Mars has vast oceans which are covered with a thick coat of ice.

31. The newspaper reported that a gigantic balloon had reached an altitude of 28,000 meters in (a) relatively short time.

D.   The following sentences involving word order in clauses with the subjunctive should be omitted at this point, **unless the student has mastered indirect statements and questions, contrary-to-fact conditions, and the subjunctive of modal auxiliaries:**

1. He could have traveled if he had had the money.
2. He asked me whether I had understood him.
3. She said that her older brother had stayed at home.
4. I asked him whether he had seen her.
5. We asked them whether they had ever been in Europe.
6. She said that she had wanted (wollen) to do it.
7. He said that he should have done it.
8. Our old German doctor said that he could have helped the little boy.
9. My dear friend said that he would write me an interesting letter.
10. He said that we should have helped those poor people.
11. I asked her whether she had been able to solve the cross-word puzzle (das Kreuzworträtsel).
12. She said that she preferred to read a good book.
13. A scientist told us that hundreds of research rockets had ascended into (the) world space.
14. We know that the flyer could have remained longer in the higher layers of air.

CHAPTER 19 **Conjunctions**

67. COÖRDINATING CONJUNCTIONS

Read the following sentences very carefully. Note the word order in each:

A. Und:

Das Auto hält, **und wir steigen ein.**
The auto stops and we get in.

B. Aber:

(1) Er sah mich, **aber ich sah** ihn nicht.
He saw me, but I did not see him.

(2) Er war nicht zu Hause, **aber sein Bruder war** da.
He was not at home, but his brother was there.

C. Sondern:

Er ging nicht in die Stadt, **sondern er blieb** auf dem Lande.
He did not go to the city but remained in the country.

D. Denn:

Sie konnte nicht kommen, **denn sie hatte** Besuch.
She could not come, for she had company (or guests).

E. Oder:

Tue deine Pflicht, **oder du wirst** es später bereuen!
Do your duty, or you will regret it later.

Summary: The above sentences indicate that the more common coördinating conjunctions are: **und** (*and*), **aber** (*but*), **sondern** (*but*), **denn** (*for*), and **oder** (*or*).

Note:

(1) **Coördinating conjunctions take normal word order** (*cf.* § 63).

(2) *But* may be translated by either **aber** or **sondern:**[1]

(*a*) **Aber** is used **after a positive** (*cf.* ¶ **B** (1) above), and after a negative when *but* is the equivalent of *however* (*cf.* **B** (2) above). It is also frequently used in the sense of *however*, **provided it does not head a clause:**

> Der alte Mann **aber** wollte es nicht zugeben.
> *The old man, **however**, did not want to admit it.*

Caution: **Aber**, unlike the English *however*, **is never set off by commas.**

(*b*) **Sondern** is used only **after a negative**, and means *on the contrary* when it connects two clauses having a common subject (*cf.* ¶ **C** above). Whereas **aber** merely modifies a previous statement, **sondern** introduces a statement which excludes or contradicts that of the preceding clause.

(3) **Denn** must not be confused with **dann** (*then*), which takes inverted word order.

(4) In addition to the coördinating conjunctions listed above, note that the combination **sowohl . . . als auch** (*both . . . and*) also requires normal word order:

> **Sowohl** die Reichen **als auch** die Armen haben gelitten.
> *Both rich and poor suffered.*

(5) (*a*) Correlatives such as **entweder . . . oder** (*either . . . or*), **weder . . . noch** (*neither . . . nor*), and **nicht nur . . . sondern auch** (*not only . . . but also*) take normal word order when they connect different subjects of the same verb, or when the subjects are emphasized:

> **Entweder** er **oder** sein Freund wird uns helfen.
> *Either he or his friend will help us.*

> **Entweder du** bleibst, **oder ich** bleibe.
> *Either you stay, or I (will) stay.*

---

[1] The conjunction **allein** is a forceful equivalent of *but* when introducing a contradictory statement, and must always stand at the head of the clause.

Weder er **noch** seine Frau konnte das Auto fahren.
Neither he nor his wife could drive the car.
Nicht nur die Kinder **sondern auch** die Eltern wollten die
Ausstellung besuchen.
*Not only the children but also the parents wanted to visit the
exposition.*

(*b*) These correlatives otherwise use inverted word order:

Weder kann noch will er es tun.
He neither can, nor wants to do it.

Caution: The inverted order may be avoided, however, by placing the
emphatic word first:

Entweder **du** machst die Arbeit, oder ich rufe deine Mutter.
Either you will do the work, or I shall call your mother.

68. SUBORDINATING CONJUNCTIONS

Read the following sentences very carefully.   Note the word order in
each:

A. Als:

Als wir gestern nach Hause **kamen,** regnete es.
When we came home yesterday, it was raining.

B. Als ob:

(1) Er tat, **als ob er** krank **wäre.**
He acted as if he were ill.

(2) Sie sehen aus, **als ob Sie** nicht geschlafen **hätten.**
You look as if you had not slept.

C. Bis:

Er arbeitete, **bis es** dunkel **wurde.**
He worked until it grew (or became) dark.

D. Da:

Er konnte nicht arbeiten, **da der Lärm** zu groß **war.**
He could not work since (or because) the noise was too great.

E. Damit:

Ich sage es dir, **damit du** es **weißt.**
I am telling you, so that you may know it.

F. Daß:

Wir wissen, **daß die Erde** rund **ist.**
We know that the earth is round.

G. Ehe (or **bevor**):

Er wird mich besuchen, **ehe** (or **bevor**) **er** nächsten Monat **abreist.**
He will visit me before he leaves next month.

H. Falls:

Falls er kommen **sollte,** würden wir ihn freundlich empfangen.
If (or *in case*) *he should come, we would welcome him cordially* (or *in friendly fashion*).

I. Nachdem:

Nachdem er angekommen **war,** besuchte er seine Freunde.
After he (had) arrived, he visited his friends.

J. Ob:

Er fragte mich, **ob ich** ihn verstanden **hätte.**
He asked me whether I had understood him.

K. Obgleich (**obwohl** or **obschon**):

Er ist nicht glücklich, **obgleich er** reich **ist.**
Although he is rich, he is not happy.

L. Seitdem:

Seitdem sie uns vor fünf Jahren besucht **hat,** haben wir sie nicht gesehen.
We have not seen her since (the time that) she visited us five years ago.

M. Sobald:

Sobald sie angekommen **war,** ließ sie einen Arzt holen.
As soon as she (had) arrived, she sent for a doctor.

N. Solange:

Solange ich krank **war,** ist er bei mir geblieben.
He stayed with me as long as I was sick.

O. Sooft:

Sooft Sie mich **bitten,** werde ich Ihnen helfen.
As often as you ask me, I shall help you.

P. Während (or **indem**):

(1) **Während ich** krank **war,** konnte ich nicht arbeiten.
I could not work, while I was sick.

(2) **Indem sie** das **sagte,** trat sie ins Zimmer herein.
As she said that, she entered the room.
lit.:   *While she was saying that, she entered the room.*

Q. Weil:

Er trägt einen Überrock, **weil es** kalt **ist.**
He wears an overcoat because it is cold.

R. Wenn:

(1) **Wenn ich** Zeit **habe,** so werde ich ihn besuchen.
If I have time, I shall visit him.

(2) **Wenn man** heutzutage **reist,** benutzt man die Eisenbahn, das
Flugzeug, oder ein Strahlflugzeug (*jet*).
*When(ever) one travels nowadays, one uses the railroad, the airplane, or
a jet.*

Summary: The above sentences indicate that the more common
subordinating conjunctions are: **als** (*when*), **als ob** (*as if*), **bis** (*until*),
da [*as, since (causal)*], **damit** [*in order* (or *so*) *that*], **daß** (*that*), **ehe** (or
bevor) (*before*), **falls** (*if, in case, provided that*), **indem** [*while, as* (temporal)], **nachdem** (*after*), **ob** (*whether, if*), **obgleich** (**obwohl** or **obschon**)
(*although*), **seitdem** [*since* (temporal)], **sobald** (*as soon as*), **solange** (*as
long as*), **sooft** (*as often as*), **während** (*while*), **weil** (*because*), and **wenn**
[*if, when(ever)*].

Note:

(1) **Subordinating conjunctions require the dependent word
order** (*cf.* § 65).

(2) *When* may be translated by either **als, wann,** or **wenn:**

(*a*) **Als** refers to a single, definite past action (*cf.* ¶ **A** above).

(*b*) **Wann** is used only in questions, both direct and indirect:

> Wann ist er nach Hause gekommen?
> *When did he come home?*
>
> Ich fragte ihn, wann er nach Hause gekommen wäre.
> *I asked him when he had come home.*

(*c*) **Wenn** is often used in the sense of *when* or *whenever* to express a customary or habitual action, either with the present (*cf.* ¶ **R** (2) above) or with the imperfect tense:

> Wenn ich ihn besuchte, war er immer beschäftigt.
> *When(ever) I visited him, he was always busy.*

It is commonly rendered by *if* in conditional sentences.

Caution: Interrogatives such as **wann, seit wann, warum, wo, woher, wohin, womit, worauf,** *etc.*, which take the inverted word order in direct questions, function as subordinating conjunctions when used in indirect questions and, therefore, require that the verb stand at the end of a clause:

> Direct: „Woher wissen Sie das?"
> *How do you know that?*
>
> Indirect: Ich fragte ihn, woher er das wisse (or wüßte).
> *I asked him how he knew that.*
>
> Direct: „Warum haben Sie das getan?"
> *Why did you do that?*
>
> Indirect: Ich fragte ihn, warum er das getan hätte.
> *I asked him why he had done that.*

(3) **Als ob** may be shortened to **als,** causing **inverted** word order, without change of meaning (*cf.* ¶ **B** above):

> Er tat, **als** wäre er müde.
> or: Er tat, als ob er müde wäre.
> *He acted as if he were tired.*

(4) (*a*) **Damit** is very often followed by the indicative in modern German:

> Er trägt das Geld auf die Bank, **damit es** Zinsen **bringt.**
> *He takes his money to the bank so (or in order) that it may bear interest.*

(*b*) **Um zu** with the infinitive is often used instead of **damit** to denote purpose, **provided there is no change of subject:**

> Das Geld wird auf die Bank getragen, **um** Zinsen **zu** bringen.
> *Money is taken to the bank so (or in order) that it may bear interest.*

Damit must be used in ¶ **E** above, since the subjects of the clauses are different (*i.e.,* **ich** and **du**).

(5) The forms **bevor** (or **ehe**), **vor,** and **vorher** are not to be confused:

(*a*) **Bevor** (or **ehe**) is a conjunction (*cf.* ¶ **G** above).

(*b*) **Vor** is a preposition:

> Das ist vor Weihnachten geschehen.
> *That happened before Christmas.*

(*c*) **Vorher** is an adverb:

> Das war vorher geschehen.
> *That had happened before.*

(6) The forms **nachdem, nach,** and **nachher** are not to be confused:

(*a*) **Nachdem** is a conjunction (*cf.* ¶ **I** above).

(*b*) **Nach** is a preposition:

> Nach dem Tanz gingen sie nach Hause.
> *After the dance, they went home.*

(*c*) **Nachher** is an adverb:

> Sie tanzten nachher.
> *They danced afterwards.*

(7) The forms **seitdem, seit,** and **seither** are not to be confused:

(*a*) **Seitdem** may serve as a conjunction (*cf.* ¶ **L** above). It is also frequently used as an adverb:

> Seitdem ist er krank.
> *Since then (or that time) he has been sick.*

Caution: The conjunctions **da** and **seitdem,** both meaning since, are not to be confused. **Da** is causative (i.e., *because*), **seitdem** is temporal (*cf.* ¶ **D** and ¶ **L** above).

(*b*) **Seit** is a preposition:

Er ist schon seit einem Monat hier.
He has been here for a month.

(*c*) **Seither** is an adverb.   **Seitdem** is more commonly used (*cf.* (*a*) above).

(8)   The forms **wenn** and **ob** are not to be confused:

(*a*) **Wenn** is commonly rendered by *if* in conditional sentences (*cf.* ¶ **R** (1) above).

(*b*) **Ob** may be translated by *if,* but is used only in indirect questions in the sense of *whether* (*cf.* ¶ **J** above).

(9)   The forms **weil**[1] and **während** are not to be confused:

(*a*) **Weil,** in modern German, means *because* (*cf.* ¶ **Q** above).

(*b*) **Während** as a conjunction means *while* (*cf.* ¶ **P** (1) above).

(10) (*a*) **Indem** (*while* or *as*) with the verb it introduces is often equivalent to the English present participle, thus denoting that the action of both clauses took place at the same time (*cf.* ¶ **P** (2) above):

Er grüßte den König, **indem er sich tief verbeugte.**
Bowing deeply, he saluted the king.

(*b*) **Während** (*while*) may have the additional implication of *as long as* (*cf.* ¶ **P** (1) above), or *during the time that.*

(11) Two conjunctions should not come together: *She said that if it had rained, she would not have come.*   To avoid the juxtaposition of **daß** and **wenn,** translate in any one of the following ways:

Sie sagte, daß sie nicht gekommen wäre, wenn es geregnet hätte.
Sie sagte, sie wäre nicht gekommen, wenn es geregnet hätte.
Sie sagte, wenn es geregnet hätte, wäre sie nicht gekommen.

---

[1] Note that the conjunction **weil** (*because*) requires the dependent word order, but that **darum, deswegen,** and **deshalb** (*therefore*) require the inverted word order. This is due to the fact that conjunctive **adverbs** regularly cause inversion.

(12) Distinguish between *as* in a temporal sense (*cf.* ¶ **P** (2) above), meaning *while*, and *as* in a causal sense (*cf.* **D** above), meaning *since*.

(13) **Wenn ... auch** (*even though*) requires the dependent word order:

> **Wenn** er **auch** sehr schwer gearbeitet **hat,** so hat er doch nicht viel Geld gespart.
> *Even though he has worked very hard, he has, nevertheless, not saved much money.*

(14) Attention has already been called to the three prepositions, **ohne, um,** and **(an)statt,** which require **zu** with a dependent infinitive (*cf.* § 27). Other prepositions in similar constructions require **da**-forms (dar**auf,** da**mit,** dar**an,** *etc.*), which serve to anticipate a **daß**-clause or an infinitive.[1] A **daß**-clause is usually used when there is a change of subject; an infinitive, when there is no such change. Note, too, that **da**-forms vary according to the idiom:

(*a*) Ich verlasse mich **darauf, daß** Sie mir helfen.
  I count on your helping me.

(*b*) Ich habe nichts **dagegen, daß** Sie Klavier spielen.
  I have no objection to your playing the piano.

(*c*) Er ist schuld **daran, daß** ich arm bin.
  He is to blame for my being poor.

(*d*) Das kommt **davon, daß** Sie zu viel rauchen.
  That comes from (your) smoking too much.

(*e*) Das Buch unterscheidet sich **darin, daß** es viele Beispiele enthält.
  The book is distinguished by the fact that it contains many examples.

(*f*) Er besteht **darauf,** die beiden Fahrpreise **zu bezahlen.**
  He insists on paying both fares.

(*g*) Er hat nie **daran** gedacht, so etwas **zu tun.**
  He never thought of doing such a thing.

(*h*) **Daran** ist nicht **zu denken.**
  That is not to be thought of.

---

[1] The preposition **um** must also be combined with **da,** if the idiom requires it:
Sie bat **darum,** das Bild zu sehen.
She asked to see the picture.

(*i*) Es handelt sich **darum, ob** er der erste gewesen ist.[1]
It is a question of whether he was the first.

EXERCISE

A. Rewrite the following sentences and connect them with the appropriate conjunctions in parentheses:

1. Man nimmt den Hut ab.   Man grüßt eine Dame.   (*when*)
2. Sie trägt eine Brille.   Sie will besser sehen.   (*because*)
3. Ich bin im Theater gewesen.   Ich (omit) habe die neueste Oper gesehen.   (*and*)
4. Man füllt einen Freiballon mit Helium.   Es ist unverbrennbar und leichter als Luft.   (*because*)
5. Er konnte nicht arbeiten.   Der Lärm war zu groß.   [*since* (causal)]
6. Der Junge war nicht in der Schule.   Er war krank.   (*for*)
7. Sie war krank.   Sie ging zum Arzt.   (*therefore*)
8. Besuchen Sie mich!   Ich werde böse auf Sie sein.   (*or*)
9. Sagen Sie es mir!   Ich weiß es auch.   (*so that*)
10. Er konnte nicht früher kommen.   Er war sehr beschäftigt. (*for*)
11. Er besucht unsere Schule.   Er ist in Amerika angekommen. [*since* (temporal)]
12. Ich fragte ihn.   Er hatte mich verstanden.   (*whether*)   (If necessary, change the mood.)
13. Er sprach.   Er wußte alles.   (*as if*)   (If necessary, change the mood.)
14. Er ist nicht hier.   Sein Bruder wird mit uns sprechen.   (*but*)
15. Er schrieb den Satz an die Tafel.   Er hatte ihn gelesen.   (*after*)
16. Er ist viel älter als die Schwester.   Er ist nicht so klug.   (*but*)
17. Sein Bruder schlief.   Er spielte Ball.   (*while*)
18. Er ging nach Hause.   Er war fertig.   (*as soon as*)
19. Ich fragte sie.   Sie hatte ihn gesehen.   (*whether*)   (If necessary, change the mood.)
20. Er besuchte mich.   Er reiste ab.   (*before*)
21. Das ist alles sehr schön.   Ich glaube es nicht.   (*but*)
22. Sie war in der Stadt.   Er war auf dem Lande.   (*but*)

---

[1] This sentence indicates that an indirect question may follow a **da**-form. For the use of the indicative, *cf.* **Note** (5) of § 77.

23. Ich sah, daß sie unzufrieden war.   Sie sagte nichts.   (*although*)
24. Wir müssen arbeiten.   Es wird dunkel.   (*until*)
25. Heute morgen spielte ich Klavier.   Er trat ins Zimmer.   (*when*)
26. Ich amüsierte mich herrlich.   Ich war auf dem Lande.   (*as long as*)
27. Sie kauft Blumen.   Sie geht aus.   (*as often as*)
28. Wir würden uns sehr freuen.   Er sollte kommen.   (*in case*)
29. Sie war nie zu Hause.   Ich wollte sie besuchen.   (*when*)
30. Ich weiß nicht.   Er ist hier.   (*whether*)
31. Ich werde ihn besuchen.   Er ist hier.   (*if*)
32. Man mußte die Form des Ballon-Spiegelteleskops verändern. Bei dem schnellen Aufstieg des Ballons ist das Instrument starken Temperaturschwankungen ausgesetzt.   (*since*)

B.   Translate:

1. If the weather is good, we shall take a long walk.
2. Although he knew me, he did not greet me.
3. My friend wrote me that he would arrive day after tomorrow.
4. He wanted to know whether this was a good book.
5. She is much younger than her brother, but she can speak German just as fluently.
6. That was all very fine (schön), but he did not believe it.
7. Not he, but she, was to blame for that.
8. The auto stopped and we got in.
9. They were not in the country but in the city.
10. When I was in Germany last summer, I saw many famous castles on the Rhine.
11. He acted as if he had not understood it.
12. We come to school in order to learn something.
13. He gives much money to the poor so that they may have something to eat.
14. She could not come yesterday, for she was ill.
15. Visit me next month, or I shall be angry with you.
16. This morning I could not go along because I was too tired.
17. After he had read the German book, he went to bed.
18. My old friend was always busy when I visited him.
19. Our dear father was ill; therefore he went to the doctor.
20. While it was raining this morning, I wrote a long letter.
21. As soon as I had written the letter, I mailed it.

22. In case the father lost (*i.e.*, should lose) his position, the family would have no money.
23. They worked until it became dark.
24. Do you know if Mr. Smith is at home?
25. If he is not at home, I shall call on him next month.
26. Both teachers and pupils were looking forward with pleasure to the vacation.
27. Neither Fred not his sister wanted to stay at home.
28. Not only the parents, but also the children, had gone to the theater.
29. Mother had company; therefore she did not go along today.
30. Either she or her brother will drive the car.
31.¹ He is provoked at your doing that.
32. He counts (*or* relies) on my helping him.
33. I have no objection to your opening the window.
34. You are to blame that I am poor.
35. That comes from (your) eating too much.
36. He always insists on paying my fare.
37. He had never thought of doing such a thing.
38. That is not to be thought of.
39. He asked to see the book.
40. It is a question of how long the trip will take (dauern).
41. See to it that the children don't make so much noise (der Lärm).
42. Although there were many difficulties to overcome, rocket research has already made great advances.
43. If I have the money, I shall fly by jet.

C. The following sentences involve not only conjunctions but also other words which should be thoroughly mastered because of their sound, English meaning, or idiomatic use. (The use of these words has been explained in previous sections.) Note particularly such combinations as the following: **bevor** (or **ehe**), **vor, vorher; nachdem, nach, nachher; seitdem, seit, seither; als, wann, wenn; ob, als ob, obgleich; denn, dann; das, daß; weil, während; etwas, einige; ohne, um,** and **anstatt** with **zu** and an infinitive; **wo, wohin; je ... desto; da-** and **wo-**forms; **dessen** and **wessen:**

1. That happened before the war.
2. What had happened before?

---

¹ Sentences 31–41 involve the construction explained in **Note** (14) above.

3. Before I go to school, I always read the German newspaper.
4. After he (had) read the paper, he went to school.
5. My little brother read the story afterwards.
6. After the dance, they took a long walk.
7. Our old doctor has been in this country for (*i.e.*, since) thirty years.
8. What has happened since (then)?
9. Since (the time that) he became ill, he cannot work so hard.
10. When I was at home this morning, my little sister was playing.
11. When I visited him, he was always busy.
12. If I have time today, I shall write him a long letter.
13. She looks as if she were tired.
14. They acted (tun) as if they had heard the story.
15. He was in school, although he was quite (ganz) ill.
16. We asked them whether they had understood us.
17. Her older brother stayed at home, for he had a headache.
18. The little children came into the large room; then they sat down.
19. The German book that belongs to my little brother is very interesting.
20. That (Das) smaller book belongs to my younger sister.
21. I know that he has read this short story.
22. They were very tired because they had worked all morning.
23. While they were working, it began to rain.
24. During the rain, they stood under a tree.
25. Have you some money in your pocket?
26. I have no money because I bought some books yesterday.
27. We come to school in order to learn.
28. Without working, we cannot learn.
29. Instead of working, one little girl talked continually (fort-während).
30. Instead of his brother, his sister appeared.
31. Where do you live? Where are you going?
32. The more I read those short stories, the more interesting I find them.
33. " Of what are you thinking? " " I am thinking of him (*or* it)."
34. " On what are you sitting? " " I am sitting on a chair (*or* on it)."

35. " With what are you writing? "   " I am writing with a pen (*or* with it)."
36. Whose book have you in your hand?
37. The man whose book I have is not at home today.
38. Helium is heavier than hydrogen.   Nevertheless, scientists now fill free balloons (Freiballone) with helium, since this gas is incombustible.
39. The first radio-relay satellite proved for the first time that it is possible, with the help of such satellites, to transmit information (Nachrichten) over thousands (*acc.*) of kilometers.

CHAPTER 20

Separable
and
Inseparable Prefixes

69. INSEPARABLE PREFIXES[1]

Read the following sentences very carefully. Note the bold-faced prefix and the form a verb assumes in its various tenses:

A. Be–:

Tiefer Schnee **be**deckte die Erde.   Was **be**deutet das Wort?
Deep snow covered the earth.   *What does the word mean?*

Ich bin ihm auf der Straße **be**gegnet.   Wo **be**fand er sich?
I met him on the street.   *Where was he?*

B. Emp–:

Sie hat mich freundlich **emp**fangen.
She welcomed me cordially (or *in friendly fashion*).

Er hatte mir diese Firma **emp**fohlen.
He had recommended this firm to me.

Ich habe es peinlich **emp**funden.
It pained me.

Er läßt sich Ihrem Herrn Vater **emp**fehlen.
He wants to be remembered to your father.

C. Ent–:

Kolumbus hat Amerika **ent**deckt.   **Ent**schuldigen Sie mich!
Columbus discovered America.   *Pardon* (or *excuse*) *me.*

Er wird den unehrlichen Diener **ent**lassen.
He will discharge the dishonest servant.

Der Rhein **ent**springt in der Schweiz.
The Rhine has its source in Switzerland.

---

[1] For the various meanings of these prefixes, *cf.* § 91 **B.**

D. Er–:

Erklären Sie die Aufgabe!   Ich habe mich erkältet.
Explain the lesson.   *I have caught cold.*
                     or: *I have a cold.*

Sie hatte mir diese Geschichte erzählt.
She had told me this story.

Der Sage nach ist Friedrich Barbarossa in einem Fluß ertrunken.
According to legend, Friedrich Barbarossa drowned in a river.

E. Ge–:

Wie gefällt Ihnen das Buch?   Es gehört meiner Schwester.
How do you like the book?   *It belongs to my sister.*

Er mußte dem Vater gehorchen.
He had to obey his father.

Wir haben die schöne Musik genossen.
We enjoyed the beautiful music.

Es ist mir noch nicht gelungen, meinen Plan auszuführen.
I have not yet succeeded in carrying out my plan.

F. Ver–:

Er hatte sein Geld verloren.   Ich vermisse meine alten Freunde.
He had lost his money.   *I miss my old friends.*

Er hat den ersten Zug verpaßt (*or* versäumt).
He missed the first train.

Verstehen Sie diesen Satz?
Do you understand this sentence?

G. Zer–:

Der Wolf zerfleischte ihn.   Er wurde in Stücke zerrissen.
The wolf mangled him.   *He was torn to pieces.*

Er hatte seine Füllfeder zerbrochen.
He had broken his fountain pen.

Der Feind wird die Stadt zerstören.
The enemy will destroy the city.

H. Miß–:

Sie haben mich mißverstanden.   Man mißhandelte ihn.
You misunderstood me.   *He was mistreated.*

Es ist ihm völlig **miß**lungen.   Es **miß**fällt mir.
He failed completely.   *I am not pleased with it.*

Er **miß**deutete meine Worte.
He misconstrued my words.

Summary: The above sentences indicate that the inseparable prefixes[1]
—so-called because they are not separated from the verb—are: **be–**,
emp–, **ent–**, **er–**, **ge–**, **ver–**, **zer–**, and **miß–**.

Note:

(1) (*a*) The past participle of verbs with these prefixes usually avoids
the customary **ge**-prefix.   Common exceptions, however, are mißgebildet
and mißgestaltet (both meaning *misshapen* or *deformed*), and mißgestimmt
(*discordant*, or fig., *depressed, in ill humor*).

(*b*) Certain verbs with the prefix **miß–** admit a participial form
with **ge–**:   mißhandelt (*or* gemißhandelt), *mistreated;*   mißtraut (*or*
gemißtraut), *mistrusted.*   The prefix, however, is never written separately
from the verb.   Its accent varies—before an unaccented prefix it is
stressed (*e.g.*, mißverstehen); in most other verbs it is either not at all, or
just slightly, stressed.

(2) Verbs with inseparable prefixes accent the **root** of the verb and not
the prefix.

(3) Study very carefully the following synopsis of an inseparable verb
(**besuchen**):

PRES.:	Er besucht mich. *He is visiting me.*	PERF.:	Er hat mich besucht. *He has visited me.*
PAST:	Er besuchte mich. *He was visiting me.*	PAST PERF.:	Er hatte mich besucht. *He had visited me.*
	FUT.:	Er wird mich besuchen. *He will visit me.*	
	FUT. PERF.:	Er wird mich besucht haben. *He will have visited me.*	

---

[1] For the complete conjugation of verbs with inseparable prefixes, *cf.* § 106 of the
Appendix.

EXERCISE

A. Supply the proper forms of verbs in parentheses:

1. Der Kaufmann hatte sein Geld —— (verlieren).
2. Das Dienstmädchen hat viele Teller —— (zerbrechen).
3. Wie —— (gefallen) Ihnen der neue Hut?
4. Gestern —— [begegnen (perf.)] er mir auf der Straße ——.
5. —— (Sich erkälten) Sie —— nicht!
6. Die Großmutter wird uns morgen die Geschichte —— (erzählen).
7. Warum hat er die beiden Diener —— (entlassen)?
8. Er hatte alles —— (beschreiben), was er gesehen hatte.
9. Sie hat es schmerzlich —— (empfinden).
10. Wer hat Amerika —— (entdecken)?
11. Wem —— (gehören) die Bücher?
12. Das wilde Tier hat den armen Mann —— (zerfleischen).
13. Haben Sie mich —— (vermissen), als ich fort war?
14. Ich habe ihn —— (mißverstehen).
15. Er hat mich sehr freundlich —— (empfangen).
16. Wissen Sie, was das lange Wort —— (bedeuten)?
17. Haben Sie das Konzert —— (genießen)?
18. Ich habe den Zug —— (verpassen or versäumen).
19. Für moderne Spiegelteleskope haben Forscher Quarz —— (verwenden). Die Verwendung eines Quarzspiegels ist erforderlich (an Stelle eines solchen aus Glas), weil dieses Material gegen Temperatureinflüsse weit weniger empfindlich ist.

B. Translate:

1. Did you enjoy the meal?
2. Does she like (gefallen) these short stories?
3. He cannot describe the thief.
4. She met (begegnen) her old friend on the street.
5. He recommended that firm to them.
6. Who received (empfangen) you?
7. I have explained the third sentence.
8. We had caught cold.
9. He will discharge that dishonest servant.
10. The little children had misunderstood me.
11. The angry animal tore the man to pieces.

12. The enemy was destroying a small village.
13. Did you miss the first train?
14. I always miss my dear friends.
15. When did you lose your book?
16. How do you like (gefallen) my new hat?
17. We enjoyed the music very much.
18. She told (erzählen) me an interesting story.
19. What altitude did the flyer reach (*perf.*)?

I. Prefixes that are usually inseparable. Read the following sentences very carefully. Note the bold-faced prefix in each:

(1) **Voll–:**

Der Bildhauer hat das große Werk **voll**bracht.
The sculptor has completed the great work.

(2) **Hinter–:**

Er hat seinen Kindern viel Geld **hinter**lassen.
He left (or bequeathed) his children much money.

(3) **Wider–:**

Widersprechen Sie mir nicht!
Don't contradict me.

Summary: The above sentences indicate that **voll–, hinter–,** and **wider–** are usually inseparable when used as verbal prefixes.

Note: Verbs compounded with the prefix **voll–** are inseparable when they denote **completion**—*e.g.,* vollbríngen, vollénden, vollfúhren; but when the literal meaning is preserved, the verb is separable—*e.g.,* vóllpfropfen and vóllstopfen (*to stuff full*), vóllmachen (*to make full*), etc.

70. SEPARABLE PREFIXES

Read the following sentences very carefully. Note the bold-faced prefix and the form that a verb assumes in its various tenses:

A. (1) Heute reist er **ab.**   Er kehrt bald **zurück.**
         He is leaving today.   *He will return soon.*

     (2) Wenn er die Tür **zu**macht, wird es zu warm im Zimmer sein.
         If he closes the door, it will be too warm in the room.

Note: Observe the use of the present tense for the future in the second sentence of (1) above.

B. Er machte die Tür **zu.**
He closed the door.

C. Wann ist er **an**gekommen?   Er war früh **fort**gegangen.
When did he arrive?   *He had left early.*

D. Er wird das Buch **auf**machen.
He will open the book.

E. (1) Er will **fort**gehen.   (2) Er wünscht **fort**zugehen.
    He wants to go away.   *He desires to go away.*

F. Stehen Sie schnell **auf!**   Drehen Sie das Licht **an**!
Get up quickly.   *Turn on the light.*

Drehen Sie das Wasser **ab**!
Turn off the water.

Note:

(1) Separable prefixes[1] are separable only **in independent clauses in the present, imperfect, or imperative** (*cf.* ¶¶ **A** (1), **B,** and **F** above).

(2) In infinitives and participles, a prefix may **not** be separated from the verb (*cf.* ¶¶ **C, D,** and **E** above).

(3) The past participle of verbs with separable prefixes has **ge–** between the prefix and the verb (*cf.* ¶ **C** above).

(4) **Zu,** when required by a verb together with the infinitive, comes between prefix and verb (*cf.* ¶ **E** (2) above).

Caution: **Zu** is omitted when the infinitive depends on a modal auxiliary (*cf.* ¶ **E** (1) above).

(5) **Prefixes are not separated from their verbs at the end of dependent clauses**—*i.e.,* in dependent (or transposed) word order (*cf.* ¶ **A** (2) above).

---

[1] For the complete conjugation of verbs with separable prefixes, *cf.* § 105 of the Appendix.

(6) **Separable prefixes are accented.**

(7) Study carefully the following synopsis of a separable verb and compare it with that of an inseparable verb (*cf.* § 69):

PRES.:	Ich stehe früh **auf.**
	I rise early.
PAST:	Ich stand früh **auf.**
	I rose early.
PERF.:	Ich bin früh **auf**gestanden.
	I have risen early.
PAST PERF.:	Ich war früh **auf**gestanden.
	I had risen early.
FUT.:	Ich werde früh **auf**stehen.
	I shall rise early.
FUT. PERF.:	Ich werde früh **auf**gestanden sein.
	I shall have risen early.

G. The more common separable prefixes. Most verbal prefixes not listed in § 69 are separable. It is very important to sense the meaning of separable prefixes (which usually have the force of adverbs), since they are used to form a great number of German verbs. Some of the more common separable prefixes are listed below:[1]

ab, *off, down:* abnehmen, *to take off;* absteigen, *to come down from*

an, *at, on:* ansehen, *to look at;* anziehen, *to put on*

auf, *up:* aufstehen, *to get up*

aus, *out:* ausführen, *to carry out, execute*

bei, *by, with:* beistehen, *to render aid, assist*

ein, *into:* eintreten, *to enter*

empor, *up:* emporsteigen, *to climb up*

entzwei, *in two:* entzweibrechen, *to break in two*

entgegen, *toward:* entgegeneilen, *to hasten toward*

fort, *away:* fortgehen, *to go away*

heim, *home:* heimgehen, *to go home;* heimkommen, *to come home*

her, *hither:* herkommen, *to come hither* (toward the speaker)

hin, *thither:* hingehen, *to go there* (away from the speaker)

los, *loose:* loslassen, *to release*

mit, *with, along:* mitbringen, *to bring along*

---

[1] For the principal parts of verbs used to illustrate the use of these prefixes, *cf.* Vocabulary.

nach, *after:* nachlaufen, *to run after*
nieder, *down:* sich niederlegen, *to lie down*
vor, *before:* vorgehen, *to precede; be fast* (of a clock)
weg, *away:* weggehen, *to go away* (*cf.* **fort**gehen above)
zu, *to:* zuhören, *to listen to*
zurück, *back:* zurückkehren, *to turn* (or *come*) *back, return*
zusammen, *together:* zusammenbringen, *to bring together*

Note:

(1) **Her,** in addition to being a separable prefix, may also indicate **past time.** It is often used with the present tense where the English idiom requires the past:

Das **ist** schon lange her.
*That **was** (a) long (time) ago.*

(2) Observe the force of **hin** and **her** with verbs of motion:

Er war **dort.**	but: Er ging **dorthin.**
He was there.	*He went there.*
Er ist **hier.**	but: Er kommt **hierher.**
He is here.	*He is coming here.*

(3) **Heim,** as a separable prefix, must not be capitalized:

Er geht heim.
He goes home.

(4) It must not be assumed that the prefixes in this section **always** have the meanings given above—*e.g.,* **an**rufen, *to call up* (on the phone); **auf**schreiben, *to write down; etc.*

H. Verbs compounded with her **and** hin.

(1) Many verbs are compounded with the separable prefixes **her** and **hin: herkommen, hingehen, herausbringen, hinaufsteigen, herunterkommen, hineingehen,** *etc.*

Note: In all such compounds **her** denotes **motion toward,** whereas **hin** denotes **motion away from** the speaker or observer. Therefore, **it is highly important to determine** *the observer's position:*

Der Hund springt zum Fenster **her**ein. (The observer is inside.)
but: Der Hund springt zum Fenster **hin**ein. (The observer is outside.)
The dog jumps (in) through the window.

Here the English translation is the same for both sentences, but fails to bring out the difference of viewpoint clearly indicated by **her**ein and **hin**ein.

(2) Verbs of motion with prepositional prefixes expressing locality — *e.g.*, **aus**gehen, **auf**gehen, *etc.*—denote motion of a **general and indefinite** character, unless compounded with the prefixes **her** and **hin**. With these additional prefixes, such verbs denote motion of a **definite** nature:

(*a*) Sie geht immer gern **aus.**   but: Sie geht **hinaus.**
She always likes to go out.   *She goes out.*

In the first sentence the motion is indefinite—we do not know from what point it is directed; the sentence is a general statement of what she likes to do. In the second, the motion is definitely away from the speaker or observer.

(*b*) Die Sonne geht **auf.**   but: Er geht die Treppe **hinauf.**
The sun rises.   *He goes upstairs.*

In the first sentence a general upward direction is indicated; in the second, definite motion away from the observer.

(*c*) Das kommt oft **vor.**
That often happens.

but: Er kam aus seinem Versteck **hervor.**
He came forth from his hiding place.

In the first sentence the verb is used figuratively; in the second, it is used literally to denote motion of a definite nature toward the speaker.

(*d*) Similarly: **unter**gehen, *to set* (of the sun and moon) and **hinunter**gehen, *to go down* (*e.g.*, a mountain); **ein**kommen, *to come in*, *be collected* (*e.g.*, of money) and **herein**kommen, *to come in, enter* (*e.g.*, a room), *etc.*

EXERCISE

Translate the following sentences illustrating points that have been brought out in this section:

1. The moon was setting. He was going down the mountain (*away from the observer*).

2. Much money is coming in now. He comes slowly into the room (*toward the speaker*).

3. She never liked to go out. She went out (*away from the speaker*).

4. The sun has risen. He has gone upstairs (*away from the speaker*).

5. The cat jumped (in) through the window. (*Translate in two ways, according to the position of the observer.*)

71. DOUBTFUL PREFIXES

Read the following sentences very carefully. Note how meaning and form vary according to the type of prefix (separable or inseparable) a verb has:

A. Durch:

(1) Ich fuhr dúrch.
    I drove through.

(2) Der Blitz durchfúhr die Luft.
    Lightning pierced the air.

B. Um:

(1) Er hat sich úmgekleidet.
    He has changed clothes.

(2) Er hat seine Gedanken mit schönen Worten umkleídet.
    He has clothed his thought(s) in beautiful language.

C. Über:

(1) Er hat mich úbergesetzt.
    He ferried me across.

(2) Er hat den Satz übersétzt.
    He translated the sentence.

D. Unter:

(1) Ich schenke ihm ein Glas Wein ein.   Er hält das Glas únter.
    I give (or *pour*) *him a glass of wine.*   *He holds the glass under.*

(2) Er unterhált sich mit mir.
    He converses with me.

E. Wieder:

(1) Holen Sie das Buch wiéder!
    Go get the book.
lit.: *Get the book again.*

(2) Wiederhólen Sie den Satz!
    Repeat the sentence.

Summary: The above sentences indicate that the more common doubtful prefixes are: **durch, um, über, unter,** and **wieder.**

Note:

(1) By " doubtful " is meant separable **or** inseparable.

(2) (*a*) When used in a **literal** sense, verbs with these prefixes have the accent on the prefix and are **separable** (*cf.* ¶¶ **A** (1), **B** (1), **C** (1), **D** (1), and **E** (1) above).

(*b*) The participial prefix **ge–** of verbs so used comes between prefix and verb (*cf.* ¶¶ **B** (1) and **C** (1) above).

(3) (*a*) When used in a **figurative** sense—*i.e.*, with a derived meaning—verbs with these prefixes have the accent on the root and are **inseparable** (*cf.* ¶¶ **A** (2), **B** (2), **C** (2), **D** (2), and **E** (2) above).

(*b*) The participle of such verbs has no **ge–** prefix (*cf.* ¶¶ **B** (2) and **C** (2) above).

(4) For prefixes that are usually inseparable but sometimes separable, *cf.* also § 69 **I.**

Study very carefully the following synopsis of a verb with a doubtful prefix (*cf.* ¶ **E** above):

PRES.:	Der Hund holt den Stein wiéder.
	Der Junge wiederhólt den Satz.
PAST:	Der Hund holte den Stein wiéder.
	Der Junge wiederhólte den Satz.
PERF.:	Der Hund hat den Stein wiédergeholt.
	Der Junge hat den Satz wiederhólt.
PAST PERF.:	Der Hund hatte den Stein wiédergeholt.
	Der Junge hatte den Satz wiederhólt.
FUT.:	Der Hund wird den Stein wiéderholen.
	Der Junge wird den Satz wiederhólen.
FUT. PERF.:	Der Hund wird den Stein wiédergeholt haben.
	Der Junge wird den Satz wiederhólt haben.

Caution: Adverbs and prepositions must not be confused with verbal prefixes:

Oben (adv.) ist die Decke.   Die Decke ist **über** (prep.) uns.
Unten (adv.) ist der Fußboden.   Er ist **unter** (prep.) uns.
Vorn (adv.) ist der Tisch.   Der Tisch ist **vor** (prep.) uns.
Hinten (adv.) ist die Tafel.   Die Tafel ist **hinter** (prep.) uns.

EXERCISE

A. Form sentences with the following combinations in the present, past, perfect, past perfect, and future:

1. Schüler —— Tür —— aufmachen.
2. Freund —— in Amerika —— ankommen
3. Gepäckträger —— Koffer —— forttragen
4. Kellner —— Geld —— einstecken
5. Schule —— im September —— anfangen
6. Marie —— Treppe —— hinaufgehen
7. Onkel —— Kinder —— einladen
8. Karl —— Hut —— abnehmen
9. Fritz —— um sechs Uhr —— aufstehen
10. Er —— schnell —— sich anziehen
11. Jemand —— Treppe —— heraufkommen
12. Kind —— um sieben Uhr —— einschlafen
13. Familie —— im Oktober —— zurückkehren
14. Vater —— Plan —— ausführen.
15. Heinrich —— Bücher —— mitbringen
16. Aufklärungssatellit —— die geplante Kreisbahn um die Erde —— erreichen

B. Complete the following sentences with the proper **hin-** and **her**-words:

1. Karl (oben) sagt zu Fritz (unten): „Komm —auf!"
2. Karl (unten) sagt zu Fritz (unten): „Geh —auf!"
3. Karl (unten) sagt zu Fritz (oben): „Komm —unter!"
4. Karl (oben) sagt zu Fritz (oben): „Geh —unter!"
5. Karl (vor der Tür) sagt zu Fritz (vor der Tür): „Geh —ein!"
6. Karl (an der Tür) sagt zu Fritz (im Zimmer): „Komm —aus!"
7. Karl (im Zimmer) sagt zu Fritz (an der Tür): „Komm —ein!"

8. Karl (im Zimmer) sagt zu Fritz (im Zimmer): „Geh —aus!"
9. Der Freiballon wird bald an einem Fallschirm langsam zur Erde —absinken.

C. Translate:

1. The sun rises at six o'clock.
2. The boy gets up at half past seven.
3. The little girl had opened her German book.
4. When did your dear friends arrive?
5. The best train leaves (abfahren) at half past ten.
6. If we close the door, it will be too warm in the room.
7. Carl, open the door. Children, open the door. Mr. Smith, please open the door.
8. Do you wish (*or* desire) to go away? (*Translate first with* wollen, *then with* wünschen.)
9. While we were in the room, a large black cat jumped (in) through the window. (*Cf.* § 70 **H.**)
10. The old lady was returning home.
11. My little brother had dressed quickly.
12. The porter is carrying away my heavy trunk.
13. The sun sets at half past six.
14. Translate the thirtieth sentence.
15. Repeat the last word, please.
16. He had carried out his plan.
17. They went away at half past four.
18. We returned at ten o'clock.
19. For months they (German **man**) have been preparing the chimpanzee for his long space flight.

CHAPTER 21 The Passive Voice

72. ACTIVE AND PASSIVE FORMS

Compare the following sentences very carefully:

A. The active voice.

  (1) Present:
    Er lobt den Jungen.
    He praises (is praising or
    does praise) the boy.

  (2) Past:
    Er lobte den Jungen.
    He praised (or was praising)
    the boy.

  (3) Perfect:
    Er hat den Jungen gelobt.
    He (has) praised the boy.

  (4) Past Perfect:
    Er hatte den Jungen gelobt.
    He had praised the boy.

  (5) Future:
    Er wird den Jungen loben.
    He will praise the boy.

B. The passive voice.

  (1) Present:
    Der Junge wird von ihm
    gelobt.
    The boy is (being) praised by
    him.

  (2) Past:
    Der Junge wurde von ihm
    gelobt.
    The boy was (being) praised
    by him.

  (3) Perfect:
    Der Junge ist von ihm gelobt
    worden.
    The boy has been (or was)
    praised by him.

  (4) Past Perfect:
    Der Junge war von ihm
    gelobt **worden.**
    The boy had been praised by
    him.

  (5) Future:
    Der Junge wird von ihm
    gelobt werden.
    The boy will be praised by him.

A. The active voice (*cont.*):	**B. The passive voice** (*cont.*):
(6) Future perfect:	(6) Future perfect:
Er wird den Jungen gelobt haben.	Der Junge wird von ihm gelobt **worden** sein.
He will have praised the boy.	*The boy will have been praised by him.*

Summary: The above sentences, both German and English, indicate that the direct object of an active verb (*cf.* ¶ **A** above) becomes the subject of a passive verb (*cf.* ¶ **B** above) and that the past participle occurs in each tense of the passive voice.

Note:

(1) The auxiliary of the German passive[1] is **werden.**
(2) **Worden** follows the past participle in the three perfect tenses.
(3) The future tense ends in werden.
(4) *Sein* is always used to form the three perfect tenses.
(5) *By* becomes **von,** which is followed by the dative case.

C. Additional examples of the passive voice. Additional examples of the passive voice follow:

Er wird von dem Barbier rasiert.
or: Er läßt sich vom Barbier rasieren.[2]
He is being shaved by the barber.

Das Bild wurde von dem Maler gemalt.
The picture was being painted by the artist.

Alles ist von dem Feinde verwüstet worden.
Everything was (lit. *has been*) *laid waste by the enemy.*

Er war von seiner Tante erzogen worden.
He had been reared by his aunt.

Mein Auto wird morgen repariert werden.
My car will be repaired tomorrow.

---

[1] For a complete conjugation of the passive voice, *cf.* § 108 of the Appendix.

[2] For the use of **lassen** with a dependent infinitive as a substitute construction for the passive, *cf.* § 75 **D.**

EXERCISE

Change the following sentences from the active to the passive voice. Make sure of the principal parts of a verb and that its tense is the same in the passive:

1. Der Schüler buchstabierte das Wort.
2. Der Junge hat die Geschichte gelesen.
3. Ich rufe den Kellner.
4. Er sah mich.
5. Sie wird das Buch lesen.
6. Wir hatten das Lied gesungen.
7. Sie besucht ihn.
8. Die Mutter hatte die Tochter begleitet.
9. Karl zerriß den Anzug.
10. Der alte Mann hat einen kurzen Spaziergang gemacht.
11. Sein jüngerer Bruder wird einen neuen Hut kaufen.
12. Ich binde die Krawatte.
13. Der fleißige Schüler hat einen langen Satz geschrieben.
14. Er hat viele Briefmarken gesammelt.
15. Mein alter Freund verkaufte ein großes Haus.
16. Der Barbier hat ihn heute morgen rasiert.
17. Unser freundlicher Arzt liebt die kleinen Kinder.
18. Sie verwöhnte den kleinen Jungen.
19. Die jungen Mädchen hatten die deutsche Aufgabe geschrieben.
20. Jene faulen Jungen schrieben nichts.
21. Diese kleinen Kinder haben die roten Äpfel gegessen.
22. Ein berühmter Maler hat dieses Bild gemalt.
23. Unser reicher Onkel hat die beiden Freunde mitgebracht.
24. Sie (*They*) werden die Tür aufmachen.
25. Sie tadelte ihn immer.
26. Er wird den Regenschirm wohl gefunden haben.

73. THE ACTIONAL AND STATAL PASSIVES

Compare the following sentences carefully:

A. The actional passive:

(1) Die Tür **wird** zugemacht.
*The door **is being** closed.*

B. The statal passive:

(1) Die Tür **ist** zugemacht.
*The door **is** closed.*

A. The actional passive (*cont.*):

(2) Die Kleider **werden** gewaschen.
*The clothes **are being** washed.*

(3) Das Haus **wird** grün angestrichen.
*The house **is being** painted green.*

(4) Der Zaun **wurde** aus kleinen Brettern gemacht.
*The fence **was** (**being**) made of small boards.*

B. The statal passive (*cont.*):

(2) Die Kleider **sind** gewaschen.
*The clothes **are** washed.*

(3) Das Haus **ist** grün angestrichen.
*The house **is** painted green.*

(4) Der Zaun **war** aus kleinen Brettern gemacht.
*The fence **was** made of small boards.*

Summary:

(1) The sentences under ¶ **A** above indicate that the **actional** (**real or true**) passive (*cf.* § 72) is formed with **werden** and denotes an **action as going on at the time indicated by the tense of the verb.**

(2) The sentences under ¶ **B** above indicate that the **statal** (or **apparent**) passive—in reality no passive at all—is formed with **sein** and denotes a **state or condition that has already resulted from some previous action.**

Note: In the statal passive, the participle is often used as an **adjective**.

74. ADDITIONAL FEATURES OF THE PASSIVE

Observe the following features of the passive voice:

A. The passive to denote a *customary occurrence*. The passive voice is often used to denote a **customary occurrence**:

Die Tür **wird** um zehn Uhr **geschlossen.**
The door is closed (regularly) *at ten o'clock.*

Tee **wird** um fünf Uhr **serviert.**
Tea is served (regularly) *at five o'clock.*

B.   The use of wurde geboren **and** ist geboren.   **Wurde geboren** is used for the dead;   **ist geboren,** for the living:

Schiller **wurde** im Jahre 1759 **geboren.**   Wann **sind** Sie **geboren?**
Schiller was born in 1759.   *When were you born?*

C.   *Means* or *instrument* in the passive.   **Means** or **instrument** in the passive voice is usually expressed by **durch** with the accusative:

Die Bretter wurden **durch** einen Nagel zusammengehalten.
The boards were held together by a nail.

Der Löwe wurde **durch** einen Schuß getötet.
The lion was killed by a shot.

D.   Intransitive verbs used impersonally in the passive.   For the impersonal use of intransitive verbs in the passive, *cf.* § 62 **D.**

E.   The passive imperative.   Read the following very carefully:

(1)   Es **sei** ferner erwähnt, daß andere Gründe vorliegen.
It is furthermore to be noted that there are other reasons.

(2)   **Seien** Sie gegrüßt!   (3) Der Herr **sei** gelobt!
Be greeted.   *May the Lord be praised.*

(4) Er **werde** hereingeführt!
Have him brought in.

Note:

(1)   The passive imperative is usually formed with **sein** (*cf.* (1), (2), and (3) above), but sometimes with **werden** (*cf.* (4) above).

(2)   The present subjunctive is used for the third person (*cf.* (1), (3), and (4) above) and quite frequently as an optative subjunctive[1] (*cf.* (3) above).

(3)   **Lassen** with a dependent active infinitive is a common equivalent of the second person passive imperative:

Lassen Sie sich nicht täuschen!
Don't be deceived.

---

[1] For the optative subjunctive, *cf.* § 79 **A.**

75. SUBSTITUTE CONSTRUCTIONS FOR THE PASSIVE

Observe the following substitute constructions for the passive voice:

A. The active voice with man.   The active voice with **man** is a common equivalent of the passive voice:

Man tut das nicht.   Man muß es tun.
That is not done.   *It must be done.*

Wie buchstabiert man das Wort?   Man gab ihm die Gelegenheit.
How is that word spelled?   *He was given the opportunity.*

Note: In the last sentence **er** could not be the subject. A passive verb, however, may be used with **Gelegenheit** as subject:

Die Gelegenheit wurde ihm gegeben.
or: Ihm wurde die Gelegenheit gegeben.
The opportunity was given (to) him.

B.   Reflexive verbs.   For the common use of a reflexive verb instead of the passive, *cf.* § 61 **E.**

C.   The active infinitive preceded by zu.   After the verb **sein,** the active infinitive preceded by **zu** has passive force:

Er ist telefonisch nicht zu erreichen.
He cannot be reached by telephone.
lit.:   *He is not **to be reached** by telephone.*

D.   Lassen with a dependent infinitive.   Lassen with a dependent infinitive is equivalent to the passive:

Ich habe mir das Haar schneiden lassen.
I had my hair cut.

E.   Verbs equivalent to the English passive.   Verbs equivalent to the English passive are: **dürfen** (*to be allowed*), **sollen** (*to be said*), **heißen** (*to be called*), **ertrinken** or **ersaufen** [*to be drowned* (*i.e., to drown* used intransitively)], and **erschrecken** (*to be frightened*):

Das Kind **darf nicht** auf der Straße spielen.
*The child **is not allowed** to play on the street.*

Transitive verbs for *to drown* are ersäufen or ertränken.

Er **soll** sehr klug sein.   Wie **heißt** es?
*He **is said** to be very clever.*   *What **is** it **called?***
                              or: *What is its name?*

Er **ist ertrunken.**   Sie **erschrak.**
*He **was drowned.***   *She **was frightened.***

EXERCISE

A.   Translate:

1. A short letter is being written.   The letter is written.
2. He was reared by his grandparents.
3. The German newspaper was being printed.
4. Many beautiful houses had been built.
5. Much tea is drunk in England.
6. The window was being closed.   The window was closed.
7. As a rule German nouns are capitalized.
8. The house is being sold.   It is sold.
9. He has been bitten by a large black dog.
10. My new car is being repaired today.
11. He will be praised by his friends.
12. The door is closed at half past nine.   It is (already) closed.
13. A huge tiger was killed by the hunter.
14. The animal was killed by one shot.
15. The little boy had been spoiled by his aunt.
16. When were you born?
17. Goethe was born in 1749.
18. My brother is now getting (*or* being) shaved by the barber.
19. The mistakes will be corrected by the pupils.
20. The short sentences have been read by the whole class.
21. The door was being closed by the little girl.
22. A large house had been built by the old carpenter.
23. The notebooks will be returned (zurückgeben) tomorrow.
24. He has not been seen by his neighbors.
25. The boards are held together by a nail.
26. He is being followed.   (*Cf.* § 62 **D.**)
27. She was not helped.   (*Cf.* § 62 **D.**)
28. He was publicly thanked.   (*Cf.* § 62 **D.**)
29. Numerous biological tests with dogs and rabbits are being carried out (ausführen) in (the) world space.

B. The following sentences involve substitute constructions for the passive:

1. That is easily said.
2. Why were the children not allowed to play?
3. What was to be seen?
4. He is said to be a famous artist.
5. No bread was to be had.
6. What is your friend's name? [*Translate by* is called (heißt).]
7. That is not done (*use* man) in the United States.
8. That is a matter of course (*or* understood).
9. Those books are said to be very interesting.
10. Nothing was to be seen.
11. When was he drowned (*or* did he drown)?
12. I was frightened (*intr.*).
13. It will soon be seen who is wrong. (*Cf.* § 61 **E.**)
14. May the Lord be praised.
15. They were given (*use* German **man**) the opportunity.
16. Altitude-research rockets are used (*use* German **man** *with active voice of* verwenden) to acquire valuable information (Kenntnisse) about (the) air density and the composition of the air.

C.   Complete the following sentences:

1. Wissenschaftliche Probleme —— (*will be solved*).
2. Große Raketen —— (*are being developed*, entwickeln).
3. Ein künstlicher Satellit —— von vielen Leuten —— (*had been seen*).
4. Einige Schimpansen —— auf einen Weltraumflug —— (*have been prepared*, vorbereiten).
5. Viele Untersuchungen —— (*were being carried out*, durchführen).
6. Zahllose Himmelskörper —— (*will be discovered*).
7. Die Erforschung des Weltraumes —— (*is being continued*, fortsetzen, *wk.*).
8. Am 26. April 1962 —— von Cape Canaveral aus ein künstlicher Erdsatellit in eine elliptische Umlaufbahn (orbit) —— (*was brought*, bringen).
9. Das Weltraum-Recht muß von den auf der Erde gültigen Rechtsnormen (current legal norms *or* standards) —— (*be derived*, ableiten, *wk.*).
10. Über die Verwendung (use) von Raketen für die Weltraumforschung, für Satellitenstarts und andere Flugmissionen —— bereits zahlreiche Artikel —— (*have been written*).

CHAPTER 22 **Indirect Discourse and the Use of the Subjunctive in Independent Sentences**

76. INDIRECT STATEMENTS

A direct statement is one in which the words of a speaker or writer are quoted **directly.** Such a statement is put in quotation marks: *The boy said: " The lesson is easy."* Stated **indirectly,** this sentence would read: *The boy said that the lesson was easy.*

Note:

(1) If the introductory verb is **past,** the present tense of a direct statement in English (here *is*) becomes the past tense of the corresponding indirect statement: *The boy **said** that the lesson **was** easy.*

(2) If the introductory verb is **present,** the present tense of a direct statement in English is retained in the corresponding indirect statement: *The boy **says** that the lesson **is** easy.*
Compare the following sentences very carefully. Note the differences between direct and indirect statement:

A. Direct statement:

(1) Er sagte: „Ich **habe** Glück."
He said: "I am lucky."

B. Indirect statement:

(1) Er sagte, er **habe** (or **hätte**) Glück.
Er sagte, daß er Glück **habe** (or **hätte**).
He said that he was lucky.

A. Direct statement (*cont.*):

(2) Er sagte: „Ich **hatte**
Glück."
He said: " *I was lucky.*"
Er sagte: „Ich **habe**
Glück **gehabt.**"
He said: "*I have been
lucky.*"
Er sagte: „Ich **hatte**
Glück **gehabt.**"
He said: "*I had been lucky.*"

(3) Er sagte: „Ich **werde**
Glück **haben.**"
He said: "*I shall be lucky.*"

(4) Er sagte: „Ich **werde**
Glück **gehabt haben.**"
He said: "*I shall have
been lucky.*"

B. Indirect statement (*cont.*):

(2) Er sagte, er **habe** (or **hätte**)
Glück **gehabt.**
Er sagte, daß er Glück **gehabt habe** (or **hätte**).
*He said that he had been
lucky.*

(3) Er sagte, er **werde** (or
würde) Glück **haben.**
Er sagte, daß er Glück
haben werde (or **würde**).
*He said that he would be
lucky.*

(4) Er sagte, er **werde** (or
würde) Glück **gehabt
haben.**
*He said that he would have
been lucky.*

Quotation marks characterize direct statements, but are omitted in indirect statements.

The distinctive form of the subjunctive must be used when the subjunctive form of an indirect statement would be identical with the indicative form of the corresponding direct statement:

Er sagte: „Die Schüler kommen."
but: Er sagte, die Schüler **kämen.**
Er sagte: „Sie werden kommen."
but: Er sagte, sie **würden** kommen.
Er sagte: „Die Schüler haben gegessen."
but: Er sagte, die Schüler **hätten** gegessen.

C. Changes of tense from direct to indirect statement. The sentences under ¶¶ **A** and **B** above indicate that the following changes occur when a direct statement is put into indirect form:

(1) A present indicative becomes present **or** past subjunctive.[1]

(2) Any past tense (past, perfect, or past perfect) of the indicative becomes perfect or past perfect subjunctive.

(3) A future indicative becomes future subjunctive **or** present conditional.

Summary: These changes may be summed up graphically as follows:

DIRECT STATEMENT   INDIRECT STATEMENT

INDICATIVE	SUBJUNCTIVE
Present	Present (or Past)
Past	
Perfect	Perfect (or Past Perfect)
Past Perfect	
Future	Future (or Present Conditional)
Future Perfect	Future Perfect (or Past Conditional)

Note:

(1) The sentences under ¶¶ **A** and **B** above indicate that **a direct statement is in the indicative mood;**[2] **an indirect statement, in the subjunctive.**

(2) The indicative mood states something as a fact. It is, therefore, natural for a speaker or writer to employ this mood in making statements which he considers true.

(3) The subjunctive mood repeats a statement indirectly as the thought or opinion of **someone else,** especially if the statement is not believed. However, in modern spoken German the indicative is used more and more commonly, and is even preferred after an introductory verb in the present tense.

(4) Normal word order is used in indirect statements, provided the conjunction **daß** is omitted. If **daß** is used, the verb must stand at the end of the clause.

(5) A study of the conjugation of the subjunctive as given in §§ 102–109

---

[1] For a complete conjugation of the subjunctive, *cf.* §§ 102–109 of the Appendix.

[2] For the use of the subjunctive in independent sentences, *cf.* § 79.

of the Appendix shows that the present and past subjunctive have the same endings:

singular: **–e, –est, –e**
plural: **–en, –et, –en**

(A common exception is ich **sei** and er **sei**, present subjunctive forms of the verb sein.)

(6) The auxiliary verbs **haben, sein,** and **werden** whose present tense is used to form the perfect, past perfect, future and future perfect tenses have the same subjunctive tense endings as those listed under (5) above (including the irregular forms of the verb sein), *viz.,* **ich habe, du habest,** *etc.;* **ich sei, du seiest,** *etc.;* **ich hätte, du hättest,** *etc.;* **ich wäre, du wärest,** *etc.;* **ich werde, du werdest,** *etc.*

(7) The vowel **e** appears in all endings of the present and past subjunctive, and also in the auxiliary verb forms listed under (6) above.

(8) The stem vowel never changes in the present subjunctive, *e.g.,* **ich sehe, du sehest,** *etc.,* but present indicative **ich sehe, du siehst,** *etc.*

(9) The present subjunctive differs from the present indicative only in the second and third persons singular, and in the second person plural.

(10) The past subjunctive of a strong verb is formed by adding the endings **–e, –est, –e, –en, –et, –en** to the past indicative stem, *e.g.,* indicative **ich ging, du gingst** becomes subjunctive **ich ginge, du gingest.** The stem vowels **a, o,** and **u** take umlaut, *e.g.,* indicative **ich kam, du kamst** becomes subjunctive **ich käme, du kämest. Sollen** and **wollen,** however, do not take umlaut.

(11) Weak verbs have identical forms in the past indicative and past subjunctive. However, the past subjunctive of **haben** is **ich hätte, du hättest,** *etc.*

(12) In the future and future perfect only the second and third persons singular of the subjunctive are different from the indicative forms of the same tenses.

D. Verbs of *knowing* followed by the indicative. Verbs such as **wissen** (*to know*), **sehen** (*to see*) and phrases such as **es ist klar** (*it is clear*), **es ist nicht zu leugnen** (*it cannot be denied*) are followed by the indicative. This use of the indicative is particularly common after the **first person** present of such verbs as **wissen.** Verbs of *knowing* emphasize, support, or endorse the truth of what follows—thus giving to the sentence as a whole the force of a direct statement,—and the indicative, as the mood of **fact,** is used to express this certainty:

> Wir wissen alle, daß Sie recht **haben.**
> *We all know that you are right.*
>
> Ich weiß, daß er morgen **abfährt.**
> *I know that he will leave tomorrow.*
>
> Es ist nicht zu leugnen, daß der Blitz manchmal **einschlägt.**
> *It cannot be denied that lightning often strikes.*

Note: Similarly, verbs of *saying*—especially in the present tense and particularly in the first person—are frequently followed by the indicative:

> Ich sage Ihnen, daß der Mann unschuldig **ist.**
> *I tell you that the man is innocent.*
>
> Ich sage Ihnen nochmals, daß ich furchtbar müde **bin.**
> *I tell you again (or repeat) that I am terribly tired.*

E.   Verbs that introduce indirect statements.   Indirect statements are **introduced** by verbs of **saying, thinking,** and **feeling** such as: **sagen** (*to say, tell*), **erzählen** (*to tell, relate*), **schreiben** (*to write*), **antworten** (*to answer*), **berichten** (*to report*), and **fürchten** (*to fear*):

> Er sagte, er würde mich um acht Uhr besuchen.
> *He said (that) he would call on me at eight o'clock.*
>
> Sie schrieb mir, die ganze Familie hätte einen Ausflug ins Gebirge gemacht.
> *She wrote me that the whole family had taken a trip to the mountains.*
>
> Die Zeitung berichtete, daß ein berühmter europäischer Schauspieler angekommen wäre.
> *The newspaper reported that a famous European actor had arrived.*

Note: Such an introductory verb is usually in the **indicative.**

F.   Change of pronouns and possessives from direct to indirect statement.   In changing sentences from the direct to the indirect form, care must be taken to change not only the verb but also pronouns and possessives.   Note particularly changes in **reflexive** forms:

> Karl sagte: „**Ich** habe **mein** Buch verloren."
> INDIR.: Karl sagte, **er** hätte **sein** Buch verloren.
> *Carl said (that) he had lost his book.*

Sie schrieb mir: „**Ich** bin bei **meiner** Tante."
INDIR.: Sie schrieb mir, **sie** wäre bei **ihrer** Tante.
She wrote me that she was at her aunt's house.

Er sagte zu mir: „**Ich** kann es **mir** nicht leisten."
INDIR.: Er sagte mir, **er** könnte es **sich** nicht leisten.
He told me that he could not afford it.

Note: **Zu** after **sagen** is dropped in an indirect statement.

EXERCISE

A. Rewrite the following sentences as indirect statements both with and without **daß**:[1]

1. Er sagte: „Ich war gestern im Theater. Mein Freund Fritz blieb zu Hause."
2. Sie schrieb mir: „Wir werden morgen abfahren."
3. Die Zeitung berichtete: „Die Flieger sind heute angekommen."
4. Die Kinder sagten: „Die Geschichte gefällt uns."
5. Der Lehrer antwortete: „Ich werde noch eine Geschichte vorlesen."
6. Sie erzählte uns: „Ich habe einen neuen Hut gekauft. Meine Mutter hat mir das Geld dazu gegeben."
7. Mein Freund schrieb mir: „Ich war vorigen Monat sehr beschäftigt."
8. Karl sagte: „Es ist heute sehr heiß."
9. Fritz antwortete: „Es war letzte Woche noch heißer."
10. Er schrieb uns: „Ich hatte kein Glück."
11. Wir antworteten: „Es wird Ihnen das nächste Mal gelingen."
12. Die Zeitung berichtete: „Ein großes Unglück ist geschehen."
13. Er schrieb mir: „Das Gewitter war um acht Uhr am heftigsten."
14. Ich sagte zu ihm: „Ich werde nächsten Sommer eine Reise machen."
15. Sie erzählte mir: „Der Dieb hat mein Geld gestohlen. Er sitzt aber jetzt im Gefängnis."

---

[1] For the **passive** subjunctive, *cf.* § 108 of the Appendix. For practice rewrite in the passive and introduce by **er sagte** sentences at the end of § 72. Changes of tense are to be made in accordance with rules stated in ¶ **C** above.

16. Der Vater telefonierte: „Ich habe den Zug versäumt. Ich komme erst morgen an."
17. Er sagte: „Ich habe kein Geld bei mir."
18. Sie sagte zu mir: „Ich interessiere mich für die Kunst."
19. Er schrieb mir: „Der Plan ist mir noch nicht gelungen."
20. Marie erzählte uns: „Die Mutter hat mir zu Weihnachten ein schönes Bilderbuch gegeben."
21. Er sagte zu mir: „Ich habe mich an alles gewöhnt."
22. Unsere Freunde schrieben uns: „Wir amüsieren uns herrlich auf dem Lande."

B. Complete the following sentences with the proper verb form:

1. Der Redner im wissenschaftlichen Verein sagte, daß Tonbandgeräte in einer Raumkapsel Meldungen an die Bodenbeobachtungsstation —— (*had played back*, abspielen).
2. Die Zeitung berichtete, daß Experimente mit Versuchstieren in höheren Luftschichten von großer Bedeutung —— (*would be*).
3. Mein Freund schrieb mir, daß die Flieger mehrere Stunden in der Atmosphäre —— (*had remained*).

C. Translate the following sentences, paying particular attention to tenses and mood:

1. My friend wrote me that he had seen the high buildings of our beautiful city.
2. She says that it is too warm in the room.
3. He said that he would write the simple sentence on the board.
4. They told us that the famous men would arrive tomorrow.
5. The old lady said that her friends had been in the country.
6. Her younger brother said that he preferred to play ball.
7. She wrote me that she took a long walk every day.
8. He said that he had been there day before yesterday.
9. They said that they would answer these easy questions.
10. She told me that she had visited those beautiful German villages.
11. He said that the little boys were not allowed to play on the street.
12. The pupil said that he usually studied at home.
13. His sister wrote him that she would arrive day after tomorrow.

14. The newspaper reported that the President was ill.
15. I heard that he had caught cold recently.
16. He said that he was looking forward with pleasure to the trip.
17. I told him that I could not afford it.
18. He said that his father had given him a beautiful fountain pen for Christmas.
19. Mother telephoned me that my cousin (*masc.*) had just left.
20. She wrote us that she was recovering from a severe illness.
21. The hotelkeeper said that he had sold much beer. He added that he had only two bottles left.
22. He said that it reminded him of old times.
23. I read recently in a scientific book that the " canals " on the planet Mars are huge clefts in oceans of ice.
24. A technician told me the space-flight experiments with mice, rats, rabbits and chimpanzees had been successful.
25. He also told me that air-traffic laws would regulate space flights in the future.

77. INDIRECT QUESTIONS

Compare the following sentences very carefully:

A. Direct question:

(1) Ich fragte ihn: „Was **haben Sie** in der Hand?"
I asked him: "What have you in your hand?"

(2) Ich fragte ihn: „Wo **waren Sie** heute morgen?"
I asked him: "Where were you this morning?"

(3) Ich fragte ihn: „**Haben** die Leute das **verstanden?**"
I asked him: "Did the people understand that?"

B. Indirect question:

(1) Ich fragte ihn, was **er** in der Hand **habe** (or **hätte**).
I asked him what he had in his hand.

(2) Ich fragte ihn, wo **er** heute morgen **gewesen sei** (or **gewesen wäre**).
I asked him where he had been this morning.

(3) Ich fragte ihn, ob die Leute das **verstanden hätten.**
I asked him whether the people had understood that.

A. Direct question (*cont.*):

(4) Ich fragte ihn: „**Werden**
Ihre Freunde **mitkommen?**"
*I asked him: "Will your
friends come along?"*

B. Indirect question (*cont.*):

(4) Ich fragte ihn, ob seine
Freunde **mitkommen wür-
den.**
*I asked him whether his
friends would come along.*

Summary: The above sentences indicate that **direct questions are in
the indicative mood;**[1] **indirect questions, in the subjunctive.**[2]

Note:

(1) Direct questions have question and quotation marks; indirect
questions have neither.

(2) The same rules for changes of tense apply to indirect questions as
to indirect statements (*cf.* § 76).

(3) An indirect question is a **dependent** clause. The verb must
therefore come **at the end of the clause.**

(4) (*a*) If no interrogative word (such as **wann?, wo?, warum?, was?,
etc.**) occurs in a direct question, the subordinating conjunction **ob**
(*whether* or *if*) introduces the corresponding indirect question: „War sie
krank?" Er fragte, **ob** sie krank gewesen wäre.

(*b*) If an interrogative word does occur in a direct question, it is
retained in the corresponding indirect question and functions there as a
subordinating conjunction: „**Wo** war sie gestern?" Er fragte, **wo** sie
gestern gewesen wäre.

(5) The indicative is used in indirect questions after a present tense or
an imperative:

Er fragt, ob sie noch **schläft.**
He asks whether she is still asleep.

Erzählen Sie mir, was geschehen **ist!**
Tell me what happened.

---

[1] For the use of the subjunctive in independent sentences, *cf.* § 79.
[2] For exceptions to this rule, *cf.* **Note** (5) below.

(6) In both German and English, a question mark comes at the end of a sentence consisting of a direct and an indirect question:

Wissen Sie, ob das Kind sich vor der Katze fürchtet?
Do you know whether the child is afraid of the cat?

Strictly speaking, however, the question mark applies only to the first part (Wissen Sie?), since the **ob**-clause is an **indirect** question.

EXERCISE

A. Rewrite the following as indirect questions after: (1) Er fragte den Mann; (2) Er fragte die Männer; and (3) Er fragte mich:

1. „Woher haben Sie so viel Geld?"
2. „Wann sind Sie geboren?"
3. „Haben Sie schon gegessen?"
4. „Warum antworten Sie nicht auf die Frage?"
5. „Wo waren Sie gestern?"
6. „Waren Sie auf dem Lande?"
7. „Werden Sie nächstes Jahr nach Deutschland reisen?"
8. „Werden Ihre Freunde Sie heute besuchen?"
9. „Freuen Sie sich auf den Besuch?"
10. „Haben Sie sich amüsiert?"
11. „Was haben Sie getan?"
12. „In was für einem Haus wohnen Sie?"
13. „Wo spielten Ihre Kinder gestern?"
14. „Haben Sie Geld bei sich?"
15. „Woher wissen Sie das denn eigentlich?"
16. „Was wollen Sie damit sagen?"
17. „Haben Sie sich erkältet?"
18. „Worüber ärgern Sie sich so sehr?"
19. „Haben Sie sich weh getan?"
20. „Wofür interessieren Sie sich?"

B. Complete the following sentences:

1. Ich fragte den Wissenschaftler, —— (*whether*) eine direkte Beobachtung des Planeten Venus möglich —— (*were*).
2. Wir fragten den Astronauten, —— (*when*) der Aufklärungssatellit die geplante Kreisbahn um die Erde —— (*had reached*).

3. Wir fragten ihn auch, —— (*whether*) das Ballon-Spiegelteleskop beim schnellen Aufstieg des Ballons starken Temperaturschwankungen —— (*had been exposed to*).

C. Translate the following sentences, considering carefully the proper tense and mood:

1. He asked me how I was.
2. She asked him whether he had seen her little brown dog.
3. They asked her when she would visit them.
4. He asked me whether I was hungry.
5. I asked him when he was born.
6. She asked me whether I had understood the German sentences.
7. He asked them whether they had a house in the country.
8. I asked the little boys whether they had brought their books (along).
9. She asked him what time it was.
10. He asked her whether she had a watch.
11. He asked me why I had not written him a letter. (*Translate* not a *by* kein.)
12. I asked him how he knew that.
13. She asked him whether he was interested in music.
14. We asked the children whether they had hurt themselves.
15. They asked us whether we had caught cold.
16. He asked me why I was bothering about that.
17. She asked me whether I had had a good time.
18. I asked him why he didn't answer my question.
19. She asked me where I had seen him.
20. He asked me what I was interested in.
21. They didn't know what it was all about.
22. The technician asked us whether we had learned many new technical expressions.
23. We asked him where we could buy a good English-German technical dictionary.
24. He asked us how much money we wanted to pay for such a book.
25. The professor asked the students whether they had read about the manned flight into the ionosphere (die Ionosphäre).

78. INDIRECT COMMANDS

Compare the following sentences very carefully:

A. Direct command:

  (1) Er sagte zu mir: „Stehen
    Sie auf!"
    He said to me: "Get up!"

  (2) Ich sagte zu ihm: „**Vergessen**
    Sie das nicht!"
    I said to him: " Don't forget
    that."

  (3) Wir sagten zu ihr: „**Lesen**
    Sie das deutsche Buch!"
    We said to her: " Read the
    German book."

B. Indirect command:

  (1) Er sagte mir, ich **solle** (or
    sollte) **aufstehen.**
  or: Er sagte mir, daß ich **auf-**
    stehen solle (or **sollte**).
    He told me to get up.
  or: *He told me that I should get*
    up.

  (2) Ich sagte ihm, er **solle** (or
    sollte) das nicht **vergessen.**
  or: Ich sagte ihm, daß er das
    nicht **vergessen solle** (or
    sollte).
    I told him not to forget that.
  or: *I told him that he should not*
    forget that.

  (3) Wir sagten ihr, sie **solle** (or
    sollte) das deutsche Buch
    lesen.
  or: Wir sagten ihr, daß sie das
    deutsche Buch **lesen solle**
    (or **sollte**).
    We told her to read the
    German book.
  or: *We told her that she should*
    read the German book.

Summary: The above sentences indicate that **direct commands are
in the imperative mood; indirect commands, in the subjunctive.**

Note:

(1) Direct commands (like direct statements and direct questions) are
enclosed in quotation marks; indirect commands are not.

(2) Direct commands in German are punctuated with an exclamation
mark; indirect commands, with a period.

(3) **Zu** is used with **sagen** in direct commands (and statements); it is omitted in indirect commands (and statements).

(4) An indirect command is customarily expressed by the present or imperfect subjunctive of **sollen** and a dependent present infinitive.

(5) **The English infinitive** often represents an indirect command:

He told me to come.

also: *He told me that I should come.*

Er sagte mir, daß ich kommen sollte.

Caution: The German infinitive cannot be used in this construction, except when it depends on such a form as **sollte**.

EXERCISE

A. Rewrite as indirect commands according to the model:

DIRECT: Ich sagte zu dem kleinen Jungen: „Sei fleißig!"

INDIRECT: Ich sagte dem kleinen Jungen, er solle (or sollte) fleißig sein.

or: Ich sagte dem kleinen Jungen, daß er fleißig sein solle (or sollte).

1. Sie sagte zu mir: „Kommen Sie morgen wieder!"
2. Der Arzt sagte zu ihm: „Rauchen Sie nicht!"
3. Ich sagte zu den Kindern: „Geht schnell!"
4. Wir sagten zu ihnen: „Bleibt hier!"
5. Der Lehrer sagte zu uns: „Lernen Sie das deutsche Gedicht auswendig!"
6. Er sagte zu mir: „Schreiben Sie den zweiten Satz an die Tafel!"
7. Er sagte zu dem Schüler: „Setze dich!"
8. Er sagte zu mir: „Setzen Sie sich!"
9. Die Mutter sagte zu mir: „Kaufe für einen Dollar Briefmarken!"
10. Mein Freund telegrafierte mir: „Fahre mit dem ersten Schnellzug!"
11. Marie schrieb ihrer Freundin: „Komme bald aufs Land!"
12. Sie sagte zu ihr: „Amüsiere dich!"
13. Fritz schrieb mir: „Amüsiere dich!"
14. Herr Wagner schrieb uns: „Amüsieren Sie sich!"

B.   Complete the following sentences:

1. Ich sagte dem Vater, daß er mir —— (*should buy a model airplane*).
2. Der Lehrer sagte uns, daß wir —— (*should learn new technical expressions*).
3. Die Mutter sagte mir, daß ich —— (*should attend scientific lectures*).

C.   Translate:

1. He told me to sit down.
2. I told her to be industrious.
3. She told him to learn the poem by heart.
4. I told him to be careful.
5. The teacher told us to write the short sentences on the board.
6. He told me to copy the exercise five times.
7. She told him not to bother about it.
8. He told me to (tele)phone him at half past three.
9. Her mother told her to buy a dollar's worth of sugar.
10. We told them to have a good time.
11. Father telegraphed me to come at once.
12. Mother told my little brother to behave (sich anständig benehmen).
13. I told my friend to meet (treffen) me at the (auf dem) station.
14. He told me not to hurry.
15. My best friends told me again and again to study foreign languages and science.   I am now studying biology.
16. Some students in this class cannot read German, so the teacher told me to read (vorlesen) them my translation of an interesting scientific article which I had translated into English.
17. I told the teacher to let me know if I might help out in this way later on.

D.   The following connected passages involve indirect statements, questions, and commands:

(1)   Rewrite in **indirect** discourse:

Mein Freund schrieb mir: „Komme bald zu mir! Hier[1] auf dem Lande ist allerlei Schönes zu sehen.   Hast Du Dich noch nicht entschlos-

---

[1] Change **hier** to **dort** in the indirect statement.

sen, diese kurze Reise zu machen? Du kannst Dich darauf verlassen, daß es der Mühe wert ist, hierher zu kommen.[1] Hier[2] kannst Du es Dir bequem machen, alte Kleider tragen, jeden Tag fischen oder rudern gehen und nachts unter freiem Himmel schlafen. Aus welchem Grunde hast Du mir noch gar keinen Brief geschrieben? Telegrafiere mir sogleich, ob Du nächste Woche reisen kannst. Ich werde Dich vom Bahnhof abholen."

(2) Rewrite in **direct** discourse:

Herr Wagner sagte mir, er hätte letztes Jahr eine Reise nach Deutschland gemacht. Dort hätte er die schönen Weinberge und die alten Schlösser am Rhein gesehen, mehrere Wochen in Süddeutschland verbracht und endlich eine Fußtour durch den Harz gemacht. Er würde sich sehr freuen, nächsten Sommer mit mir nach Europa zu fahren. Ich sollte ihm sagen, ob ich lieber erster oder zweiter Klasse reiste. Ein paar Wochen vor der Abreise würde er die Fahrkarten lösen. Ich sollte einen leichten Mantel mitbringen, denn auch während der Sommermonate wäre es ziemlich kühl auf dem Wasser. Er fragte mich, mit welchem Schiff ich reisen möchte.

If additional exercises are needed, use sentences in previous chapters introduced by **Er sagte, daß** . . . , **Ich fragte ihn, ob** (**wann, warum**) . . . , **Er sagte mir, daß ich,** *etc.* (in an indirect command), according to the sense of the sentence. See also ¶ **D** § 66.

79. THE USE OF THE SUBJUNCTIVE IN INDEPENDENT SENTENCES

The subjunctive may also be used in independent sentences to express **wish, command, possibility, doubt,** *etc.*

A. The subjunctive in wishes. Read the following sentences very carefully:

(1) Es **lebe** die Freiheit!   Gott **gebe** es!
May freedom live.   *May God grant it.*

Seine Seele **ruhe** in Frieden!
May his soul rest in peace.

Möge das neue Jahr Ihnen viel Glück bringen!
May the new year bring you much good fortune.

---

[1] Change **hierher zu kommen** to **dorthin zu gehen** in the indirect statement.
[2] Change **hier** to **dort** in the indirect statement.

(2) **Wäre** ich nur reich!   **Hätte** er doch Geduld!

or: Wenn ich nur reich **wäre**!   or: Wenn er doch Geduld **hätte**!

Would that I were rich.   *Would that he had patience.*

or: *If I were only rich!*   or: *If he only had patience!*

(3) **Wäre** er nur hier **gewesen**!

or: Wenn er nur hier **gewesen wäre**!

Would that he had been here.

or: *If he had only been here!*

Hätte sie mir doch **geschrieben**!

or: Wenn sie mir doch **geschrieben hätte**!

Would that she had written me.

or: *If she had only written me!*

Summary: The above sentences indicate that the subjunctive may be used to express a **wish**. This is known as the " optative subjunctive."

Note:

(1) (*a*) The **present subjunctive** is used—chiefly in set phrases, prayers, and formal greetings—to express a wish that may be fulfilled. The present subjunctive of **mögen** with a dependent infinitive is also used in this construction (*cf.* last sentence under ¶ **A** (1) above).

(*b*) In addition to the examples given under ¶ **A** (1) above may be added the common execration:

Hol' ihn der Teufel (or Kuckuck)!

May the devil take him!

(2) (*a*) The **past subjunctive** is used to express a wish that is equivalent to a present contrary-to-fact condition[1] of which the conclusion is to be supplied (*cf.* ¶ **A** (2) above). This tense is used both when a wish is incapable and when it is capable of fulfillment—although the idea of unreality may be obvious at the time a wish is expressed:

Wenn ich nur Flügel **hätte**!   Wenn der Zug nur **käme**!

or: **Hätte** ich nur Flügel!   or: **Käme** der Zug nur!

If I only had wings!   *If only the train would come!*

(*b*) The past subjunctive may indicate **impatience** on the part of the speaker (*cf.* second sentence under (2) (*a*) of this **Note**).

---

[1] For a detailed explanation of contrary-to-fact conditions, *cf.* ¶¶ **A** and **B** of § 82.

(*c*) The past subjunctive (used in wishes and otherwise) often conveys the additional idea of **modesty** on the part of the speaker, when a statement concerns him:

> Möge es ihm gelingen! ⎫
> *May he succeed!*   ⎬ PRESENT
>
> **Möchte** es mir nur bald gelingen! ⎫
> **Gelänge** es mir nur bald!   ⎬
> but: Wenn es mir nur bald **gelänge**! ⎬ PAST
> *May I succeed soon!*   ⎭

(3) The **past perfect subjunctive** is used to express a wish that is equivalent to a past contrary-to-fact condition[1] of which the conclusion is to be supplied (*cf.* ¶ **A** (3) above).

(4) **Doch** or **nur** usually accompanies the past or past perfect subjunctive, when used to express a wish.

B.   The subjunctive in commands.   Read the following sentences very carefully:

(1) **Lesen** wir jetzt weiter!   **Fangen** wir jetzt **an**!
     Let us now continue reading.   *Let us begin now.*

     Reden wir nicht mehr davon!   **Vergessen** wir das nicht!
     Let us talk no more about it.   *Let us not forget that.*

(2) „Edel **sei** der Mensch.“[2]   Er **komme**! (or **Komme** er!)
     Let man be noble.   *Let him come.*

             Jeder **kehre** vor seiner Tür!
             Mind your own business.
lit.:   *Let each one sweep before his (own) door.*

             Man **beachte** die Vorschriften!
             Let everybody (lit. *one*) *observe the rules.*

Summary: The above sentences indicate that the subjunctive may be used to express a **command.**

Note:

(1) Since the imperative forms of a verb are used only for the second person (singular and plural), commands in the first and third persons

---

[1] For a detailed explanation of contrary-to-fact conditions, *cf.* ¶¶ **A** and **B** of § 82.
[2] This is a quotation from Goethe.

must be expressed otherwise. The **present subjunctive** supplies these missing forms of the imperative.

(*a*) The first person plural regularly has the inverted word order and is, therefore, easily distinguished from the indicative (*cf.* ¶ **B** (1) above and also **Note** under ¶ **B** of § 87).

(*b*) The third person singular of the present subjunctive, when used as an imperative, may have either the normal or the inverted word order (*cf.* ¶ **B** (2) above): Er gehe (or Gehe er)!

(*c*) The third person plural is less common than the third singular in this construction, since the form is the same as that of the indicative:

Alle **setzen** sich!

(*Let*) *all be seated.*

(2) The imperative forms of **lassen** with the present infinitive are very often used instead of the subjunctive forms of a simple verb:

Laß (laßt or **lassen Sie)** uns gehen!

Let us go.

Laß (laßt or **lassen Sie)** ihn kommen!

Let him come.

C. The subjunctive to express *possibility* and *doubt*.   Read the following sentences very carefully:

(1) Wie **wäre** es mit einer Partie Schach?
     How would you like to play a game of chess?
colloq.:   *How about a game of chess?*

(2) **Wäre** es möglich, daß Fritz das Schachbrett **verlegt hätte**?
     Is it possible that Fred misplaced the chessboard?

(3) Nicht daß ich **wüßte.**   (4) Das **wäre** schade!
     Not that I am aware of.   *That would be a pity.*

(5) Wo **könnte** (or **dürfte**) es wohl sein?
     Where might it possibly be?

Summary: The above sentences indicate that the past and past perfect subjunctives are often used to express **possibility, uncertainty,** or **doubt.**

Note:

(1) The subjunctive is used for this purpose especially in **modest, mild, polite,** or **diplomatic expressions of opinion** and in **questions.**

(2) The **modal auxiliaries** are frequently employed in this same sense (*cf.* ¶ **C** (5) above and also **Note** (3) (*b*) of § 87 **E**):

> Sie **dürften** sich geirrt haben.
> *You may possibly have made a mistake.*

> Das **sollte** ich doch meinen!
> *I should think so!*

> **Dürfte** ich Sie um Ihr Opernglas bitten?
> *Might I ask you for your opera glass?*

> Es **möchte** wohl besser sein, wenn wir es unterließen.
> *It would probably be better if we did not do it.*

D.   Additional uses of the subjunctive in independent sentences. For additional uses of the subjunctive in independent sentences, *cf.* Chapter XXIV on Modal Auxiliaries.

80. THE USE OF THE SUBJUNCTIVE IN CONCESSIVE CLAUSES

Read the following sentences very carefully:

> **A.   Sei** die Gefahr auch noch so groß, ich werde mich nicht fürchten.
> or: Die Gefahr **sei** auch noch so groß, ich werde mich nicht fürchten.
> *Be the danger ever so great, I shall not be afraid.*
> or: *Although the danger be ever so great, I shall not be afraid.*

> **B.   Sei** es früh, **sei** es spät, er ist immer auf seinem Posten.
> *(Be it) early or (be it) late, he is always at his post.*

Summary: The above sentences indicate that the subjunctive may be used to express **concession.**

Note:

(1) The inverted word order is not used in a clause following one of concessive force, since the two clauses were originally independent (*cf.* § 51).

(2) Concession may be expressed in several ways without the subjunctive—*e.g.*, the first clause of ¶ **A** above might also have read:

Mag die Gefahr auch noch so groß sein, . . .
Die Gefahr mag auch noch so groß sein, . . .
Ist die Gefahr auch noch so groß, . . .

EXERCISE

The following sentences for translation involve the uses of the subjunctive which have been explained in §§ 79–80:

1. If she only had patience!
2. If they only had been here!
3. Let us work now.
4. Let him enter.
5. Let's take a walk.
6. " Did he really do that (*indic.*)? "   " Not that I am aware of."
7. Where can he possibly be?
8. Is it possible that he did such a thing?
9. That would be stupid indeed.
10. It might perhaps be in order.
11. Can he have said that?
12. That would be a pity.
13. Be the lesson ever so difficult, the pupils will write it.
14. Be it early or be it late, she is always working.
15. Might I ask you for the book?
16. Where might my book (possibly) be?
17. Is it possible that my little brother misplaced it?
18. Let us not forget his advice.
19. If you had only studied your lesson!
20. If I had only worked harder!
21. Be the danger ever so great, more experiments will be carried out in (the) world space.

CHAPTER 23 Conditional Sentences

8I. CONDITIONAL SENTENCES WITH THE INDICATIVE

Read the following sentences very carefully. Note mood and word order:

A. Wenn er Zeit **hat,** (so) **wird** er mich **besuchen.** ⎫
    Hat er Zeit, so **wird** er mich **besuchen.**   ⎬
    Er **wird** mich **besuchen,** wenn er Zeit **hat.**   ⎭
    If he has time, he will visit me.
or: *He will visit me if he has time.*

B. Wenn es stark **regnet,** (so) **wird** er zu Hause **bleiben.** ⎫
    Regnet es stark, so **wird** er zu Hause **bleiben.**   ⎬
    Er **wird** zu Hause **bleiben,** wenn es stark **regnet.** ⎭
    If it rains hard, he will stay at home.
or: *He will stay at home if it rains hard.*

Summary: The above sentences indicate that the indicative mood is used in both clauses of a conditional sentence, if nothing in the *if*-clause is contrary to fact.

As to the various types of word order in the illustrative sentences, see § 65 **Note** (1) and § 66 **B.**

Note:

(1) The use of **so** (not to be translated but felt as a weak suppressed *then*) may introduce a main clause, provided an *if*-clause precedes; **so** is usually used if **wenn** is omitted in the preceding clause. **So** in such sentences serves to sum up the thought of a preceding clause. It is required in short sentences having the inverted word order in both main and dependent clauses, provided the meaning is not clear otherwise:

    Muß er, so kommt er.
    If he has to, he will come.

(2) **So** as connective is used chiefly after clauses of **condition** (*cf.* first sentences under ¶¶ **A** and **B** above) or **concession**:

Wenn er auch viel geleistet hat, so ist er doch nicht zufrieden.
Even though he has accomplished much, he is nevertheless not satisfied.

82. CONTRARY-TO-FACT CONDITIONS

Conditions that are **contrary to fact** (*i.e.*, not true) may refer both to the **present** and to the **past**:

A. Present contrary-to-fact conditions. Read the following sentences very carefully. Note mood and tense:

(1) Wenn er das Geld **hätte,** (so) **würde** er es mir **geben.** ⎞
    Wenn er das Geld **hätte,** (so) **gäbe** er es mir. ⎟
    Hätte er das Geld, so **würde** er es mir **geben.** ⎟
    Hätte er das Geld, so **gäbe** er es mir. ⎠
    If he had the money, he would give it to me.

(2) Wenn er hier **wäre,** (so) **würde** er ins Theater **gehen.** ⎞
    Wenn er hier **wäre,** (so) **ginge** er ins Theater. ⎟
    Wäre er hier, so **würde** er ins Theater **gehen.** ⎟
    Wäre er hier, so **ginge** er ins Theater. ⎠
    If he were here, he would go to the theater.

Summary: The above sentences indicate that the *if*-clauses in these examples are **contrary to fact;** thus it is clear from (1) that *he does not have the money* and from (2), that *he is not here.*

Note:

(1) These *if*-clauses **refer to present time, although both German and English use a past tense of the verb.**

(2) If a condition is contrary to fact in present time, the past subjunctive[1] **must** be used in the *if*-clause. Either the present conditional or the past subjunctive may be used in the main clause. (The present conditional is more common in modern spoken German.) This is graphically expressed as follows:

---

[1] For a complete conjugation of the subjunctive, *cf.* §§ 102–109 of the Appendix.

<table>
<tr><td>IF-CLAUSE</td><td>MAIN CLAUSE</td></tr>
<tr><td>PAST SUBJUNCTIVE</td><td>PRESENT CONDITIONAL</td></tr>
<tr><td></td><td>OR</td></tr>
<tr><td></td><td>PAST SUBJUNCTIVE</td></tr>
</table>

B.   Past contrary-to-fact conditions.   Read the following sentences very carefully.   Note mood and tense:

(1)   Wenn er das Geld **gehabt hätte,** (so) **hätte** er es mir **gegeben.**
Wenn er das Geld **gehabt hätte,** (so) **würde** er es mir **gegeben haben.**
Hätte er das Geld **gehabt,** so **hätte** er es mir **gegeben.**
Hätte er das Geld **gehabt,** so **würde** er es mir **gegeben haben.**
If he had had the money, he would have given it to me.

(2)   Wenn er hier **gewesen wäre,** (so) **wäre** er ins Theater **gegangen.**
Wenn er hier **gewesen wäre,** (so) **würde** er ins Theater **gegangen sein.**
Wäre er hier **gewesen,** so **wäre** er ins Theater **gegangen.**
Wäre er hier **gewesen,** so **würde** er ins Theater **gegangen sein.**
If he had been here, he would have gone to the theater.

Summary: The above sentences indicate that the *if*-clauses in these examples are contrary to fact; thus it is clear from ¶ **B** (1) that *he did not have the money* and from ¶ **B** (2) that *he was not here.*

Note:

(1)   These *if*-clauses **refer to past time.**   Both German and English use the past perfect tense of the verb.

(2)   If a condition is contrary to fact in the past time, the past perfect subjunctive[1] **must** be used in the *if*-clause.   Either the past perfect subjunctive or the past conditional may be used in the main clause.   This is graphically expressed as follows:

<table>
<tr><td>IF-CLAUSE</td><td>MAIN CLAUSE</td></tr>
<tr><td>PAST PERFECT SUBJUNCTIVE</td><td>PAST PERFECT SUBJUNCTIVE</td></tr>
<tr><td></td><td>OR</td></tr>
<tr><td></td><td>PAST CONDITIONAL</td></tr>
</table>

---

[1] For a complete conjugation of the subjunctive, *cf.* §§ 102–109 of the Appendix.

C. Mixed contrary-to-fact conditions. Read the following sentence very carefully:

> Wenn Sie die Tür nicht **zugemacht hätten,** (so) **wäre** es jetzt nicht so warm im Zimmer.
> *If you had not closed the door, it would not be so warm in the room now.*

Summary: The above sentence indicates that it is possible to have two kinds of contrary-to-fact conditions in one sentence. Note that **zugemacht hätten** is past perfect because it refers to the past; **wäre** is past because it refers to the present.

D. Als ob clauses with implied contrary-to-fact ideas.

(1) Sie kleidet sich, **als ob** sie reich **wäre.**
Sie kleidet sich, **als wäre** sie reich.
She dresses as if she were rich.

(2) Sie taten, **als ob** sie es nicht **verstanden hätten.**
Sie taten, **als hätten** sie es nicht **verstanden.**
They acted as if they had not understood it.

Summary: The above sentences indicate that the subjunctive mood is often used in clauses introduced by **als ob.** Note that the past subjunctive denotes present time (*cf.* (1) above) and the past perfect subjunctive, past time (*cf.* (2) above). If **als ob** is shortened to **als,** the inverted word order is required (*cf.* alternative sentences under (1) and (2) above).

E. Hätte können **and** hätte sollen **indicating past contrary-to-fact conditions.**

(1) Er **hätte** es **tun können,** wenn er das Geld gehabt hätte.
He could have done it, if he had had the money.

(2) Ich **hätte** nach Hause **gehen sollen.**
I should have gone home.

(3) Wenn er es **hätte tun können,** (so) hätte er es mir gesagt.
If he could have done it, he would have told me so.

Summary: The above sentences indicate that constructions with *could have* and *should have* (with a dependent infinitive) require the subjunctive, since contrary-to-fact ideas are involved. Note that the past perfect subjunctive is used, since there is reference to the past. *Could have* becomes **hätte ...** (dependent infinitive) **können,** which is the past perfect subjunctive (*cf.* 1 and 3 above). *Should have* becomes **hätte ...** (dependent infinitive) **sollen,** which is past perfect subjunctive (*cf.* 2 above). Observe the position of **hätte** necessitated by a double infinitive construction (*cf.* 3 above; also **Note** 5 of § 65).

Caution: **Können** and **sollen** are used instead of **gekonnt** and **gesollt** since they are used with dependent infinitives.

F.   Optative subjunctive as equivalent of contrary-to-fact conditions.   Attention has already been called to the fact that the optative subjunctive is frequently the equivalent of contrary-to-fact conditions [*cf.* § 79 **A** (2) and (3)].   This use is confined, of course, to the **past** and **past perfect** tenses of the subjunctive:

Hätte ich nur einen Regenschirm!   **Hätten** wir es nur **gewußt**!
If I only had an umbrella!   *If we had only known it!*

Note:

Considered as contrary-to-fact conditions, the conclusion of each of the above sentences is **to be supplied.**

EXERCISE

A.   Complete the following sentences by supplying the proper forms of verbs in parentheses:

1. Wenn er —— (kommen), (so) werden wir ihn freundlich empfangen.
2. Wenn der Arzt hier —— (sein), (so) wäre das Kind nicht gestorben.
3. Wenn das Wetter schön —— (sein), (so) werde ich einen Spaziergang machen.

4. Wenn er das Geld —— (haben), (so) hätte er das Haus gekauft.
5. Wenn er einfacher —— (leben), (so) wäre er reich.
6. Wenn ich Zeit —— (haben), (so) werde ich einen Brief schreiben.
7. Wenn der Preis nicht so hoch wäre, (so) —— er das Buch —— (kaufen).
8. Wenn sie Geld hat, (so) —— sie dieses Jahr —— (reisen).
9. Wenn er nicht so müde gewesen wäre, (so) —— er nicht —— (einschlafen).
10. Wenn es nicht so weit wäre, (so) —— ich dorthin —— (fahren).
11. Wenn das Buch interessant ist, (so) —— ich es —— (lesen).
12. Wenn es nicht geregnet hätte, (so) —— ich nicht zu Hause —— (bleiben).
13. Bäte er mich um Hilfe, so —— ich ihm —— (helfen).
14. Wäre er da gewesen, so —— er das —— (wissen).
15. Hätte er mich eingeladen, so —— ich ihn —— (besuchen).
16. Wäre ich ein Vogel, so —— ich zu dir —— (fliegen).
17. Der Schüler hätte nicht so viele Fehler gemacht, wenn er aufmerksam —— (sein).
18. Ich würde den Arzt nicht kommen lassen, wenn ich gesund —— (sein).
19. Er hätte mich nicht gefragt, wenn er das —— (wissen).
20. Wenn er mehr Geduld hätte, (so) —— es ihm —— (gelingen).
21. Er —— die Sätze an die Tafel —— (*could have written*).
22. Er —— keine Fehler —— (*should have made*).
23. Wir —— zu Hause —— (*should have stayed*).
24. Ich —— die Aufgabe —— (*could have written*).
25. Sie sah aus, als ob sie müde —— (*were*).
26. Er tat, als ob er es nicht —— (*had heard*).
27. Sie tat, als ob sie es nicht —— (*had understood*).
28. Er sah aus, als ob er schläfrig —— (*were*).
29. —— (*Had*) ich nur eine gute Feder!
30. —— (*Were*) der Vater nur hier!
31. —— er es nur —— (*Had known*)!
32. —— er nur zu Hause —— (*Had stayed*)!
33. Wenn er das deutsche Buch —— (*could have read*), (so) hätte er es getan.
34. Wenn Sie das —— (*could have done*), (so) hätte ich mich sehr gefreut.

35. Wenn Sie das Fenster nicht zugemacht hätten, (so) —— es jetzt nicht so warm im Zimmer (sein).

36. Er sah aus, als ob er hungrig —— (*were*).

37. Er —— das nicht —— (*should have said*).

38. Wenn er —— (kommen), (so) hätte ich ihn gesehen.

39. Wenn mein alter Freund hier wäre, (so) —— ich ihn —— (besuchen).

40. —— (Haben) ich Zeit, so würde ich viele Bücher lesen.

41. Wenn die Atmosphäre des Planeten Venus nicht wolkenerfüllt —— (*were*), —— (*could*) man die Oberfläche dieses Himmelskörpers sehen.

42. Wenn die Nationen unserer Erde ihre Ansprüche auf Bodenerwerb außerhalb des von ihren Völkern besiedelten Territoriums stützen —— (*can*), —— (*must*) diese Nationen sich mit der Frage des Weltraum-Rechts befassen.

B. Translate:

1. If I had phoned him, he would have met me at the station.

2. If they had a good airplane, they would fly to New York.

3. If I have time, I shall read an interesting German book.

4. If the book were interesting, he would read it.

5. If it had rained, my dear friends would have stayed at home.

6. If it does not rain this morning, I shall take a long walk.

7. If I do not find his new address, I shall not be able to visit him.

8. If he had had the money, he would have bought that large house.

9. If he read more German books, he would speak German better.

10. If they had been punctual, he would not have been angry.

11. If he had lived more simply, he would have become rich.

12. If our dear friend had the money, he would give it to me at once.

13. If he had the time today, he would accompany me.

14. If he had studied the grammar, he would have known the answers to these simple questions.

15. If he would help the poor men, they would thank him.

16. You should have visited me last summer.

17. He could have visited them last winter.

18. Had I only known it!

19. If he were only here!

20. If I only had more money.
21. If they had only paid attention!
22. He looked as if he were sleepy.
23. She acted as if she had not understood the last sentence.
24. They looked as if they were tired.
25. He ate as if he had not eaten anything for (seit) a week.
26. You should have read that interesting story in the German newspaper.
27. He could have taken a long trip if he had had the money.
28. His father would have given him the money if he had earned more this year.
29. He would earn more if times (die Zeiten) were not so bad (schlecht).
30. If he earns more next year, he will take a trip.
31. If you had worked harder last month, you would not be so poor now.
32. If you only had more patience!
33. You should have learned more.
34. Your younger brother could have worked harder.
35. Your older sister should have helped you.
36. If he were here, they would be happy.
37. If the old men had visited me, I should have thanked them.
38. If it rains, I shall stay at home.
39. If he had known that, he would not have gone.
40. He looked as if he had grown (werden) much older.
41. If the huge space-research rocket had not ascended into the higher layers of air, the astronauts would have been disappointed.
42. Scientists would fill free balloons with hydrogen instead of helium, if hydrogen were incombustible. Hydrogen is lighter than helium.

83. THE MODAL AUXILIARIES WITH AND WITHOUT A DEPENDENT INFINITIVE

Read the following sentences very carefully:

A. Modals without an infinitive:	B. Modals with an infinitive:
(1) **Können:**	(1) **Können:**
Er kann es.[1]	Er kann es tun.
He can.	*He can do it.*
Er konnte es.	Er konnte es tun.
He could.	*He could do it.*
Er hat es **gekonnt.**	Er hat es tun **können.**
He has been able to.	*He has been able to do it.*
Er hatte es **gekonnt.**	Er hatte es tun **können.**
He had been able to.	*He had been able to do it.*
Er wird es können.	Er wird es tun können.
He will be able to.	*He will be able to do it.*
Er wird es **gekonnt** haben.	Er wird es haben tun **können.**
He will have been able to.	*He will have been able to do it.*
(2) **Müssen:**	(2) **Müssen:**
Wir müssen es.	Wir müssen es tun.
We must.	*We must do it.*
Wir mußten es.	Wir mußten es tun.
We had to.	*We had to do it.*
Wir haben es **gemußt.**	Wir haben es tun **müssen.**
We have had to.	*We have had to do it.*

---

[1] *Cf.* **Caution** under **Note** (2) (*a*) below.

A. Modals without an infinitive (*cont.*):

> Wir hatten es **gemußt.**
> *We had had* (or *been obliged*) *to.*
>
> Wir werden es müssen.
> *We shall have to.*
>
> Wir werden es **gemußt** haben.
> *We shall have had* (or *been obliged*) *to.*

(3) **Dürfen:**

> Er darf es.
> *He may.*
>
> Er hat es **gedurft.**
> *He has been allowed to.*

(4) **Mögen:**

> Er mag es.
> *He likes to.*
>
> Er hat es **gemocht.**
> *He has liked to.*

(5) **Wollen:**

> Ich will es.
> *I want to.*
>
> Ich habe es **gewollt.**
> *I have wanted to.*

(6) **Sollen:**

> Ich soll es.
> *I am to.*
>
> Ich habe es **gesollt.**
> *I have been required* (or *called upon*) *to.*

B. Modals with an infinitive (*cont.*):

> Wir hatten es tun **müssen.**
> *We had had* (or *been obliged*) *to do it.*
>
> Wir werden es tun müssen.
> *We shall have to do it.*
>
> Wir werden es haben tun **müssen.**
> *We shall have had* (or *been obliged*) *to do it.*

(3) **Dürfen:**

> Er darf es tun.
> *He may do it.*
>
> Er hat es tun **dürfen.**
> *He has been allowed to do it.*

(4) **Mögen:**

> Er mag es tun.
> *He likes to do it.*
>
> Er hat es tun **mögen.**
> *He has liked to do it.*

(5) **Wollen:**

> Ich will es tun.
> *I want to do it.*
>
> Ich habe es tun **wollen.**
> *I have wanted to do it.*

(6) **Sollen:**

> Ich soll es tun.
> *I am to do it.*
>
> Ich habe es tun **sollen.**
> *I have been required* (or *called upon*) *to do it.*

Summary: The above sentences indicate that the six modal auxiliaries are:

können, konnte, hat gekonnt, er kann	*to be able, can, could, etc.*
müssen, mußte, hat gemußt, er muß	*to have to, must, etc.*
dürfen, durfte, hat gedurft, er darf	*to be allowed*
mögen, mochte, hat gemocht, er mag	*to like to, care for*
wollen, wollte, hat gewollt, er will	*to want, desire*
sollen, sollte, hat gesollt, er soll	*to be (required) to*

Note:

(1) **All modal auxiliaries are conjugated with haben.**

(2) (*a*) The meaning of a sentence in which a modal auxiliary is the only verb, **depends on the verb to be supplied,** just as in English; thus *He can* may be in answer to *Can he do (write, understand, sing, etc.) it?*

Caution: Contrary to English usage, however, German may **retain** a direct object (particularly **es** and **das**) with a modal auxiliary:

„Kann er das beweisen?"   „Er **kann es**" (or „**Das kann** er").
"Can he prove that?"   *"He can."*

Here **es** and **das** are direct objects of the verb **beweisen,** which is understood.

(*b*) As independent transitive verbs, German modals may take their own direct objects (*cf.* § 16 **B**):

Er kann Deutsch.
He knows German.

(3) If there is no dependent infinitive with a modal auxiliary, the forms **gekonnt, gemußt, gedurft, gemocht, gewollt,** and **gesollt** are used in the perfect, past perfect, and future perfect tenses (*cf.* bold-faced forms in ¶ **A** above).

(4) If there is a dependent infinitive with a modal auxiliary, the forms **gekonnt, gemußt, gedurft, gemocht, gewollt,** and **gesollt** are replaced by **können, müssen, dürfen, mögen, wollen,** and **sollen** (the older participial forms), which regularly **follow the dependent infinitive** (*cf.* bold-faced forms in ¶ **B** above). This is the so-called "double infinitive" construction.

(5) Since **haben** is the tense auxiliary of all modals, *has had to* . . . must be translated by **hat** . . . (dependent infinitive) müssen:

> *He has had to go home.*
> Er **hat** nach Hause gehen müssen.

Here **gehen** is dependent on the main verb **müssen.**

(6) The preposition **zu** cannot be used with an infinitive depending on a modal auxiliary:

> Er muß gehen.   Er will arbeiten.
> *He has to go.*   *He wants to work.*

(7) In the future perfect **haben** precedes both infinitive forms of the double infinitive construction.

(8) The English equivalents of German modal auxiliaries are often defective: *I must, I had to; he can, he will be able; etc.* German modals, however, are quite regular: **ich muß, ich mußte; er kann, er wird können; etc.**

(9) For the conjugation of modals, *cf.* § 109 of the Appendix and observe the following:

(*a*) The present indicative singular of modals (and also of the verb **wissen**) resembles the past indicative singular of strong verbs; first and third persons of both are identical in form and have no endings:

> Modal: ich kann, er kann; ich darf, er darf; *etc.*
> Strong Verb: ich begann, er begann; ich warf, er warf; *etc.*

These verbs are, therefore, known as " preterit-present " verbs.

(*b*) **Sollen** is the only modal that does not change the vowel of the infinitive in the present indicative singular: ich **soll;** but: ich kann, ich muß, ich darf, ich mag, and ich will.

(*c*) **Sollen** and **wollen** are the only modals that retain the infinitive vowel in the past indicative: ich **sollte** and ich **wollte.**

(*d*) The present indicative **plural** of all modals has the form of the infinitive: wir **können,** wir **müssen,** wir **dürfen,** wir **mögen,** wir **wollen,** and wir **sollen.**

(*e*) The past subjunctive forms of **können, müssen, dürfen,** and **mögen** are: **könnte, müßte, dürfte,** and **möchte;** those of **wollen** and **sollen** are identical with the corresponding past indicative forms: **wollte** and **sollte**.

(*f*) **Wollen** is the only modal auxiliary that has an imperative form.

84. THE DOUBLE INFINITIVE CONSTRUCTION WITH VERBS OTHER THAN MODALS

The double infinitive construction may also occur with the following verbs:

A. Lassen:

(1) Er läßt den Arzt holen.   Er hat den Arzt holen **lassen.**
He sends for the doctor.   *He sent for the doctor.*

(2) Ich lasse mir das Haar schneiden.
I am having my hair cut.

Ich habe mir das Haar schneiden **lassen.**
I had my hair cut.

(3) Sie läßt sich ein neues Kleid machen.
She is having a new dress made.

Sie hat sich ein neues Kleid machen **lassen.**
She had a new dress made.

B. Sehen:

Ich sehe ihn kommen.   Ich habe ihn kommen **sehen.**
I see him coming.   *I saw him coming.*

C. Heißen:

Er heißt mich gehen.   Er hat mich gehen **heißen.**
He orders me to go.   *He ordered me to go.*

D. Helfen:

Ich helfe das Geschäft begründen.
I am helping to establish the business.

Ich habe das Geschäft begründen **helfen.**

or: Ich habe geholfen, das Geschäft zu begründen.
I helped to establish the business.

E. Hören:

Hören Sie die Dame singen?
Do you hear the lady singing?

Haben Sie die Dame singen **hören?**
Did you hear the lady sing?

F. Lernen:

Er lernt fliegen.
He is learning to fly.

Ich habe ihn gestern kennen**gelernt** (or kennen**lernen**).
I made his acquaintance yesterday.

G. Lehren:

Ich lehre ihn schreiben.
I am teaching him to write.

Ich habe ihn schreiben **lehren** (or **gelehrt**).
I taught him to write.

Summary: The above sentences indicate that some of the more common verbs (in addition to the modal auxiliaries) requiring a dependent infinitive without **zu** are: **lassen, sehen, heißen, helfen, hören, lernen,** and **lehren.**

Note:

(1) The verbs listed in above summary assume an infinitive instead of a past participial form when used with a dependent infinitive—*i.e.*, the double infinitive construction (*cf.* bold-faced infinitive forms above).

(2) **The dependent infinitive must precede,** just as it does with modal auxiliaries (*cf.* **Note** (4) of § 83).

(3) English often has the present participle where German requires the present infinitive (*cf.* ¶¶ **B** and **E** above).

(4) (*a*) **Zu** may be used with the dependent infinitive after **lehren, lernen,** and occasionally after **heißen** and **helfen**—particularly when the infinitive has modifiers:

Ich lehrte ihn, sein möglichstes zu **tun.**
I taught him to do his utmost.

(*b*) The dependent infinitive with **zu** is the more usual construction in compound tenses of **helfen** (*cf.* alternative for the second sentence under ¶ **D** above).

(5) The dependent infinitive with **lassen** has passive force (*cf.* ¶ **A** above).

85. VERBS OTHER THAN MODALS REQUIRING A DEPENDENT INFINITIVE WITHOUT ZU

Additional verbs (not used in the double infinitive construction) that require a dependent infinitive without **zu** are:

A. (1) **Gehen:**

Er **geht** spazieren.
He goes walking.

(2) **Reiten** (or **fahren**):

Wir **reiten** (or **fahren**) spazieren.
We are going riding (or *driving*).

B. (1) **Stehenbleiben:**

Sie **bleibt** stehen.
She stops.

Sie **blieb** stehen.
She stopped.

(2) **Sich schlafen legen:**

Er **legt sich** schlafen.
He lies down to sleep.

Summary: The above sentences indicate that verbs of motion such as **gehen, reiten, fahren,** *etc.* and also **bleiben** and **sich legen** are followed by an infinitive without **zu,** especially in set phrases.

Note:

(1) Here again, the use of the English present participle is not to be confused with that of the German infinitive (*cf.* **Note** (3) of § 84).

(2) Observe the **participial** forms in the perfect tenses of the sentences given above:

Er ist spazierengegangen.
He went walking.

Wir sind spazierengeritten (or spazierengefahren).
We went riding (or *driving*).

Sie ist stehengeblieben.   Meine Uhr ist stehengeblieben.
She stopped.   *My watch stopped.*

Er hat sich schlafen gelegt.
He lay down to sleep.

(3) After a verb of motion German sometimes employs the **past participle** (instead of the present infinitive as in the above sentences) **with present sense,** where the English idiom requires the present participle:

Er kam **gelaufen.**   Sie kommt **gesprungen.**
*He came **running.***   *She comes **jumping** along.*

86. MODAL AUXILIARIES WITH PASSIVE FORMS

Read the following sentences very carefully and note bold-faced forms:

Das kann **gemacht werden.**   Eine Brücke soll **gebaut werden.**
That can be done.   *A bridge is to be built.*

Das muß **gesagt werden.**
That must be said.

Das Radarsignal konnte sofort **identifiziert werden.**
The radar signal could be identified at once.

Summary: The above sentences indicate that modal auxiliaries do not have a passive voice but may be followed by a passive infinitive.

Note:

(1) The active infinitive may be used instead, however, provided a sentence is reconstructed:

Man muß das sagen.
That must be said.

(2) *Cannot be* is often rendered by **sein** followed by **nicht zu** and an active infinitive:

Es **ist nicht zu** leugnen.   Er **ist** telefonisch **nicht zu** erreichen.
*It **cannot be** denied.*   *He **cannot be** reached by telephone.*

87.　IDIOMATIC USES OF MODAL AUXILIARIES

For purposes of comparison, some of the literal meanings of modals have been included in the following sentences (*cf.* § 83 carefully):

A.　Sollen:

(1)　Was **soll** ich tun?
　　*What **am** I to* (or **shall** I) *do?*

(2)　Sie **sollen** arbeiten.
　　*You **are to** work.*

(3)　Sie **sollten** arbeiten.
　　*You **should*** (or **ought to**) *work.*

(4)　Er **soll** sehr arm sein.
　　*He **is said** to be very poor.*

(5)　Du **sollst** nicht stehlen.
　　*Thou **shalt** not steal.*

(6)　Er **hätte** zu Hause **bleiben sollen.**
　　*He **should have stayed** at home.*

Note:

(1)　English *should* (or *ought to*), denoting obligation, is rendered by the past of **sollen** (*cf.* ¶ **A** (3) above).　**Sollte(n)** in this sense is the past **subjunctive** which is used to express an unaccomplished possibility.

Caution:　The past **indicative,** identical in form with the past subjunctive, may be illustrated by such a sentence as:

> Gestern **sollte** ich abfahren, aber leider mußte ich in der Stadt bleiben.
> *Yesterday I **was** (supposed) **to** leave, but unfortunately I had to stay in the city.*

(2)　English *should have* with a dependent verb is rendered by **hätte** ... (dependent infinitive) **sollen** (*cf.* (6) above).　This form is the past perfect subjunctive denoting unreality in the past.

(3)　*Shall* in deliberative questions (*cf.* ¶ **A** (1) above) and *shalt* in commands (*cf.* ¶ **A** (5) above) are rendered by **sollen.**

Caution: Do not use **sollen** for *shall* to denote future time; **werden** denotes futurity.

B. Wollen:

(1) Er **will** morgen abfahren.
     *He **intends** to leave tomorrow.*

(2) Er **will** es getan haben.
     *He **claims** to have done it.*

(3) Sie **will** einen reichen Onkel haben.
     *She **professes** to have a rich uncle.*

(4) Was **wollen** Sie damit **sagen?**
     *What do you **mean** by that?*

(5) **Wir wollen** (or **Wollen wir**) nicht mehr davon **sprechen.**
     *Let's not **talk** any more about it.*

(6) **Wollen Sie** Tee oder Kaffee?
     ***Will you take** tea or coffee?*

Note: **Wollen** with a dependent infinitive is commonly used in conversation with the force of an imperative (*cf.* ¶ **B** (5) above). Although present subjunctive in form (*cf.* § 79 **B**), **wollen** is an exception in that it frequently employs normal word order in the first person plural.

Caution: German **will** is not to be used for English *will* to denote future time:

> He *will* go home.   He *wants* to go home.
> Er **wird** nach Hause gehen.   Er **will** nach Hause gehen.

C. Mögen:

(1) Er **mag** das Essen nicht.
     *He does not **like** the food* (or *meal*).

(2) Das **mag** (*or* kann) sein.
     *That **may** be.*

(3) Er **möchte** (gern) ins Theater gehen.
     *He **would like** to go to the theater.*

(4) **Möchten Sie** mit?
Would you like to go along?

(5) Er **mochte wohl** dreißig Jahre alt sein.
He was probably thirty years old.

(6) Das Buch **mag** auch noch so schwer sein, er wird es lesen.

or: **Mag** das Buch auch noch so schwer sein, er wird es lesen.[1]
Although the book be ever so difficult, he will read it.

(7) **Möge** Gott dir helfen![2]
May God help you.

Note:

(1) English **would** (or **should**) **like** is commonly rendered by the past subjunctive of **mögen** (*cf.* ¶ **C** (3) and (4) above).

(2) Modal auxiliaries are commonly used with the dependent infinitive **understood** (*cf.* ¶ **C** (4) above).

(3) **Mögen** often denotes **probability** (*cf.* ¶ **C** (5) above) and **concession** (*cf.* ¶ **C** (6) above).

D. Können:

(1) Letzten Monat **konnte** ich ihn nicht besuchen.
I could not (i.e., was unable to) visit him last month.

(2) Ich **könnte** ihn jetzt besuchen, wenn ich Zeit **hätte**.
I could (i.e., should be able to) visit him now if I had time.

(3) Er **kann** nichts dafür.　　　Was **kann** ich dafür?
It is not his fault.　　　　　*How can I help it?*
or: *He can't help it.*

(4) Ich **konnte nicht umhin,** ihm die Wahrheit zu sagen.
I couldn't help telling him the truth.

(5) Er **kann** Deutsch.[3]
He knows German.

---

[1] *Cf.* § 80 and **Note.**
[2] *Cf.* § 79 **A** (1).
[3] *Cf.* **Note** (2) (*b*) of § 83.

(6)   Das **kann** (or mag) sein.
     *That **may** be.*

(7)   Es **könnte** nützlich sein.[1]
     *It **might** be useful.*

(8)   Sie **hätten** ein deutsches Buch lesen **können.**
     *You **could** have read a German book.*

Note:

(1)   If English *could* is the equivalent of *was able*, it is rendered by the past indicative **konnte** (*cf.* ¶ **D** (1) above); if it is the equivalent of *should* (or *would*) *be able*, it is rendered by the past subjunctive **könnte.** The subjunctive is used, of course, because of the present contrary-to-fact condition (*cf.* § 82 **A**).

Caution: The weak, unstressed English *should* [**not** denoting obligation (*cf.* **Note** (1) of ¶ **A** of this section)], which occurs frequently in conditional sentences, must not be rendered by **sollte** (*cf.* ¶ **D** (2) above).

(2)   **Nicht umhin können** is the equivalent of **müssen** but, unlike the latter, requires **zu** with a dependent infinitive (*cf.* (4) above).

(3)   The conditional mood (*i.e.*, **würde**-forms) of modal auxiliaries is extremely rare and should be avoided. Use in its place the proper subjunctive form (*cf.* (2) above).

(4)   For the difference between **können, kennen,** and **wissen,** *cf.* § 16 **B.**

(5)   English *could have* with a dependent verb is rendered by **hätte** . . . (dependent infinitive) **können** (*cf.* (8) above). This form is the past perfect subjunctive denoting unreality in the past.[2]

Caution: Such a sentence as *He could have written it* must not be translated by: Er könnte es geschrieben haben (which would mean *It might be that he wrote it*) but by: **Er hätte es schreiben können.**

(6)   For a translation of *cannot be*, *cf.* **Note** (2) of § 86.

---

[1] *Cf.* § 79 **C.**
[2] For a similar construction with **sollen** *cf.* **Note** (2) of § 87 **A.**

E. Dürfen:

(1) Das **dürfen** Sie **nicht** tun.
*You **must not** do that.*

(2) **Dürfte** ich Sie um das Buch bitten?[1]
Might I ask you for the book?

Darf ich Sie um das Brot bitten?
May I ask you for the bread?

(3) Es **dürfte** (*or* könnte) sein.[1]
*It **might** (**possibly**) be.*

(4) Er **durfte** es tun.
*He **was allowed** to do it.*

(5) Sie **dürften** ihn mißverstanden haben.[1]
You may possibly have misunderstood him.

Note:

(1) English *must not* is very often rendered by **dürfen** with a negative (*cf.* ¶ **E** (1) above).

Caution: **Müssen** used negatively is much less forceful than **dürfen.**

„Das weiß ich ja auswendig; du mußt auch nicht immer dasselbe erzählen."[2]
"I know that by heart; don't always tell the same thing over again."

(2) **Dürfen** is quite frequently equivalent to the English passive (*cf.* ¶ **E** (4) above).[3]

(3) (*a*) Sometimes **möchte** as well as **könnte** (*cf.* ¶ **E** (3) above) is used in the sense of **dürfte.**

(*b*) A number of the sentences under **können, dürfen,** and **mögen** indicate that these three auxiliaries frequently express **possibility** or **probability.**

---

[1] *Cf.* § 79 **C.**
[2] This quotation is from Storm's „Immensee."
[3] *Cf.* also § 75 **E.**

F. Müssen:

(1) Ich **muß** gleich an die Arbeit (gehen).
I must go to work at once.

(2) Er **mußte** die Miete bezahlen.
He had to pay the rent.

(3) Wir **haben** es tun **müssen.**
We were compelled to do it.

(4) Er **hatte** es tun **müssen.**
He had been obliged to do it.

(5) Er **hätte** es tun **müssen.**
He would have been obliged to do it.

(6) Er **muß** es **getan haben.**
He must have done it.

Note:

(1) A statement of fact requires the indicative (*cf.* ¶ **F** (1), (2), (3), and (4) above).

(2) The past perfect subjunctive is used in an abbreviated past contrary-to-fact condition (*cf.* ¶ **F** (5) above).[1]

(3) When **the inference is that the action implied in a sentence took place, muß** with the perfect infinitive is required (*cf.* ¶ **F** (6) above).

(4) The future perfect indicative is frequently used to express a **past probability,** which may be brought out in translation by *must have* (*cf.* § 39 ¶ **B**):

Er wird seine Füllfeder wohl verlegt haben.
He must have (i.e., He probably) misplaced his fountain pen.

(5) *Not to have to* in the sense of *not to need to* is rendered by **brauchen** with **nicht zu** and a dependent infinitive:

Ich **brauche** es **nicht zu** tun.
I don't have (i.e., need) to do it.

---

[1] For the use of **hätte ... sollen** and **hätte ... können,** *cf.* also **Note** (2) of ¶ **A** and **Note** (5) of ¶ **D** above.

(6) For the use of **dürfen** to replace **müssen** in negative sentences, *cf.* part (1) and **Note** (1) of ¶ **E** of this section.

EXERCISE

A. Rewrite each of the following sentences in the future, perfect, and past perfect indicative:

1. Ich muß den ganzen Tag arbeiten.
2. Das Kind durfte nicht auf der Straße spielen.
3. Er kann nicht schlafen.
4. Er wollte Deutsch sprechen.
5. Wir hören die alte Dame sprechen.
6. Er läßt den Arzt holen.
7. Ich sah ihn kommen.
8. Ich muß gleich an die Arbeit gehen.
9. Ich kann es mir nicht leisten.
10. Mein kleiner Bruder läßt sich das Haar schneiden.
11. Seine jüngere Schwester muß zu Hause bleiben.
12. Ich sah den alten Mann arbeiten.
13. Er kann den langen Brief nicht lesen.
14. Sie wollte ins Kino gehen.
15. Ich kann den Fehler nicht finden.
16. Sein lieber Freund muß bis in die Nacht arbeiten.
17. Man darf nicht im Theater rauchen.
18. Das schöne Mädchen läßt sich ein neues Kleid machen.
19. Wir hörten den weltbekannten Tenor singen.
20. Er will viel Geld verdienen.

B. Rewrite the following sentences with **hätte ... können** and **hätte ... sollen,** and translate them into English according to the following model:

Er geht aufs Land.
He goes to the country.

Er **hätte** aufs Land gehen **können.**
He could have gone to the country.

Er **hätte** aufs Land gehen **sollen.**
He should have gone to the country.

1. Mein reicher Onkel macht eine lange Reise.
2. Ich las ein deutsches Buch.
3. Er besuchte seinen alten Freund.
4. Sie gibt dem armen Mann etwas Geld.
5. Er steht früh auf.
6. Mein älterer Bruder arbeitet fleißig.

C. Translate:

1. We have to go to school.
2. My little brother was unable to go to school today.
3. You should (or ought to) stay at home.
4. Yes, you are right. I should have stayed at home.
5. Do you know German?
6. Carl does not know his lesson.
7. Those little boys never wanted to study.
8. When will your dear friend have to go home?
9. We could have gone home at half past eleven.
10. Might I ask you for your new German dictionary?
11. The little children were not allowed to play on the street.
12. Have they ever been allowed to play there?
13. He wants to visit me next month.
14. I was on the point of going out, when I received your long, interesting letter.
15. She intends to go to the country next week.
16. She claims to have seen him in the country.
17. He professes to have a rich aunt.
18. You should have visited her.
19. You could have taken a long trip.
20. Next summer you should visit your old parents.
21. Yesterday I could go. Today I could go if I had the time.
22. Would you like to take a long walk this morning?
23. I don't like (**mögen**) the meal.
24. It is not her fault.
25. If he could have done it, he would have written me.
26. You should have visited those beautiful German villages.
27. My dear friend is said to be very ill.
28. He should not work so hard.

29. He should have stayed in bed.
30. What are we to do this afternoon?
31. He wants to give the little children some beautiful gifts.
32. They were about to sit down when I entered the room.
33. She claims to have read that short story. That may be.
34. We shall not be able to give them those interesting books.
35. Last year we could do it. This year, however, we could not do it, even if we earned twice as much money.
36. Can he understand these simple German sentences?
37. When did your older brother have his hair cut?
38. A week ago my younger sister had a beautiful dress made.
39. Why did you send for the doctor?
40. Have you ever seen that lazy boy working?
41. He will be unable to read this long letter.
42. Does your poor neighbor have to work all night?
43. He had been unable to sleep.
44. She has always wanted to earn much money.
45. Did you hear that famous tenor sing?
46. They (*use* **man**) were not allowed to smoke in the theater.
47. Were you unable (*perfect tense*) to find those mistakes?
48. Might I ask you for a good pencil?
49. I should like to read a good German book.
50. You should have translated these short German sentences.
51. That may be. That might (possibly) be.
52. Thou shalt not kill.
53. Will you take tea or coffee?
54. He claims to have heard him.
55. She was probably thirty years old. (*Use a modal auxiliary.*)
56. Might I ask you for another (*i.e.*, an additional) pen?
57. Might I ask you for another (*i.e.*, a different) chair?
58. They must have done that. (*The inference is that they did it.*)
59. They would have been obliged to do it.
60. That might be dangerous.

D. Complete the following sentences:

1. Man befaßte sich mit der Frage, ob Himmelskörper durch die Staaten unserer Erde —— (*be occupied*) könnten.

2. Wir —— den künstlichen Satelliten mit einem Teleskop ——
(*could have seen*).

3. Das große Radarteleskop —— (*is said*) Echos von Radar-
strahlen, die auf Planeten in unserem Sonnensystem gerichtet
werden, —— (*to receive*) und außerdem Signale von Himmels-
körpern —— (*to pick up*), die Millionen, ja vielleicht sogar
Milliarden Lichtjahre von der Erde entfernt sind.

88. GERMAN IDIOMS AND THEIR ENGLISH EQUIVALENTS

Note very carefully in what respect a German idiom differs from its English equivalent, giving particular attention to the use of prepositions. **Use idioms in different tenses** and **form sentences** with additional idioms to be listed as they occur in your reading.[1]

1. Er denkt an ihn. *He thinks of him.*
2. Ich warte auf den Mann. *I am waiting for the man.*
3. Er ist stolz auf den Sohn. *He is proud of his son.*
4. Er geht in die Schule. *He goes to school.*
5. Er ist in der Schule. *He is in school.*
6. Nach der Schule spielt er Ball. *He plays ball after school.*
7. Hat er recht oder unrecht? *Is he right or wrong?*
8. Wie geht es Ihnen? *How are you?*
9. (*a*) Ich lese gern. *I like to read.*
   (*b*) Ich habe es gern. *I like it.*
10. (*a*) Er liest lieber. *He prefers to read.*
    (*b*) Er hat es lieber. *He prefers it.*
11. (*a*) Sie liest am liebsten. *She likes best to read.*
    (*b*) Sie hat es am liebsten. *She likes it best.*
12. Er ist auf dem Lande. *He is in the country.*
13. Er geht aufs Land. *He is going to the country.*
14. Sie ist zu Hause. *She is at home.*
15. Sie geht nach Hause. *She is going home.*
16. Es wird immer heißer. *It is getting hotter and hotter.*
17. Was fehlt Ihnen? *What is the matter with you?*
18. Es tut mir leid. *I am sorry.*
19. Er bittet mich um den Bleistift. *He asks me for the pencil.*
20. Je öfter ich das Buch lese, desto besser gefällt es mir. *The oftener I read the book, the better I like it.*

---

[1] For various classroom idioms, *cf.* § 112 of the Appendix.

21. Er sprach vor sich (acc. refl.) hin. *He spoke to himself.*
22. Er hat gar nichts. *He has nothing at all.*
23. Ich verstehe es gar nicht. *I do not understand it at all.*
24. Er kommt, nicht wahr? *He is coming, is he not?*
25. Es tut mir weh. *It hurts me.*
26. Das geht Sie nichts an. *That does not concern you.*
27. Erinnern Sie sich an den Jungen? *Do you remember the boy?*
28. Auf Wiedersehen! *Goodbye.*
29. Leben Sie wohl! *Farewell.*
30. Er ist noch nicht da. *He has not yet come.*
31. Er hat ein Paar Schuhe. *He has a pair of shoes.*
32. Er hat ein paar Bücher. *He has several books.*
33. Geben Sie mir noch ein Buch! *Give me another (i.e., an additional) book.*
34. Geben Sie mir ein anderes Buch! *Give me another (i.e., a different) book.*
35. Wir lernten ihn kennen. *We made his acquaintance.*
36. Er soll sehr reich sein. *He is said to be very rich.*
37. Sie denkt sich (dat. refl.) das. *She imagines that.*
38. Er ist es los. *He is rid of it.*
39. Kümmern Sie sich nicht um ihn! *Don't worry (or bother) about him.*
40. Er fürchtet sich vor dem Hunde. *He is afraid of the dog.*
41. Sie ist toll vor Schmerz. *She is frantic with pain.*
42. Er ist außer sich vor Zorn. *He is beside himself with anger.*
43. Sie ging auf und ab. *She walked up and down (or to and fro).*
44. Es ist mir nicht gelungen, ihn zu überzeugen. *I didn't succeed in convincing him.*
45. Er bleibt stehen. *He stops.*
46. Ich kann es mir nicht leisten. *I can't afford it.*
47. Fahren Sie mit dem Dampfer oder mit der Eisenbahn? *Are you going by steamer or by rail?*
48. Heute über acht Tage wird er kommen. *He will come a week from today.*
49. Schreiben Sie das auf deutsch! *Write that in German.*
50. Nehmen Sie sich in acht! *Be careful (or Take care).*
51. Es geschah vor acht Tagen. *It happened a week ago.*
52. Ich freue mich auf den Besuch. *I am looking forward with pleasure to the visit.*
53. Ich freue mich über Ihren Erfolg. *I am happy about your success.*

54. Es kommt darauf an. *That depends.*
55. Um so besser. *All the better.*
56. (*a*) Er ist bei mir. *He is at my house.*
    (*b*) Ich habe kein Geld bei mir. *I have no money with me.*
57. Er klopft an die Tür. *He is knocking at the door.*
58. Ich war im Begriff zu gehen. *I was on the point of going.*
59. Er tat es auf diese Weise. *He did it in this manner.*
60. Das Haus besteht aus sechs Zimmern. *The house consists of six rooms.*
61. Man machte ihn zum Führer. *They made him* (or *He was made*) *leader.*
62. Man gewöhnt sich an alles. *One gets used to everything.*
63. Ich ärgere mich über ihn. *I am provoked at him.*
64. Es macht mir Freude. *It gives me pleasure.*
65. Sie lachten ihn aus. *They laughed at him.*
66. Er verliebte sich in das Mädchen. *He fell in love with the girl.*
67. Er verlobte sich mit dem Mädchen. *He became engaged to the girl.*
68. Er antwortet auf meine Frage. *He answers my question.*
69. Ich habe mich erkältet. *I have caught cold* (or *I have a cold*).
70. Was wird aus ihm werden? *What will become of him?*
71. (*a*) Ich bin es. *It is I.*
    (*b*) „Ist er es?" „Er ist es." *"Is it he?" "It is he."*
72. Ich wohne ihm gegenüber. *I live opposite him.*
73. Er ließ mich holen. *He sent for me.*
74. Sie wohnte in meiner Nähe. *She lived near me.*
75. Er setzte sich an den Tisch. *He sat down at the table.*
76. Ich schrieb einen Brief an meinen Vetter. *I wrote my cousin a letter.*
77. Der wievielte ist heute? *What is today's date?*
78. Um wieviel Uhr kommt er? *At what time is he coming?*
79. Es geschieht ihm recht. *It serves him right.*
80. Ich habe ihm einen großen Gefallen getan. *I did him a great favor.*
81. Es freut mich. *I am glad.*
82. (*a*) Die Reihe ist an mir (or Ich bin an der Reihe). *It is my turn.*
    (*b*) Ich bin an die Reihe gekommen. *My turn has come.*
83. Der Stuhl gefällt mir. *I like the chair.*
84. Auf einmal begann es zu regnen. *Suddenly it began to rain.*
85. (*a*) Meine Uhr geht vor. *My watch is fast.*
    (*b*) Meine Uhr geht nach. *My watch is slow.*

86. Wir hoffen auf günstiges Wetter. *We are hoping for favorable weather.*

87. Er hat entweder eine Feder oder einen Bleistift. *He has either a pen or a pencil.*

88. Er hat weder das eine noch das andere. *He has neither the one nor the other.*

89. Sowohl sein Vater als auch seine Mutter sind gekommen. *Both his father and his mother came.*

90. Passen Sie auf! *Pay attention.*

91. Es hat noch nicht geklingelt. *The bell has not yet rung.*

92. Amüsieren Sie sich! *Have a good time.*

93. Er hat Kopfweh. *He has a headache.*

94. Das macht nichts aus. *That makes no difference.*

95. Er arbeitet in der Nacht. *He works at night.*

96. Er schläft am Tage. *He sleeps in the daytime.*

97. Er geht auf einen Monat aufs Land. *He is going to the country for a month.*

98. Was gibt's Neues? *What is the news?*

99. Gehen Sie ins Theater? *Are you going to the theater?*

100. Was ißt er zum Frühstück? *What does he eat for breakfast?*

101. Er sieht zum Fenster hinaus. *He is looking out of the window.*

102. Ich gehe an ihm vorbei. *I pass him.*

103. Sie spricht von ihm. *She is speaking about him.*

104. Sie setzt (sich) den Hut auf. *She is putting on her hat.*

105. Sie zieht sich die Handschuhe an. *She is putting on her gloves.*

106. Er ist Student auf der Universität. *He is a student at the university.*

107. Er ist Professor an der Universität. *He is a professor at the university.*

108. Es ist nicht der Mühe (gen.) wert [or Es lohnt sich nicht der Mühe (gen.)]. *It is not worth while (or It does not pay).*

109. Ich bin derselben Meinung (gen.). *I am of the same opinion.*

110. Er möchte eine Reise (einen Spaziergang) machen. *He would like to take a trip (a walk).*

111. Er fährt lieber zweiter Klasse. *He prefers to travel second class.*

112. Wir haben viel Schönes gesehen. *We saw many beautiful things.*

113. Er ist auf einen Baum geklettert. *He climbed a tree.*

114. (a) Seien Sie nicht grausam gegen den Hund! *Don't be cruel to the dog*
(b) Er ist gegen jeden Menschen freundlich (gütig, höflich, kalt). *He is friendly (kind, polite, cold) to every human being.*

115. Seien Sie nicht böse auf mich! *Don't be angry with me.*
116. Das Land ist reich (arm) an Wäldern. *The country is rich (poor) in forests.*
117. Besten Gruß an Ihren Bruder. *Best regards to your brother.*
118. Fangen Sie von vorn an! *Begin at the beginning.*
119. Er erhielt viele schöne Geschenke zum Geburtstag (zu Weihnachten). *He received many beautiful gifts for his birthday (for Christmas).*
120. Köln ist durch den Dom (*or* wegen des Domes) berühmt. *Cologne is famous for its* (lit. *the*) *cathedral.*
121. Sie wird den Brief auf die Post bringen. *She will mail the letter.*
122. Lernen Sie das Gedicht auswendig! *Learn the poem by heart.*
123. Er benimmt sich schlecht. *He behaves badly.*
124. Das Pferd ist blind auf beiden Augen. *The horse is blind in both eyes.*
125. Das schmeckt nach saurer Milch. *That tastes of sour milk.*
126. Es riecht nach frischem Heu. *It smells of fresh hay.*
127. Er wird es nicht tun, **es sei denn, daß**[1] sie ihn darum bitten. *He will not do it **unless** they ask him (to).*

EXERCISE

A. Complete the following sentences:
  1. Ich warte schon eine Stunde —— mein— lieb— Freund.
  2. Er kann es —— nicht —— (*afford*).
  3. —— (*A week from today*) werde ich Sie besuchen.
  4. Sein Vetter war früher Professor —— d— Universität.
  5. Haben Sie —— mi— gedacht?
  6. Schreiben Sie diesen Satz —— (*in German*)!
  7. Sein ältester Sohn ist Student —— d— Universität.
  8. Die Mutter war sehr stolz —— d— klein— Mädchen.
  9. Sie —— die Handschuhe —— (*was putting on*).
  10. Sein kleiner Bruder geht noch nicht —— (*to school*).
  11. Der kleine Junge ist —— (*in the country*).
  12. Karl, —— (*be careful*)! Kinder, —— (*be careful*)!
      Herr Schmidt, —— (*be careful*)!
  13. Er —— den Hut —— (*was putting on*).
  14. Es geschah —— (*a week ago*).

---

[1] **After a negative statement** *unless* is usually rendered by **es sei denn, daß.**

15. Fährt er —— (*by steamer*) oder —— (*by rail*)?
16. Das kleine Mädchen ist —— (*in school*).
17. Er geht schon anderthalb Stunden —— (*up and down*).
18. —— (*After school*) wird er einen langen Spaziergang machen.
19. Sie sprach —— (*about*) mi—.
20. Was essen Sie —— (*for breakfast*)?
21. Er klopfte —— d— Tür.
22. Ich werde es —— dieselb— Weise tun.
23. Das Essen besteht —— sechs Gäng—.
24. Er war —— (*to the country*) gegangen.
25. Ich bin außer mi— —— Zahnweh.
26. Mein Bruder ist —— (*to the*) Theater gegangen.
27. Man machte —— (*him*) König.
28. Sie ist nicht —— (*at home*).
29. Ärgern Sie sich nicht —— (*about it*)!
30. Wann wird er —— (*home*) gehen?
31. Er ist toll —— Schmerz.
32. Schlafen Sie auch —— (*in the daytime*)?
33. Das Kind fürchtet sich —— d— groß— Katze.
34. Er lachte —— (*at her*).
35. Ich kümmere —— nicht —— (*about him*).
36. Sind Sie —— (*it*) endlich los geworden?
37. Es wurde —— (*colder and colder*).
38. Was fehlt —— (*those little children*)?
39. Arbeiten Sie —— (*at night*)?
40. Ich habe —— (*a headache*).
41. Hat er sich —— d— Mädchen verliebt?
42. Er hat sich schon —— d— Mädchen verlobt.
43. Er hat —— d— Tisch gesetzt.
44. Antworten Sie —— dies— kurz— Frage!
45. Das Kind hat —— (*neither*) Vater —— (*nor*) Mutter.
46. Es tat d— alt— Mann leid.
47. Es geschieht —— (*you*) recht.
48. Ich werde —— (*him*) —— ein— gut— Bleistift bitten.
49. Tut es —— (*you*) weh?
50. Erinnern Sie sich —— d— freundlich— Leute?
51. Ich muß —— (*either*) einen Bleistift —— (*or*) eine Feder haben.
52. Wir hoffen schon lange —— gut— Wetter.

53. Das geht —— (*him*) nichts an.
54. Er hat einen Brief —— sein— alt— Freund geschrieben.
55. Er hat mi— ein— groß— Gefallen getan.
56. —— (*Both*) sein Bruder —— (*and*) seine Schwester sind zu Hause geblieben.
57. Es ist nicht d— Mühe —— (*worth while*).
58. Sind Sie —— (*of the same*) Meinung?
59. Wir werden es nicht tun, —— (*unless*) sie uns darum bitten.
60. Friedrich der Große war sehr stolz —— (*of his*) Flötenspiel [*flute playing* (neut.)].
61. Wir werden morgen ein— kurz— Spaziergang ——.
62. Karl, —— (*behave*) anständig!
63. Nicht alle Reichen fahren erst— Klasse.
64. Fritz, hast du vergessen, meinen Brief —— (*to mail*)?
65. Der Soldat war —— d— link— Auge blind.
66. Die Kinder mußten das Gedicht —— (*by heart*) lernen.
67. Es roch —— ein— faul— Ei.
68. Die Speise schmeckt —— Knoblauch [*garlic* (masc.)].
69. Er hat mir etwas —— (*interesting*) erzählt.
70. Haben Sie nichts —— (*new*) gehört?
71. Unsere Bibliothek ist reich —— (*books*) über Goethe.
72. Dresden ist —— sein— Museen berühmt.
73. Besten Gruß —— Ihr— lieb— Eltern.
74. Der kleine Junge —— d— Dach —— (*had climbed*).
75. Sie hat viele interessant— Bücher —— Geburtstag erhalten.
76. Er ist —— (*angry with*) sein— Nachbar.
77. Sie singt nie, —— (*unless*) man sie darum bittet.

B. Translate:

1. I am looking forward with pleasure to the vacation.
2. My best friend will come a week from today.
3. The old man is looking out of the window.
4. That happened a week ago.
5. He stopped in front of the house.
6. I have not succeeded in finding my old umbrella.
7. She was thinking of her dear mother.
8. How long have you been waiting for me?
9. Is she right or wrong?
10. After school the little boys play ball.

11. " Will you go to the country for a week? "   " That depends."
12. Fred is already in school. His brother does not yet go to school.
13. Look out of the window.
14. Last month we were at their house.
15. Their house consists of twelve large rooms.
16. Do you live near them?
17. Do you remember those little children?
18. Their parents are said to be very poor.
19. I am sorry for them.
20. Last summer we made their acquaintance.
21. Do they still live in the country?
22. He had fallen in love with a rich girl.
23. Two months ago he became engaged to her.
24. They went to the theater yesterday evening.
25. The more I read Goethe, the more I admire him.
26. He liked to travel.
27. He was a student at the university of Leipzig.
28. Schiller was a professor at the university of Jena.
29. She likes to read. She prefers to sing. She likes best to dance.
30. Do you like it? Do you prefer it? Do you like it best? (*Use* gern.)
31. They had sent for a good physician.
32. Put on your hat and gloves.
33. Did you pass those old houses?
34. He was speaking of his friends.
35. What do you eat for breakfast?
36. In the daytime we must all work hard.
37. I don't like to work at night. (*Use* gern.)
38. That makes no difference.
39. Suddenly he stopped.
40. We can't afford it.
41. I shall travel either by steamer or by rail.
42. He never worries about the future.
43. Why should he worry about it?
44. You will visit me next winter, will you not?
45. He has been walking up and down for an hour and a half.
46. Have a good time when you are in the country.

47. I have a headache.   I am frantic with pain.
48. " When did you catch cold? "   " A week ago."
49. We caught cold last month when we were at their house.
50. (*a*) " Is it he? "   " It is he."
     (*b*) " Is it they? "   " It is they."
     (*c*) " Is it you? "   " It is I."
51. Our dear friend was on the point of going home.
52. We shall get used to it.
53. It gives the little boy pleasure.
54. What will become of those lazy children?   -
55. What time is it?
56. What is today's date?
57. It serves you right.
58. He did me a great favor.
59. It is your turn.
60. Most children are afraid of the dark.
61. Are you (*perf. of* werden) finally rid of it?
62. I like this pencil.   Bring me another one.
63. I don't like this pen.   Bring me another one.
64. She bought a pair of gloves.
65. Several books are (lying) on the table.
66. " Farewell."   " Goodbye."
67. It hurts me.   I am sorry.
68. What is the matter with that old lady?
69. She is talking to herself.
70. She is very proud of her grandson.
71. Both the grandfather and the grandmother are over a hundred years old.
72. They never take a walk unless we ask them to.
73. They always say, " It isn't worth while."
74. They are both of the same opinion.
75. Perhaps they are right.
76. Would you like to take a long trip to Europe?
77. The little child was behaving badly.
78. Do you usually travel second class?
79. I shall learn that short poem by heart.
80. Please mail this letter.
81. We had seen many beautiful things. (*Use the adjective as noun.*)

82. Heidelberg is famous for its old university.
83. The fox had climbed a high tree.
84. Did you receive many beautiful gifts for Christmas?
85. Don't be angry with him.
86. Please begin at the beginning.
87. Best regards to your charming sister.
88. The country is rich in coal.
89. It tastes of onions (die Zwiebel, —, –n).
90. The whole hall smells of roses.
91. In which eye is the poor animal blind?
92. He never does it unless he has to (*supply* es).
93. They have done nothing at all for her.
94. He just imagines that.
95. The old hotelkeeper is said to be very rich.
96. Don't bother about it.
97. Is he happy about it?
98. He will never get used to it.
99. When did the bell ring?
100. He was always friendly to his neighbors.

CHAPTER 26

Word Formation

89. COMPOUND NOUNS

The German language comprises a very large percentage of compounded words, which abound not only in technical and scientific but also in common parlance: der **Handschuh** (*glove*), der **Fingerhut** (*thimble*), der **Maulkorb** (*muzzle*), *etc.* A student should acquire the habit of analyzing compounded words into their component parts. With a comparatively small number of root words and a knowledge of prepositions, adverbs, prefixes, and suffixes, he can usually determine the meaning of a long compounded word without the help of a dictionary.

A. The formation of compound nouns. German forms compounds chiefly from simpler **German** words rather than coining words with Latin and Greek roots, as English so frequently does: das **Bindewort** (*conjunction*), die **Ausnahme** (*exception*), der **Wasserstoff** (*hydrogen*), die **Rolltreppe** (*escalator*).

B. The gender of compound nouns. Compound nouns have the gender of their **last** component:

> der Hausschlüssel (= das Haus + der Schlüssel), *housekey*
> die Eisenbahn (= das Eisen + die Bahn), *railroad*
> der Birnbaum (= die Birne + der Baum), *pear tree*
> das Vaterland (= der Vater + das Land), *native land*
> die Raumkapsel (= der Raum + die Kapsel), *space capsule*
> die Kernenergie (= der Kern + die Energie), *nuclear energy*
> die Feuerversicherungsgesellschaft (= das Feuer + die Versicherung + die Gesellschaft), *fire insurance company*

Note:

(1) A connective –**(e)s**– often appears in the compound, irrespective of the gender of a noun:

der Geburtstag (= die Geburt + der Tag), *birthday*
das Hochzeitskleid (= die Hochzeit + das Kleid), *wedding dress*
die Jahreszeit (= das Jahr + die Zeit), *season*

(2) (*a*) A connective –(e)n– is also common in compounds: der Hirtenknabe (= der Hirt + der Knabe), *shepherd boy.*

(*b*) This –(e)n– sometimes shows the old genitive form of certain feminine nouns, which otherwise rarely occurs in modern German:

der Sonnenstrahl (= die Sonne + der Strahl), *sunbeam*

EXERCISE

Form compounds with the following:

A. Nouns having no connective: der Rat + das Haus; das Haus + der Herr; das Haus + die Frau; die Luft + die Dichte.

B. Nouns having connective –(e)s–: der Frühling + die Blume; der Tod + die Angst; die Liebe + der Brief; der Himmel + der Körper.

C. Nouns having connective –(e)n–: der Knabe + das Alter; das Ohr + die Krankheit; die Sonne + der Schein; die Rakete + die Forschung.

90. SUFFIXES

Originally most suffixes and prefixes were independent words; in modern German, however, they have lost their independent identity and become associated with other words to which they have been affixed.

A. Noun suffixes. Noun suffixes occur in all three genders; some of the more common ones are listed below:

(1) Feminine noun suffixes: **–e, –ei, –heit, –keit, –kunft, –in, –schaft, –ung, –ion,** and **–tät.**

(*a*) **–e:** This suffix forms from adjectives abstract nouns denoting *quality*, *state*, or *condition:*

die Güte, *goodness* or *kindness* (from gut, *good*)
die Kürze, *shortness* or *brevity* (from kurz, *short*)

Note: Nouns formed with the suffix –e have umlaut whenever possible.

(*b*) **–ei:** This suffix forms from nouns of occupation nouns denoting (*place of*) *business* or *trade:*

> die Bäckerei, *bakery* (from der Bäcker, *baker*)
> die Druckerei, *printing office* (from der Drucker, *printer*)
> die Brauerei, *brewery* (from der Brauer, *brewer*)

(*c*) **–heit** and **–keit:** These suffixes form from adjectives and nouns abstract nouns denoting *state, condition, quality,* or *character:*

> die Schönheit, *beauty* (from schön, *beautiful*)
> die Fruchtbarkeit *fruitfulness* or *fertility* (from fruchtbar, *fertile*)
> die Folgsamkeit, *obedience* (from folgsam, *obedient*)
> die Leitfähigkeit, *conductivity* (from leitfähig, *conductive*)

Note:

The suffix **–heit** is often equivalent to the English suffix **–hood:** die Kindheit, *childhood.*

The suffix **–keit** (rather than **–heit**) is usually appended to adjectives ending in **–bar, –lich, –sam, –er,** and **–ig.**

(*d*) **–kunft:** This suffix forms from prepositions and adverbs of motion nouns denoting *coming:*

> die Ankunft, *arrival* (from an, *at* or *to*)
> die Zukunft, *future* (from zu, *to* or *towards*)

Note: The suffix **–kunft** was formerly a noun meaning *coming* and is etymologically related to the verb **kommen,** as its modern German compounds indicate.

(*e*) **–in:** This suffix forms feminines from masculine nouns:

> die Gräfin, *countess* (from der Graf, *count*)
> die Lehrerin, *woman teacher* (from der Lehrer, *teacher*)
> die Amerikanerin, *American woman* (from der Amerikaner, *American*)
> die Königin, *queen* (from der König, *king*)

Note: Nouns formed with the suffix **–in** usually have umlaut.

(*f*) **–schaft:** This suffix forms from nouns abstract and collective nouns denoting *state, condition,* or *quality; office, dignity,* or *profession:*

die Feindschaft, *enmity* (from der Feind, *enemy*)
die Mannschaft, *crew* or *team* (in a game) (from der Mann, *man*)
die Herrschaft, *dominion* (from der Herr, *master* or *ruler*)

Note: The suffix –**schaft** is often equivalent to the English suffix –*ship*:
die Freundschaft, *friendship;* die Gemeinschaft, *fellowship.*

(*g*) –**ung:** This suffix forms from verbal roots nouns denoting an *action* or the *result of an action:*

die Erfindung, *discovery* (from erfinden, *to discover*)
die Erziehung, *education* (from erziehen, *to educate*)
die Spaltung, *cleavage, splitting* (from spalten, *to cleave* or *split up*);
cf. Kernspaltung, *nuclear fission.*

Note: The suffix –**ung** is often equivalent to the English suffix –*ing:*
die Warnung, *warning;* die Endung, *ending.*

(*h*) –**ion:** This suffix occurs with nouns of foreign origin, many of which occur in English in about the same form: die Million, *million;* die Religion, *religion;* die Nation, *nation;* die Lektion, *lesson;* die Erdrotation (= die Erddrehung), *rotation of the earth.*

(*i*) –**tät:** This suffix occurs with nouns of foreign origin: die Universität, *university;* die Elektrizität, *electricity;* die Qualität, *quality;* die Quantität, *quantity;* die Relativität, *relativity;* die Radioaktivität, *radioactivity.*

Note: The suffix –**tät** often equals the English suffix –*ty.*

(2) Neuter noun suffixes: –**chen,** –**lein,** –**nis,** –**sal,** and –**tum.**

(*a*) –**chen** and –**lein:** These suffixes form from nouns diminutives and nouns denoting *endearment:*

das Bächlein, *little brook* or *brooklet* (from der Bach, *brook*)
das Bäumchen, *little tree* (from der Baum, *tree*)
das Blümlein, *little flower* (from die Blume, *flower*)
das Mütterchen, *dear mother* (from die Mutter, *mother*)
das Väterchen, *dear father* (from der Vater, *father*)
das Körperchen, *corpuscle* or *particle* (from der Körper, *body*)

Note:

The suffix –**chen** is equivalent to the English suffix –*kin:* das Lämmchen, *lambkin.*

The suffix –**lein** originated in South Germany and is used there in ordinary conversation and various dialect forms to the exclusion of the suffix –**chen.**

Nouns formed with –**chen** and –**lein** usually have umlaut.

(*b*) –**nis:** This suffix forms from verbal roots neuter (and sometimes feminine) nouns, usually with umlaut, denoting the *result* or *object of an activity* implied in the verbal stem of a compound:

> das Ergebnis, *result* (from sich ergeben, *to result*)
> das Verständnis, *understanding* (from verstehen, *to understand*)

Note:

The suffix –**nis** is sometimes equivalent to the English suffix –**ness,** as in darkness.

Nouns formed with –**nis** usually have umlaut, as in das Vermächtnis, *testament* or *legacy* (from vermachen, *to bequeath*).

Two common feminines formed with –**nis** are:

> die Erlaubnis, *permission* (from erlauben, *to permit*)
> die Kenntnis, *knowledge* (from kennen, *to know*)

(*c*) –**sal:** This suffix forms from verbal roots nouns similar to those ending in –**nis** but often with a more comprehensive and intensive force:

> das Schicksal, *fate* (*i.e., that which is sent*) (from schicken, *to send*)
> das Wirrsal, *confusion* (from wirren, *to entangle*)

(*d*) –**tum:** This suffix forms from noun, adjective, and verbal roots neuter nouns (with only two exceptions) denoting *dignity* or *rank, condition* or *state,* or *a collective idea:*

> das Königtum, *royalty* or *kingship* (from der König, *king*)
> das Siechtum, *state of poor health* (from siech, *sickly*)
> das Bürgertum, *citizenry* (from der Bürger, *citizen*)

Note:

The suffix –**tum** is often equivalent to the English suffix –*dom,* as in *martyrdom* (Märtyrtum).

Two **masculine** nouns are formed with –**tum:**

> der Reichtum, *riches* (from reich, *rich*)
> der Irrtum, *error* (from irr(e),[1] *in error*)

---

[1] *Cf.* also **irren,** *to err.*

(3) Masculine noun suffixes: –**er**, –**el**, and –**ling**.

(*a*) –**er**: This suffix forms from verbal roots masculine nouns denoting *the personal agent;* from noun stems, nouns of *nationality:*

> der Räuber, *robber* (from rauben, *to rob*)
> der Maler, *painter* (from malen, *to paint*)
> der Arbeiter, *worker* or *workman* (from arbeiten, *to work*)
> der Diener, *servant* (from dienen, *to serve*)
> der Engländer, *Englishman* (from England, *England*)
> der Spanier, *Spaniard* (from Spanien, *Spain*)
> der Sender, *sender*, *transmitter*, *broadcasting station* (from senden, *to send*)

Note:

The suffix –**er** is equivalent to the English suffix –*er*.

Nouns formed with –**er** often have umlaut.

Nouns denoting the personal agent are sometimes formed with the suffixes –**ler** or –**ner**:

> der Künstler, *artist* (from die Kunst, *art*)
> der Kellner, *waiter* (from der Keller, *cellar*)

(*b*) –**el**: This suffix forms from verbal roots nouns—usually masculine—denoting *instrument:*

> der Schlüssel, *key* (from schließen, *to close* or *lock*)
> der Deckel, *lid* (from decken, *to cover*)
> der Zügel, *rein* (from ziehen,[1] *to draw*)

(*c*) –**ling**: This suffix forms from adjective, noun, and verbal roots masculine nouns denoting people (sometimes animals) who appear *young*, *small*, or *contemptible:*

> der Jüngling, *young man* or *youth* (from jung, *young*)
> der Feigling, *coward* (from feig, *cowardly*)
> der Emporkömmling, *upstart* [from empor (*up*) + kommen (*to come*)]
> der Sprößling, *scion* or *descendant* (from der Sproß, *sprout*)

---

[1] Note that the principal parts of **ziehen** are: ziehen, zog, gezogen.

Note:

The suffix –**ling** is equivalent to the English suffix –*ling,* as in *duckling (i.e., young duck)* and *darling = dear–ling (i.e., little dear).*

Nouns formed with –**ling** usually have umlaut.

B.   Adjective suffixes.   Some of the more common adjective suffixes are: –**er,** –**(e)n** and –**ern,** –**haft,** –**bar,** –**isch,** –**lich,** –**ig,** –**los,** –**sam,** –**reich,** and –**voll.**

(1) –**er:** This suffix forms from names of cities indeclinable adjectives:

eine Münch(e)ner Zeitung, *a Munich newspaper* (from München, *Munich*)

das Heidelberger Schloß, *Heidelberg Castle* (from Heidelberg, *Heidelberg*)

(2) –**(e)n** and –**ern:** These suffixes form from nouns adjectives of *material:*

ledern, *of leather* (from das Leder, *leather*)

hölzern, *wooden* (from das Holz, *wood*)

bleiern, *of lead* or *leaden* (from das Blei, *lead*)

stählern, *of steel* (from der Stahl, *steel*)

Note:

The suffixes –**(e)n** and –**ern** are often equivalent to the English suffix –*en,* as in *wooden.*

Derivatives in –**(e)n** and –**ern** sometimes have umlaut.

(3) –**haft:** This suffix forms from nouns adjectives that denote *having the nature of:*

knabenhaft, *boyish* (from der Knabe, *boy*)

schmerzhaft, *painful* (from der Schmerz, *pain*)

meisterhaft, *masterly* (from der Meister, *master*)

fabelhaft, *fabulous* (from die Fabel, *fable*)

vorteilhaft, *advantageous, profitable* (from der Vorteil, *advantage, profit*)

Note: The suffix –**haft** is related to **haben,** *to have.*

(4) –**bar:** This suffix forms from verbal and noun roots adjectives denoting *ability, fitness,* or *worthiness:*

lesbar, *legible* (from lesen, *to read*)
eßbar, *edible* (from essen, *to eat*)
denkbar, *thinkable* or *conceivable* (from denken, *to think*)
sichtbar, *visible* (from sehen, *to see*)

Note:

The suffix –**bar** is usually equivalent to the English suffix *–able* or *–ible*. The negative prefix **un**– is frequently used with adjectives ending in –**bar**: unlesbar (*illegible*), undenkbar (*unthinkable*), unauflösbar, *insoluble*.

(5) –**isch**: This suffix forms from nouns and proper names adjectives that denote *belonging to* or *of the nature of*:

teuflisch, *devilish* (from der Teufel, *devil*)
himmlisch, *heavenly* (from der Himmel, *heaven*)
regnerisch, *rainy* (from der Regen, *rain*)
englisch, *English* (from England, *England*)
römisch, *Roman* (from Rom, *Rome*)
französisch, *French* (from der Franzose, *Frenchman*)

Note: The suffix –**isch** is usually equivalent to the English suffix *–ish*, as in *childish*.

Caution: Do not confuse the following forms (*cf.* ¶ **B** (6) below): **kindisch,** *childish* and **kindlich,** *childlike;* **weibisch,** *womanish* (*i.e.,* un-manly or effeminate) and **weiblich,** *womanly* (*i.e., feminine*).

(6) –**lich**: This suffix forms from nouns adjectives denoting *full of* or *like in appearance, manner,* or *nature*:

göttlich, *godly* or *divine* (from der Gott, *God*)
gefährlich, *dangerous* (from die Gefahr, *danger*)
schädlich, *harmful* (from der Schaden, *harm*)

Note: The suffix –**lich** is usually equivalent to the English suffixes *–ly*, *–ous,* and *–ful* (*cf.* (5) above).

(7) –**ig**: This suffix forms from nouns adjectives denoting *full of, characterized by,* or *pertaining to*:

blutig, *bloody* (from das Blut, *blood*)
mutig, *courageous* (from der Mut, *courage*)
freudig, *joyful* (from die Freude, *joy*)

Note:

The suffix **–ig** is usually equivalent to the English suffixes *–y*, *–ful,* and *–ous.*

The **g** in **–ig** and final *y* in English words such as *hungry* are cognates.

(8) **–los:** This suffix forms from nouns adjectives denoting *lack of:*

endlos, *endless* (from das Ende, *end*)
grundlos, *groundless* or *bottomless* (from der Grund, *ground* or *bottom*)
zahllos, *countless* (from die Zahl, *number*)
hilflos, *helpless* (from die Hilfe, *help*)

Note: The suffix **–los** is usually equivalent to the English suffix *–less.*

(9) **–sam:** This suffix forms from nouns, adjectives, and verbs adjectives that denote *causing,* or *a considerable degree* of the thing or quality denoted in the first part of a compound:

mühsam, *troublesome* or *toilsome* (from die Mühe, *trouble* or *toil*)
langsam, *slow* (from lang, *long*)
biegsam, *flexible* (from biegen, *to bend*)
wirksam, *effective*, *operative* (from wirken, *to effect*, *to operate*)

Note: The suffix **–sam** is usually, but not always, equivalent to the English suffix *–some.*

(10) **–reich:** This suffix forms from nouns adjectives denoting *full of, rich* (or *abounding*) *in:*

silberreich, *rich in silver* (from das Silber, *silver*)
liebreich, *loving* or *affectionate* (from die Liebe, *love*)
ideenreich, *rich in ideas* (from die Idee, –, Ideen, *idea*)

Note:

Distinguish between **steínreich** (with the accent on the first syllable) meaning *stony* and **steinreích** (with full stress on the second syllable) meaning *very rich.*

Similarly **blútarm** means *of poor blood;* **blútárm,** *very poor.*

(11) –**voll:** This suffix forms from nouns adjectives denoting *full of:*

> gefahrvoll, *full of danger* or *risky* (from die Gefahr, *danger*)
> liebevoll, *loving* or *affectionate* (from die Liebe, *love*)

Note: **Liebevoll** is the equivalent of **liebreich** above.

C. Verbal suffixes. Some of the more common verbal suffixes are: –**eln,** –**igen,** –**en,** –**ern,** –**ieren,** and –**zen.**

(1) –**eln:** This suffix forms from adjectives, nouns, and other verbs, verbs denoting a *diminutive idea* or the *repetition* of an activity:

> säuseln, *to rustle* [from sausen, *to roar* (as wind)]
> handeln, *to trade* (from die Hand, *hand*)

Note:

Sometimes the verb combines the ideas of diminution and iteration: kränkeln, *to be sickly* (from krank, *sick*).

In the case of verbs derived from nouns in –**el,** the verbal suffix –**eln** can hardly be said to have any meaning other than to convert the noun into a verb:

> gurgeln, *to gargle* (from die Gurgel, *throat*)
> prügeln, *to fight* or *thrash* (from der Prügel, *cudgel* or *stick*)

(2) –**igen:** This suffix forms verbs from adjectives and nouns:

> steinigen, *to stone* (from der Stein, *stone*)
> befestigen, *to fasten* or *make secure* (from fest, *firm*)

(3) –**en:** This suffix forms factitive verbs from the positive or comparative of adjectives to which it is affixed:

> zähmen, *to tame* (from zahm, *tame*)
> heizen, *to heat* (from heiß, *hot*)
> wärmen, *to warm* (from warm, *warm*)

Note: The suffix –**en,** however, often forms verbs that stand in various relations to the root words: bluten, *to bleed;* tafeln, *to eat.*

Caution: Weak verbs in **–nen** (which is really not a suffix) are derived from nouns or adjectives in **–en:**

> regnen, *to rain* (from der Regen, *rain*)
> trocknen, *to dry* (from trocken, *dry*)
> zeichnen, *to draw* or *sketch* (from das Zeichen, *sign, mark*)

(4) **–ern:** This suffix forms from verbs and nouns intensives, iteratives, and factitives:

> klappern, *to rattle* (from klappen, *to clap* or *clatter*)
> räuchern, *to (expose to) smoke* (from der Rauch, *smoke*)
> steigern, *to raise, strengthen,* or *enhance* (from steigen, *to mount*)

(5) **–ieren:** This suffix forms derivatives which are usually of foreign origin. For examples, *cf.* **Note** (4) of § 14.

(6) **–zen:** This suffix forms verbs that mean *to utter the word* or *sound* of the root word:

> duzen, *to address with* du (from du, *you*)

EXERCISE

A. Form feminine nouns with the suffix:

(1) **–e,** from: breit, dicht, lang, hart, treu, and groß.

(2) **–ei,** from: der Metzger (*butcher*), der Färber (*dyer*), der Schnitzer (*woodcarver*), and der Gerber (*leather dresser*).

(3) **–heit** or **–keit,** from: gesund, selig, blind, fröhlich, klug, dankbar, frei, tapfer, and dunkel.

(4) **–kunft,** from: zusammen and her.

(5) **–in,** from: der Schüler (*pupil*), der Tänzer (*dancer*), and der Sänger (*singer*).

(6) **–schaft,** from: der Bürger (*citizen*), der Meister (*master*), das Land (*country*), das Wissen (*knowledge*), and der Wirt (*innkeeper*).

(7) **–ung,** from: sich erkälten (*to catch cold*), sich versammeln (*to assemble*), entdecken (*to discover*), entzünden (*to inflame*), mischen (*to mix*), and entwickeln (*to develop*).

B. (1) Form neuter diminutives with the suffix **–chen** or **–lein** from:

der Sohn, der Brief, der Vogel, der Fuß, die Tochter, die Rose, die Stadt, die Nase, and der Hund.

(2) Form neuter nouns with the suffix:

(*a*) **–nis,** from: begraben (*to bury*), hindern (*to hinder*), and sich ereignen (*to occur*).

(*b*) **–sal,** from: laben (*to refresh*) and trüben (*to trouble*).[1]

(*c*) **–tum,** from: der Ritter (*knight*), der Besitz (*possession*), heilig (*holy*), eigen (*own*), das Alter (*age*), der Priester (*priest*), Christen (*Christians*), and Juden (*Jews*).

C. Form masculine nouns with the suffix:

(1) **–er,** from: schneiden (*to cut*), jagen[2] (*to chase*), morden[2] (*to murder*), Italien (*Italy*), Japan (*Japan*), Amerika[3] (*America*), reiten (*to ride*), reden[3] (*to speak*), kaufen[2] (*to buy*), and verkaufen[2] (*to sell*).

(2) **–el,** from: heben (*to lift*) and sich gürten (*to put on a girdle*).

(3) **–ling,** from: das Nest (*nest*), lieb (*dear*), finden (*to find*), weich (*weak*), and die Flucht[2] (*flight*).

D. Form adjectives with the suffix:

(1) **–er,** derived from the nouns in parentheses: der —— (Cologne) Dom; eine —— (Vienna) Wurst; das —— (Berlin) Leben; eine —— (Hamburg) Zeitung.

(2) **–(e)n** or **–ern,** from: das Gold[4] (*gold*), das Glas[5] (*glass*), der Stein[5] (*stone*), das Zinn[5] (*tin*), die Wolle[4] (*wool*), and die Seide[4] (*silk*).

(3) **–haft,** from: das Mädchen (*girl*), der Fehler (*mistake*), der Mangel (*fault*), die Tugend (*virtue*), die Dauer (*duration*), der Schalk (*rogue*), and der Spaß (*fun* or *joking*).

(4) **–bar,** from: die Furcht (*fear*), danken (*to thank*), heilen (*to cure*), trinken (*to drink*), fruchten (*to bear fruit*),[6] brennen (*to burn*), brauchen (*to use*), and übertragen (*to transmit, relay*).

---

[1] The derivative from **trüben** is usually feminine.
[2] The derivative takes umlaut.
[3] The derivative ends in **–ner.**
[4] The derivative ends in **–en**; it takes no umlaut.
[5] The derivative ends in **–ern**; only that of **Glas** takes umlaut.
[6] *Cf.* the noun **Frucht.**

(5) **–isch,** from: der Sturm[1] (*storm*), die Stadt[1] (*city*), der Verschwender (*spendthrift*), Italien (*Italy*), Spanien (*Spain*) (derivative drops the –ien), der Narr[1] (*fool*), der Dichter (*poet*), der Maler (*artist*), der Redner (*speaker* or *orator*), and die Stratosphäre (*stratosphere*).

(6) **–lich,** from: der König, das Herz, der Freund, der Feind, der Vater,[1] die Mutter,[1] der Mann,[1] das Weib, die Sache[1] (derivative drops the –e), der Tag,[1] die Woche[1] (derivative adds –nt–), der Monat, das Jahr,[1] die Nacht,[1] die Natur,[1] der Tod,[1] and Ehre (compound drops the –e).

(7) **–ig,** from: das Salz, der Hunger, der Durst, der Fleiß, die Macht,[1] die Kraft,[1] die Sonne, das Gift, die Luft, die Geduld, der Sand, and heute (compound drops the –e).

(8) **–los,** from: der Schmerz (*pain*), der Schlaf (*sleep*), die Treue (*fidelity*), die Hoffnung (*hope*) (derivative adds –s–), die Wolke (*cloud*) (derivative adds –n before the suffix).

(9) **–sam,** from: schweigen (*to be silent*), die Furcht (*fear*), gemein (*common*), folgen (*to follow*), wirken (*to effect*), aufmerken (*to pay attention*), and sich enthalten (*to abstain from*).

(10) **–reich,** from: das Wasser (*water*), der Fisch (*fish*), die Zahl (*number*), die Lehre (*instruction*), and die Kunst (*art*).

(11) **–voll,** from: das Wunder (*wonder* or *miracle*), der Kummer (*grief* or *trouble*), and die Pracht (*splendor*).

E. Form verbs with the suffix:

(1) **–eln,** from: lachen[1] (*to laugh*), klingen (*to sound*).

(2) **–igen,** from: Huld[2] (*grace* or *favor*), rein (*clean*), Kraft[1] (*strength*).

(3) **–en,** factitives from: warm[1] (*warm*), stark[1] (*strong*), hart[1] (*hard*), rot[1] (*red*), frei (*free*) (derivative adds **be–**).

(4) **–ern,** from: einschlafen[1] (*to fall asleep*).

(5) **–zen,** from: ach[1] (*oh* or *alas*).

---

[1] The derivative takes umlaut.
[2] The derivative takes no umlaut.

91. PREFIXES

Many German words are formed with prepositions, adverbs, and other parts of speech as prefixes—*e.g.*, aúfstehen (*to get up*), fórtgehen (*to go away*).[1]

A. Noun and adjective prefixes. A few of the more common noun and adjective prefixes are: **ge–**, **ur–**, **un–**, and **erz–**:

(1) **ge–:** This prefix forms from noun stems nouns denoting *collectivity;* from verbal roots, nouns denoting the *action of a verb* itself:

> das Gebirge, *mountain range* or *mountainous region* (from der Berg, *mountain*)
> das Gebüsch, *bushes* (from der Busch, *bush*)
> der Geschmack, *taste* (from schmecken, *to taste*)
> der Geruch, *smell* (from riechen, *to smell*)

Note:

The prefix **ge–** is often equivalent to the English prefix *com–*:

> der Gefährte, *comrade* or *fellow traveler* (from fahren, *to travel*)
> der Geselle, *companion* (lit. *roommate*) (from der Saal, *room*)

Observe the plural forms **Gebrüder,** *brothers,* and **Geschwister,** *brothers and sisters.*

(2) **ur–:** This prefix forms from nouns and adjectives nouns and adjectives denoting *primitive, original,* or *very ancient:*

> uralt, *very old* (from alt, *old*)
> der Urgroßvater, *great-grandfather* (from der Großvater, *grandfather*)
> die Ururgroßmutter, *great-great-grandmother* (from die Großmutter, *grandmother*)
> der Urwald, *primeval forest* (from der Wald, *forest*)
> die Ursache, *the (first) cause* (from die Sache, *thing* or *cause*)
> der Urzustand, *original condition* (from der Zustand, *condition*)
> das Urgestein, *primitive rock, mother* or *igneous rock* (from das Gestein, *rock*)

(3) **un–:** This prefix forms from adjectives negative adjectives; from nouns, either negative nouns or nouns which strongly intensify the meaning of the original:

---

[1] For prepositions and separable and inseparable prefixes, *cf.* Chapters 10 and 20.

unmöglich, *impossible* (from möglich, *possible*)
unverständlich, *unintelligible* or *incomprehensible* (from verständlich, *comprehensible*)
der Undank, *ingratitude* (from der Dank, *thanks*)
eine Unzahl, *a great number* (from die Zahl, *number*)
unbemannt, *unmanned* (from bemannt, *manned*)
unverdünnt, *undiluted* (from verdünnt, *diluted*)

Note:
The prefix **un–** is usually equivalent to the English prefixes *un–*, *in–*, and *im–*.

Observe that **die Untiefe** may mean either *shallowness* (the negative of die Tiefe) or *great depth* (the intensified meaning of die Tiefe).

(4) **erz–:** This prefix forms from nouns, nouns denoting *chief*, *principal*, or *master;* from adjectives, adjectives in which the meaning of the original has been intensified:

der Erzengel, *archangel* (from der Engel, *angel*)
der Erzbischof, *archbishop* (from der Bischof, *bishop*)
erzfaul, *extremely lazy* (from faul, *lazy*)

Note: The prefix **erz–** is equivalent to the English prefix *arch–*.

EXERCISE

Form nouns with the prefix **ge–** from: die Wolke (*cloud*), der Stein (*stone*), das Wasser (*water*), fühlen (*to feel*), and brüllen (*to roar*).

Explain the meaning of der Tischgenosse (from genießen, *to enjoy*).

Form nouns or adjectives with the prefix:

ur–, from: der Enkel (*grandson*), die Enkelin (*granddaughter*), Einwohner (*inhabitants*), der Zweck (*purpose*), die Zeit (*time*), die Geschichte (*history*), der Grund (*cause*), verwandt (*related*), germanisch (*Germanic*), and der Wald (*forest*).

un–, from: sichtbar (*visible*), höflich (*polite*), abhängig (*dependent*), die Masse (*mass* or *crowd*), ruhig (*quiet*), angenehm (*pleasant*), and denkbar (*conceivable*).

erz–, from: der Herzog (*duke*), dumm (*stupid*), der Lügner (*liar*), and der Dieb (*thief*).

B. Verbal prefixes. Verbal prefixes may be either **separable** or **inseparable.**

(1) For separable verbal prefixes, *cf.* § 70.

(2) Inseparable verbal prefixes[1] originally had certain fundamental meanings, which are still preserved in some verbs although lost in many others. The meaning of one (**zer–**), however, has remained constant. These prefixes are: **be–, ent–** (or **emp–**), **er–, ge–, ver–,** and **zer–**:

(*a*) **be–:** This prefix serves to make a verb transitive (*i.e.*, a verb formed with it may take a direct object): bedienen, *to serve;* bekommen, *to receive;* beantworten, *to answer*. [*Cf.* § 35 ¶ I. (1).]

(*b*) **ent–** (or **emp–**): This prefix denotes the *beginning of an action* or *separation;* entstehen, *to arise* (or *come into existence*); entzünden, *to inflame;* entlassen, *to dismiss;* entgehen, *to escape;* entlaufen, *to run away;* entsäuern, *to deacidify, to neutralize.*

(*c*) **er–:** This prefix denotes *origin* or *accomplishment:* erblühen, *to blossom;* erwachen, *to wake;* erleben, *to experience;* erreichen, *to attain;* erraten, *to guess correctly.*

(*d*) **ge–:** This prefix denotes *result* or *completeness* (as shown also in the past participle prefix **ge–**) and often *successful action:* gelangen, *to arrive at;* genesen, *to get well;* gewinnen, *to gain.*

Note: The prefix **ge–** originally denoted *with* or *together* (*cf.* noun prefix **ge–** in ¶ **A** (1) above) and had perfective force equivalent to the Latin prefix *con–*, as in "*conficere,*" *to accomplish.*

(*e*) **ver–:** This prefix often denotes that the action of a verb *miscarried:* verführen, *to lead astray;* verspielen, *to lose money in playing;* verkennen, *to misjudge;* verlegen, *to misplace;* sich verschlafen, *to oversleep;* verdrehen, *to distort.*

Note: The prefix **ver–** is sometimes equivalent to the English prefix *for–:* vergeben, *to forgive;* vergessen, *to forget;* verbieten, *to forbid.*

---

[1] *Cf.* also Chapter 20.

(*f*) **zer–:** This prefix is the most constant in meaning of any of the inseparable prefixes. It regularly denotes *going asunder, apart,* or *in pieces;* or *destruction* or *damage* resulting from the action of the original verb: zerreißen, *to tear to pieces* (or *damage by tearing*); zerbrechen, *to break to pieces;* zerschneiden, *to cut to pieces;* zerfallen, *to fall to pieces;* zerlegen, *to take apart;* zerstreuen, *to scatter;* zerknallen, *to explode, to detonate.*

92. COGNATES

The ability to recognize English-German cognates (*i.e.,* words etymologically related) enables a student to understand words which might otherwise be unintelligible to him without the aid of a dictionary.

A. Changes in form and meaning of cognates. Certain cognates are identical in both form and meaning (Arm, *arm;* Hand, *hand*), others differ slightly in form but have the same meaning (Distel, *thistle*), and some differ in both form and meaning (Stube, *stove*). These changes take place in accordance with definite phonetic laws; thus if the cognate forms of **D**istel and **D**urst are *thistle* and *thirst*, we may look for a similar change in many other words—*e.g.,* Le**d**er and *leather.*

Note: It does not, of course, follow that each German word has an English cognate.

B. Common cognates. It is beyond the province of this type of book to give a detailed treatment of cognates—including vowels, diphthongs, and the less common consonants. The following are merely some of the more common English-German cognates arranged in groups according to consonant changes:

(1) English *p* >¹ German **f, ff,** or **pf:**

sharp, scharf	*open*, offen
up, auf	*ship*, Schiff
leap, laufen	*plant*, Pflanze
deep, tief	*penny*, Pfennig

---

¹ The symbol > means *becomes.*

(2) English *t* > German **z** or **ß**:

twig, Zweig   ten, zehn
to, zu   curt, kurz
timber, Zimmer   foot, Fuß

(3) English *k* > German **ch**:

week, Woche   make, machen
lark, Lerche   sake, Sache
token, Zeichen   book, Buch

(4) English *d* > German **t**:

day, Tag   word, Wort
deal, Teil   God, Gott
wide, weit   blade, Blatt
side, Seite   deer, Tier
old, alt   fodder, Futter

(5) English *th* > German **d**:

thou, du   earth, Erde
three, drei   brother, Bruder
thine, dein   seethe, sieden

(6) English *v* or *f* > German **b**:

silver, Silber   evil, übel
harvest, Herbst   deaf, taub

(7) English *y* > German **g**:

day, Tag   holy, heilig
way, Weg   yester(day), gestern
fly, fliegen   yard, Garten

EXERCISE

Give cognate forms—**not *necessarily* a translation**—of the following:[1]

A. helfen, Schlaf, hoffen, Haufe, Affe, Pfad, Pfund, Pfeife, Pfeffer, Apfel, reif, Schaf, Seife, Stiefvater, Pfanne, Pflaume, Pflaster, Waffe, Pfau.

---

[1] Paragraphs A–G of this exercise correspond to parts (1)–(7) of § 92 **B** above.

B. Zeit, Zoll, Salz, Malz, Zunge, Holz, groß, weiß, Haß, essen, Straße, reißen, grüßen, beißen, vergessen, Zahn, zwölf, zahm, Zinn, Zug.

C. brechen, suchen, wachen, auch, Grieche, Eiche, sprechen, Joch, Milch, Storch, streichen, weich, Deich, bleich.

D. Tisch, laut, tief, hart, Bett, Tür, Tochter, tot, Traum, traurig, trinken, tun, tüchtig, Tanz, Blut, falten, Not.

E. Nord, daß, dies–, dünn, dick, denken, baden, beide, Feder, Heide, Leder, danken, Ding, Donner, Kleid, Herd, Bude, Dorn, Eid, Schmied, Durst, dreschen, Distel, Dieb, würdig.

F. haben, leben, lieben, sterben, heben, treiben, eben, sieben, über, Taube, Grab, Knabe, Leber, Rabe, Schaufel, Stube, weben, Stab, schieben, Sieb, streben, Dieb.

G. gelb, traurig, tüchtig, sagen, Auge, mag (from mögen), lag (from liegen), gern, gelten, hungrig, Pfennig, bergen, Garn.

Appendix

93. THE DEFINITE ARTICLE

| | SINGULAR | | | PLURAL |
	MASCULINE	FEMININE	NEUTER	ALL GENDERS
Nom.	der	die	das	die
Gen.	des	der	des	der
Dat.	dem	der	dem	den
Acc.	den	die	das	die

94. THE DEMONSTRATIVE DIESER

| | SINGULAR | | | PLURAL |
	MASCULINE	FEMININE	NEUTER	ALL GENDERS
Nom.	dieser	diese	dieses	diese
Gen.	dieses	dieser	dieses	dieser
Dat.	diesem	dieser	diesem	diesen
Acc.	diesen	diese	dieses	diese

Note: All **der**-words are declined like **dieser** (*cf.* § 8 **C**).

95. THE INDEFINITE ARTICLE

| | SINGULAR | | |
	MASCULINE	FEMININE	NEUTER
Nom.	ein	eine	ein
Gen.	eines	einer	eines
Dat.	einem	einer	einem
Acc.	einen	eine	ein

Note: **Ein** has no plural forms.

96. THE POSSESSIVE MEIN

	SINGULAR			PLURAL
	MASCULINE	FEMININE	NEUTER	ALL GENDERS
Nom.	mein	meine	mein	meine
Gen.	meines	meiner	meines	meiner
Dat.	meinem	meiner	meinem	meinen
Acc.	meinen	meine	mein	meine

Note: All **ein**-words are declined like **mein** (*cf.* **Summary** of § 10 **B**).

97. THE DEMONSTRATIVE DERSELBE

	SINGULAR			PLURAL
	MASCULINE	FEMININE	NEUTER	ALL GENDERS
Nom.	derselbe	dieselbe	dasselbe	dieselben
Gen.	desselben	derselben	desselben	derselben
Dat.	demselben	derselben	demselben	denselben
Acc.	denselben	dieselbe	dasselbe	dieselben

Note: **Derjenige** is declined like **derselbe**.

98. NOUN DECLENSION

A. The strong declension:

(1) Class I:

SINGULAR

Nom.	der Vater	der Onkel	die Mutter	das Mädchen
Gen.	des Vaters	des Onkels	der Mutter	des Mädchens
Dat.	dem Vater	dem Onkel	der Mutter	dem Mädchen
Acc.	den Vater	den Onkel	die Mutter	das Mädchen

PLURAL

Nom.	die Väter	die Onkel	die Mütter	die Mädchen
Gen.	der Väter	der Onkel	der Mütter	der Mädchen
Dat.	den Vätern	den Onkeln	den Müttern	den Mädchen
Acc.	die Väter	die Onkel	die Mütter	die Mädchen

Note: Class I comprises:

Masculine and neuter nouns (sometimes with umlaut in the plural) ending in **–el, –en,** and **–er.**

Caution: This does not include mixed nouns such as der **Bauer,** *peasant* and der **Vetter,** *male cousin* listed under ¶ **C** below.

The two feminine nouns die **Mutter** (pl. Mütter), *mother* and die **Tochter** (pl. Töchter), *daughter.*

Neuter diminutives in **–chen** and **–lein.**

Neuter nouns with the prefix **ge–** and ending in **–e:** das Gebäude, *building;* das Gebirge, *mountain range* (or *mountainous region*).

(2) Class II:

SINGULAR

Nom.				
der Baum	der Arm	die Hand	der König	das Ereignis
Gen.				
des Baumes	des Armes	der Hand	des Königs	des Ereignisses
Dat.				
dem Baume	dem Arme	der Hand	dem König	dem Ereignis
Acc.				
den Baum	den Arm	die Hand	den König	das Ereignis

PLURAL

Nom.				
die Bäume	die Arme	die Hände	die Könige	die Ereignisse
Gen.				
der Bäume	der Arme	der Hände	der Könige	der Ereignisse
Dat.				
den Baümen	den Armen	den Händen	den Königen	den Ereignissen
Acc.				
die Bäume	die Arme	die Hände	die Könige	die Ereignisse

Note: Class II comprises:

Monosyllables:

Many masculines, usually with umlaut: der Sohn.

Caution: The following common nouns, however, do not take umlaut: der Arm, der Dom, der Hund, der Laut, der Mond, der Park, der Schuh, der Tag.

Some feminines which always take umlaut: die Wand.

Some neuters which almost always do not take umlaut: das Jahr, das Haar.

Caution: Two neuter nouns of this group that do take umlaut, however, are das (less often der) **Floß** (pl. Flöße), *raft* and das **Chor** (pl. Chöre), *choir* (*i.e.*, that part of a church in which the choir—**der** Chor—*sits*).

Polysyllables (usually without umlaut):

Masculine nouns ending in –**ig** and –**ling**: der König, *king;* der Honig, *honey;* der Frühling, *spring.*

Nouns ending in –**nis** and –**sal** (usually neuter but sometimes feminine): das Erlebnis, *experience;* die Erlaubnis, *permission;* das Schicksal, *fate;* die (or das) Trübsal, *affliction.*

Caution: Nouns in –**nis** double the final **s** before an ending.

Neuters with the prefix **ge**–: das Gedicht, *poem;* das Gesetz, *law.*

Words of foreign origin accented on the last syllable: der Vokal, *vowel;* das Papier, *paper.*

(3) Class III:

SINGULAR

Nom.	der Mann	das Haus	das Eigentum
Gen.	des Mannes	des Hauses	des Eigentums
Dat.	dem Manne	dem Hause	dem Eigentum
Acc.	den Mann	das Haus	das Eigentum

PLURAL

Nom.	die Männer	die Häuser	die Eigentümer
Gen.	der Männer	der Häuser	der Eigentümer
Dat.	den Männern	den Häusern	den Eigentümern
Acc.	die Männer	die Häuser	die Eigentümer

Note:

Class III comprises:

Many neuter nouns of one syllable.

A few masculines of one syllable.

Neuters ending in **–tum.**

Caution: There are only two masculines ending in **–tum:** der Reichtum, *riches* and der Irrtum, *error.*

Some neuters with the prefix **ge–:** das Gesicht, *face;* das Gespenst, *ghost.*

Class III contains no feminine nouns.

Nouns in Class III take umlaut in the plural whenever possible.

B. The weak declension:

SINGULAR

Nom.	der Junge	die Frau	der Student	die Feder
Gen.	des Jungen	der Frau	des Studenten	der Feder
Dat.	dem Jungen	der Frau	dem Studenten	der Feder
Acc.	den Jungen	die Frau	den Studenten	die Feder

PLURAL

Nom.	die Jungen	die Frauen	die Studenten	die Federn
Gen.	der Jungen	der Frauen	der Studenten	der Federn
Dat.	den Jungen	den Frauen	den Studenten	den Federn
Acc.	die Jungen	die Frauen	die Studenten	die Federn

Note:

The weak declension comprises:

All feminines of more than one syllable except die **Mutter** and die **Tochter** and the few feminine nouns ending in **–nis** and **–sal.**

Many feminines of one syllable.

Masculine nouns of one syllable denoting living beings: der Herr, *gentleman (master, Mr.,* or *lord); der Bär, bear;* der Mensch, *man.*

Masculine nouns of more than one syllable ending in **–e** and denoting living beings: der Junge, *boy;* der Neffe, *nephew;* der Ochse, *ox;* der Affe, *ape* (or *monkey*).

Masculine nouns of foreign origin accented on the last syllable: der Soldat, *soldier;* der Elefant, *elephant;* der Präsident, *president;* der Student, *student.*

The weak declension contains no neuter nouns.

Nouns of the weak declension never add umlaut in the plural.

C. The mixed (or irregular) declension:

SINGULAR

Nom.	der Staat	der Professor	das Auge
Gen.	des Staates	des Professors	des Auges
Dat.	dem Staate	dem Professor	dem Auge
Acc.	den Staat	den Professor	das Auge

PLURAL

Nom.	die Staaten	die Professoren	die Augen
Gen.	der Staaten	der Professoren	der Augen
Dat.	den Staaten	den Professoren	den Augen
Acc.	die Staaten	die Professoren	die Augen

Note:

The mixed (or irregular) declension comprises:

A few native German or naturalized words: der Schmerz, *pain;* der Staat, *state;* das Auge, *eye;* das Bett, *bed;* das Ende, *end;* das Hemd, *shirt;* das Ohr, *ear;* der Vetter, *male cousin;* der Bauer, *peasant* (or *farmer*).[1]

Masculines of foreign origin ending in –**or** in which the short **o** becomes long in the plural by a shift in accent: *e.g.,* der Proféssor but die Professóren.

Foreign neuters in –**um** with the plural in –**en:**

das Gymnasium	die Gymnasien
des Gymnasiums	der Gymnasien
dem Gymnasium	den Gymnasien
das Gymnasium	die Gymnasien

Other nouns of this type are: das Museum (des Museums, die Museen), *museum;* das Partizipium (des Partizipiums, die Partizipien), *participle.*

---

[1] Der **Bauer** often has weak endings (–**n**) in the singular.

Foreign neuters in –il and –al with the plural in –ien: das Fossil (des Fossils, die Fossilien), *fossil;* das Mineral (des Minerals, die Mineralien), *mineral.*

Foreign nouns with plural forms in –s (in all cases): das Hotel (des Hotels, die Hotels), *hotel;* das Sofa (des Sofas, die Sofas), *sofa;* das Auto (des Autos, die Autos), *auto;* das Kino, (des Kinos, die Kinos), *cinema;* das Radio (des Radios, die Radios), *radio;* der Tee (des Tees, die Tees), *tea;* das Echo (des Echos, die Echos), *echo.*

A few foreign nouns ending in –s have the same form throughout the singular and plural, e.g., das Relais, —, — (*relay*), a word now common in technical vocabulary, especially in compounded forms: der Funk-Relais-Satellit (*radio-relay satellite*).

99. ADJECTIVE DECLENSION

A. The strong declension:

SINGULAR

Nom.	guter	Tee	rote Seide	kaltes	Bier
Gen.	guten	Tees	roter Seide	kalten	Bieres
Dat.	gutem	Tee	roter Seide	kaltem	Biere
Acc.	guten	Tee	rote Seide	kaltes	Bier

PLURAL

Nom.	treue	Freunde	schöne Frauen	reiche Länder
Gen.	treuer	Freunde	schöner Frauen	reicher Länder
Dat.	treuen	Freunden	schönen Frauen	reichen Ländern
Acc.	treue	Freunde	schöne Frauen	reiche Länder

B. The weak declension:

SINGULAR

Nom.	der gute Freund	die liebe Tochter	das große Haus
Gen.	des guten Freundes	der lieben Tochter	des großen Hauses
Dat.	dem guten Freunde	der lieben Tochter	dem großen Hause
Acc.	den guten Freund	die liebe Tochter	das große Haus

PLURAL

Nom.			
die	guten Freunde	die lieben Töchter	die großen Häuser

Gen.

der	guten Freunde	der lieben Töchter	der großen Häuser

Dat.

den	guten Freunden	den lieben Töchtern	den großen Häusern

Acc.

die	guten Freunde	die lieben Töchter	die großen Häuser

Note:

The weak adjective declension occurs after any **der**-word (*cf.* § 8 **C**). Weak endings are also added to comparative and superlative stems:

> der ältere Junge (des älteren Jungen, *etc.*), *the older boy*
> der älteste Junge (des ältesten Jungen, *etc.*), *the oldest boy*

C. The mixed declension:

SINGULAR

Nom.

ein	kleiner Stuhl	eine rote Rose	ein	kleines Zimmer

Gen.

eines	kleinen Stuhles	einer roten Rose	eines	kleinen Zimmers

Dat.

einem	kleinen Stuhle	einer roten Rose	einem	kleinen Zimmer

Acc.

einen	kleinen Stuhl	eine rote Rose	ein	kleines Zimmer

Note:

The mixed adjective declension occurs after **ein**-words (*cf.* **Summary** of § 10 **B**).

Adjectives after **ein**-words admitting a plural are declined in the same manner as those having the weak declension: meine lieben Kinder (meiner lieben Kinder, meinen lieben Kindern, meine lieben Kinder), *my dear children.*

Observe that the same endings are also added to comparative and superlative stems:

> ein reicherer Mann (eines reicheren Mannes, *etc.*), *a richer man*
> sein reichster Freund (seines reichsten Freundes, *etc.*), *his richest friend.*

100. THE DECLENSION OF PROPER NAMES

Nom.	Goethe	Amerika	Karl der Große
Gen.	Goethes	Amerikas	Karls des Großen
Dat.	Goethe	Amerika	Karl dem Großen
Acc.	Goethe	Amerika	Karl den Großen

Nom.	König Friedrich	der König Friedrich
Gen.	König Friedrichs	des Königs Friedrich
Dat.	König Friedrich	dem König Friedrich
Acc.	König Friedrich	den König Friedrich

101. THE DECLENSION OF PRONOUNS

A. Personal pronouns:

SINGULAR

Nom.	ich (*I*)	du (*you*)	er (*he*)	sie (*she*)	es (*it*)	Sie (*you*)
Gen.	(meiner)	(deiner)	(seiner)	(ihrer)	(seiner)	(Ihrer)
Dat.	mir	dir	ihm	ihr	ihm	Ihnen
Acc.	mich	dich	ihn	sie	es	Sie

PLURAL

Nom.	wir (*we*)	ihr (*you*)	sie [*they* (all genders)]	Sie (*you*)
Gen.	(unser)	(euer)	(ihrer)	(Ihrer)
Dat.	uns	euch	ihnen	Ihnen
Acc.	uns	euch	sie	Sie

Note: The genitive forms are given in parentheses because they are rare.

B. Interrogative pronouns:

	MASCULINE AND FEMININE	NEUTER
Nom.	wer	was
Gen.	wessen	(wes, wessen)
Dat.	wem	———
Acc.	wen	was

Note:

The genitive forms of the neuter interrogative **was** are rare.

Interrogative **was** has no dative form.

C. Demonstrative pronouns:

(1) **Dieser** and **jener** are declined like the definite article (*cf.* § 94 of the Appendix).

(2) For the declension of **derselbe** and **derjenige** (*cf.* § 97 of the Appendix).

(3) **Der** as demonstrative pronoun is declined like the relative pronoun (*cf.* ¶ **D** of this section).

Note:

For both possible forms of the genitive plural of **der**, *cf.* **Note** (2) of § 58.

(*a*) **Dieser, jener, derselbe, derjenige,** and **der** are also demonstrative adjectives.

(*b*) As demonstrative adjective, **der** is declined like the definite article.

D. Relative pronouns:

SINGULAR

	MASCULINE	FEMININE	NEUTER
Nom.	der, welcher	die, welche	das, welches
Gen.	dessen	deren	dessen
Dat.	dem, welchem	der, welcher	dem, welchem
Acc.	den, welchen	die, welche	das, welches

PLURAL

ALL GENDERS
die,   welche
deren
denen, welchen
die,   welche

Note: As relative pronouns, **wer** and **was** are declined like the interrogatives **wer** and **was** (*cf.* ¶ **B** of this section).

102. THE AUXILIARY VERBS HABEN, SEIN, **AND** WERDEN

A. The indicative mood:

(1) Present (*I have, am, become; etc.*):

SINGULAR

ich habe	ich bin	ich werde
du hast	du bist	du wirst
er hat	er ist	er wird

PLURAL

wir haben	wir sind	wir werden
ihr habt	ihr seid	ihr werdet
sie haben	sie sind	sie werden

(2) Past (*I had, was, became; etc.*):

SINGULAR

ich hatte	ich war	ich wurde
du hattest	du warst	du wurdest
er hatte	er war	er wurde

PLURAL

wir hatten	wir waren	wir wurden
ihr hattet	ihr wart	ihr wurdet
sie hatten	sie waren	sie wurden

(3) Perfect (*I have had, have been, have become; etc.*):

SINGULAR

ich habe gehabt	ich bin gewesen	ich bin geworden
du hast gehabt	du bist gewesen	du bist geworden
er hat gehabt	er ist gewesen	er ist geworden

PLURAL

wir haben gehabt	wir sind gewesen	wir sind geworden
ihr habt gehabt	ihr seid gewesen	ihr seid geworden
sie haben gehabt	sie sind gewesen	sie sind geworden

(4) Past Perfect (*I had had, had been, had become; etc.*):

SINGULAR

ich hatte gehabt	ich war gewesen	ich war geworden
du hattest gehabt	du warst gewesen	du warst geworden
er hatte gehabt	er war gewesen	er war geworden

PLURAL

wir hatten gehabt	wir waren gewesen	wir waren geworden
ihr hattet gehabt	ihr wart gewesen	ihr wart geworden
sie hatten gehabt	sie waren gewesen	sie waren geworden

(5) Future (*I shall have, shall be, shall become; etc.*):

SINGULAR

ich werde haben	ich werde sein	ich werde werden
du wirst haben	du wirst sein	du wirst werden
er wird haben	er wird sein	er wird werden

PLURAL

wir werden haben	wir werden sein	wir werden werden
ihr werdet haben	ihr werdet sein	ihr werdet werden
sie werden haben	sie werden sein	sie werden werden

(6) Future Perfect (*I shall have had, shall have been, shall have become; etc.*):

SINGULAR

ich werde gehabt haben	ich werde gewesen sein
du wirst gehabt haben	du wirst gewesen sein
er wird gehabt haben	er wird gewesen sein

ich werde geworden sein
du wirst geworden sein
er wird   geworden sein

PLURAL

wir werden gehabt haben	wir werden gewesen sein
ihr werdet gehabt haben	ihr werdet gewesen sein
sie werden gehabt haben	sie werden gewesen sein

wir werden geworden sein
ihr werdet geworden sein
sie werden geworden sein

B. The subjunctive mood.

(1) Present:

SINGULAR

ich habe	ich sei	ich werde
du habest	du seiest	du werdest
er habe	er sei	er werde

PLURAL

wir haben	wir seien	wir werden
ihr habet	ihr seiet	ihr werdet
sie haben	sie seien	sie werden

(2) Past:

SINGULAR

ich hätte	ich wäre	ich würde
du hättest	du wärest	du würdest
er hätte	er wäre	er würde

PLURAL

wir hätten	wir wären	wir würden
ihr hättet	ihr wäret	ihr würdet
sie hätten	sie wären	sie würden

(3) Perfect:

SINGULAR

ich habe gehabt	ich sei gewesen	ich sei geworden
du habest gehabt	du seiest gewesen	du seiest geworden
er habe gehabt	er sei gewesen	er sei geworden

PLURAL

wir haben gehabt	wir seien gewesen	wir seien geworden
ihr habet gehabt	ihr seiet gewesen	ihr seiet geworden
sie haben gehabt	sie seien gewesen	sie seien geworden

(4) Past Perfect:

SINGULAR

ich hätte gehabt	ich wäre gewesen	ich wäre geworden
du hättest gehabt	du wärest gewesen	du wärest geworden
er hätte gehabt	er wäre gewesen	er wäre geworden

PLURAL

wir hätten gehabt	wir wären gewesen	wir wären geworden
ihr hättet gehabt	ihr wäret gewesen	ihr wäret geworden
sie hätten gehabt	sie wären gewesen	sie wären geworden

(5) Future:

SINGULAR

ich werde haben	ich werde sein	ich werde werden
du werdest haben	du werdest sein	du werdest werden
er werde haben	er werde sein	er werde werden

PLURAL

wir werden haben	wir werden sein	wir werden werden
ihr werdet haben	ihr werdet sein	ihr werdet werden
sie werden haben	sie werden sein	sie werden werden

(6) Future Perfect:

SINGULAR

ich werde gehabt haben	ich werde gewesen sein
du werdest gehabt haben	du werdest gewesen sein
er werde gehabt haben	er werde gewesen sein

ich werde geworden sein
du werdest geworden sein
er werde geworden sein

PLURAL

wir werden gehabt haben	wir werden gewesen sein
ihr werdet gehabt haben	ihr werdet gewesen sein
sie werden gehabt haben	sie werden gewesen sein

wir werden geworden sein
ihr werdet geworden sein
sie werden geworden sein

Note: Since the meaning of the subjunctive depends upon its use in a particular sentence, no English equivalents have been given for the various tenses of the subjunctive.

C. The conditional mood:

(1) Present:

SINGULAR

ich würde haben	ich würde sein	ich würde werden
du würdest haben	du würdest sein	du würdest werden
er würde haben	er würde sein	er würde werden

PLURAL

wir würden haben	wir würden sein	wir würden werden
ihr würdet haben	ihr würdet sein	ihr würdet werden
sie würden haben	sie würden sein	sie würden werden

(2) Past:

SINGULAR

ich würde gehabt haben	ich würde gewesen sein
du würdest gehabt haben	du würdest gewesen sein
er würde gehabt haben	er würde gewesen sein

ich würde geworden sein
du würdest geworden sein
er würde geworden sein

PLURAL

wir würden gehabt haben	wir würden gewesen sein
ihr würdet gehabt haben	ihr würdet gewesen sein
sie würden gehabt haben	sie würden gewesen sein

wir würden geworden sein
ihr würdet geworden sein
sie würden geworden sein

D. The imperative mood:

SINGULAR

| habe | sei | werde |
| haben Sie | seien Sie | werden Sie |

PLURAL

habt	seid	werdet
haben Sie	seien Sie	werden Sie

E. Infinitives:

(1) Present: haben, sein, werden.

(2) Perfect: gehabt haben, gewesen sein, geworden sein.

F. Participles:

(1) Present: habend, seiend, werdend.

(2) Past: gehabt, gewesen, geworden.

Note: The present participles of **haben, sein,** and **werden** are rarely used.

103. THE WEAK CONJUGATION

The weak verb **lernen (lernte, hat gelernt)** is conjugated as follows:

A. The indicative mood: **B. The subjunctive mood:**

(1) Present (*I learn, etc.*):   (1) Present:

SINGULAR   SINGULAR

ich lerne	ich lerne
du lernst	du lernest
er lernt	er lerne

PLURAL   PLURAL

wir lernen	wir lernen
ihr lernt	ihr lernet
sie lernen	sie lernen

(2) Past (*I learned, etc.*):   (2) Past:

SINGULAR   SINGULAR

ich lernte	ich lernte
du lerntest	du lerntest
er lernte	er lernte

A. The indicative mood (*cont.*): **B. The subjunctive mood** (*cont.*):

PLURAL

wir lernten
ihr lerntet
sie lernten

PLURAL

wir lernten
ihr lerntet
sie lernten

(3) Perfect (*I have learned, etc.*):

(3) Perfect:

SINGULAR

ich habe gelernt
du hast gelernt
er hat gelernt

SINGULAR

ich habe gelernt
du habest gelernt
er habe gelernt

PLURAL

wir haben gelernt
ihr habt gelernt
sie haben gelernt

PLURAL

wir haben gelernt
ihr habet gelernt
sie haben gelernt

(4) Past Perfect (*I had learned, etc.*):

(4) Past Perfect:

SINGULAR

ich hatte gelernt
du hattest gelernt
er hatte gelernt

SINGULAR

ich hätte gelernt
du hättest gelernt
er hätte gelernt

PLURAL

wir hatten gelernt
ihr hattet gelernt
sie hatten gelernt

PLURAL

wir hätten gelernt
ihr hättet gelernt
sie hätten gelernt

(5) Future (*I shall learn, etc.*):

(5) Future:

SINGULAR

ich werde lernen
du wirst lernen
er wird lernen

SINGULAR

ich werde lernen
du werdest lernen
er werde lernen

PLURAL

wir werden   lernen
ihr werdet   lernen
sie werden   lernen

PLURAL

wir werden lernen
ihr werdet lernen
sie werden lernen

(6) Future Perfect (*I shall have learned, etc.*):

SINGULAR

ich werde gelernt haben
du wirst   gelernt haben
er wird   gelernt haben

PLURAL

wir werden gelernt haben
ihr werdet gelernt haben
sie werden gelernt haben

(6) Future Perfect:

SINGULAR

ich werde   gelernt haben
du werdest gelernt haben
er werde   gelernt haben

PLURAL

wir werden gelernt haben
ihr werdet gelernt haben
sie werden gelernt haben

C. The conditional mood:

(1) Present:

SINGULAR

ich würde   lernen
du würdest lernen
er würde   lernen

PLURAL

wir würden lernen
ihr würdet lernen
sie würden lernen

(2) Past:

SINGULAR

ich würde   gelernt haben
du würdest gelernt haben
er würde   gelernt haben

PLURAL

wir würden gelernt haben
ihr würdet gelernt haben
sie würden gelernt haben

D. The imperative mood:

SINGULAR

lerne
lernen Sie

PLURAL

lernt
lernen Sie

E. Infinitives:

(1) Present: lernen
(2) Perfect: gelernt haben

F. Participles:

(1) Present: lernend
(2) Past: gelernt

Note: Passive forms are given in § 108 of the Appendix.

104. THE STRONG CONJUGATION

A. Sehen. The strong verb **sehen (sah, hat gesehen)** is conjugated as follows:

(1) The indicative mood:

(a) Present (*I see, etc.*):

SINGULAR

ich sehe
du siehst
er   sieht

PLURAL

wir sehen
ihr seht
sie sehen

(b) Past (*I saw, etc.*):

SINGULAR

ich sah
du sahst
er   sah

PLURAL

wir sahen
ihr saht
sie sahen

(2) The subjunctive mood:

(a) Present:

SINGULAR

ich sehe
du sehest
er   sehe

PLURAL

wir sehen
ihr sehet
sie sehen

(b) Past:

SINGULAR

ich sähe
du sähest
er   sähe

PLURAL

wir sähen
ihr sähet
sie sähen

(c) Perfect (*I have seen, etc.*):

(c) Perfect:

SINGULAR

ich habe gesehen
du hast gesehen
er hat gesehen

SINGULAR

ich habe gesehen
du habest gesehen
er habe gesehen

PLURAL

wir haben gesehen
ihr habt gesehen
sie haben gesehen

PLURAL

wir haben gesehen
ihr habet gesehen
sie haben gesehen

(d) Past Perfect (*I had seen, etc.*):

(d) Past Perfect:

SINGULAR

ich hatte gesehen
du hattest gesehen
er hatte gesehen

SINGULAR

ich hätte gesehen
du hättest gesehen
er hätte gesehen

PLURAL

wir hatten gesehen
ihr hattet gesehen
sie hatten gesehen

PLURAL

wir hätten gesehen
ihr hättet gesehen
sie hätten gesehen

(e) Future (*I shall see, etc.*):

(e) Future:

SINGULAR

ich werde sehen
du wirst sehen
er wird sehen

SINGULAR

ich werde sehen
du werdest sehen
er werde sehen

PLURAL

wir werden sehen
ihr werdet sehen
sie werden sehen

PLURAL

wir werden sehen
ihr werdet sehen
sie werden sehen

(f) Future Perfect (*I shall have seen, etc.*):

SINGULAR

ich werde gesehen haben
du wirst gesehen haben
er wird   gesehen haben

PLURAL

wir werden gesehen haben
ihr werdet gesehen haben
sie werden gesehen haben

(f) Future Perfect:

SINGULAR

ich werde   gesehen haben
du werdest gesehen haben
er werde   gesehen haben

PLURAL

wir werden gesehen haben
ihr werdet gesehen haben
sie werden gesehen haben

(3) The conditional mood:

(a) Present:

SINGULAR

ich würde   sehen
du würdest sehen
er würde   sehen

PLURAL

wir würden sehen
ihr würdet sehen
sie würden sehen

(b) Past:

SINGULAR

ich würde   gesehen haben
du würdest gesehen haben
er würde   gesehen haben

PLURAL

wir würden gesehen haben
ihr würdet gesehen haben
sie würden gesehen haben

(4) The imperative mood:

SINGULAR

sieh
sehen Sie

PLURAL

seht
sehen Sie

(5) Infinitives:

(a) Present: sehen
(b) Perfect: gesehen haben

(6) Participles:

(a) Present: sehend
(b) Past: gesehen

Note: Passive forms of the verb **sehen** are given in § 108 of the Appendix.

B. Kommen. The strong verb **kommen (kam, ist gekommen)** is conjugated as follows:

(1) The indicative mood:

(2) The subjunctive mood:

(*a*) Present (*I come, etc.*):

(*a*) Present:

SINGULAR

ich komme
du kommst
er kommt

SINGULAR

ich komme
du kommest
er komme

PLURAL

wir kommen
ihr kommt
sie kommen

PLURAL

wir kommen
ihr kommet
sie kommen

(*b*) Past (*I came, etc.*):

(*b*) Past:

SINGULAR

ich kam
du kamst
er kam

SINGULAR

ich käme
du kämest
er käme

PLURAL

wir kamen
ihr kamt
sie kamen

PLURAL

wir kämen
ihr kämet
sie kämen

(*c*) Perfect (*I have come, etc.*):

(*c*) Perfect:

SINGULAR

ich bin gekommen
du bist gekommen
er ist gekommen

SINGULAR

ich sei gekommen
du seiest gekommen
er sei gekommen

PLURAL

wir sind gekommen
ihr seid gekommen
sie sind gekommen

PLURAL

wir seien gekommen
ihr seiet gekommen
sie seien gekommen

(*d*) Past Perfect (*I had come, etc.*):

SINGULAR

ich war   gekommen
du warst gekommen
er war   gekommen

PLURAL

wir waren gekommen
ihr wart   gekommen
sie waren gekommen

(*e*) Future (*I shall come, etc.*):

SINGULAR

ich werde kommen
du wirst   kommen
er wird   kommen

PLURAL

wir werden kommen
ihr werdet kommen
sie werden kommen

(*f*) Future Perfect (*I shall have come, etc.*):

SINGULAR

ich werde gekommen sein
du wirst   gekommen sein
er wird   gekommen sein

PLURAL

wir werden gekommen sein
ihr werdet gekommen sein
sie werden gekommen sein

(*d*) Past Perfect:

SINGULAR

ich wäre   gekommen
du wärest gekommen
er wäre   gekommen

PLURAL

wir wären gekommen
ihr wäret gekommen
sie wären gekommen

(*e*) Future:

SINGULAR

ich werde   kommen
du werdest kommen
er werde   kommen

PLURAL

wir werden kommen
ihr werdet kommen
sie werden kommen

(*f*) Future Perfect:

SINGULAR

ich werde   gekommen sein
du werdest gekommen sein
er werde   gekommen sein

PLURAL

wir werden gekommen sein
ihr werdet gekommen sein
sie werden gekommen sein

(3) The conditional mood:

(a) Present: (b) Past:

SINGULAR   SINGULAR

ich   würde   kommen   ich   würde   gekommen   sein
du   würdest kommen   du   würdest gekommen   sein
er   würde   kommen   er   würde   gekommen   sein

PLURAL   PLURAL

wir   würden   kommen   wir   würden   gekommen   sein
ihr   würdet   kommen   ihr   würdet   gekommen   sein
sie   würden   kommen   sie   würden   gekommen   sein

(4) The imperative mood:

SINGULAR   PLURAL

komme   kommt
kommen Sie   kommen Sie

(5) Infinitives: (6) Participles:

(a) Present: kommen   (a) Present: kommend
(b) Perfect: gekommen sein   (b) Past: gekommen

105. SEPARABLE VERBS

The separable verb **anfangen (fing an, hat angefangen)** is conjugated as follows:

A. The indicative mood: **B. The subjunctive mood:**

(1) Present (*I begin, etc.*):   (1) Present:
ich fange an   ich fange an
du fängst an, *etc.*   du fangest an, *etc.*

(2) Past (*I began, etc.*):   (2) Past:
ich fing an, *etc.*   ich finge an, *etc.*

(3) Perfect (*I have begun, etc.*):

ich habe angefangen
du hast angefangen, *etc.*

(4) Past Perfect (*I had begun, etc.*):

ich hatte angefangen, *etc.*

(5) Future (*I shall begin, etc.*):

ich werde anfangen
du wirst anfangen, *etc.*

(6) Future Perfect (*I shall have begun, etc.*):

ich werde angefangen haben
du wirst angefangen haben, *etc.*

(3) Perfect:

ich habe angefangen
du habest angefangen, *etc.*

(4) Past Perfect:

ich hätte angefangen, *etc.*

(5) Future:

ich werde anfangen
du werdest anfangen, *etc.*

(6) Future Perfect:

ich werde angefangen haben
du werdest angefangen haben, *etc.*

C. The conditional mood:

(1) Present: ich würde anfangen, *etc.*

(2) Past: ich würde angefangen haben, *etc.*

D. Imperatives:

SINGULAR	PLURAL
fange an	fangt an
fangen Sie an	fangen Sie an

E. Infinitives:

(1) Present: anfangen
(2) Perfect: angefangen haben

F. Participles:

(1) Present: anfangend
(2) Past: angefangen

106. INSEPARABLE VERBS

The inseparable verb **beginnen (begann, hat begonnen)** is conjugated as follows:

A. The indicative mood:

(1) Present (*I begin, etc.*):
ich beginne
du beginnst, *etc.*

(2) Past (*I began, etc.*):
ich begann, *etc.*

(3) Perfect (*I have begun, etc.*):
ich habe begonnen
du hast begonnen, *etc.*

(4) Past Perfect (*I had begun, etc.*):
ich hatte begonnen, *etc.*

(5) Future (*I shall begin, etc.*):
ich werde beginnen
du wirst beginnen, *etc.*

(6) Future Perfect (*I shall have begun, etc.*):
ich werde begonnen haben
du wirst begonnen haben, *etc.*

B. The subjunctive mood:

(1) Present:
ich beginne
du beginnest, *etc.*

(2) Past:
ich begönne (*or* begänne), *etc.*

(3) Perfect:
ich habe begonnen
du habest begonnen, *etc.*

(4) Past Perfect:
ich hätte begonnen, *etc.*

(5) Future:
ich werde beginnen
du werdest beginnen, *etc.*

(6) Future Perfect:
ich werde begonnen haben
du werdest begonnen haben, *etc.*

C. The conditional mood:

(1) Present: ich würde beginnen, *etc.*

(2) Past: ich würde begonnen haben, *etc.*

D. The imperative mood:

SINGULAR	PLURAL
beginne	beginnt
beginnen Sie	beginnen Sie

E. Infinitives:

(1) Present: beginnen
(2) Perfect: begonnen haben

F. Participles:

(1) Present: beginnend
(2) Past: begonnen

107. REFLEXIVE VERBS

A. Direct reflexives. The direct reflexive verb **sich setzen** (**setzte sich, hat sich gesetzt**) is conjugated as follows:

(1) The indicative mood:

(2) The subjunctive mood:

(*a*) Present (*I sit down, etc.*):

(*a*) Present:

SINGULAR

ich setze mich
du setzt dich
er setzt sich

SINGULAR

ich setze   mich
du setzest dich
er setze   sich

PLURAL

wir setzen uns
ihr setzt euch
sie setzen sich

PLURAL

wir setzen uns
ihr setzet euch
sie setzen sich

(*b*) Past (*I sat down, etc.*):

(*b*) Past:

SINGULAR

ich setzte   mich
du setztest dich
er setzte   sich

SINGULAR

ich setzte   mich
du setztest dich
er setzte   sich

PLURAL

wir setzten uns
ihr setztet euch
sie setzten sich

PLURAL

wir setzten uns
ihr setztet euch
sie setzten sich

(*c*) Perfect (*I have sat down, etc.*):

ich habe mich gesetzt
du hast dich gesetzt, *etc.*

(*c*) Perfect:

ich habe mich gesetzt
du habest dich gesetzt, *etc.*

(*d*) Past Perfect (*I had sat down, etc.*):

ich hatte mich gesetzt, *etc.*

(*d*) Past Perfect:

ich hätte mich gesetzt, *etc.*

(*e*) Future (*I shall sit down, etc.*):

ich werde mich setzen
du wirst dich setzen, *etc.*

(*e*) Future:

ich werde mich setzen
du werdest dich setzen, *etc.*

(*f*) Future Perfect (*I shall have sat down, etc.*):

ich werde mich gesetzt haben
du wirst dich gesetzt haben, *etc.*

(*f*) Future Perfect:

ich werde mich gesetzt haben
du werdest dich gesetzt haben, *etc.*

(3) The conditional mood:

(*a*) Present: ich würde mich setzen, *etc.*

(*b*) Past: ich würde mich gesetzt haben, *etc.*

(4) The imperative mood:

SINGULAR	PLURAL
setze dich	setzt euch
setzen Sie sich	setzen Sie sich

(5) Infinitives:

(*a*) Present: sich setzen
(*b*) Perfect: sich gesetzt haben

(6) Participles:

(*a*) Present: sich setzend
(*b*) Past: sich gesetzt

B.   Reflexives that take the dative. The reflexive verb **sich schaden (schadete sich, hat sich geschadet)** is conjugated as follows:

(1) The indicative mood:

(*a*) Present (*I hurt myself, etc.*):

(2) The subjunctive mood:

(*a*) Present:

SINGULAR			SINGULAR		
ich	schade	mir	ich	schade	mir
du	schadest	dir	du	schadest	dir
er	schadet	sich	er	schade	sich

PLURAL	PLURAL
wir schaden uns	wir schaden uns
ihr schadet euch	ihr schadet euch
sie schaden sich	sie schaden sich

(b) Past: (*I hurt myself, etc.*):

(b) Past:

ich schadete mir, *etc.*

ich schadete mir, *etc.*

(c) Perfect (*I have hurt myself, etc.*):

(c) Perfect:

ich habe mir geschadet
du hast dir geschadet, *etc.*

ich habe mir geschadet
du habest dir geschadet, *etc.*

(d) Past Perfect: (*I had hurt myself, etc.*):

(d) Past Perfect:

ich hatte mir geschadet, *etc.*

ich hätte mir geschadet, *etc.*

(e) Future (*I shall hurt myself, etc.*):

(e) Future:

ich werde mir schaden
du wirst dir schaden, *etc.*

ich werde mir schaden
du werdest dir schaden, *etc.*

(f) Future Perfect (*I shall have hurt myself, etc.*):

(f) Future Perfect:

ich werde mir geschadet haben
du wirst dir geschadet
haben, *etc.*

ich werde mir geschadet haben
du werdest dir geschadet haben,
etc.

(3) The conditional mood:

(a) Present: ich würde mir schaden, *etc.*

(b) Past: ich würde mir geschadet haben, *etc.*

(4) The imperative mood:

SINGULAR	PLURAL
schade dir	schadet euch
schaden Sie sich	schaden Sie sich

(5) Infinitives: (6) Participles:

(*a*) Present: sich schaden   (*a*) Present: sich schadend
(*b*) Perfect: sich geschadet   (*b*) Past: sich geschadet
haben

108. THE PASSIVE VOICE

The passive of **sehen (sah, hat gesehen)** is conjugated as follows:

A. The indicative mood: **B. The subjunctive mood:**

(1) Present [*I am (being)*   (1) Present:
seen, etc.]:

SINGULAR			SINGULAR		
ich	werde	gesehen	ich	werde	gesehen
du	wirst	gesehen	du	werdest	gesehen
er	wird	gesehen	er	werde	gesehen

PLURAL			PLURAL		
wir	werden	gesehen	wir	werden	gesehen
ihr	werdet	gesehen	ihr	werdet	gesehen
sie	werden	gesehen	sie	werden	gesehen

(2) Past [*I was (being)*   (2) Past:
seen, etc.]:

SINGULAR			SINGULAR		
ich	wurde	gesehen	ich	würde	gesehen
du	wurdest	gesehen	du	würdest	gesehen
er	wurde	gesehen	er	würde	gesehen

PLURAL			PLURAL		
wir	wurden	gesehen	wir	würden	gesehen
ihr	wurdet	gesehen	ihr	würdet	gesehen
sie	wurden	gesehen	sie	würden	gesehen

(3) Perfect (*I have been seen,*   (3) Perfect:
etc.):

A. The indicative mood (*cont.*):

B. The subjunctive mood (*cont.*):

SINGULAR

ich bin gesehen worden
du bist gesehen worden
er ist gesehen worden

SINGULAR

ich sei gesehen worden
du seiest gesehen worden
er sei gesehen worden

PLURAL

wir sind gesehen worden
ihr seid gesehen worden
sie sind gesehen worden

PLURAL

wir seien gesehen worden
ihr seiet gesehen worden
sie seien gesehen worden

(4) Past Perfect (*I had been seen, etc.*):

(4) Past Perfect:

SINGULAR

ich war gesehen worden
du warst gesehen worden
er war gesehen worden

SINGULAR

ich wäre gesehen worden
du wärest gesehen worden
er wäre gesehen worden

PLURAL

wir waren gesehen worden
ihr wart gesehen worden
sie waren gesehen worden

PLURAL

wir wären gesehen worden
ihr wäret gesehen worden
sie wären gesehen worden

(5) Future (*I shall be seen, etc.*):

(5) Future:

SINGULAR

ich werde gesehen werden
du wirst gesehen werden
er wird gesehen werden

SINGULAR

ich werde gesehen werden
du werdest gesehen werden
er werde gesehen werden

PLURAL

wir werden gesehen werden
ihr werdet gesehen werden
sie werden gesehen werden

PLURAL

wir werden gesehen werden
ihr werdet gesehen werden
sie werden gesehen werden

(6) Future Perfect (*I shall have been seen, etc.*):

SINGULAR

ich werde gesehen worden sein
du wirst gesehen worden sein
er wird gesehen worden sein

PLURAL

wir werden gesehen worden sein
ihr werdet gesehen worden sein
sie werden gesehen worden sein

(6) Future Perfect:

SINGULAR

ich werde gesehen worden sein
du werdest gesehen worden sein
er werde gesehen worden sein

PLURAL

wir werden gesehen worden sein

ihr werdet gesehen worden sein

sie werden gesehen worden sein

C. The conditional mood:

(1) Present:

SINGULAR

ich würde gesehen werden

du würdest gesehen werden

er würde gesehen werden

PLURAL

wir würden gesehen werden
ihr würdet gesehen werden
sie würden gesehen werden

(2) Past:

SINGULAR

ich würde gesehen worden sein

du würdest gesehen worden sein

er würde gesehen worden sein

PLURAL

wir würden gesehen worden sein
ihr würdet gesehen worden sein
sie würden gesehen worden sein

D. The imperative mood:

SINGULAR

sei (*or* werde) gesehen
seien (*or* werden) Sie gesehen

PLURAL

seid (*or* werdet) gesehen
seien (*or* werden) Sie gesehen

Note: The passive imperative is quite rare (*cf.* § 74 **E** for details).

E. Infinitives: **F. Participles:**

(1) Present: gesehen werden   (1) Present: —

(2) Perfect: gesehen worden sein (2) Past: gesehen

Note: The present passive participle is wanting.

109. THE MODAL AUXILIARIES

The modals **können, wollen, müssen, mögen, dürfen,** and **sollen**
are conjugated as follows:

A. The indicative mood:
(1) Present:

SINGULAR

ich:	kann	will	muß	mag	darf	soll
du:	kannst	willst	mußt	magst	darfst	sollst
er:	kann	will	muß	mag	darf	soll

PLURAL

wir:	können	wollen	müssen	mögen	dürfen	sollen
ihr:	könnt	wollt	müßt	mögt	dürft	sollt
sie:	können	wollen	müssen	mögen	dürfen	sollen

(2) Past: ich: konnte, wollte, mußte, mochte, durfte, sollte; *etc.*

(3) Perfect: ich habe: gekonnt, gewollt, gemußt, gemocht, gedurft,
gesollt; *etc.*

Note: Participles assume the form of an infinitive when used with
dependent infinitives (*cf.* **Note** (4) of § 83).

(4) Past Perfect:[1] ich hatte: gekonnt, gewollt, gemußt, gemocht,
gedurft, gesollt; *etc.*

(5) Future: ich werde: können, wollen, müssen, mögen, dürfen, sollen;
etc.

---

[1] *Cf.* **Note** under ¶ **A** (3) above.

(6) Future Perfect:[1] ich werde: gekonnt haben, gewollt haben, gemußt haben, gemocht haben, gedurft haben, gesollt haben; *etc.*

B. The subjunctive mood:

(1) Present: ich: könne, wolle, müsse, möge, dürfe, solle; *etc.*

(2) Past: ich: könnte, wollte, müßte, möchte, dürfte, sollte; *etc.*

(3) Perfect:[1] ich habe: gekonnt, gewollt, gemußt, gemocht, gedurft, gesollt; *etc.*

(4) Past Perfect:[1] ich hätte: gekonnt, gewollt, gemußt, gemocht, gedurft, gesollt; *etc.*

(5) Future: ich werde: können, wollen, müssen, mögen, dürfen, sollen; *etc.*

(6) Future Perfect:[1] ich werde: gekonnt haben, gewollt haben, gemußt haben, gemocht haben, gedurft haben, gesollt haben; *etc.*

C. The conditional mood. The conditional of modals is quite rare and should be avoided.

D. The imperative mood:

SINGULAR	PLURAL
wolle	wollt
wollen Sie	wollen Sie

Note: **Wollen** is the only modal having imperative forms.

E. Infinitives:

(1) Present: können, wollen, müssen, mögen, dürfen, sollen.

(2) Perfect: gekonnt haben, gewollt haben, gemußt haben, gemocht haben, gedurft haben, gesollt haben.

F. Participles:

(1) Present: könnend, wollend, müssend, mögend, dürfend, sollend.

(2) Past:[1] gekonnt, gewollt, gemußt, gemocht, gedurft, gesollt.

Note: The present participle of modals is very rarely used.

---

[1] *Cf.* **Note** under ¶ **A** (3) above.

110. IRREGULAR WEAK VERBS AND THE PRESENT INDICATIVE OF WISSEN

A. Irregular Weak Verbs:

INFINITIVE	PAST INDICATIVE	PERFECT INDICATIVE	PRESENT INDICATIVE	PAST SUBJUNCTIVE	IMPERATIVE (2d sing. fam.)	MEANING
brennen	brannte	hat gebrannt	er brennt	brennte	brenn(e)	*to burn*
rennen	rannte	ist gerannt	er rennt	rennte	renn(e)	*to run*
kennen	kannte	hat gekannt	er kennt	kennte	kenn(e)	*to know*
nennen	nannte	hat genannt	er nennt	nennte	nenn(e)	*to name*
senden	sandte (*or* sendete)	hat gesandt (*or* gesendet)	er sendet	sendete	send(e)	*to send*
wenden	wandte (*or* wendete)	hat gewandt (*or* gewendet)	er wendet	wendete	wend(e)	*to turn*
denken	dachte	hat gedacht	er denkt	dächte	denk(e)	*to think*
bringen	brachte	hat gebracht	er bringt	brächte	bring(e)	*to bring*
wissen	wußte	hat gewußt	er weiß	wüßte	wisse	*to know*

B. The present indicative of wissen. Although not a modal auxiliary, **wissen** resembles one in the conjugation of its present indicative:

SINGULAR	PLURAL
ich weiß	wir wissen
du weißt	ihr wißt
er weiß	sie wissen

III. PRINCIPAL PARTS OF STRONG AND IRREGULAR VERBS

INFINITIVE	PAST INDICATIVE	PERFECT INDICATIVE	PRESENT INDICATIVE	PAST SUBJUNCTIVE	IMPERATIVE (2d sing. fam.)	MEANING
backen	buk	hat gebacken	er bäckt	büke	back(e)	to bake
befehlen	befahl	hat befohlen	er befiehlt	beföhle	befiehl	to command
beginnen	begann	hat begonnen	er beginnt	begönne (or begänne)	beginn(e)	to begin
beißen	biß	hat gebissen	er beißt	bisse	beiß(e)	to bite
bergen	barg	hat geborgen	er birgt	bürge (or bärge)	birg	to hide
bersten	barst	ist geborsten	er birst	börste (or bärste)	birst	to burst
betrügen	betrog	hat betrogen	er betrügt	betröge	betrüg(e)	to deceive
bewegen[1]	bewog	hat bewogen	er bewegt	bewöge	beweg(e)	to induce
biegen	bog	hat gebogen	er biegt	böge	bieg(e)	to bend
bieten	bot	hat geboten	er bietet	böte	biet(e)	to offer
binden	band	hat gebunden	er bindet	bände	bind(e)	to bind
bitten	bat	hat gebeten	er bittet	bäte	bitte	to ask
blasen	blies	hat geblasen	er bläst	bliese	blas (blase)	to blow
bleiben	blieb	ist geblieben	er bleibt	bliebe	bleib(e)	to remain
braten	briet	hat gebraten	er brät	briete	brat(e)	to roast
brechen	brach	hat gebrochen	er bricht	bräche	brich	to break

[1] **Bewegen** meaning *to move*, is weak.

dringen	drang	dring(e)	dränge	er dringt	hat gedrungen	to press
dürfen	durfte	—	dürfte	er darf	hat gedurft	to be allowed
einladen (cf. **laden**)						
empfehlen	empfahl	empfiehl	empföhle (or empfähle)	er empfiehlt	hat empfohlen	to recommend
erlöschen	erlosch	erlisch	erlösche	er erlischt	ist erloschen	to go out, be extinguished (as a light)
erschrecken[1]	erschrak	erschrick	erschräke	er erschrickt	ist erschrocken	to be frightened
essen	aß	iß	äße	er ißt	hat gegessen	to eat
fahren	fuhr	fahr(e)	führe	er fährt	ist gefahren	to drive, ride, go
fallen	fiel	fall(e)	fiele	er fällt	ist gefallen	to fall
fangen	fing	fang(e)	finge	er fängt	hat gefangen	to catch
fechten	focht	ficht	föchte	er ficht	hat gefochten	to fight
finden	fand	find(e)	fände	er findet	hat gefunden	to find
flechten	flocht	flicht	flöchte	er flicht	hat geflochten	to braid
fliegen	flog	flieg(e)	flöge	er fliegt	ist geflogen	to fly
fliehen	floh	flieh(e)	flöhe	er flieht	ist geflohen	to flee
fließen	floß	fließ(e)	flösse	er fließt	ist geflossen	to flow
fressen	fraß	friß	fräße	er frißt	hat gefressen	to eat (of animals)
frieren	fror	frier(e)	fröre	er friert	hat gefroren	to freeze
gebären	gebar	gebier	gebäre	sie gebiert	hat geboren	to bear, give birth to

---

[1] The transitive verb **erschrecken**, *to frighten*, is weak.

INFINITIVE	PAST INDICATIVE	PERFECT INDICATIVE	PRESENT INDICATIVE	PAST SUBJUNCTIVE	IMPERATIVE (2d sing. fam.)	MEANING
geben	gab	hat gegeben	er gibt	gäbe	gib	to give
gedeihen	gedieh	ist gediehen	er gedeiht	gediehe	gedeih(e)	to thrive
gehen	ging	ist gegangen	er geht	ginge	geh(e)	to go
gelingen	gelang	ist gelungen	es gelingt	gelänge	—	to succeed
gelten	galt	hat gegolten	er gilt	gölte (or gälte)	gilt	to be worth
genesen	genas	ist genesen	er genest	genäse	genese	to recover
genießen	genoß	hat genossen	er genießt	genösse	genieß(e)	to enjoy
geschehen	geschah	ist geschehen	es geschieht	geschähe	—	to happen
gewinnen	gewann	hat gewonnen	er gewinnt	gewönne (or gewänne)	gewinn(e)	to win, gain
gießen	goß	hat gegossen	er gießt	gösse	gieß(e)	to pour
gleichen	glich	hat geglichen	er gleicht	gliche	gleich(e)	to be like, resemble
gleiten	glitt	ist geglitten	er gleitet	glitte	gleit(e)	to glide
graben	grub	hat gegraben	er gräbt	grübe	grab(e)	to dig
greifen	griff	hat gegriffen	er greift	griffe	greif(e)	to seize
haben	hatte	hat gehabt	er hat	hätte	hab(e)	to have
halten	hielt	hat gehalten	er hält	hielte	halt(e)	to hold
hangen	hing	hat gehangen	er hängt	hinge	hang(e)	to hang (intr.)
hauen	hieb	hat gehauen	er haut	hiebe	hau(e)	to hew
heben	hob	hat gehoben	er hebt	höbe (or hübe)	heb(e)	to lift

Infinitive	Past	Past subjunctive	er- present	Perfect	Imperative	Meaning
heißen	hieß	hieße	er heißt	hat geheißen	heiß(e)	to be named; order
helfen	half	hülfe (or hälfe)	er hilft	hat geholfen	hilf	to help
klingen	klang	klänge	er klingt	hat geklungen	kling(e)	to sound
kommen	kam	käme	er kommt	ist gekommen	komm(e)	to come
können	konnte	könnte	er kann	hat gekonnt	—	to be able
kriechen	kroch	kröche	er kriecht	ist gekrochen	kriech(e)	to creep
laden	lud (or ladete)	lüde (or ladete)	er ladet (or lädt)	hat geladen	lad(e)	to invite (usually **einladen**)
lassen	ließ	ließe	er läßt	hat gelassen	laß	to let
laufen	lief	liefe	er läuft	ist gelaufen	lauf(e)	to run
leiden	litt	litte	er leidet	hat gelitten	leid(e)	to suffer
leihen	lieh	liehe	er leiht	hat geliehen	leih(e)	to lend
lesen	las	läse	er liest	hat gelesen	lies	to read
liegen	lag	läge	er liegt	hat gelegen	lieg(e)	to lie
lügen	log	löge	er lügt	hat gelogen	lüg(e)	to (tell a) lie
meiden	mied	miede	er meidet	hat gemieden	meid(e)	to avoid
messen	maß	mäße	er mißt	hat gemessen	miß	to measure
mögen	mochte	möchte	er mag	hat gemocht	—	to like; may
müssen	mußte	müßte	er muß	hat gemußt	—	to have to, **must**
nehmen	nahm	nähme	er nimmt	hat genommen	nimm	to take
pfeifen	pfiff	pfiffe	er pfeift	hat gepfiffen	pfeif(e)	to whistle
preisen	pries	priese	er preist	hat gepriesen	preis (preise)	to praise
quellen	quoll	quölle	er quillt	ist gequollen	quill	to gush forth

INFINITIVE	PAST INDICATIVE	PERFECT INDICATIVE	PRESENT INDICATIVE	PAST SUBJUNCTIVE	IMPERATIVE (2d sing. fam.)	MEANING
raten	riet	hat geraten	er rät	riete	rat(e)	to advise; guess
reiben	rieb	hat gerieben	er reibt	riebe	reib(e)	to rub
reißen	riß	hat gerissen	er reißt	risse	reiß(e)	to tear
reiten	ritt	ist geritten	er reitet	ritte	reit(e)	to ride
riechen	roch	hat gerochen	er riecht	röche	riech(e)	to smell
rufen	rief	hat gerufen	er ruft	riefe	ruf(e)	to call
saufen	soff	hat gesoffen	er säuft	söffe	sauf(e)	to drink (of animals)
schaffen[1]	schuf	hat geschaffen	er schafft	schüfe	schaff(e)	to create
scheiden	schied	ist geschieden	er scheidet	schiede	scheid(e)	to part
scheinen	schien	hat geschienen	er scheint	schiene	schein(e)	to seem; shine
schelten	schalt	hat gescholten	er schilt	schölte (or schälte)	schilt	to scold
schieben	schob	hat geschoben	er schiebt	schöbe	schieb(e)	to shove
schießen	schoß	hat geschossen	er schießt	schösse	schieß(e)	to shoot
schlafen	schlief	hat geschlafen	er schläft	schliefe	schlaf(e)	to sleep
schlagen	schlug	hat geschlagen	er schlägt	schlüge	schlag(e)	to strike
schleichen	schlich	ist geschlichen	er schleicht	schliche	schleich(e)	to creep
schließen	schloß	hat geschlossen	er schließt	schlösse	schließ(e)	to shut
schleifen	schliff	hat geschliffen	er schleift	schliffe	schleif(e)	to whet

[1] **Schaffen** meaning *to work*, is weak.

Infinitive	Past	Subjunctive	Present	Perfect	Imperative	Meaning
schmelzen	schmolz	schmölze	er schmilzt	ist geschmolzen	schmilz	to melt
schneiden	schnitt	schnitte	er schneidet	hat geschnitten	schneid(e)	to cut
schreiben	schrieb	schriebe	er schreibt	hat geschrieben	schreib(e)	to write
schreien	schrie	schriee	er schreit	hat geschrie(e)n	schrei(e)	to cry
schreiten	schritt	schritte	er schreitet	ist geschritten	schreit(e)	to stride
schweigen	schwieg	schwiege	er schweigt	hat geschwiegen	schweig(e)	to be silent
schwellen	schwoll	schwölle	er schwillt	ist geschwollen	schwill	to swell
schwimmen	schwamm	schwömme (*or* schwämme)	er schwimmt	ist geschwommen	schwimm(e)	to swim
schwinden	schwand	schwände	er schwindet	ist geschwunden	schwind(e)	to vanish (usually **verschwinden**)
schwingen	schwang	schwänge	er schwingt	hat geschwungen	schwing(e)	to swing
schwören	schwur (*or* schwor)	schwüre	er schwört	hat geschworen	schwör(e)	to swear
sehen	sah	sähe	er sieht	hat gesehen	sieh	to see
sein	war	wäre	er ist	ist gewesen	sei	to be
sieden	sott (*or* siedete)[1]	sötte	es siedet	hat gesotten	sied(e)	to boil
singen	sang	sänge	er singt	hat gesungen	sing(e)	to sing
sinken	sank	sänke	er sinkt	ist gesunken	sink(e)	to sink
sinnen	sann	sönne (*or* sänne)	er sinnt	hat gesonnen	sinn(e)	to think
sitzen	saß	säße	er sitzt	hat gesessen	sitz(e)	to sit

[1] The weak past (**siedete**) occurs especially when **sieden** is used figuratively.

INFINITIVE	PAST INDICATIVE	PERFECT INDICATIVE	PRESENT INDICATIVE	PAST SUBJUNCTIVE	IMPERATIVE (2d sing. fam.)	MEANING
sollen	sollte	hat gesollt	er soll	sollte	—	to be (required) to; shall (denoting obligation)
speien	spie	hat gespie(e)n	er speit	spiee	spei(e)	to spit
spinnen	spann	hat gesponnen	er spinnt	spönne (or spänne)	spinn(e)	to spin
sprechen	sprach	hat gesprochen	er spricht	spräche	sprich	to speak
sprießen	sproß	ist gesprossen	es sprießt	sprösse	sprieß(e)	to sprout
springen	sprang	ist gesprungen	er springt	spränge	spring(e)	to jump
stechen	stach	hat gestochen	er sticht	stäche	stich	to prick
stehen	stand	hat gestanden	er steht	stände (or stünde)	steh(e)	to stand
stehlen	stahl	hat gestohlen	er stiehlt	stöhle (or stähle)	stiehl	to steal
steigen	stieg	ist gestiegen	er steigt	stiege	steig(e)	to climb
sterben	starb	ist gestorben	er stirbt	stürbe	stirb	to die
stieben	stob	ist gestoben	er stiebt	stöbe	stieb(e)	to scatter
stoßen	stieß	hat gestoßen	er stößt	stieße	stoß(e)	to push
streichen	strich	hat gestrichen	er streicht	striche	streich(e)	to stroke
streiten	stritt	hat gestritten	er streitet	stritte	streit(e)	to contend
tragen	trug	hat getragen	er trägt	trüge	trag(e)	to carry
treffen	traf	hat getroffen	er trifft	träfe	triff	to meet; hit

treiben	trieb	er treibt	hat getrieben	treib(e)	triebe	*to drive*
treten	trat	er tritt	ist getreten	tritt	träte	*to step*
trinken	trank	er trinkt	hat getrunken	trink(e)	tränke	*to drink*
tun	tat	er tut	hat getan	tu(e)	täte	*to do*
verderben[1]	verdarb	er verdirbt	hat verdorben	verdirb	verdürbe	*to ruin, spoil*
vergessen	vergaß	er vergißt	hat vergessen	vergiß	vergäße	*to forget*
verlieren	verlor	er verliert	hat verloren	verlier(e)	verlöre	*to lose*
verschwinden (*cf.* **schwinden**)						
verzeihen	verzieh	er verzeiht	hat verziehen	verzeih(e)	verziehe	*to pardon*
wachsen	wuchs	er wächst	ist gewachsen	wachs(e)	wüchse	*to grow*
waschen	wusch	er wäscht	hat gewaschen	wasch(e)	wüsche	*to wash*
weichen	wich	er weicht	ist gewichen	weich(e)	wiche	*to recede*
weisen	wies	er weist	hat gewiesen	weis(e)	wiese	*to show*
werben	warb	er wirbt	hat geworben	wirb	würbe	*to woo*
werden	wurde (*or* ward)	er wird	ist geworden	werd(e)	würde	*to become*
werfen	warf	er wirft	hat geworfen	wirf	würfe	*to throw*
wiegen	wog	er wiegt	hat gewogen	wieg(e)	wöge	*to weigh*
winden	wand	er windet	hat gewunden	wind(e)	wände	*to wind*
wollen	wollte	er will	hat gewollt	wolle	wollte	*to wish*
ziehen[2]	zog	er zieht	hat gezogen	zieh(e)	zöge	*to pull*
zwingen	zwang	er zwingt	hat gezwungen	zwing(e)	zwänge	*to force*

[1] As an intransitive verb, **verderben** is conjugated with the auxiliary **sein.**
[2] As an intransitive verb, **ziehen** (*to move*) is conjugated with **sein.**

112. COMMON CLASSROOM EXPRESSIONS

The following sentences make use of expressions commonly used in the classroom:

1. Der Schüler geht um acht Uhr in die Schule.
    The pupil goes to school at eight o'clock.

2. Marie ist schon in der Schule.
    Mary is already in school.

3. Nach der Schule spielen die Jungen Ball.
    After school the boys play ball.

4. Ihr Bruder war schon im Zimmer.
    Her brother was already in the room.

5. Bald kamen andere Schüler ins Zimmer.
    Other pupils soon entered the room.

6. Er setzt sich.
    He sits down.

7. Er sitzt am Fenster.
    He sits by the window.

8. Er geht ans Fenster.
    He goes to the window.

9. Heinrich macht das Buch auf.
    Henry opens his book.

10. Karl sitzt in der ersten Reihe.
    Carl sits in the first row.

11. Es hat noch nicht geklingelt.
    The bell hasn't rung yet.

12. Fritz kommt immer zu spät in die Schule.
    Fred always comes late to school.

13. Die anderen Schüler waren schon in der Klasse.
    The other pupils were already in class.

14. Die erste Klasse fängt um neun Uhr an.
    The first class begins at nine o'clock.

15. Es sind sechzehn Schüler und sechs Schülerinnen in der Klasse.
    There are sixteen boy-pupils and six girl-pupils in the class.

16. Wer fehlt heute?
Who is absent today?

17. In dieser Klasse fällt niemand durch.
No one is failing in this class.

18. Er macht die Prüfung.
He takes the examination.

19. Er besteht die Prüfung.
He passes the examination.

20. Der Lehrer steht vor der Klasse.
The teacher stands in front of the class.

21. Er tritt vor die Klasse.
He steps before the class.

22. Er hat die Kreide in der Hand.
He has the chalk in his hand.

23. Er nimmt die Kreide in die Hand.
He takes the chalk in his hand.

24. Er liest einen kurzen Satz.
He reads a short sentence.

25. Karl wiederhólt den Satz.
Carl repeats the sentence.

26. Wilhelm hebt die Hand, weil er den Satz nicht versteht.
William raises his hand because he does not understand the sentence.

27. Luise fragt: „Auf welcher Seite fängt die Aufgabe an?"
Louise asks, "On what page does the lesson begin?"

28. Wie viele Seiten haben Sie heute gelesen?
How many pages did you read today?

29. Lesen Sie die zwanzigste Zeile!
Read the twentieth line.

30. Karl konnte diese beiden Zeilen nicht verstehen.
Carl couldn't understand these two lines.

31. Welche Seite war am schwersten?
Which page was most difficult?

32. Weil der Schüler zu schnell liest, sagt der Lehrer: „Lies langsamer!"
Because the pupil reads too rapidly, the teacher says, "Read more slowly."

33. Weil das Mädchen zu leise spricht, sagt der Lehrer: „Sprich lauter!"
Because the girl speaks in too low a voice, the teacher says, "Speak (in a) louder (voice)."

34. Achten Sie auf Ihre Aussprache!
or: Beachten Sie Ihre Aussprache!
Be careful of your pronunciation.

35. Sie machen Fortschritte.
You are making progress.

36. Warten Sie einen Augenblick!
Wait a moment.

37. Lesen Sie jetzt weiter!
Now continue reading.

38. Ein Junge hat nicht aufgepaßt.
One boy didn't pay attention.

39. Er sah zum Fenster hinaus.
He was looking out of the window.

40. Er spricht das Wort nicht richtig aus.
He doesn't pronounce the word correctly.

41. Ihre Aussprache ist schauderhaft.
Your pronunciation is terrible.

42. Er antwortet auf meine Frage.
or: Er beantwortet meine Frage.
He answers my question.

43. Was ist die Antwort auf diese Frage?
What is the answer to this question?

44. Der Schüler stellt eine Frage an den Lehrer.
The pupil asks the teacher a question.

45. Er bittet mich um einen Bleistift.
He asks me for a pencil.

46. Ich habe die deutsche Sprache gern.
I like the German language.

47. Ich spreche Deutsch gern.
    I like to speak German.

48. Diese kurze Geschichte gefällt mir.
    I like this short story.

49. Im Deutschen hat er eine gute Zensur (*or* Note) erhalten.
    He received a good mark in German.

50. Nach der Prüfung gehen Sie nach Hause, nicht wahr?
    You are going home after the examination, are you not?

51. Seine Schwester hat eine schlechte Zensur in der Mathematik erhalten.
    His sister received a poor mark in mathematics.

52. Schreiben Sie das auf deutsch!
    Write that in German.

53. Fangen Sie von vorn an!
    Begin at the beginning.

54. Sie haben zu viele Fehler gemacht.
    You made too many mistakes.

55. Verbessern Sie diesen Fehler!
    Correct this mistake.

56. Geben Sie mir noch ein Buch!
    Give me another (i.e., an additional) book.

57. Geben Sie mir ein anderes Buch!
    Give me another (i.e., a different) book.

58. Nehmen Sie sich in acht!
    Be careful.

59. Ich freue mich auf die Ferien.
    I am looking forward with pleasure to (the) vacation.

60. Nehmen Sie Platz!
    Be seated.

61. Der wievielte ist heute?
or: Den wievielten haben wir heute?
    What is today's date?

62. Wieviel Uhr ist es?
    What time is it?

63. Er steht an der Tafel.
    He is standing at the (black)board.

64. Er geht an die Tafel.
    He goes to the (black)board.

65. Er schreibt den Satz an die Tafel.
    He writes the sentence on the (black)board.

66. Machen Sie das Fenster auf!
    Open the window.

67. Wenn es zu kühl wird, machen Sie es (*i.e.,* das Fenster) wieder zu!
    If it gets too cool, close it (i.e., the window) again.

68. Stehen Sie auf, bitte!
    Please rise.

69. Übersetzen Sie den dritten Satz!
    Translate the third sentence.

70. Was bedeutet das vierte Wort?
    What does the fourth word mean?

71. Ergänzen Sie den Satz auf passende Weise!
    Complete the sentence in a suitable way (or *appropriately*).

72. Was ist das Gegenteil von „schwarz"?
    What is the opposite of "black"?

73. Schreiben Sie einen Aufsatz von etwa 200 Worten!
    Write a composition of about 200 words.

74. Er kann seine Aufgabe nicht.
    He doesn't know his lesson.

75. Heute haben wir Diktat.
    We have dictation today.

76. Wir haben Deutsch fünfmal die Woche.
    We have German five times a week.

113. COMMON PROVERBS

The following proverbs are common to both German and English:

1. Jeder ist seines Glückes Schmied.
   Every man is the founder of his own fortune.

2. Ehrlich währt am längsten.
   Honesty is the best policy.

3. Reden ist Silber, Schweigen ist Gold.
   Speech is silver, silence is golden.

4. Man muß das Eisen schmieden, solange es heiß ist.
   Strike the iron while it is hot.

5. Einigkeit macht stark.
   In union there is strength.

6. Übung macht den Meister.
   Practice makes perfect.

7. Besser ein Sperling in der Hand als eine Taube auf dem Dache.
   A bird in the hand is worth two in the bush.

8. Jedem Narren gefällt seine Kappe.
   Every fool likes his own hobby best.

9. Not bricht Eisen.
   Necessity knows no law.

10. Gleich und gleich gesellt sich gern.
    Birds of a feather flock together.

11. Ende gut, alles gut.
    All's well that ends well.

12. Der Apfel fällt nicht weit vom Stamm.
    He's a chip of the old block.

13. Ein gutes Gewissen ist ein sanftes Ruhekissen.
    A clear conscience makes a soft pillow.

14. Man soll den Tag nicht vor dem Abend loben.
    Don't crow too soon.

15. Jeder kehre vor seiner Tür!
    Mind your own business.

16. Ein Unglück kommt selten allein.
    It never rains but it pours.

17. Nach getaner Arbeit ist gut ruhen.
    Rest is pleasant after work.

18. Hunger ist der beste Koch.
    Hunger is the best sauce.

19. Aller Anfang ist schwer.
    All beginnings are difficult.

20. Das dicke Ende kommt noch (*or* nach).
    The worst is yet to come.

21. Müßiggang ist aller Laster Anfang.
    Idleness is the root of all evil.

22. Morgenstunde hat Gold im Munde.
    The early bird catches the worm.

23. Erst wägen, dann wagen!
    Look before you leap.

24. Morgen, morgen, nur nicht heute, sagen alle faulen Leute.
    Tomorrow, tomorrow, not today, all the lazy people say.

25. Frisch gewagt ist halb gewonnen.
    Well begun is half done.

26. Gesagt, getan.
    No sooner said than done.

114. VERBS THAT ARE SIMILAR IN SOUND AND SPELLING

The following verbs are commonly confused because of similarity in sound or spelling:

A. Beten, bieten, and bitten:

beten	betete	hat gebetet	*to pray*
bieten	bot	hat geboten	*to offer*
bitten	bat	hat gebeten	*to ask, request*

B. Danken and denken:

| danken | dankte | hat gedankt | *to thank* |
| denken | dachte | hat gedacht | *to think* |

C. Brechen and bringen:

| brechen | brach | hat gebrochen | *to break* |
| bringen | brachte | hat gebracht | *to bring* |

D. Kennen, können, and wissen: *Cf.* **Note** 2 of § 16.

E. Legen, liegen, and lügen:

legen	legte	hat gelegt	*to lay*
liegen	lag	hat gelegen	*to lie*
lügen	log	hat gelogen	*to tell a lie*

Note: **Sich legen** means *to lie down*.

F. Reisen, reißen, and reizen:

reisen	reiste	ist gereist	*to travel*
reißen	riß	hat gerissen	*to tear*
reizen	reizte	hat gereizt	*to excite, irritate*

G. Setzen and sitzen:

setzen	setzte	hat gesetzt	*to set*
sitzen	saß	hat gesessen	*to sit*

Note: **Sich setzen** means *to sit down*.

H. Lassen and lesen:

lassen	ließ	hat gelassen	*to let*
lesen	las	hat gelesen	*to read*

I. Fallen, gefallen, and fällen:

fallen	fiel	ist gefallen	*to fall*
gefallen	gefiel	hat gefallen	*to please*
fällen	fällte	hat gefällt	*to fell*

J. Reiten, raten, and retten:

reiten	ritt	ist geritten	*to ride* (*on horseback*)
raten	riet	hat geraten	*to advise; guess*
retten	rettete	hat gerettet	*to save, rescue*

K. Fliegen and fliehen:

fliegen	flog	ist geflogen	*to fly*
fliehen	floh	ist geflohen	*to flee*

L. Erschrecken, transitive and intransitive:

erschrecken	erschrak	ist erschrocken	*to be(come) frightened* (intr.)
erschrecken	erschreckte	hat erschreckt	*to frighten* (tr.)

M. Schneien and schneiden:

| schneien | schneite | hat geschneit | *to snow* |
| schneiden | schnitt | hat geschnitten | *to cut* |

N. Fahren and führen:

| fahren | fuhr | ist gefahren | *to ride, travel* |
| führen | führte | hat geführt | *to lead* |

O. Lernen and lehren:

| lernen | lernte | hat gelernt | *to learn, study* |
| lehren | lehrte | hat gelehrt | *to teach* |

P. Leiden and leiten:

| leiden | litt | hat gelitten | *to suffer* |
| leiten | leitete | hat geleitet | *to lead* |

Q. Wachsen and waschen:

| wachsen | wuchs | ist gewachsen | *to grow* |
| waschen | wusch | hat gewaschen | *to wash* |

R. Ziehen and zeigen:

| ziehen | zog | hat gezogen | *to draw, pull* |
| zeigen | zeigte | hat gezeigt | *to show* |

S. Reichen, riechen, and rauchen:

reichen	reichte	hat gereicht	*to reach*
riechen	roch	hat gerochen	*to smell*
rauchen	rauchte	hat geraucht	*to smoke*

115. SYNONYMS AND ANTONYMS

The following are synonyms and antonyms for common words:

WORD	SYNONYM	ANTONYM
ähnlich:	gleich	unähnlich
alt:	bejahrt (only of people)	jung, neu
das Antlitz:	das Gesicht	
sich ánziehen:	sich ánkleiden	sich aúsziehen

WORD	SYNONYM	ANTONYM
die Backe:	die Wange	
brauchen:	nötig haben, bedürfen	
die Burg:	das Schloß	
dunkel:	finster	hell
dünn:	mager	dick
edel:	adlig	unedel, gemein
endlich:	zuletzt, schließlich	zuerst
eng:	schmal	weit, breit
ernst:	feierlich	heiter
essen:	speisen	fasten
faul:	nachlässig	fleißig
feucht:	naß	trocken
früh:	(früh)zeitig	spät
die Gabe:	das Geschenk	
gerade:	direkt	krumm, ungerade
gewiß:	sicher	ungewiß
glücklich:	froh, fröhlich	unglücklich
gut:	fromm	schlecht, böse
hart:	fest	weich
das Haupt:	der Kopf	
heiß:	hitzig (figuratively *hot*)	kalt
herrschen:	regieren	
hoch:	erhaben (*elevated;* often used figuratively)	niedrig
höflich:	artig	unhöflich, grob
immer:	stets	nie
kalt:	frostig	heiß
klar:	hell	unklar, dunkel
klein:	winzig	groß
klug:	verständig	dumm
krank:	leidend	gesund
kurz:	klein	lang
langsam:	träge	schnell
leicht:	einfach	schwer
leise:	ruhig	laut
das Meer:	die See, der Ozean	das Land
müde:	erschöpft	frisch

WORD	SYNONYM	ANTONYM
nah:	naheliegend, in der Nähe	fern
neu:	modern	alt
das Observatorium:	die Sternwarte	
das Pferd:	das Roß	
die Quelle:	der Brunnen	
reich:	wohlhabend	arm
rufen:	schreien	
scharf:	spitz	stumpf
schlau:	klug	dumm
schmutzig:	unrein	rein, sauber
schön:	hübsch	häßlich
schweigen:	verstummen	sprechen
selten:	spärlich	häufig
treu:	ergeben	untreu
ungefähr:	etwa	
vergessen:	verlernen	sich erinnern
zornig:	böse	

116. HOMONYMS

A. Homonyms of different gender with identical plural forms:

der Heide, –n, –n, *heathen* die Heide, —, –n, *heath*
das Messer, –s, —, *knife* der Messer, –s, —, *measurer*
der See, –s, –n, *lake* die See, —, –n, *sea, ocean*
der Verdienst, –es, –e, *wages* das Verdienst, –es, –e, *merit*

B. Homonyms of different gender with one plural form lacking or rare:

der Erbe, –n, –n, *heir* das Erbe, –s, *inheritance*
das Harz, –es, –e, *resin* der Harz, –es, *Harz Mountains*
der Hut, –es, ⸚e, *hat* die Hut, —, *guard*
der Kunde, –n, –n, *customer* die Kunde, —, *knowledge*
die Mark, —, –en, *border-land* { das Mark, –es, *marrow*
  { die Mark, —, *mark* (German coin)
das Tau, –(e)s, –e, *rope* der Tau, –(e)s, *dew*

C. Homonyms differing in both gender and plural forms:

der Band, –(e)s, ¨e, *volume*
{ das Band, –(e)s, ¨er, *ribbon*
{ das Band, –(e)s, –e, *bond, tie*

der Bund, –(e)s, ¨e, *alliance*
das Bund, –(e)s, –e, *bundle* (also das Bündel)

der Flur, –(e)s, –e, *vestibule, hall*
die Flur, —, –en, *field, plain*

der Gehalt, –(e)s, –e, *contents*
das Gehalt, –(e)s, ¨er (or –e), *salary*

der Kiefer, –s, —, *jaw*
die Kiefer, —, –n, *pine tree*

der Leiter, –s, —, *conductor*
die Leiter, —, –n, *ladder*

der Schild, –(e)s, –e, *shield*
das Schild, –(e)s, –er, *signboard, doorplate*

die Steuer, —, –n, *tax*
das Steuer, –s, —, *rudder, helm*

der Reis, –es, –e, *rice*
das Reis, –es, –er, *twig*

der Tor, –en, –en, *fool*
das Tor, –(e)s, –e, *gate*

die Wehr, —, –en, *defense*
das Wehr, –(e)s, –e, *dike, dam*

D. Homonyms of the same gender with different plural forms:

die Bank, —, ¨e, *bench*
die Bank, —, –en, *bank* (for money)

der Bauer, –s (or –n), –n, *farmer*
der (or das) Bauer, –s, —, *bird cage*

das Gesicht, –(e)s, –er, *face*
das Gesicht, –(e)s, –e, *apparition*

das Wort, –(e)s, –e, *word;* (pl.) *connected words*
das Wort, –(e)s, ¨er, *word;* (pl.) *disconnected words*

117. NOUN PECULIARITIES

A. Nouns used only in the plural. Some of the more common nouns used only in the plural are: Eltern (*parents*), Leute (*people*), Gebrüder (*brothers*), Geschwister (*brothers and sisters*), Ferien (*vacation*), Masern (*measles*), Insignien (*insignia*). Weihnachten (*Christmas*) and Pfingsten (*Whitsuntide*) occur as plurals and also as neuter and feminine singulars. Ostern (*Easter*) may be either plural or neuter singular.

B. Nouns used only in the singular. Some of the more common nouns used only in the singular are:

der Adel, –s, *nobility*   der Hafer, –s, *oats*
die Beute, —, *booty*   das Publikum, –s, *public*

der Bodensatz, –es, *sediment,*   die Mathematik, —, *mathematics*
dregs
das Elend, –(e)s, *misery*   die Musik, —, *music*

C. Nouns having irregular compound plural forms. A number
of abstract and collective nouns have compound forms in the plural.
These plural forms are often derivatives in which the singular noun
functions as a component part.   Some of the more common nouns of this
type are:

SINGULAR	PLURAL
der Atem, *breath*	Atemzüge
der Dank, *thanks*	Danksagungen, *expressions of gratitude*
das Glück, *luck*	Glücksfälle, *pieces of good fortune*
der Rat, *advice*	Ratschläge, *counsels*
der Regen, *rain*	Regenfälle (*or* Niederschläge)
der Streit, *dispute*	Streitigkeiten
der Tod, *death*	Todesfälle
das Unglück, *misfortune*	Unglücksfälle
die Vorsicht, *precaution*	Vorsichtsmaßregeln, *precautionary measures*

118. PUNCTUATION

Rules for punctuation in German differ in many respects from those
in English and should be noted carefully.

A. Punctuation marks. The more common punctuation marks
used in German are:

,   (= das Komma), *comma*
.   (= der Punkt), *period*
:   (= der Doppelpunkt), *colon*
;   (= das Semikolon), *semicolon*
!   (= das Ausrufungszeichen), *exclamation mark* (*or point*)
?   (= das Fragezeichen), *question mark*
„" [= Anführungszeichen (pl.)], *quotation marks*
—   (= der Gedankenstrich), *dash*
-   (= der Bindestrich), *hyphen*
( ) [= runde Klammern (pl.)], *parentheses*

B. Uses of various punctuation marks. Characteristic uses of the various punctuation marks follow:

(1) Commas are used:

(*a*) To set off dependent (*or* subordinate) clauses:

Die Dame, die uns jetzt besucht, ist sehr reich.
The lady who is visiting us now is very rich.

(*b*) Before **ohne . . . zu, um . . . zu,** and **(an)statt . . . zu** (all of which are followed by an infinitive):

Er ging an mir vorbei, ohne etwas zu sagen.
He passed me without saying anything.

Note: Phrases with **zu** are also preceded by a comma when the following infinitive has modifiers, and when **zu** is the equivalent of **um . . . zu:**

Gewöhne dich daran, immer früh aufzustehen.
Accustom yourself to early rising.

Es lebt ein Gott, zu strafen und zu rächen.
There is (lit. *lives*) *a God, to punish and take revenge.*

but: Es fing an zu regnen.
It began to rain.

(*c*) Before the coördinating conjunctions **und** and **oder,** provided the following clause contains both subject and verb:

Die Luft ist blau, und die Felder sind grün.
The air is blue and the fields are green.

but: Er legte sich hin und schlief sogleich ein.
He lay down and fell asleep at once.

Note:

(*a*) Contrary to English usage, **aber** meaning *however* is not set off by commas:

Der alte Mann aber verlor den Mut nicht.
The old man, however, did not lose courage.

(*b*) Contrary to English usage, no comma is used before **und** or **oder** in a series:

Karl, Fritz und Johann sind meine besten Freunde.
Carl, Fred, and John are my best friends.

(2) Periods are used when the endings of ordinals have been omitted: den 4. (= 4ten *or* vierten) März, *March 4.*

Note: Similarly:

Friedrich II. (= der Zweite), *Frederick II*

(3) Exclamation marks (*or* points) are used:

(*a*) Usually after the salutation in letters:

Lieber Vater! *Dear Father,*

Note: In English, the salutation is followed by a **comma** in personal letters but by a **colon** in business letters.

(*b*) Regularly after emphatic commands:

Folgen Sie mir! *Follow me.*

(4) Question marks are used at the end of interrogative sentences as in English:

Haben Sie ihn gesehen?
Did you see him?

Note: Indirect questions, however, end with a **period:**

Er fragte mich, ob ich den Mann gesehen hätte.
He asked me whether I had seen the man.

(5) Quotation marks are used to enclose a direct quotation, as in English:

Der Fuchs sprach: „Die Trauben sind mir zu sauer."
The fox said, "The grapes are too sour for me."

Note:

(*a*) In German, the first quotation mark is written **below** the line; the second, **above** the line.

(*b*) In German, the first quotation mark is preceded by a **colon;** in English, by either a **comma** or a **colon.**

(6) Hyphens are used:

(*a*) To divide words at the end of a line.

(b) To indicate the omission of the last component common to two or more compounds in a series:

Haupt- und Nebensatz, *main and dependent clause*
Feld- und Gartenfrüchte, *field and garden fruits*

(c) Rarely to form compound nouns.

Note: A German hyphen consists of one small dash (as in English) when the Roman type is used, and two small dashes when the Fraktur (German print) is used.

119. CAPITALIZATION

Capitalization is much more common in German than it is in English. The conditions under which it occurs should be noted very carefully.

A. Words that must be capitalized. Capitalization is required by:

(1) Neuter adjectives **used as nouns after etwas** (*something*), **viel** (*much*), **nichts** (*nothing*), **alles** (*all*), **allerlei** [*all kinds (or sorts) of*)], and **wenig** (*little, not much*):

etwas Schönes, *something beautiful*
viel Wichtiges, *much of importance*
nichts Schlechtes, *nothing bad*
alles Gute, *all good things* (or *all that is good*)
allerlei Unverständliches, *all kinds of unintelligible things*
wenig Nützliches, *little of use*

(2) Words of all kinds **used as nouns:**

der Arme, *the poor man*	eine Fünf, (*a (figure) five*
Gutes und Böses, *good and evil*	Altes und Neues, *old and new*

jedem das Seine, *to each one his own*

Das Lesen fällt ihm schwer.	Die Armen haben nichts zu essen.
Reading is difficult for him.	*The poor (people) have nothing to eat.*

(3) The pronoun of formal address **Sie** (*you*), and its corresponding adjective **Ihr** (*your*):

Haben Sie Ihr Buch?
Have you your book?

Caution:

(*a*) The reflexive **sich** is **not** capitalized:

> Setzen Sie sich! *Sit down.*

(*b*) **Du, dein, ihr,** and **euer** are **not** capitalized unless used in direct address in letters:

> Karl, hast du dein Buch?   Kinder, was tut ihr?
> *Carl, have you your book?*   *Children, what are you doing?*
> but: Lieber Karl!

> Hoffentlich hast **Du Di**ch nicht erkältet.
> **D**ein **Di**ch liebender Fritz.

(4) The first word of a direct quotation (following a quotation mark preceded by a colon):

> Der Schüler sagte: „**J**etzt verstehe ich diesen Satz.“
> *The pupil said, "Now I understand this sentence."*

Caution:

(1) If a direct quotation is divided, the word resuming a quotation is **not** capitalized:

> „Die Trauben,“ sprach der Fuchs, „**s**ind mir zu sauer.“

(2) The word directly after a question mark or an exclamation mark is **not** capitalized if what follows completes the sentence:

> „Was wollen Sie?“ **f**ragte der Mann.
> *"What do you wish?" asked the man.*

> „Karl, mache deine Aufgabe!“ **s**agte der Lehrer.
> *"Carl, do your lesson!" said the teacher.*

B.   Words that are *not* capitalized.   Capitalization does **not** occur with:

(1) Combinations with **heute, morgen,** and **gestern:**[1]

> **h**eute **m**orgen, *this morning*
> **g**estern **m**orgen, *yesterday morning*
> **g**estern **a**bend, *yesterday evening* (or *last night*)

(2) Proper adjectives such as *German, English, French, etc.*—unless they are used in titles:

---

[1] For additional examples, *cf.* § 25 **D.**

Wo ist Ihr deutsches (englisches, französisches) Buch?
Where is your German (English, French) book?

but: das Deutsche Reich, *the German empire*

Note:

(*a*) Observe the absence of capitalization in the phrase **auf deutsch,**
in German. Similarly:

auf englisch, *in English*   auf französisch, *in French*

(*b*) Observe the use of **Deutsch** as a noun:

Studieren Sie Deutsch?
Are you studying German?

(3) The following common pronouns and numerals:[1] **man,** *one;*
jemand, *someone;* **niemand,** *no one;* **jedermann,** *everyone;* **derselbe,**
the same one; **einer,** *one;* **keiner,** *no one;* (**ein**) **jeder,** *each one;* **zwei,**
two; **beide (die beiden** or **alle beide),** *both;* **der eine . . . der andere,**
the one . . . the other; **drei,** *three;* **alle drei,** *all three;* **das andere,** *the*
rest; **alles andere,** *all else;* **die anderen,** *the others;* **alle anderen,**
all others; **nichts anderes,** *nothing else;* **das übrige,** *the rest;* **alles**
übrige, *all else;* **die übrigen,** *the others;* **alle übrigen,** *all others;* **der**
erste . . . der letzte, *the first . . . the last;* **einige,** *some;* **alle,** *all;* **viele,**
many; **etwas,** *something;* **nichts,** *nothing;* **viel,** *much;* **mehr,** *more;*
das meiste, *the most;* **das mindeste,** *the least;* **der einzelne,** *the*
individual; **einzelne,** *individuals;* **alles mögliche,** *everything possible.*

(4) The following bold-faced words in verbal idioms:

Er ist **schuld** daran.
He is to blame for that.

Es tut mir **leid.**
I am sorry.

Tut es Ihnen **weh?**
Does it hurt you?

(Das ist) **schade!**
That is too bad.

Nehmen Sie sich in **acht!**
Take care (or *be careful*).

Er nimmt daran **teil.**[2]
He takes part (in it).

Sind Sie **imstande,** das
zu tun?
Can you do that?

Jetzt geht er **heim.**[2]
He is going home now.

Wann findet die Vorstellung **statt?**[2]
When will the performance take place?

---

[1] *Cf.* **Notes** (5) and (6), and ¶ **K** of § 18.
[2] **Teilnehmen, heimgehen,** and **stattfinden** are separable verbs.

120. GERMAN SCRIPT

It is usually unnecessary for foreigners to learn the German script in order to carry on correspondence with native Germans, since both English and German scripts are taught in German schools.   For the benefit of students who may wish to familiarize themselves with the German script, however, two types—the old and the 𝔖ütterlin scripts—are presented below.   The former was customary at the beginning of the century and is still used by elderly Germans; the latter is the new simplified system of 𝔏ubwig 𝔖ütterlin which was in official use in German schools until the latter part of the thirties.   The alphabet and opening lines of Schiller's „𝔚ilhelm 𝔗ell" appear in each type.

A.   The old script:

(1)   The alphabet:

(2) The opening lines of „Wilhelm Tell":

[handwritten script — German cursive]

B. The Sütterlin script:

(1) The alphabet:

[handwritten Sütterlin alphabet]

(2) The opening lines of „Wilhelm Tell":

Note: The opening lines of „Wilhelm Tell" appear as follows in German type:

> Es lächelt der See, er ladet zum Bade,
> Der Knabe schlief ein am grünen Gestade,
> Da hört er ein Klingen,
> Wie Flöten so süß,
> Wie Stimmen der Engel
> Im Paradies.

Supplement

German Poems and Lieder

A. German poems:

Die Beiden

Sie trug den Becher in der Hand
— ihr Kinn und Mund glich seinem Rand —
so leicht und sicher war ihr Gang,
kein Tropfen aus dem Becher sprang.

So leicht und fest war seine Hand:⠀⠀⠀⠀⠀⠀⠀5
er ritt auf einem jungen Pferde,
und mit nachlässiger Gebärde
erzwang er, daß es zitternd stand.

Jedoch, wenn er aus ihrer Hand
den leichten Becher nehmen sollte,⠀⠀⠀⠀⠀⠀10
so war es beiden allzu schwer:
denn beide bebten sie so sehr,
dass keine Hand die andre fand,
und dunkler Wein am Boden rollte.

Hugo von Hofmannsthal

Manche Nacht

Wenn die Felder sich verdunkeln,
fühl' ich, wird mein Auge heller;
schon versucht ein Stern zu funkeln,
und die Grillen wispern schneller.

5 Jeder Laut wird bilderreicher,
das Gewohnte sonderbarer,
hinterm Wald der Himmel bleicher,
jeder Wipfel hebt sich klarer.

Und du merkst es nicht im Schreiten,
10 wie das Licht verhundertfältigt
sich entringt den Dunkelheiten.
Plötzlich stehst du überwältigt.

Richard Dehmel

März

Über der Isar fliegen
die Möwen im knatternden Wind.
Die Enten schnattern und liegen
am Ufer dann still. Es sind

5 die Wolken nie höher gestiegen
als diese Stunde im März.
Die Möwen schreien und fliegen
der taumelnden Sonne ins Herz.

Georg Britting

Einkehr

Bei einem Wirte wundermild,
da war ich jüngst zu Gaste;
ein goldner Apfel war sein Schild
an einem langen Aste.

5 Es war der gute Apfelbaum,
bei dem ich eingekehret,
mit süßer Kost und frischem Schaum
hat er mich wohl genähret.

Es kamen in sein grünes Haus
viel leichtbeschwingte Gäste;   10
sie sprangen frei und hielten Schmaus
und sangen auf das beste.

Ich fand ein Bett zu süßer Ruh'
auf weichen, grünen Matten;
der Wirt, er deckte selbst mich zu   15
mit seinem kühlen Schatten.

Nun fragt' ich nach der Schuldigkeit,
da schüttelt' er den Wipfel;
gesegnet sei er allezeit
von der Wurzel bis zum Gipfel!   20

                    Ludwig Uhland

Erster Schnee

Aus silbergrauen Gründen tritt
ein schlankes Reh
im winterlichen Wald
und prüft vorsichtig, Schritt für Schritt,
den reinen, kühlen, frischgefallenen Schnee.   5

Und deiner denk' ich, zierlichste Gestalt.

                    Christian Morgenstern

Der Fischer

Das Wasser rauscht', das Wasser schwoll,
ein Fischer saß daran,
sah nach dem Angel ruhevoll,
kühl bis ans Herz hinan.
Und wie er sitzt, und wie er lauscht,   5
teilt sich die Flut empor;
aus dem bewegten Wasser rauscht
ein feuchtes Weib hervor.

10
Sie sang zu ihm, sie sprach zu ihm:
„Was lockst du meine Brut
mit Menschenwitz und Menschenlist
hinauf in Todesglut?
Ach, wüßtest du, wie's Fischlein ist
so wohlig auf dem Grund,
15
du stiegst herunter, wie du bist,
und würdest erst gesund.

Labt sich die liebe Sonne nicht,
der Mond sich nicht im Meer?
Kehrt wellenatmend ihr Gesicht
20
nicht doppelt schöner her?
Lockt dich der tiefe Himmel nicht,
das feuchtverklärte Blau?
Lockt dich dein eigen Angesicht
nicht her in ew'gen Tau?"

25
Das Wasser rauscht', das Wasser schwoll,
netzt' ihm den nackten Fuß;
sein Herz wuchs ihm so sehnsuchtsvoll
wie bei der Liebsten Gruß.
Sie sprach zu ihm, sie sang zu ihm;
30
da war's um ihn gescheh'n:
halb zog sie ihn, halb sank er hin,
und ward nicht mehr geseh'n.

Johann Wolfgang von Goethe

Hoffnung

Es reden und träumen die Menschen viel
von bessern, künftigen Tagen;
nach einem glücklichen goldenen Ziel
sieht man sie rennen und jagen.
5
Die Welt wird alt und wird wieder jung,
doch der Mensch hofft immer Verbesserung.

Die Hoffnung führt ihn ins Leben ein,
   sie umflattert den fröhlichen Knaben,
den Jüngling begeistert ihr Zauberschein,
   sie wird mit dem Greis nicht begraben;   10
denn beschließt er im Grabe den müden Lauf,
noch am Grabe pflanzt er — die Hoffnung auf.

Es ist kein leerer, schmeichelnder Wahn,
   erzeugt im Gehirne des Toren.
Im Herzen kündigt es laut sich an: 15
   zu was Besserm sind wir geboren;
und was die innere Stimme spricht,
das täuscht die hoffende Seele nicht.

Friedrich von Schiller

Im Nebel

Seltsam, im Nebel zu wandern!
Einsam ist jeder Busch und Stein,
kein Baum sieht den andern,
jeder ist allein.

Voll von Freunden war mir die Welt,   5
als noch mein Leben licht war;
nun, da der Nebel fällt,
ist keiner mehr sichtbar.

Wahrlich, keiner ist weise,
der nicht das Dunkel kennt,   10
das unentrinnbar und leise
von allen ihn trennt.

Seltsam, im Nebel zu wandern!
Leben ist Einsamsein.
Kein Mensch kennt den andern,   15
jeder ist allein.

Hermann Hesse

B.　German Lieder:

Ein Minnelied aus dem 12. Jahrhundert

Du bist mein, ich bin dein:
des sollst du gewiß sein;
du bist beschlossen
in meinem Herzen;
5　verloren ist das Schlüssellein:
du mußt immer drinne sein.

Wiegenlied

Guten Abend, gut' Nacht,
mit Rosen bedacht,
mit Näglein besteckt
schlupf' unter die Deck:
5　morgen früh, wenn Gott will,
wirst du wieder geweckt.

Guten Abend, gut' Nacht,
von Englein bewacht,
die zeigen im Traum
10　dir Christkindleins Baum:
schlaf' nun selig und süß,
schau' im Traum 's Paradies.

Johannes Brahms

Volkslied

Wenn ich ein Vöglein wär'
und auch zwei Flüglein hätt',
flög' ich zu dir;
weil's aber nicht kann sein,
5　bleib' ich allhier.

Bin ich gleich weit von dir,
bin ich doch im Traum bei dir
und red' mit dir;
wenn ich erwachen tu',
10　bin ich allein.

Es vergeht kein' Stund' in der Nacht,
da nicht mein Herz erwacht
und an dich denkt,
daß du mir tausendmal
dein Herz geschenkt.   15

Geistliches Lied

Die Himmel rühmen des Ewigen Ehre,
ihr Schall pflanzt seinen Namen fort.
Ihn rühmt der Erdkreis, ihn preisen die Meere,
vernimm, o Mensch, ihr göttlich Wort.
Wer trägt der Himmel unzählbare Sterne?   5
Wer führt die Sonn' aus ihrem Zelt?
Sie kommt und leuchtet und lacht uns von ferne,
und läuft den Weg gleich als ein Held.

Vernimm's und siehe die Wunder der Werke,
die Gott so herrlich aufgestellt!   10
Verkündigt Weisheit und Ordnung und Stärke
dir nicht den Herrn, den Herrn der Welt?
Kannst du der Wesen unzählbare Heere,
den kleinsten Staub fühllos beschaun?
Durch wen ist alles? Dem Ewigen Ehre!   15
„Nur mir," ruft Gott, „sollst du vertraun!"

Christian Fürchtegott Gellert

Wanderlied eines Handwerksburschen

Es, es, es und es, es ist ein harter Schluß,
weil, weil, weil und weil, weil ich aus Frankfurt muß.
Drum schlag' ich Frankfurt aus dem Sinn
und wende mich Gott weiß wohin.
Ich will mein Glück probieren,   5
marschieren.

Er, er, er und er, Herr Meister, leb' er wohl!
Ich sag's ihm grad frei ins Gesicht,
seine Arbeit, die gefällt mir nicht:
10   ich will mein Glück probieren,
marschieren.

Sie, sie, sie und sie, Frau Meistrin, leb' sie wohl!
Ich sag's ihr grad frei ins Gesicht,
ihr Kraut und Speck, das schmeckt mir nicht:
15   ich will mein Glück probieren,
marschieren.

Ihr, ihr, ihr und ihr, ihr Jungfern lebet wohl!
Ich wünsche euch zu guter Letzt
einen andern, der mein' Stell' ersetzt:
20   ich will mein Glück probieren,
marschieren.

Soldatenlied

Ich hatt' einen Kameraden,
einen bessern findst du nit.
Die Trommel schlug zum Streite,
er ging an meiner Seite
5   in gleichem Schritt und Tritt.

Eine Kugel kam geflogen;
gilt's mir oder gilt es dir?
Ihn hat es weggerissen,
er liegt mir vor den Füßen,
10   als wär's ein Stück von mir.

Will mir die Hand noch reichen,
derweil ich eben lad':
,,Kann dir die Hand nicht geben;
bleib du im ew'gen Leben
15   mein guter Kamerad."

Ludwig Uhland

Studentenlied

Alt Heidelberg, du Feine, du Stadt an Ehren reich,
am Neckar und am Rheine kein' andre kommt dir gleich.
Stadt fröhlicher Gesellen, an Weisheit schwer und Wein,
klar ziehn des Stromes Wellen, Blauäuglein blitzen drein,
Blauäuglein blitzen drein.   5

Und kommt aus lindem Süden der Frühling übers Land,
so webt er dir aus Blüten ein schimmernd Brautgewand.
Auch mir stehst du geschrieben ins Herz gleich einer Braut,
es klingt wie junges Lieben dein Name mir so traut,
dein Name mir so traut.   10

Und stechen mich die Dornen und wird mir's draus zu kahl,
geb' ich dem Roß die Sporen und reit' ins Neckartal,
und reit' ins Neckartal.

Victor von Scheffel

Jägerlied

Im Wald und auf der Heide, da such' ich meine Freude,
ich bin ein Jägersmann, ich bin ein Jägersmann.
Die Forsten treu zu hegen, das Wildpret zu erlegen,
mein' Lust hab' ich daran, mein' Lust hab' ich daran.

Refrain:
Halli, halo, halli, halo, mein' Lust hab' ich daran.   5

So streich' ich durch die Wälder und zieh' ich durch die Felder
einsam den vollen Tag, einsam den vollen Tag;
doch schwinden mir die Stunden gleich flüchtigen Sekunden,
tracht' ich dem Wilde nach, tracht' ich dem Wilde nach.—
Refrain.

10 Wenn sich die Sonne neiget, der feuchte Nebel steiget,
das Tagwerk ist getan, das Tagwerk ist getan:
dann zieh' ich von der Heide zur häuslich stillen Freude,
ein froher Jägersmann, ein froher Jägersmann.—*Refrain.*

Wilhelm Bornemann

Spinnstubenlied

„Spinn, spinn, meine liebe Tochter,
ich kauf' dir'n Paar Schuh."
„Ja, ja, meine liebe Mutter,
auch Riemen dazu!"

Refrain:
5   „Ich kann ja nicht spinnen,
es schmerzt mich mein Finger
und tut, und tut, und tut mir so weh."

„Spinn, spinn, meine liebe Tochter,
ich kauf' dir'n Paar Strümpf."
10   „Ja, ja, meine liebe Mutter
auch Zwickeln darin!"—*Refrain.*

„Spinn, spinn, meine liebe Tochter,
ich kauf' dir ein Kleid."
„Ja, ja, meine liebe Mutter,
15   nicht zu eng und nicht zu weit."—*Refrain.*

„Spinn, spinn, meine liebe Tochter,
ich kauf' dir 'nen Mann."
„Ja, ja, meine liebe Mutter,
dann streng' ich mich an.
20   Ich kann ja schon spinnen,
es schmerzt mich kein Finger
und tut, und tut, und tut nicht mehr weh."

C. Vocabulary for the German Poems and Lieder:

Words included in this vocabulary either do not occur in the general vocabulary at the end of the book, or are used in the preceding poems with special meanings. They are given for each poem individually in the order of their appearance:

(1) „Die Beiden" (by Hugo von Hofmannsthal):

l. 1. der **Becher,** –s, —, goblet, cup
 2. der **Rand,** –(e)s, ⸚er, brim. The round brim of the dainty goblet is compared to the softly curved features of the girl.
 3.   **sicher,** steady
 3. der **Gang,** –(e)s, ⸚e, gait, walk
 4. der **Tropfen,** –s, —, drop
 7.   **nachlässig,** perfunctory [denoting the playful (*or lit.*, careless) ease with which the young horse was brought to a halt]
 7. die **Gebärde,** —, –n, gesture (movement of the hand)
 8.   **erzwingen,** erzwang, erzwungen, to force
 9.   **jedoch,** however
 11.   **allzu,** far too
 12.   **beben,** to tremble, quiver
 12.   **sie** would be superfluous in prose
 14.   **rollen,** to flow (*lit.*, roll)
 14.   **am Boden,** on the ground

Note: This poem is considered by many to be one of the most beautiful love lyrics in any language, although it does not contain the word love. The rhythm and the graphic choice of words combine to create the lyric atmosphere. The first four lines, in smoothly moving iambic tetrameter, fit the girl's graceful and steady gait. The following four lines, with varied meter and altered rhyme sequence, and with words suggesting strength and vigor, portray the masculine type admirably. The action of the last six lines reveals deep emotion. To be appreciated the poem must be read aloud. The essence of such poetry, however, is found in the *connotation* of the highly musical phrases.

(2) „Manche Nacht" (by Richard Dehmel):

l. 1. sich **verdunkeln,** to become dark
 3.   **funkeln,** to sparkle
 4. die **Grille,** —, –n, cricket
   wispern, to whisper
 5.   **bilderreich,** rich in imagery (*lit.* pictures)
 6. das **Gewohnte,** –n, that which is usual (*or* customary)

7.   **hinterm** (= hinter dem), behind the
      bleich, pale
9.   **merken,** to notice
      das **Schreiten,** –s, walking; im —, as you walk
10.   **verhundertfältigt,** increased a hundredfold
11. sich **entringen,** entrang, entrungen, to break forth, escape
      die **Dunkelheit,** —, –en, darkness
12.   **überwältigen,** to overwhelm

(3) ,,März" (by Georg Britting):

l. 1. die **Möwe,** —, –n, sea-gull
      2.   **knattern,** to rattle
      3. die **Ente,** —, –n, duck
      3.   **schnattern,** to cackle
      8.   **taumeln,** to stagger (in a *fig.* sense)

(4) ,,Einkehr" (by Ludwig Uhland):
      die **Einkehr,** —, putting up at a hotel *or* inn (*cf.* **einkehren** *below*)
l. 1.   **wundermild,** exceptionally kind (*or* generous)
      2.   **jüngst,** recently
      der **Gast,** –es, ̈–e, guest; zu —e, as a guest
      3. das **Schild,** –(e)s, –er, sign(board) (*hung in front of an inn; not to be
           confused with* **der** Schild, –(e)s, –e, *shield*)
      6.   **einkehren,** kehrte ein, ist eingekehrt, to put up at a hotel
      7. die **Kost,** —, food
      der **Schaum,** –(e)s, foam (*here used in the sense of* **schäumender
           Apfelsaft;** *the verb* to foam *is* **schäumen.**)
      10.   **leichtbeschwingt,** light-winged
      11. der **Schmaus,** –es, Schmäuse, feast; — halten, to (have a) feast
      13. die **Ruhe,** —, rest; zu süßer Ruh', in sweet repose
      14. die **Matte,** —, –n, meadow
      15.   **zudecken,** deckte zu, zugedeckt, to cover (up)
      17. die **Schuldigkeit** (= die Rechnung), bill
      19.   **segnen,** to bless
            allezeit, always
      20. die **Wurzel,** —, –n, root

(5) ,,Erster Schnee" (by Christian Morgenstern):
l. 1.   **silbergrau,** silver-gray
      1. der **Grund,** –(e)s, ̈–e, valley, dale
      2. das **Reh,** –(e)s, –e, roe, doe (*or,* in a general and wider sense, deer)
      3.   **winterlich,** wintry
      4.   **prüfen,** to examine
      4.   **vorsichtig,** cautiously, carefully
      4.   **Schritt für Schritt,** step by step

5.   **frischgefallen** (*part.* as *adj.*), freshly fallen
5.   **zierlich**, graceful, pretty, dainty

(6) „Der Fischer" (by Goethe):

l. 1.   **rauschen,** to rush, roar; das Wasser rauscht', the water swirled
        schwellen, to swell, rise; das Wasser schwoll, the water rose
   3. der **Angel,** –s, — (*also* **die** Angel, —, –n), fishing hook (*or* line)
        ruhevoll, very calmly (*or* quietly)
   4.   **hinan,** up to; ans Herz —, up to his heart (*i.e.,* except his heart, which was warm)
   6.   **empórteilen,** to divide upwards; teilt sich die Flut empor, the waves divide as they rise
   7.   **bewegt,** stormy, troubled, tempestuous
        hervórrauschen, to come forth with the noise of swirling waves (*cf. line 1*)
   8.   **feucht,** wet; —es Weib, mermaid
  10.   **was** (= warum), why
        hinaúflocken, to lure up
    die **Brut,** —, –en, brood
  11. der **Menschenwitz,** –es, human wit
    die **Menschenlist,** —, human cunning (*cf.* der **Menschenwitz** *above*)
  12. die **Todesglut,** —, death-bringing heat (*The reference is to the heat and danger above.*)
  13.   **wie's** (= wie es), how it; — Fischlein ist (= wie es dem Fischlein ist), how the little fish feels
  14.   **wohlig,** comfortable
  15.   **wie,** as; — du bist, as you are (*i.e.,* without further delay)
  16.   **erst,** (for the) first (time); und würdest — gesund, and for the first time you would enjoy real health
  17. sich **laben,** to refresh oneself
  19.   **hérkehren,** kehrte her, ist hergekehrt, to come back
        wellenatmend, bathing (*lit.,* breathing) in the waves
  21.   **locken,** to lure
  22.   **feuchtverklärt,** humid (and) bright (*The blue sky is doubly beautiful when reflected in the water.*)
    das **Blau,** the blue (*Adjectives used as nouns are neuter.*)
  23. das **Angesicht** (= das Gesicht), face
  24.   **ew'gen** (= ewigen), eternal
    der **Tau,** –(e)s, dew (*i.e.,* coolness as of dew; *opposite of* die **Todesglut,** *above*)
  26.   **netzen,** to (make) wet
  27.   **sehnsuchtsvoll,** longing, yearning
  28. die **Liebste,** —, –n, beloved; wie bei der —n (*gen. sing.*) Gruß (*dat.*) (= wie bei dem Gruß der Liebsten), as at the greeting of his beloved

30. **geschehen,** geschah, ist geschehen, to happen; da war es um ihn —, then he was doomed (*i.e.*, done for)

32. **ward** (= wurde), was (*This use is frequent in poetry for metrical reasons.*)

Note: The changing rhythm of this poem is in imitation of the movement of waves, and a frequency of **s**-sounds (*cf.* lines 1 and 7) suggests the sound of water.   The mermaid personifies the poet's fascination for the water (*cf.* opening lines of the fisherboy's song in Schiller's „Wilhelm Tell").

(7) „Hoffnung" (by Schiller):

l. 2.   **künftig,** future

6. die **Verbesserung,** —, –en, improvement, change for the better

7.   **einführen,** führte ein, eingeführt, to introduce, initiate

8.   **umflattern,** umflatterte, umflattert, to flutter (*or* hover) around

9.   **begeistern,** to inspire

der **Zauberschein,** –(e)s, –e, magic gleam

10. der **Greis,** –es, –e, old man

11.   **beschließen,** beschloß, beschlossen, to conclude, finish

das **Grab,** –(e)s, ¨er, grave

der **Lauf,** –(e)s, ¨e, course

12.   **aúfpflanzen,** pflanzte auf, aufgepflanzt, to set up

13. der **Wahn,** –(e)s, delusion, erroneous idea

14.   **erzeugen,** to produce

das **Gehirn,** –(e)s, –e, brain

der **Tor,** –en, –en, fool

15. sich **ankündigen,** kündigte an, angekündigt, to announce, be announced

(8) „Im Nebel" (by Hesse):

l. 1.   **seltsam,** strange

2.   **einsam,** solitary, forsaken, lonely

6.   **licht,** light, bright, clear

8.   **sichtbar,** visible

9.   **wahrlich,** truly, indeed, (most) assuredly

10. das **Dunkel:** die Dunkelheit

11.   **unentrinnbar,** inescapably, inevitably

14. das **Einsamsein,** –s, being alone (*cf.* **einsam** *above*)

(9) Ein Minnelied aus dem 12. Jahrhundert:

l. 2.   **des,** of that; — . . . gewiß, sure of that

3.   **beschlossen** (= eingeschlossen), locked (up)

5. das **Schlüssellein,** –s, —, little key

6.   **drinne** (= darin), in it

Note: The original (Middle-High-German) version of this beautiful little **Minnelied** (*lovesong*) is:

> Dû bist mîn, ich bin dîn:
> des solt dû gewis sîn.
> Dû bist beslozzen
> in mînem herzen;
> verlorn ist daz sluzzelîn:
> dû muost immer drinne sîn.

All of the following Lieder have been set to music and should be sung.

(10) Wiegenlied (by Johannes Brahms):

		Wiegenlied, cradlesong, lullaby
l.	2.	**bedacht,** bedecked
	3. das	**Näglein,** –s, — (= Nägelchen), carnation
	3.	**besteckt,** adorned, decorated
	4.	**schlupfen** (= schlüpfen), to slip
	4. die	**Deck(e),** —, –en, cover, blanket
	6.	**wecken** (*tr. vb.*), to awaken
	8. das	**Eng(e)lein,** –s, —, little angel
	8.	**bewachen,** to watch over, guard
	12. das	**Paradies,** –es, paradise

Note: Brahms' „Wiegenlied" is one of the world's most famous lullabies. When sung, lines five and six, and lines eleven and twelve, are repeated.

(11) Volkslied:

l.	1. das	**Vöglein,** –s, —, little bird
	2. das	**Flüglein,** –s, —, little wing
	4.	**weil's** (weil es), because it
	5.	**allhier** (= hier), here
	6.	**gleich** (= obgleich), although; bin ich — weit von dir (= obgleich ich weit von dir bin), although I am far from you
	9.	**erwachen,** to awake; — tu (= erwache), awake

(12) Geistliches Lied (by Christian Fürchtegott Gellert):

		geistliches Lied, sacred song, hymn
l.	1.	**rühmen,** to praise, extol
	1.	**des Ewigen Ehre,** the glory of God (*lit.*, the Eternal)
	2. der	**Schall,** –(e)s, –e, sound
	2.	**fortpflanzen,** to transmit, spread (*fig.*)
	3. der	**Erdkreis,** –es, globe, sphere of the earth

3.   **preisen,** pries, gepriesen, to praise
4.   **vernehmen,** vernahm, vernommen, vernimmt, to hear
4.   **göttlich** (= göttliches), divine
5.   **unzählbar,** countless, innumerable
6. das   **Zelt,** –(e)s, –e, vault (*or* canopy) of heaven (*lit.*, tent)
7.   **leuchten,** to beam, shine
10.   **aufstellen,** stellte auf, aufgestellt, to arrange (*lit.*, set up)
11.   **verkünden,** to make known, proclaim
11. die   **Ordnung,** —, order
11. die   **Stärke,** —, strength
12. das   **Wesen,** –s, —, creature, living thing (*lit.*, being)
14.   **fühllos** (= gefühllos), unfeeling, without feeling
14.   **beschau(e)n,** to look at
16.   **vertrau(e)n,** to trust, to put one's trust in a person

Note: The best known musical setting of this famous hymn is the one by Beethoven. When sung, the last line of each stanza is repeated.

(13) Wanderlied eines Handwerksburschen:

      das   **Wanderlied,** –(e)s, –er, traveler's song
      der   **Handwerksbursch(e),** –en, –en, traveling journeyman
l. 3.   **drum** (= darum), therefore
         ausschlagen, schlug aus, ausgeschlagen, schlägt aus, to strike out; ich schlag' es (mir) aus dem Sinn, I forget it
   5.   **probieren,** to try, test
      die   **Meistrin** (= Meisterin, —, –nen), mistress, wife of a master tradesman
   6.   **marschieren,** to march
   8.   **sag's** (= sage es), say it
         grad (= gerade), straight(forward); — frei, point-blank, frankly
14. der   **Speck,** –(e)s, –e, bacon
17. die   **Jungfer,** —, –n (= die Jungfrau, —, –en), maiden, Miss
18.   **zu guter Letzt,** —, in conclusion
19.   **ersetzen,** to take the place of, replace

Note: A young man who wished to learn a trade was obliged to work several years without pay and live in the house of a **Meister** (*master tradesman*). Such an apprentice was called a **Lehrling.** Apprentices were boarded at the homes of master tradesmen and made frequent complaints about the food, as evidenced in numerous folksongs. When a young man had served his apprenticeship, he became a journeyman (der **Geselle** *or* **Handwerksbursche**) entitled to earn wages, although still obliged to work for master workmen only and not directly for the public.

(14) Soldatenlied, „Der gute Kamerad" (by Ludwig Uhland):

This was the favorite song of the German field marshal Paul von Hindenburg who later became the second president of the German Republic (1925–1934).

l. 2.　**einen besser(e)n find(e)st du ni(ch)t**
　　3. die **Trommel, —, –n,** drum
　　3. der **Streit, –(e)s, –e,** conflict, battle
　　4. der **Schritt, –(e)s, –e;** der **Tritt, –(e)s, –e:** both words mean step
　　7.　**wegreißen,** riß weg, weggerissen, to tear (*or* snatch) away
　　11.　**derweil ich eben lad(e),** while I am loading (my gun)

(15) Studentenlied (by Victor von Scheffel):

l. 2.　**gleich,** like, equal;　kommt dir —, is to be compared with you
　　3. der **Geselle, –n, –n,** fellow;　Stadt fröhlicher —, city of merry fellows
　　4.　**ziehn** (= ziehen), to move
　　das **Blauäuglein, –s, —,** little blue eye
　　　drein (= darein), in it
　　6.　**lind,** gentle, mild
　　　übers (= über das), over it
　　7.　**weben,** to weave
　　die **Blüte, —, –n,** blossom, flower
　　　schimmern, to glitter, gleam
　　das **Brautgewand, –(e)s, ̈er,** bridal gown
　　9.　**traut,** dear, beloved
　　11.　**mir's** = mir es
　　　draus (= draußen), out in the world
　　　kahl, barren, bleak
　　12. das **Roß,** Rosses, Rosse, horse
　　der **Sporn, –es,** Sporen, spur

(16) Jägerlied, „Im Wald und auf der Heide" (by Wilhelm Bornemann):
　　　Jägerlied, hunting song
l. 1. die **Heide, —, –n,** heath
　　2. der **Jägersmann** (= der Jäger), hunter
　　3. der **Forst, –(e)s, –e,** forest
　　3.　**hegen,** to protect, take care of, preserve
　　3. das **Wildpret** (*or* Wildbret), –es, game
　　3.　**erlegen,** to kill
　　4. die **Lust, —, ̈e,** pleasure;　Lust an etwas (*dat.*) haben, to take pleasure in something
　　6.　**streichen,** strich, gestrichen, to stroll, ramble
　　7.　**einsam,** alone
　　7.　**den vollen Tag:**　den ganzen Tag
　　8.　**schwinden:** verschwinden
　　9.　**nachtrachten,** trachtete nach, nachgetrachtet, to pursue

9. das **Wild,** −es, −e (*cf.* **Wildpret** *above*)
10. sich **neigen,** to go down (*ref.* to the sun)
10.   **feucht,** moist, damp
11. das **Tagwerk,** −(e)s, day's work
12.   **häuslich,** domestic; häuslich stille Freude, quiet joy experienced in one's home

(17) Spinnstubenlied

das **Spinnstubenlied,** −(e)s, −er, spinning room song
l. 1.   **spinnen,** to spin
   2.   **dir'n:** dir ein
   4. der **Riemen,** −s, —, shoelace, shoestring
   5.   **schmerzen,** to pain
   9. der **Strumpf,** −(e)s, ̈e, stocking
  11.   **Zwickeln,** *i.e.* **mit Zwickeln; der Zwickel,** −s, —, clock (woven or embroidered ornament on the side of a stocking, going up from the ankle)
  12. sich **anstrengen,** to make every effort, to exert oneself

Note: Folk songs (Volkslieder), such as this spinning song, are often rich in folklore.   This Lied is built around the theme that a young woman could not expect a marriage proposal until her suitor was convinced that she was proficient in the art of spinning.

Vocabulary

List of Abbreviations

abbr.	=	abbreviation	*lit.*	=	literally
acc.	=	accusative	*masc.*	=	masculine
adj.	=	adjective	*neg.*	=	negative
adv.	=	adverb(ial)	*neut.*	=	neuter
art.	=	article	*nom.*	=	nominative
aux.	=	auxiliary	*num.*	=	numeral
colloq.	=	colloquial	*obj.*	=	object
comp.	=	comparative	*opp.*	=	opposite
conj.	=	conjunction	*part.*	=	particle
correl.	=	correlative	*pers.*	=	person
dat.	=	dative	*p.p.*	=	past participle
decl.	=	declension	*pl.*	=	plural
def.	=	definite	*poss.*	=	possessive
dem.	=	demonstrative	*prep.*	=	preposition(al)
dep.	=	dependent	*pres.*	=	present
dir.	=	direct	*pres. p.*	=	present participle
e.g.	=	for example	*pret.*	=	preterit
emph.	=	emphatic	*prin.*	=	principal
etc.	=	and so forth	*pron.*	=	pronoun
excl.	=	exclamation	*ques.*	=	question
fem.	=	feminine	*ref.*	=	referring
fig.	=	figurative(ly)	*refl.*	=	reflexive
fut.	=	future	*rel.*	=	relative
gen.	=	genitive	*sci.*	=	scientific
i.e.	=	that is	*sep.*	=	separable
imperf.	=	imperfect	*sing.*	=	singular
impers.	=	impersonal	*str.*	=	strong
indecl.	=	indeclinable	*sub.*	=	subordinating
indef.	=	indefinite	*subj.*	=	subjunctive
indir.	=	indirect	*superl.*	=	superlative
inf.	=	infinitive	*tech.*	=	technical
intens.	=	intensive	*temp.*	=	temporal
inter.	=	interrogative	*th.*	=	thing
interj.	=	interjection	*tr.*	=	transitive
intr.	=	intransitive	*vb.*	=	verb
invar.	=	invariable	*w.*	=	with
			wk.	=	weak

German-English Vocabulary

Genitive singular and nominative plural endings are given for all nouns. Principal parts are given only for strong or irregular verbs. Verbs conjugated with **haben** omit the auxiliary: abnehmen, nahm ab, abgenommen, nimmt ab; those conjugated with **sein** have **ist** in the third principal part: abfahren, fuhr ab, ist abgefahren, fährt ab. Reflexive verbs have **sich** only with the present infinitive: sich ausziehen, zog aus, ausgezogen. Separable verbs accent the prefix when their principal parts are not given: ánklagen; inseparable verbs indicate the accent only when a prefix is doubtful: überráschen.

A

der **Abend,** –s, –e, evening; eines —s (*indef. time*), one evening; gestern abend, yesterday evening, last night; heute abend, this evening, tonight

das **Abendessen,** –s, —, supper, dinner (*in the evening*)

aber, but, however

abfahren, fuhr ab, ist abgefahren, fährt ab, to depart, leave

abholen, holte ab, abgeholt, to call (*or* come) for

abnehmen, nahm ab, abgenommen, nimmt ab, to take off; er nimmt den Hut ab, he takes off his hat

die **Abreise,** —, –n, departure

abreisen, reiste ab, ist abgereist, to depart, leave

abschaffen, schaffte ab, abgeschafft, to do away with, abolish

der **Abschied,** –(e)s, –e, departure

abschreiben, schrieb ab, abgeschrieben, to copy

die **Absicht,** —, –en, intention

abspielen, spielte ab, abgespielt, to play back (*referring to tape recorder*)

absteigen, stieg ab, ist abgestiegen, to come down from; er steigt vom Pferde ab, he dismounts

abwesend, absent

acht, eight

achtzehnt–, eighteenth

der **Acker,** –s, ⸚, field

der **Adler,** –s, —, eagle

die **Adresse,** —, –n, address

der **Advokat,** –en, –en, lawyer

der **Affe,** –n, –n, monkey, ape

Afrika, –s (*neut.*), Africa

ähnlich (*w. dat.*), similar (to); er ist dem Vater —, he resembles his father

der **Akkusativ,** –s, –e, accusative

alle (*pl.*), all; auf —n vieren, on all fours

allein (*adv.*), alone; (*conj.*) but

allerlei, all sorts (*or* kinds) of

allerschönst–, most beautiful of all

alles, everything, all; —, was, all that
die **Alpen,** — (*pl.*), Alps
als, than (*after a comp.*); (*conj.*) when (*refers to a def. past action*); — ob, as if
also, so, consequently, therefore
alt, old
das **Alter,** –s, —, age
Amerika, –s (*neut.*), America
amerikanisch, American
sich **amüsieren,** to have a good time
an (*prep. w. dat. or acc.*), at, on, to; — der Universität, at the university (*of a professor*)
ander–, other
ändern, to change
anders, differently, otherwise
anderthalb, one and a half
der **Anfang,** –(e)s, ¨e, beginning
anfangen, fing an, angefangen, fängt an, to begin
angehen, ging an, hat (*or* ist) angegangen, to concern; das geht ihn nichts an, that does not concern him
angenehm (*w. dat.*), pleasant, agreeable
die **Angst,** —, ¨e, fear
ánklagen (*w. acc. of the pers. & gen. of the th.*), to accuse of
ankommen, kam an, ist angekommen, to arrive
annehmen, nahm an, angenommen, nimmt an, to accept
ansehen, sah an, angesehen, sieht an, to look at
der **Anspruch,** –(e)s, ¨e, claim (*w.* auf *and acc.*)
anständig, decent, proper
(an)statt (*prep. w. gen.*), instead of
die **Antwort,** —, –en, answer
antworten, to answer; man antwortet einer Person (*dat.*),

one answers a person; man antwortet **auf** eine Frage (*acc.*), one answers a question
anwesend, present
anziehen, zog an, angezogen, to put on; (*often refl.*) sie zieht sich an, she dresses (herself); (*frequently w. dat. refl.*) du solltest **dir** ein neues Kleid —, you should put on a new dress
der **Anzug,** –(e)s, ¨e, suit of clothes
der **Apfel,** –s, ¨, apple
der **Apfelbaum,** –(e)s, ¨e, apple tree
der **Appetit,** –(e)s, –e, appetite
der **April,** –(s), –e, April
die **Arbeit,** —, –en, work
arbeiten, to work; fleißig (schwer *or* tüchtig) —, to work hard
der **Arbeiter,** –s, —, laborer
ärgerlich, vexed, provoked
sich **ärgern** über (*w. acc.*), to be provoked at
arm, poor
der **Arm,** –(e)s, –e, arm
die **Armut,** —, poverty
die **Art,** —, –en, kind
der **Arzt,** –es, ¨e, physician, doctor; den — holen (*or* kommen) lassen, to send for the doctor
Asien, –s (*neut.*), Asia
der **Ast,** –es, ¨e, branch
der **Astronaut,** –en, –en, astronaut
der **Astronom,** –en, –en, astronomer
astronomisch, celestial
der **Atem,** –s, –züge, breath
atmen, to breathe
die **Atmosphäre,** —, –n, atmosphere
atomisch, atomic; das atomische Zeitalter, the Atomic Age

auch, also, too

auf (*prep. w. dat. or acc.*), on, to; — dem Lande, in the country; — der Universität, at the university (*of a student*); — einmal, suddenly; —s Land, to the country

die **Aufgabe,** —, -n, lesson, assignment, task, exercise, homework; er macht seine —n, he does his lessons

aufgeben, gab auf, aufgegeben, gibt auf, to give up

aufhalten, hielt auf, aufgehalten, hält auf, to stop, check

aufheben, hob auf, aufgehoben, hebt auf, to pick up

aufhören, hörte auf, aufgehört, to stop, cease

der **Aufklärungssatellit,** -en, -en, reconnaissance satellite

aufmachen, machte auf, aufgemacht, to open

aufmerksam, attentive

die **Aufnahme,** —, -n, photograph

der **Aufsatz,** -es, ̈-e, composition, essay

aufsetzen, setzte auf, aufgesetzt, to put on (*as hat or glasses*); setze (dir) den Hut auf!, put on your hat

aufstehen, stand auf, ist aufgestanden, to (a)rise, get up

aufsteigen, stieg auf, ist aufgestiegen, to rise, ascend (*esp. in sci. language ref. to a rocket*)

der **Aufstieg,** -s, -e, ascent

das **Auge,** -s, -n, eye

der **Augenblick,** -(e)s, -e, moment

aus (*prep. w. dat.*), out (of), from; — welchem Grunde?, for what reason?

ausbessern, besserte aus, ausgebessert, to repair, mend

der **Ausdruck,** -(e)s, ̈-e, expression

ausführen, führte aus, ausgeführt, to execute, carry out

der **Ausländer,** -s, —, foreigner

sich **ausruhen,** ruhte aus, ausgeruht, to rest

aussehen, sah aus, ausgesehen, sieht aus, to look, appear

außen, outside; outwardly

außer (*prep. w. dat.*), besides; except; ich bin — mir vor Freude, I am beside myself with joy

außerdem, besides, moreover

außerhalb (*prep. w. gen.*), outside of

aussetzen, setzte aus, ausgesetzt, to expose

aussprechen, sprach aus, ausgesprochen, spricht aus, to pronounce

auswendig, by heart; — lernen, to learn by heart

sich **ausziehen,** zog aus, ausgezogen, to undress

das **Auto,** -s, -s, auto, car

automatisch, automatic, self-acting

B

der **Bach,** -(e)s, ̈-e, brook

backen, buk, gebacken, bäckt, to bake

der **Bäcker,** -s, —, baker

die **Bäckerei,** —, -en, bakery

das **Bad,** -(e)s, ̈-er, bath

baden, to bathe

die **Bahn,** —, -en, road, track

der **Bahnhof,** -(e)s, ̈-e, station

der **Ball,** -(e)s, ̈-e, ball

der **Ballon,** -s, -e *or* -s, balloon

das **Ballonspiegelteleskop,** -s, -e, balloon reflecting telescope, balloon reflector

das **Ballon-Teleskop,** -s, -e, balloon telescope

der **Band,** -(e)s, ̈-e, volume

das **Band,** –(e)s, ⸚er, ribbon
die **Bank,** —, ⸚e, bench
die **Bank,** —, –en, bank (*for money*)
der **Bär,** –en, –en, bear
der **Barbier,** –s, –e, barber
der **Bart,** –(e)s, ⸚e, beard
bauen, to build
der **Bauer,** –s (*or* –n), –n, farmer, peasant
der **Baum,** –(e)s, ⸚e, tree
Bayern, –s (*neut.*), Bavaria
der **Beamte,** –n, –n, official; (*w. adj. decl.*) ein —**r,** an official
beantworten (*w. acc.*), to answer
sich **bedanken,** to thank; sich **bei** einer Person **für** etwas —, to thank a person for something
bedeuten, to mean
die **Bedeutung,** —, –en, meaning, importance
bedienen, to serve
sich **bedienen** (*w. gen.*), to make use of
bedürfen (*w. gen.*), to need
bedürftig (*adj. w. gen.*), in need of
sich **beeilen,** to hurry
sich **befassen** mit, to concern oneself with, occupy oneself with
befehlen, befahl, befohlen, befiehlt (*w. dat.*), to order, command
sich **befinden,** befand, befunden, to be, fare, feel
begegnen, begegnete, ist begegnet (*w. dat.*), to meet
beginnen, begann, begonnen, to begin
begleiten, to accompany
begraben, begrub, begraben, begräbt, to bury
behalten, behielt, behalten, behält, to retain, keep
behandeln, to treat
behaupten, to maintain, assert

bei (*prep. w. dat.*), next to, with, at (the house of); — mir, at my house; das Geld, das ich — mir hatte, the money I had with me
beide, both; — (*or* die —n) Brüder, the two (*or* both) brothers
das **Bein,** –(e)s, –e, leg
das **Beispiel,** –(e)s, –e, example; zum — (*abbr.* z.B.), for example (*or* instance) (*abbr.* e.g.)
beißen, biß, gebissen, to bite
beistehen, stand bei, beigestanden (*w. dat.*), to render aid, assist
bekannt, (well-)known
der **Bekannte,** –n, –n (*w. adj. decl.*), acquaintance; ein —**r,** an acquaintance
sich **beklagen** über (*w. acc.*), to complain about
bekommen, bekam, bekommen, to receive
beliebt, beloved; favorite, popular
bellen, to bark
belohnen, to reward
bemannt, manned
bemerken, to notice
sich **benehmen,** benahm, benommen, benimmt, to behave
benutzen, to use, utilize, employ, take advantage of, avail, profit
beobachten, to observe
die **Beobachtung,** —, –en, observation, study, examination
bequem, comfortable; mache es dir —!, make yourself at home
berauben (*w. acc. of the pers. & gen. of the th.*), to rob
bereit, ready, prepared
bereiten, to prepare

bereits, already

der **Berg,** –(e)s, –e, mountain

berichten, to report

berühmt, famous; — durch (*w. acc.*) [*or* wegen (*w. gen.*)], famous for

beschäftigt, busy

beschreiben, beschrieb, beschrieben, to describe

beschuldigen (*w. acc. of the pers. & gen. of the th.*), to accuse

der **Besen,** –s, —, broom

besiedeln, to settle

besiegen, to conquer

besitzen, besaß, besessen, to possess

besonders, especially

besser (*comp. of* gut), better

best– (*superl. of* gut), best

bestehen, bestand, bestanden, to pass (*an examination*); — aus, to consist of

bestellen, to order

bestimmt, certain(ly), sure(ly); determined, destined

bestrafen, to punish

der **Besuch,** –(e)s, –e, visit

besuchen, to visit

beten, to pray

betrachten, to observe

sich **betragen,** betrug, betragen, beträgt, to behave

betrügen, betrog, betrogen, to deceive

das **Bett,** –(e)s, –en, bed

betteln, to beg

bevor (*conj.*), before

beweisen, bewies, bewiesen, to prove

sich **bewerben,** bewarb, beworben, bewirbt (*w. um & acc.*), to apply for

bewundern, to admire

bewußt (*adj. w. gen.*), conscious of

bezahlen, to pay

bezug, in bezug (*or* Bezug) auf (*w. acc.*), with reference to, with regard to, as to

die **Bibliothek,** —, –en, library

biegen, bog, gebogen, to bend

die **Biene,** —, –n, bee

das **Bier,** –(e)s, –e, beer

bieten, bot, geboten, to offer

das **Bild,** –(e)s, –er, picture

bilden, to form

die **Bildung,** —, education

binden, band, gebunden, to tie

die **Birne,** —, –n, pear

bis (*prep. w. acc.*), to, as far as; (*conj.*) until; (*often w. other preps.*) — an das Fenster, up to the window

bisher, until now

bitte, (if you) please; you are welcome

bitten, bat, gebeten, to ask; um etwas (*acc.*) —, to ask for something

bitter, bitter

blasen, blies, geblasen, bläst, to blow

blaß, pale

das **Blatt,** –(e)s, ¨er, leaf; sheet

blau, blue

das **Blei,** –(e)s, –e, lead

bleiben, blieb, ist geblieben, to remain, stay; er bleibt stehen, he stops

der **Bleistift,** –(e)s, –e, pencil

der **Blick,** –(e)s, –e, glance, look

blicken, to look

blind, blind; — auf (*w. dat.*), blind in

blitzen, to glitter, sparkle; es blitzt, it lightens

bloß, bare; mit bloßem Auge, with the naked eye

blühen, to bloom

die **Blume,** —, –n, flower

das **Blut,** –(e)s, blood

der **Boden,** –s, ¨ (*or* –), floor

die **Bodenbeobachtungsstation,** —, –en, surface-observation station

der **Bodenerwerb,** –(e)s, –e, acquisition of territory (ground, land)

der **Bogen,** –s, — (*or* ¨), arch; bow; sheet of paper

das **Boot,** –(e)s, –e, boat

die **Börse,** —, –n, purse; stock exchange

böse, angry; — sein auf (*w. acc.*), to be angry with

der **Boxer,** –s, —, boxer, pugilist

braten, briet, gebraten, brät, to roast

brauchen, to need

braun, brown

die **Braut,** —, ¨e, fiancée

brechen, brach, gebrochen, bricht, to break

breit, wide, broad; weit und —, far and wide; einen Fuß —, a foot wide

brennen, brannte, gebrannt, to burn; er brennt vor Ungeduld, he burns with impatience

das **Brett,** –(e)s, –er, board

der **Brief,** –(e)s, –e, letter

die **Briefmarke,** —, –n, stamp

die **Briefmarkensammlung,** —, –en, stamp collection

die **Brille,** —, –n, (eye)glasses, spectacles; eine — tragen, to wear glasses

bringen, brachte, gebracht, to bring

der **Brocken,** –s, Brocken (*highest peak in the Harz Mountains*)

das **Brot,** –(e)s, –e, bread

die **Brücke,** —, –n, bridge

der **Bruder,** –s, ¨, brother

die **Brust,** —, ¨e, breast

das **Buch,** –(e)s, ¨er, book

buchstabieren, to spell

sich **bücken,** to stoop

bunt, variegated, many-colored

die **Burg,** —, –en, castle

der **Bürger,** –s, —, citizen

der **Bürgermeister,** –s, —, mayor

der **Bursche,** –n, –n, fellow; lad; student

die **Butter,** —, butter

C

der **Charákter,** –s, Charaktére, character

die **Chemie,** —, chemistry

der **Chemiker,** –s, —, chemist

chemisch, chemical

die **Cousine,** —, –n, (*female*) cousin

D

da (*adv.*), there; (*conj.*) since, as

dabei, thereby; while doing it

das **Dach,** –(e)s, ¨er, roof

dafür, for it

dagegen, on the other hand; against it

daheim (= zu Hause), at home

daher, therefore

damals, at that time

die **Dame,** —, –n, lady

damit (*adv.*), with it; (*conj.*) in order that

der **Dampfer,** –s, —, steamer

das **Dampfschiff,** –(e)s, –e, steamship

der **Dank,** –(e)s, thanks

dankbar (*w. dat.*), thankful, grateful

danken (*w. dat.*), to thank; ich danke Ihnen für das Buch, I thank you for the book

dann, then

darauf, thereupon, after that; upon it (that *or* them)

darauffolgend, following, later

darin, therein; in it (that *or* them)

darum, therefore

daß (*conj.*), that

der **Dativ,** –s, –e, dative

das **Datum,** –s, Daten, date

dauernd, continually, constantly

davon, of (*or* about) it (*or* them)

dazu, for that; in addition

die **Decke,** —, –n, ceiling; cover

decken, to cover

dein, deine, dein (*poss. adj.*), your

denken, dachte, gedacht, to think; — an (*w. acc.*), to think of

denn (*causal conj.*) for; warum hat er es — getan?, why then did he do it?; es sei denn, daß . . ., unless . . .

derselbe, dieselbe, dasselbe, the same

deshalb, therefore

dessen (*masc. & neut. sing.*), **deren** (*fem. sing.*), **deren** (*pl.*) (*gen. forms of the rel. pron.* der, die, das), whose

desto, the; je . . . —, the . . . the; je höher er steigt, — kälter wird es, the higher he climbs, the colder it gets

deutlich, distinct(ly)

deutsch (*adj.*), German; auf —, in German

Deutsch (*noun*), German; lernen Sie —?, are you learning German?

der **Deutsche,** –n, –n (*w. adj. decl.*), German, native of Germany; ein —r, a German (man)

Deutschland, –s (*neut.*), Germany

dicht, dense, compact

der **Dichter,** –s, —, poet

dick, thick; einen Fuß —, a foot thick

der **Dieb,** –(e)s, –e, thief

dienen (*w. dat.*), to serve

der **Diener,** –s, —, servant

der **Dienstag,** –(e)s, –e, Tuesday

das **Dienstmädchen,** –s, —, maid, servant (girl)

dieser, –e, –es (*adj.*), this; (*pron.*) this one

diesseits (*prep. w. gen.*), on this side of

das **Ding,** –(e)s, –e, thing

direkt, direct

doch, still, however, yet

der **Doktor,** –s, –en, doctor, physician

der **Dom,** –(e)s, –e, cathedral

donnern, to thunder

der **Donnerstag,** –(e)s, –e, Thursday

doppelt (*adj.*), double; (*adv.*) doubly

das **Dorf,** –(e)s, ̈er, village

der **Dorn,** –(e)s, –en (–e *or* ̈er), thorn

dort, there (*i.e.,* in that place)

dorthin, there (*i.e.,* to that place), thither

draußen, outside

drehen (*often refl.*), to turn

drei, three

dreibeinig, three-legged

dreifach, threefold, triple

dreimal, three times

drinnen, inside

dritt–, third

drohen (*w. dat.*), to threaten

drüben, over there

dumm, stupid

die **Dummheit,** —, –en, stupidity

dunkel, dark

dünn, thin

durch (*prep. w. acc.*), through, by

durchführen, führte durch, durchgeführt, to carry out, perform, execute, accomplish, conduct

dürfen, durfte, gedurft, darf, to be allowed; das — Sie nicht tun, you must not do that; dürfte ich Sie darum bitten?, might I ask you for that?

der **Durst,** –es, thirst

durstig, thirsty

das **Dutzend,** –s, –e, dozen

E

eben, even; just

ebenso, just as; — groß wie, just as large as

das **Echo,** –s, –s, echo

echt, genuine

die **Ecke,** —, –n, corner

edel, noble

ehe (conj.), before

die **Ehre,** —, –n, honor

ehrlich, honest

das **Ei,** –(e)s, –er, egg

die **Eiche,** —, –n, oak

eigen (adj.), own

eigentlich, real(ly)

einander, each other

sich (dat.) **einbilden,** to imagine

einfach, simple

der **Einfall,** –(e)s, ̈-e, idea, notion

einfallen, fiel ein, ist eingefallen, es fällt ein, to occur; das war **mir** nie eingefallen, that had never occurred to me

einladen, lud ein, eingeladen, ladet (or lädt) ein, to invite

einmal, once; once upon a time; auf —, suddenly

einschlafen, schlief ein, ist eingeschlafen, schläft ein, to fall asleep

einseitig, one-sided, partial, biased

einstecken, steckte ein, eingesteckt, to put in; man hat ihn ins Gefängnis eingesteckt, they put him in prison

der **Einwohner,** –s, —, inhabitant

das **Eis,** –es, ice

das **Eisen,** –s, iron

die **Eisenbahn,** —, –en, railroad

der **Eis-Ozean,** –s, –e, ocean of ice

die **Elbe,** —, Elbe (River)

der **Elefant,** –en, –en, elephant

die **Eltern,** — (pl.), parents

empfangen, empfing, empfangen, empfängt, to receive

empfinden, empfand, empfunden, to feel; er empfindet es schmerzlich, it pains him

empfindlich, susceptible, sensitive, responsive

emporsteigen, stieg empor, ist emporgestiegen, to climb up

das **Ende,** –s, –n, end; zu — lesen, to finish reading, read through

enden, to end

endlich, finally, at last

eng, narrow

England, –s (neut.), England

der **Engländer,** –s, —, Englishman

entdecken, to discover

entfernt, distant, remote

entgegeneilen (w. sein & dat.), to hasten toward

entlang (w. acc.), along

entlassen, entließ, entlassen, entläßt, to dismiss

entscheiden, entschied, entschieden, to decide; often refl., to decide, make up one's mind

sich **entschließen,** entschloß, entschlossen, to decide, make up one's mind

entschuldigen (w. acc.), to excuse, pardon

die **Entstehung,** —, –en, origin, formation, genesis

entwickeln, to develop

entzünden, to inflame

entzweibrechen, brach entzwei, entzweigebrochen, bricht entzwei, to break in two

die **Erde,** —, earth, world

der **Erdsatellit,** –en, –en, earth satellite

erfahren, erfuhr, erfahren, erfährt, to learn, experience, discover (knowledge); to learn about, erfahren über (*w. acc.*)

erfinden, erfand, erfunden, to invent

der **Erfolg,** –(e)s, –e, success

erfolgreich, successful

erforderlich, necessary, required, requisite

das **Ergebnis,** –ses, –se, result

erhalten, erhielt, erhalten, erhält, to receive

sich **erholen** von, to recover (*or* recuperate) from

sich **erinnern** (*w. gen. or* an *& acc.*), to remember

sich **erkälten,** to catch cold

erkennen, erkannte, erkannt, to recognize

sich **erkundigen** nach, to make inquiries about

erlauben (*w. dat.*), to permit

die **Erlaubnis,** —, –se, permission

erleben, to experience, live through

das **Erlebnis,** –ses, –se, experience

ernst, serious

erreichen, to reach, attain

erscheinen, erschien, ist erschienen, to appear

erschrecken (*wk. tr.*), to frighten

erschrecken erschrak, ist erschrocken, erschrickt (*intr.*), to be frightened

erst– (*adj.*), first

erst (*adv.*), not until

erstaunt, astonished

erwachen, erwachte, ist erwacht (*intr.*), to awake

erwarten, to expect

erweisen, erwies, erwiesen, to show (*e.g.,* honor), render

erwidern, to reply

erzählen, to tell, relate

erziehen, erzog, erzogen, to bring up, rear, educate

der **Esel,** –s, —, donkey

essen, aß, gegessen, ißt, to eat

etliche (*pl.*), some, several

etwa, perhaps

etwas, some, something, somewhat

euer, eu(e)re, euer (*poss. adj.*), your

Europa, –s, (*neut.*), Europe

ewig, eternal

das **Examen,** –s, Examina, examination

das **Experiment,** –s, –e, experiment

F

das **Fach,** –(e)s, ̈er, subject of study

fähig (*adj. w. gen.*), capable of

fahren, fuhr, ist gefahren, fährt, to ride, travel, drive, go

die **Fahrkarte,** —, –n, ticket

die **Fahrt,** —, –en, trip, voyage, ride

das **Fahrzeug,** –s, –e, (power) craft (marine, land, *or* air), car

der **Fall,** –(e)s, ̈e, fall; case

fallen, fiel, ist gefallen, fällt, to fall; das Schreiben fällt mir schwer, writing is difficult for me

der **Fallschirm,** –s, –e, parachute

die **Familie,** —, -n, family
fangen, fing, gefangen, fängt, to catch
die **Farbe,** —, -n, color
fast, almost
faul, lazy; rotten
die **Feder,** —, -n, feather; pen
fehlen, to be absent; lack, miss; be the matter with; was fehlt Ihnen?, what is the matter with you?
der **Fehler,** -s, —, mistake
feiern, to celebrate
der **Feiertag,** -(e)s, -e, holiday
fein, fine
der **Feind,** -(e)s, -e, enemy
feindlich (*adj. w. dat.*), hostile; — gesinnt, hostile to(wards)
das **Feld,** -(e)s, -er, field; auf dem —e, in the field
der **Felsen,** -s, —, rock, cliff
das **Fenster,** -s, —, window
die **Ferien,** — (*pl.*), vacation
fern, far, distant, remote
der **Fernsehapparat,** -s, -e, television set
fertig, ready, finished
festhalten, hielt fest, festgehalten, hält fest, to cling to; keep (*emph.*)
fett, fat
das **Feuer,** -s, —, fire
die **Feuerversicherungsgesellschaft,** —, -en, fire insurance company
finden, fand, gefunden, to find
der **Finger,** -s, —, finger
der **Fisch,** -es, -e, fish
flach, flat, plain; shallow
die **Fläche,** —, -n, (plane) surface, area
die **Flamme,** —, -n, flame
die **Flasche,** —, -n, bottle, flask
das **Fleisch,** -es, meat
der **Fleiß,** -es, diligence
fleißig, diligent, industrious; —

arbeiten (studieren), to work (study) hard
fliegen, flog, ist geflogen, to fly
der **Flieger,** -s, —, aviator, flyer
die **Fliegertauglichkeitsuntersuchung,** —, -en, flyer-fitness test
fliehen, floh, ist geflohen, to flee
fließen, floß, ist geflossen, to flow
fließend, fluent(ly)
der **Flug,** -(e)s, ⸚e, flight
der **Flügel,** -s, —, wing
das **Flugzeug,** -(e)s, -e, airplane
der **Fluß,** Flusses, Flüsse, river
die **Folge,** —, -n, consequence, result
folgen, folgte, ist gefolgt (*w. dat.*), to follow
die **Form,** —, -en, form, shape
der **Forscher,** -s, —, investigator, scientist, scientific researcher
die **Forschung,** —, -en, investigation, research, inquiry, study
das **Forschungsergebnis,** -ses, -se, result of research
die **Forschungsrakete,** —, -n, research rocket
fort, away
fortgehen, ging fort, ist fortgegangen, to go away
fortlaufen, lief fort, ist fortgelaufen, läuft fort, to run away
forttragen, trug fort, fortgetragen, trägt fort, to carry away
fortwährend, continual(ly)
die **Frage,** —, -n, question; eine — an eine Person (*acc.*) stellen, to ask a person a question
fragen, to ask, question
Frankreich, -s (*neut.*), France
der **Franzose,** -n, -n, Frenchman
französisch, French

die **Frau,** —, –en, woman; wife; Mrs. (*before proper names*)

das **Fräulein,** –s, —, young lady, Miss (*before proper names*)

frei, free

der **Freiballon,** –s, –e, *or* –s, free balloon

die **Freiheit,** —, freedom, liberty

der **Freitag,** –(e)s, –e, Friday

fremd, strange, foreign; er ist mir —, he is a stranger to me

die **Freude,** —, –n, joy, happiness, pleasure; ich bin außer mir vor —, I am beside myself with joy; es macht mir —, it gives me pleasure; ich habe meine — dar**an,** I take pleasure **in** that

freuen, to make glad; es freut mich, I am glad

sich **freuen,** to be glad; er freut sich, he is glad; sich — auf (*w. acc.*), to look forward with pleasure to; sich — über (*w. acc.*), to be happy about, be pleased with, rejoice at

der **Freund,** –(e)s, –e, (*male*) friend

die **Freundin,** —, –nen, (*female*) friend

freundlich, friendly; seien Sie ihm —!, be friendly to him

die **Freundschaft,** —, –en, friendship

der **Friede(n),** –ns, peace

frieren, fror, gefroren, to freeze; vorige Nacht hat es stark gefroren, last night it froze hard

frisch, fresh

Fritz, –(ens) (*masc.*), Fred

froh, glad, happy; er wird seines Lebens nicht —, he leads an unhappy life

fröhlich, happy, cheerful

fromm, pious

die **Frucht,** —, ⸚e, fruit

früh, early

früher, earlier; sooner; formerly

der **Frühling,** –s, –e, spring; im —, in spring

das **Frühstück,** –(e)s, –e, breakfast; zum —, for breakfast

frühstücken, frühstückte, gefrühstückt, to have breakfast

fühlen, to feel

führen, to lead

der **Führer,** –s, —, leader, guide

füllen, to fill

die **Füllfeder,** —, –n, fountain pen

für (*prep. w. acc.*), for; — fünf Mark Zucker, five marks worth of sugar

fürchten, to fear; sich — vor (*w. dat.*), to be afraid of

der **Fürst,** –en, –en, prince

der **Fuß,** –es, ⸚e, foot

der **Fußboden,** –s, ⸚, floor

füttern, to feed

G

die **Gabel,** —, –n, fork

der **Gang,** –(e)s, ⸚e, course (*of a meal*); corridor

die **Gans,** —, Gänse, goose

ganz, entire(ly), all, whole

gar, quite, very; — nicht, not at all; — nichts, nothing at all

der **Garten,** –s, ⸚, garden

das **Gas,** –es, –e, gas

der **Gast,** –es, ⸚e, guest

gebären, gebar, geboren, gebiert, to give birth to (*cf.* **geboren**)

das **Gebäude,** –s, —, building

geben, gab, gegeben, gibt, to give; es gibt (gab) (*impers. w. acc.*), there is (*or* are) [was (*or* were)]

das **Gebiet,** –(e)s, –e, territory, domain; (*fig.*) field

das **Gebirge, –s, —,** mountain range, mountainous region
geboren (*p.p. of* gebären), born; **wurde —,** was born (*used for the dead*); **ist —,** was born (*used for the living*); wann sind Sie **—?,** when were you born?
gebrauchen, to use
die **Geburt, —, –en,** birth
der **Geburtstag,** –(e)s, –e, birthday; zum **—,** for one's birthday
das **Gedächtnis, –ses ,–se,** memory
der **Gedanke, –ns, –n,** thought
gedenken (*w. gen.*), to remember
das **Gedicht,** –(e)s, –e, poem
die **Geduld, —,** patience
geduldig, patient
die **Gefahr, —, –en,** danger
gefährlich, dangerous
gefallen, gefiel, gefallen, gefällt (*w. dat.*), to please; es gefällt mir, I like it
der **Gefallen, –s, —,** favor; er tut mir den **—,** he does me the favor
das **Gefängnis, –ses, –se,** prison
das **Gefühl,** –(e)s, –e, feeling
gegen (*prep. w. acc.*), against; toward; contrary to
die **Gegend, —, –en,** region
der **Gegensatz, –es, ̈e** (= das Gegenteil), contrast, opposite
gegenüber (*prep. w. dat.; usually follows noun or pronoun it governs*), opposite
die **Gegenwart, —,** present time, modern time(s); presence; in meiner **—,** in my presence
geheim, secret(ly)
das **Geheimnis, –ses, –se,** secret
geheimnisvoll, mysterious
gehen, ging, ist gegangen, to go; in die Schule **—,** to go to school; wie geht es Ihnen?, how are you?
gehorchen (*w. dat.*), to obey
gehören (*w. dat. & no prep. if ownership is denoted*), to belong to; **— zu,** to be a part (*or* member) of (*as a club*)
der **Geist, –es, –er,** mind, spirit
gelangen, gelangte, ist gelangt, to attain; come to; endlich ist er zu einem Schluße gelangt, he finally reached a conclusion
gelb, yellow
das **Geld,** –(e)s, –er, money
gelegen (*adj. w. dat.*), opportune
die **Gelegenheit, —, –en,** opportunity, occasion; bei dieser **—,** on this occasion
gelingen, gelang, ist gelungen (*w. dat.*), to succeed; es ist mir gelungen, Ihre Schrift zu entziffern, I succeeded in deciphering your writing
gelten, galt, gegolten, gilt, to be worth (*or* of value); be meant for
das **Gemüt,** –(e)s, –er, feeling, soul, heart
gemütlich, cosy, comfortable; sociable
genau, exact(ly)
genesen, genas, ist genesen, genest, to recover (*from an illness*)
genießen, genoß, genossen, genießt, to enjoy
der **Genitiv, –s, –e,** genitive
genug, enough
genügen (*w. dat.*), to be enough; satisfy
das **Gepäck,** –(e)s, –e, baggage, luggage
der **Gepäckträger, –s, —,** porter

gerade (*adj. & adv.*), straight, direct; (*adv.*) just, exactly

geraten (geriet, ist geraten, gerät (*w. in & acc.*), to get (*or* stray) into; turn out to be

das Gericht, –(e)s, –e, court (of justice); dish, course

gern (lieber, am liebsten), gladly, willingly; er hat es —, he likes it; er tut es —, he likes to do it

der Gesangverein, –(e)s, –e, glee club, singing society

das Geschäft, –(e)s, –e, business; occupation

geschehen, geschah, ist geschehen, es geschieht, to happen; es geschieht ihm recht, it serves him right

das Geschenk, –(e)s, –e, gift, present

die Geschichte, —, –n, story; history

das Geschlecht, –(e)s, –er, sex; gender; race, stock

die Geschwindigkeit, —, –en, speed, velocity

der Geschwindigkeitsmesser, –s, —, speedometer, tachometer, speed indicator

der Geselle, –n, –n, fellow; journeyman

die Gesellschaft, —, –en, society, company

das Gesetz, –es, –e, law

das Gesicht, –(e)s, –er, face

gesinnt (*adj.*), minded, disposed; feindlich —, hostile to(wards)

das Gespräch, –(e)s, –e, conversation

die Gestalt, —, –en, form, figure, stature

gestern, yesterday

gesund, well, healthy

die Gesundheit, —, –en, health

das Getränk, –(e)s, –e, drink

gewahr werden (*w. gen.*), to become conscious of, perceive

die Gewalt, —, –en, force

gewinnen, gewann, gewonnen, to win, gain

gewiß, sure(ly), certain(ly); (*adj. w. gen.*), sure (*or* certain) of

das Gewitter, –s, —, (thunder)storm

sich gewöhnen an (*w. acc.*), to get used to; ich bin nicht daran gewöhnt, I am not used to it

gewohnt, accustomed; ich bin es (*acc.*) —, I am used to it.

gießen, goß, gegossen, to pour

das Gift, –(e)s, –e, poison

der Gipfel, –s, —, top, summit

glänzen, to shine, sparkle

das Glas, –es, Gläser, glass

glatt, smooth

der Glaube, –ns, –n, belief

glauben, (*w. dat. of the pers. & acc. of the th.*), to believe; er glaubt mir, he believes me; er glaubt es, he believes it

gleich, equal; like; (= sogleich) immediately; es ist mir ganz —, it is all the same to me

gleichen (*w. dat.*), to resemble

die Glocke, —, –n, bell

das Glück, –(e)s, (good) luck, fortune, happiness

glücklich, happy

das Gold, –(e)s, gold

golden, golden(-yellow)

der Gott, –es, –er, God

graben, grub, gegraben, gräbt, to dig

der Graf, –en, –en, count

sich grämen über (*w. acc.*), to grieve at (*or* over)

das Gras, –es, Gräser, grass

grau, gray

grauen (*impers.*), to shudder; mir graut, I shudder

greifen, griff, gegriffen, to grasp, seize, take hold of

die **Grenze,** —, -n, boundary, limit

grob, rude

groß, large, big; tall; great

großartig, grand

die **Großeltern,** — (*pl.*), grandparents

die **Großmutter,** —, ⸚, grandmother

der **Großvater,** -s, ⸚, grandfather

grün, green

der **Grund,** -(e)s, ⸚e, reason; ground, bottom; aus welchem —e?, for what reason?

gründlich, thoroughly

die **Gruppe,** —, -n, group, troop

der **Gruß,** -es, ⸚e, greeting; besten Gruss an (*w. acc.*), best regards to

grüßen, to greet

günstig, favorable

gut [besser, der beste (*or* am besten)], good

das **Gymnasium,** -s, Gymnasien, gymnasium (*the German school that prepares students for the* Universität)

H

das **Haar,** -(e)s, -e, hair

haben, hatte, gehabt, hat, to have

die **Hafenstadt,** —, ⸚e, seaport

der **Hahn,** -(e)s, ⸚e, cock, rooster

halb, half

die **Hälfte,** —, -n, half

der **Hals,** -es, Hälse, neck, throat

das **Halsweh,** -(e)s, sore throat

halten, hielt, gehalten, hält, to hold; eine Rede —, to deliver a speech; er hält Wort, he keeps his word; ich halte ihn für einen ehr-

lichen Mann, I believe he is an honest man

die **Hand,** —, ⸚e, hand; mit der — winken, to wave, beckon

der **Handel,** -s, trade

sich **handeln** um (*impers.*), to concern, be a question of; um was handelt es sich?, what is it (all) about?

der **Handschuh,** -(e)s, -e, glove

hangen, hing, gehangen, hängt (*intr.*), to hang

hängen (*tr.*), to hang

hart, hard

der **Hase,** -n, -n, hare

hassen, to hate

häufig, frequent(ly)

das **Haupt,** -(e)s, ⸚er, head; chief

das **Haus,** -es, Häuser, house; zu Hause, at home; nach Hause, home(ward)

das **Haustier,** -(e)s, -e, domestic animal

die **Haustür,** —, -en, front door

heben, hob gehoben, hebt, to lift, raise, (*refl.*) to rise

das **Heer,** -(e)s, -e, army

das **Heft,** -(e)s, -e, notebook

heftig, violent

heilig, holy

die **Heimat,** —, -en, home(land)

heimlich, secret(ly)

Heinrich, -s (*masc.*), Henry

heiraten, to marry

heiß, hot

heißen, hieß, geheißen, heißt, to be called; mean; bid, command; call; wie — Sie?, what is your name?; er heißt, his name is; das heißt (*abbr.* d.h.), that is (*abbr.* i.e.)

der **Held,** -en, -en, hero

helfen, half, geholfen, hilft (*w. dat.*), to help

das **Helium,** -s, helium

hell, light, bright(ly)

das **Hemd,** –(e)s, –en, shirt
die **Henne,** —, –n, hen
herabsinken, sank herab, ist herabgesunken, to descend (*lit.*, sink down)
der **Herbst,** es, –e, fall, autumn
herkommen, kam her, ist hergekommen, to come hither, approach
der **Herr,** –n, –en, master; lord; gentleman; sir (*in address*); Mr. (*before proper names*); meine –en, gentlemen
herrlich, glorious, magnificent; sich — amüsieren, to have a wonderful time
herrschen, to rule
der **Herrscher,** –s, —, ruler
das **Herz,** –ens, –en, heart
herzlich, cordial(ly)
der **Herzog,** –(e)s, –e (*or* ˮe), duke
heute, today; — morgen, this morning; — abend, this evening, tonight
die **Hexe,** —, –n, witch
hier, here
die **Hilfe,** —, –n, help
der **Himmel,** –s, —, heaven, sky
der **Himmelskörper,** –s, —, celestial body
hinaufgehen, ging hinauf, ist hinaufgegangen, to go up
das **Hindernis,** –ses, –se, obstacle, hindrance
hingehen, ging hin, ist hingegangen, geht hin, to go there (*or* to a place)
hinten (*adv.*), in the rear
hinter (*prep. w. dat. or acc.*), behind
der **Hirt,** –en, –en, shepherd
die **Hitze,** —, heat
hoch, high; einen Fuß —, a foot high
die **Hochzeit,** —), –en, wedding
der **Hof,** –(e)s, ˮe, yard, court, estate

hoffen auf (*w. acc.*), to hope for
die **Hoffnung,** —, –en, hope
höflich, polite
die **Höhe,** —, –n, height, altitude, elevation
hohl, hollow
holen, to get, fetch; — lassen, to send for; er hat den Arzt — lassen, he sent for the doctor
das **Holz,** –es, Hölzer, wood
der **Honig,** –s, honey
hören, to hear; ich höre ihn sprechen, I hear him speaking
das **Horn,** –(e)s, ˮer, horn
das **Hotel,** –s, –s, hotel
der **Hügel,** –s, —, hill
das **Huhn,** –(e)s, ˮer, chicken
humoristischerweise, humorously, in a humorous way *or* manner
der **Hund,** –(e)s, –e, dog
hundert (*num. adj.*), hundred
das **Hundert,** –(e)s, –e, hundred
hundertmal, a hundred times
der **Hunger,** –s, hunger; ich habe —, I am hungry
hungrig, hungry
der **Hut,** –(e)s, ˮe, hat
sich **hüten** vor (*w. dat.*), to guard against

I

idiomatisch, idiomatic
ihr, ihre, ihr (*poss. adj.*), her; their; its
Ihr, Ihre, Ihr (*poss. adj.*), your
immer, always
in (*prep. w. dat. or acc.*), in(to)
indem, while
der **Indianer,** –s, —, Indian
Indien, –s (*neut.*), India
der **Inhalt,** –(e)s, contents
inner, inner

innerhalb (*prep. w. gen.*), within

die **Insel**, —, –n, island

das **Instrument**, –s, –e, instrument, device, apparatus

interessant, interesting

sich **interessieren** für, to be interested in

inzwischen, in the meantime

irgend (*used in various compounds*), any; some; — jemand, anybody

irgendwo, anywhere

sich **irren**, to be mistaken

der **Irrtum**, –(e)s, ⸚er, mistake

die **Isar** —, Isar (River)

J

ja, yes; indeed

jagen, to hunt, chase

das **Jahr**, –(e)s, –e, year

die **Jahreszeit**, —, –en, season

das **Jahrhundert**, –(e)s, –e, century

je, ever (*cf.* **desto** *and* **jemals**)

jeder, jede, jedes, each, every

jedermann, everybody

jemals, ever, at any time

jemand, someone; anyone; irgend —, anybody

jener, jene, jenes (*dem. adj.*), that; (*dem. pron.*) that one

jenseits (*prep. w. gen.*), on that side of

jetzt, now

Johann, –s (*masc.*), John

der **Juli**, –(s), –s, July

jung, young

der **Junge**, –n, –n, boy

der **Jüngling**, –s, –e, young man

der **Juni**, –(s), –s, June

K

der **Kaffee**, –s, coffee

die **Kaffeetasse**, —, –n, coffee cup

der **Kahn**, –(e)s, ⸚e, boat

der **Kaiser**, –s, —, emperor

das **Kalb**, –(e)s, ⸚er, calf

kalt, cold

die **Kälte**, —, cold

der **Kamerad**, –en, –en, comrade, companion, chum

der **Kamm**, –(e)s, ⸚e, comb

der **Kampf**, –(e)s, ⸚e, fight, struggle

kämpfen, to fight, battle

Kanada, –s (*neut.*), Canada

der **Kanal**, –s, …näle, canal

karg, stingy

die **Karte**, —, –n, card; map

die **Katze**, —, –n, cat

kaufen, to buy

der **Kaufmann**, –(e)s, Kaufleute, merchant

kaum, hardly, barely, scarcely

kein, keine, kein, no, not a, not any

keiner, keine, keines (*pron.*), none, not one (*or* any)

keineswegs (*adv.*), by no means

der **Keller**, –s, —, cellar

der **Kellner**, –s, —, waiter

kennen, kannte, gekannt, to know, be acquainted with

der **Kerl**, –(e)s, –e, fellow

das **Kind**, –(e)s, –er, child

die **Kindheit**, —, childhood

das **Kinn**, –(e)s, –e, chin

das **Kino**, –s, –s, moving pictures

die **Kirche**, —, –n, church

die **Kirsche**, —, –n, cherry

das **Kissen**, –s, —, pillow, cushion

klagen, to complain

klar, clear(ly)

die **Klärung**, —, –en, clarification, *or*, in *sci.* sense, settling, purification, clearing

die **Klasse**, —, –n, class; erster — (*gen.*) fahren, to travel first class

das **Klassenzimmer**, –s, —, classroom

klatschen, to clap; in die

Hände —, to clap one's hands

das **Klavier,** –s, –e, piano; — (*no art.*) spielen, to play the piano

das **Kleid,** –(e)s, –er, dress; (*pl. often*) clothes

sich **kleiden,** to dress (oneself)

klein, small, little

klettern auf (*w. acc.*), to climb (up)

klingeln, to ring

klingen, klang, geklungen, to sound, resound, ring

klopfen, to knock; **an** die Tür —, to knock at the door

klug, clever, intelligent, wise, bright

der **Knabe,** –n, –n, boy

das **Knie,** –s, —, knee

der **Knopf,** –(e)s, ⁓e, button

kochen, to cook

der **Koffer,** –s, —, trunk

die **Kohle,** —, –n, coal

Köln, –s, (*neut.*), Cologne

kommen, kam, ist gekommen, to come

der **König,** –(e)s, –e, king

können, konnte, gekonnt, kann, to be able, can; know; er hätte es tun —, he could have done it; er kann Deutsch, he knows German; er kann nichts dafür, it is not his fault

konstruieren, to construct, design, build

das **Konzert,** –(e)s, –e, concert

der **Kopf,** –(e)s, ⁓e, head

das **Kopfweh,** –(e)s, headache; — (*no art.*) haben, to have a headache

der **Korb,** –(e)s, ⁓e, basket

der **Körper,** –s, —, body

der **Körperbau,** –s, bodily structure, frame, build

kostbar, expensive, costly, precious

kosten, to cost; es kostete mich (*or* mir) einen Dollar, it cost me a dollar

kostspielig, expensive, costly

die **Kraft,** —, ⁓e, strength, power

krank, sick, ill

die **Krankheit,** —, –en, sickness, illness

das **Kraut,** –(e)s, ⁓er, plant, vegetable, herb; (= der Kohl), cabbage; (= das Unkraut), weed

die **Krawatte,** —, –n, necktie, cravat

die **Kreide,** —, chalk

der **Kreis,** –es, –e, circle

die **Kreisbahn,** —, –en, orbit, circular path

kriechen, kroch, ist gekrochen, to creep

der **Krieg,** –(e)s, –e, war

krumm, crooked

die **Küche,** —, –n, kitchen

die **Kugel,** —, –n, bullet, ball; globe

die **Kuh,** —, ⁓e, cow

kühl, cool

sich **kümmern** um, to trouble (*or* concern) oneself about, worry (*or* bother) about

die **Kunst,** —, ⁓e, art

der **Künstler,** –s, —, (*male*) artist

die **Künstlerin,** —, –nen (*female*) artist

künstlerisch, artistic

künstlich, artificial, synthetic

kurz, short

L

lächeln, to smile

lachen, to laugh; — über (*w. acc.*), to laugh at

der **Laden,** –s, ⁓, store

lahm, lame

das **Lamm,** (–e)s, ⁓er, lamb

die **Lampe,** —, –n, lamp

das **Land,** –(e)s, ⁻er, land, country; aufs —, to the country; auf dem —e, in the country

lang, long; einen Fuß —, a foot long

lange, (for) a long time

langsam, slow(ly)

langweilig, tedious, boring

der **Lärm,** –(e)s, noise

lassen, ließ, gelassen, läßt, to let, leave; have done; sich (*dat.*) das Haar schneiden —, to have one's hair cut

laufen, lief, ist gelaufen, läuft, to run; Schlittschuh —, to skate

laufend, current (of time), auf dem laufenden, up-to-date; running, mit laufendem Motor, with engine running

die **Laune,** —, –n, mood, humor; guter — (*gen.*) sein, to be in good humor (*or* spirits)

lauschen, to listen

laut, loud(ly), aloud

der **Laut,** –(e)s, –e, sound

das **Leben,** –s, —, life

leben, to live

das **Leder,** –s, —, leather

leer, empty

legen, to lay, place, put

sich **lehnen** an (*w. acc.*), to lean on

lehren, to teach; sie lehrte **ihn** das Lied, she taught him the song

der **Lehrer,** –s, —, (*male*) teacher

die **Lehrerin,** —, –nen, (*female*) teacher

der **Lehrling,** –s, –e, apprentice

leicht, easy; light; —en Herzens, with a light heart

leiden, litt, gelitten, to suffer

leider (*adv.*), unfortunately; (*interj.*) alas

leid tun (*impers.*), to be sorry; es tut mir leid, I am sorry

leisten, to perform, accom-

plish; sich (*dat.*) —, to afford

leiten, to lead, guide

die **Lerche,** —, –n, lark

lernen, to learn, study

lesen, las, gelesen, liest, to read

letzt–, last

die **Leute,** — (*pl.*), people

das **Licht,** –(e)s, –er, light

das **Lichtjahr,** –(e)s, –e, light year

lieb, dear

die **Liebe,** —, –n, live

lieben, to love

lieber (*adj. comp. of* lieb), dearer; (*adv. comp. of* gern), rather

lieblich, lovely, sweet

der **Liebling,** –s, –e, favorite; darling

das **Lied,** –(e)s, –er, song

liefern, to supply, furnish, deliver, render, yield

liegen, lag, gelegen, to lie; be situated

die **Linde,** —, –n, linden tree

der **Lindenbaum,** –(e)s, ⁻e, linden tree

link–, left

links, on the left; nach —, to the left

die **Lippe,** —, –n, lip

die **Literatur,** —, –en, literature

loben, to praise

das **Loch,** –(e)s, ⁻er, hole

der **Löffel,** –s, —, spoon

los, rid of; ich bin es —, I am rid of it; was ist —?, what is the matter?

das **Löschblatt,** –(e)s, ⁻er, (sheet of) blotting paper

löschen, to blot; quench

lösen, to loosen; solve (*e.g. a puzzle*); buy (*a ticket*); (*refl.*), to loosen, become detached, be released (*esp. in tech. language*)

loslassen, ließ los, losgelassen, läßt los, to release, let go
der **Löwe,** –n, –n, lion
die **Luft,** —, ⁻e, air
die **Luftdichte,** —, air density, atmospheric density
die **Luftschicht,** —, –en, air layer, stratum of air, atmospheric layer
das **Luftschiff,** –(e)s, –e, airship
der **Luftverkehr,** –s, air traffic
das **Luftverkehrsgesetz,** –es, –e, air-traffic law
die **Lüge,** —, –n, lie falsehood
lügen, log, gelogen, to (tell a) lie
lustig, merry, gay

M

machen, to make; do; eine Reise (einen Spaziergang, eine Prüfung) —, to take a trip (a walk, an examination); sich (*dat.*) Sorgen — um, to worry (*or* be anxious) about; man machte ihn zum Präsidenten, he was made (*lit.*, they made him) president
die **Macht,** —, ⁻e, might, power
mächtig, mighty; (*w. gen.*) master (*or* in control) of
das **Mädchen,** –s, —, girl
die **Mahlzeit,** —, –en, meal
der **Mai,** –(e)s (*or* —), –e, May
das **Mal,** –(e)s, –e, time; das erste — (*or* erstemal), the first time
malen, to paint
der **Maler,** –s, —, painter; artist
malerisch, artistic, picturesque
man (*indef. pron.*), one, they, people
mancher, manche, manches, many a; (*pl.*) some

manchmal, sometimes, many a time
der **Mann,** –(e)s, ⁻er, man
der **Mantel,** –s, ⁻, cloak; overcoat
die **Mark,** —, mark (*German coin*)
der **Markt,** –(e)s, ⁻e, market
das **Maß,** –es, –e, measure
das **Material,** –s, –ien, material, substance, matter
der **Mathematiker,** –s, —, mathematician
die **Mauer,** —, –n, (*outside*) wall
die **Maus,** —, Mäuse, mouse
das **Meer,** –(e)s, –e, sea, ocean
mehr (*comp. of* viel), more
mehrere (*pl.*), several
die **Meile,** —, –n, mile (statute mile)
mein, meine, mein (*poss. adj.*), my
meinen, to mean (*only of people*), think, believe
die **Meinung,** —, –en, opinion
meist– (*superl. of* viel), most
der **Meister,** –s, —, master; expert; master tradesman
die **Meldung,** —, –en, message, report
der **Mensch,** –en, –en, man, human being
das **Merkmal,** –s, . . . male, characteristic, feature
die **Messe,** —, –n, fair
messen, maß, gemessen, mißt, to measure
das **Messer,** –s, —, knife
das **Metall,** –s, –e, metal
das **Meter,** –s, —, meter (39.37 U.S. inches)
die **Milch,** —, milk
die **Milliarde,** —, –n, milliard, one thousand millions
die **Million,** —, –en, million
das **Minnelied,** –(e)s, –er, love song (*love poem of the minnesingers*)
die **Minute,** —, –n, minute
mischen, to mix

mißverstehen, mißverstand, mißverstanden, to misunderstand

mit (*prep. w. dat.*), with

mitbringen, brachte mit, mitgebracht, to bring along

das **Mitglied,** –(e)s, –er, member

mithelfen, half mit, mitgeholfen, hilft mit, to give assistance, lend a (helping) hand

der **Mittag,** –(e)s, –e, noon; am —, at noon

die **Mitte,** —, middle

mitten in, in the middle of

der **Mittwoch,** –(e)s, –e, Wednesday

mögen, mochte, gemocht, mag, to like to, care for; er möchte (gern) mitgehen, he would like to go along; er mochte wohl dreißig Jahre alt sein, he was probably thirty years old; das mag sein, that may be

möglich, possible

der **Monat,** –(e)s, –e, month

monatelang, for months

der **Mond,** –(e)s, –e, moon

der **Montag,** –(e)s, –e, Monday

morgen (*adv.*), tomorrow

der **Morgen,** –s, —, morning; am — (des —s *or* morgens), in the morning; eines —s (*indef. time*), one morning; heute morgen, this morning

morgens (*adv.*), in the morning

müde (*adj. w. gen. or acc.*), tired; ich bin des Lebens —, I am tired of life; ich bin es —, I am tired of it

die **Mühe,** —, –n, trouble; der — (*gen.*) wert sein, to be worth the trouble

die **Mühle,** —, –n, mill

der **Müller,** –s, —, miller

der **Mund,** –(e)s, Münder (rarely Munde and Münde), mouth

das **Museum,** –s, Museen, museum

die **Musik,** —, music

müssen, mußte, gemußt, muß, to be obliged, have to, must

das **Muster,** –s, —, model, sample, pattern

der **Mut,** –(e)s, courage

mutig, courageous

die **Mutter,** —, ‥, mother

N

nach (*prep. w. dat.*), after; toward; according to; — Hause, home (*w. vbs. of motion*), homeward

der **Nachbar,** –s (*or* –n), –n, (*male*) neighbor

die **Nachbarin,** —, –nen, (*female*) neighbor

nachdem (*conj.*), after

nachher (*adv.*), afterwards

nachlaufen, lief nach, ist nachgelaufen, läuft nach (*w. dat.*), to run after

der **Nachmittag,** –(e)s, –e, afternoon; am — (des —s *or* nachmittags), in the afternoon; eines —s (*indef. time*), one afternoon; **heute nachmittag,** this afternoon

nachmittags (*adv.*), in the afternoon

die **Nachricht,** —, –en, news, information

nächst– (*superl. of* nah), next, nearest; —es Jahr, next year

die **Nacht,** —, ‥e, night; in der —, at night

nackt, naked, bare

die **Nadel,** —, –n, needle

der **Nagel,** –s, ‥, nail

nah(e) (näher, nächst–) (*w. dat.*), near

die **Nähe,** —, –n, vicinity, neighborhood; in seiner —, near him

sich **nähern** (*w. dat.*), to approach

nähren, to nourish

der **Name,** –ns, –n, name; er nannte ihn beim —, he called him by name

namens, named, by the name of; ein Mann — Schmidt, a man named (*or* by the name of) Smith

nämlich, namely

der **Narr,** –en, –en, fool

die **Nase,** —, –n, nose

naß, wet

die **Natur,** —, –en, nature

natürlich, natural(ly)

der **Nebel,** –s, —, fog

neben (*prep. w. dat. or acc.*), beside, by the side of, next to

das **Nebenzimmer,** –s, —, adjoining (*or* next) room

necken, to tease

der **Neffe,** –n, –n, nephew

nehmen, nahm, genommen, nimmt, to take

nein, no

nennen, nannte, genannt, to name, call; er nannte ihn beim Namen, he called him by name

das **Nest,** –es, –er, nest

nett, pleasant; pretty; tidy; (*colloq.*) nice; ein —es Mädchen, a nice girl

das **Netz,** –es, –e, net

neu, new

neulich, recently

neutral, neutral

nicht, not; gar —, not at all; noch —, not yet; — einmal, not even; — nur ... sondern auch, not only ... but also; — wahr? (= *French*

"*n'est-ce pas?*"), isn't (*or* wasn't) it?, not so?, will he not?, *etc.* (*always implies an affirmative answer*)

der **Nicht-Mediziner,** –s, –, nonmedical man, man who is not a physician

nichts, nothing; gar —, nothing at all; das geht ihn — an, that does not concern him

die **Niederlande,** — (*pl.*), Netherlands

sich **niederlegen,** legte nieder, niedergelegt, to lie down

niedrig, low

nie(mals), never

niemand, –(e)s, nobody

nirgend (*neg. of* irgend; *used in various compounds*), no–

nirgends, nowhere

nirgendwo, *cf.* **nirgends**

noch, still, yet; — einmal, again; — ein, another; — immer (*or* immer —), still; — nicht, not yet; weder ... —, neither ... nor; was —?, what else?

der **Nominativ,** –s, –e, nominative

der **Norden,** –s, north

die **Not,** —, ⸚e, need, necessity; trouble

nötig, necessary; ich habe es —, I need it

die **Nummer,** —, –n, number

nun (*adv.*), now; (*part.*) now, well

nur, only

die **Nuß,** —, Nüsse, nut

nützlich, useful

O

ob (*conj.*), whether, if; als —, as if

oben (*adv.*), above, at the top of, up; upstairs

oberhalb (*prep. w. gen.*), above
die **Oberfläche**, —, –n, surface
obgleich (*conj.*), although
das **Observatorium**, –s, ...ien, observatory
das **Obst**, –es, fruit
der **Obstbaum**, –(e)s, ̈–e, fruit tree
obwohl (*conj.*), although
der **Ochse**, –n, –n, ox
oder (*conj.*), or
der **Ofen**, –s, ̈–, stove
offen (*adj.*), open
öffnen, to open
oft, often
ohne (*prep. w. acc.*), without
das **Ohr**, –(e)s, –en, ear
der **Oktober**, –(s), —, October
das **Öl**, –(e)s, –e, oil
der **Onkel**, –s, —, uncle
die **Oper**, —, –n, opera
das **Opfer**, –s, —, victim, sacrifice
opfern, to sacrifice
organisch, organic
die **Orgel**, —, –n, organ
der **Ort**, –(e)s, –e (*or* rarely ̈–er), place
der **Osten**, –s, east
Ostern (*pl. w. sing. vb.*), Easter
der **Ozean**, –s, –e, ocean

P

das **Paar**, –(e)s, –e, pair; ein paar, several, a few
packen, to pack (*as a trunk*); to seize
das **Papier**, –s, –e, paper
der **Park**, –(e)s, –e, park
passen (*w. dat.*), to fit; be convenient, suit
die **Perle**, —, –n, pearl
die **Person**, —, –en, person
die **Pfeife**, —, –n, pipe; whistle
pfeifen, pfiff, gepfiffen, to whistle
der **Pfennig**, –s, –e, pfennig (= $\frac{1}{100}$ mark)

das **Pferd**, –(e)s, –e, horse
die **Pflanze**, —, –n, plant
pflanzen, to plant
pflegen, to take care of; be accustomed; wie er zu sagen pflegt, as he usually says
das **Pfund**, –(e)s, –e, pound
der **Physiker**, –s, —, physicist
physiologisch, physiological
der **Plan**, –(e)s, ̈–e, plan
planen, to plan
der **Planet**, –en, –en, planet
die **Planetenoberfläche**, —, –n, surface of a planet
das **Platin**, –s, platinum
der **Platz**, –es, ̈–e, place; seat; square; nehmen Sie —!, be seated (*lit.*, take a seat)
plötzlich, sudden(ly)
der **Polizist**, –en, –en, policeman
die **Post**, —, –en, mail; post office; auf die — bringen, to mail
die **Postkarte**, —, –en, postal card
der **Präsident**, –en, –en, president
der **Preis**, –es, –e, price; prize
Preußen, –s (*neut.*), Prussia
der **Prinz**, –en, –en, prince
der **Professor**, –s, –en, professor; — **an** einer Universität sein, to be professor **at** a university
die **Prüfung**, —, –en, examination
das **Pult**, –(e)s, –e, desk
der **Punkt**, –(e)s, –e, point; — zwei Uhr, at two o'clock sharp, on the dot of two
pünktlich, punctual(ly)
putzen, to clean, shine; (*refl.*) to dress up

Q

der **Quarz**, –es, –e, quartz, crystal
die **Quelle**, —, –n, spring; source
die **Quittung**, —, –en, receipt

R

die **Rache**, —, revenge

sich **rächen an** (*w. dat.*), to take revenge on

das **Rad**, –(e)s, ̈er, wheel; bicycle

der **Radarstrahl**, –(e)s, –en, radar beam

das **Radarteleskop**, –s, –e, radar telescope

der **Rand**, –(e)s, ̈er, edge

rasch, quick(ly)

rasieren, to shave (*often refl.*)

der **Rat**, –(e)s, –schläge, (piece of) advice

der **Rat**, –(e)s, ̈e, councilor, adviser

raten, riet, geraten, rät (*w. dat.*), to advise; (*w. acc.*) to guess

das **Rathaus**, –es, … –häuser, city (*or* town) hall

das **Rätsel**, –s, —, riddle, puzzle

die **Ratte**, —, –n, rat

der **Räuber**, –s, —, robber

rauchen, to smoke

der **Raum**, –(e)s, ̈e, room, space

das **Raumfahrzeug**, –s, –e, space ship, space vehicle, space craft

der **Raumflug**, –(e)s, ̈e, space flight; interplanetary *or* interstellar flight

das **Raumflugexperiment**, –s, –e, space-flight experiment

die **Raumforschungsrakete**, —, –n, space-research rocket

die **Raumkapsel**, –, –n, space capsule

rauschen, to rustle

die **Rechnung**, —, –en, bill

recht, right; er hat —, he is right; es geschieht ihm —, it serves him right

rechts, on the right; nach —, to the right

die **Rede**, —, –n, speech, discourse

reden, to speak, talk

der **Redner**, –s, —, speaker, orator

die **Regel**, —, –n, rule; in **der** —, as a rule

regelmäßig, regular(ly)

der **Regen**, –s, –fälle (*or* Niederschläge), rain

der **Regenschirm**, –(e)s, –e, umbrella

regieren, to rule

die **Regierung**, —, –en, government

regnen, to rain; stark —, to rain hard

regulieren, to regulate, govern, control

reiben, rieb, gerieben, to rub

reich, rich; — an (*w. dat.*), rich in

das **Reich**, –(e)s, –e, empire, realm, state; system of government

reif, ripe; mature

die **Reihe**, —, –n, row; ich bin an der — (*or* die — ist an mir), it is my turn

rein, pure, clean; — klingen, to ring out clearly (*as a bell*)

reinigen, to clean

die **Reise**, —, –n, trip, journey; eine — machen, to take a trip

reisen, reiste, ist gereist, to travel

das **Reiseziel**, –(e)s, –e, goal *or* destination of a trip (journey, voyage)

reißen, riß, gerissen, to tear

reiten, ritt, ist geritten, to ride (horseback)

der **Reiter**, –s, –e, rider, horseman

reizen, to excite, irritate

reizend (*pres. p. used as adj.*), charming

rennen, rannte, ist gerannt, to run

die **Republik**, —, –en, republic

retten, to save, rescue

der **Rhein**, –(e)s, Rhine (River)

der **Richter**, –s, —, judge

richtig, correct

riechen, roch, gerochen, to smell; — nach, to smell of

der **Riese,** –n, –n, giant

der **Riesenballon,** –s, –e, *or* –s, giant balloon

riesig, gigantic

der **Ring,** –(e)s, –e, ring

der **Ritter,** –s, —, knight

der **Rock,** –(e)s, ˝e, coat

roh, raw

rollen, rollte, ist gerollt, to roll

die **Rose,** —, –n, rose

rot, red

der **Rücken,** –s, —, back

rücken, to move

die **Rücksicht,** —, –en, consideration

rufen, rief, gerufen, to call

die **Ruhe,** —, peace, quiet, rest

ruhig, quiet(ly)

der **Ruhm,** –(e)s, fame

sich **rühmen** (*w. gen.*), to boast of

rühren, to stir, move; (*often refl.*) — Sie sich nicht von der Stelle!, don't move from the spot!

rund, round

S

der **Saal,** –(e)s, Säle, hall

die **Sache,** —, –n, thing; matter; er ist seiner — gewiß, he knows what he is about

der **Sack,** –(e)s, ˝e, sack

die **Sage,** —, –n, legend, tradition; der — nach, according to the legend

sagen, to say, tell; — wollen, mean

das **Salz,** –es, –e, salt

sammeln, to collect

der **Samstag,** –(e)s, –e, Saturday

der **Sand,** –(e)s, –e, sand

sanft, mild(ly), gentle, gently

der **Sänger,** –s, —, (*male*) singer

die **Sängerin,** —, –nen, (*female*) singer

der **Satellit,** –en, –en, satellite

der **Satz,** –es, ˝e, sentence

sauber, clean

sauer, sour

schade (*interj.*), that is too bad, what a pity

schaden (*w. dat.*), to hurt, injure

das **Schaf,** –(e)s, –e, sheep

sich **schämen,** (*w. gen.* or über & *acc.*), to be ashamed of

scharf, sharp

der **Schatten,** –s, —, shade, shadow

der **Schatz,** –es, ˝e, treasure; sweetheart

schätzen, to appreciate

schauen, to look

scheiden, schied, geschieden (*tr.*), to separate; (*intr. w.* sein) to take leave

der **Schein,** –(e)s, –e, light, brilliancy

scheinen, schien, geschienen, to shine; appear, seem

schelten, schalt, gescholten, schilt, to scold; call (names)

schenken, to give, present (*as a gift*)

die **Schicht,** —, –en, layer, stratum

schicken, to send

das **Schicksal,** –(e)s, –e, fate, destiny

schieben, schob, geschoben, to shove

schief, uneven, crooked, wry

schießen, schoß, geschossen, to shoot

das **Schiff,** –(e)s, –e, ship

der **Schild,** –(e)s, –e, shield

das **Schild,** –(e)s, –er, sign(board); door plate

der **Schimpanse,** –n, –n, chimpanzee

der **Schirm,** –(e)s, –e, shelter; shade, screen

die **Schlacht,** —, –en, battle

der **Schlaf,** –(e)s, sleep

schlafen, schlief, geschlafen, schläft, to sleep

schläfern (*impers*.), to be sleepy; mich schläfert, I am sleepy

schläfrig, sleepy

der **Schlag,** –(e)s, ⸚e, blow; stroke

schlagen, schlug, geschlagen, schlägt, to strike, hit

schlank, slender, slim

schlau, sly, cunning

schlecht, bad

schließen, schloß, geschlossen, to close, lock

schlimm, bad(ly)

der **Schlittschuh,** –(e)s, –e, skate; — laufen, to skate

das **Schloß,** Schlosses, Schlösser, castle

der **Schluß,** Schlusses, Schlüsse, end

der **Schlüssel,** –s, —, key

schmal, narrow; thin, slender

schmecken, to taste

schmeicheln (*w. dat.*), to flatter; (*refl.*) to flatter oneself; du schmeichelst **dir,** you flatter yourself

schmelzen, schmolz, ist geschmolzen, schmilzt, to melt

der **Schmerz,** –es, –en, pain; toll vor —, frantic with pain

schmerzlich, painful(ly); er empfindet es —, it pains him

schmücken, to adorn

schmutzig, dirty

der **Schnee,** –s, snow

schneiden, schnitt, geschnitten, to cut

der **Schneider,** –s, —, tailor

schneien, to snow

schnell, quick(ly)

der **Schnellzug,** –(e)s, ⸚e, express train

schon, already

schön, beautiful(ly)

die **Schönheit,** —, –en, beauty

der **Schrank,** –(e)s, ⸚e, cupboard, cabinet

schreiben, schrieb, geschrieben, to write; ich schreibe meinem Freund einen Brief (*or* ich schreibe einen Brief an meinen Freund), I write my friend a letter

schreien, schrie, geschrie(e)n, to scream

die **Schrift,** —, –en, writing

schriftlich, in writing, written

der **Schuh,** –(e)s, –e, shoe

die **Schuld,** —, –en, guilt; debt

schuldig, guilty; indebted; ich bin ihm nichts —, I owe him nothing

die **Schule,** —, –n, school; in der —, in school; nach der —, after school; in die (*or* zur) — gehen, to go to school

der **Schüler,** –s, —, (*male*) pupil

die **Schülerin,** —, –nen, (*female*) pupil

die **Schulter,** —, –n, shoulder

der **Schupo,** –s, –s (*abbr. for* der Schutzpolizist), policeman

die **Schüssel,** —, –n, dish; platter; bowl

schütteln, to shake

schützen, to protect

schwach, weak

der **Schwager,** –s, ⸚, brother-in-law

schwarz, black

der **Schwarzwald,** –(e)s, Black Forest

schweben, to hover, float, hang, be suspended

schweigen, schwieg, geschwiegen, to be silent

die **Schweiz,** —, Switzerland

schwer, heavy; difficult; — arbeiten, to work hard

die **Schwester,** —, -n, sister

schwierig, hard, difficult

schwimmen, schwamm, ist geschwommen, to swim

der **See,** -s, -n, lake

die **See,** —, -n, ocean, sea

die **Seele,** —, -n, soul

segeln, to sail

sehen, sah, gesehen, sieht, to see; haben Sie ihn kommen —?, did you see him coming?

sich **sehnen** nach, to long for

sehr, very (much)

die **Seide,** —, -n, silk

sein, war, ist gewesen, ist, to be; mir ist, it seems to me; mir ist schlecht zumute, I am out of sorts (or in a bad humor)

sein, seine, sein (poss. adj.), his, its

seiner, seine, seines (poss. pron.), his, its

seit (prep. w. dat.), since, for; — wann?, since when?

seitdem (adv. & conj.), since

die **Seite,** —, -n, side; page

seither (adv.), since then

die **Sekunde,** —, -n, second

selbst (indecl. adj. and pron.), self; (adv.) even

selig, blessed; blissful(ly)

selten, seldom, rare(ly)

seltsam, peculiar

senden, sandte, gesandt, to send

der **September,** -(s), —, September

setzen, to set, place; (refl.) to sit down; er setzt sich an den Tisch, he sits down at the table

sicher (adj. & adv.), sure(ly); safe(ly); (adj. w. gen.) sure of

der **Sieg,** -(e)s, -e, victory

siegen, to conquer

das **Signal,** -s, -e, signal, sign

das **Silber,** -s, silver

silbern (adj.), silver(y), of silver

singen, sang, gesungen, to sing

sinken, sank, ist gesunken (intr.), to sink

der **Sinn,** -(e)s, -e, mind; sense

sitzen, saß, gesessen (intr.), to sit; er sitzt am Tisch, he sits at the table

so, so, thus, as

sobald, as soon as

sofort, at once

sogar, even

sogleich, at once, immediately

der **Sohn,** -(e)s, ⸚e, son

solcher, solche, solches, such

der **Soldat,** -en, -en, soldier

sollen, sollte, gesollt, soll, to be (required) to (e.g., I am to . . .); be said; er hätte arbeiten —, he should have worked; er soll reich sein, he is said to be rich; er sollte (imperf. subj.) arbeiten, he should (or ought) to work

der **Sommer,** -s, —, summer

der **Sommermonat,** -(e)s, -e, summer month

sonderbar, unusual, peculiar, queer

sondern, but; nicht nur . . . — auch, not only . . . but also

der **Sonnabend,** -s, -e (= der Samstag), Saturday

die **Sonne,** —, -n, sun

die **Sonnenfinsternis,** –, –se, solar eclipse, eclipse of the sun

die **Sonnennähe,** –, nearness to the sun, perihelion (the tech. term to indicate that point in *the orbit of a planet or comet nearest to the sun)*

die **Sonnenoberfläche,** —, surface of the sun

der **Sonnenschein,** –(e)s, sunshine

das **Sonnensystem,** –s, –e, solar system

sonnig, sunny

der **Sonntag,** –(e)s, –e, Sunday

sonst, otherwise

die **Sorge,** —, –n, care, worry; sich (*dat.*) —n machen um, to worry (*or* be anxious) about

sorgen für, to care for, take care of

sorgfältig, careful(ly)

die **Spalte,** —, –n, crack, cleft, fissure, split, gap

sparen, to save, economize

der **Spaß,** –es, ⸚e, joke

spät, late

spazierengehen, to go walking, take a walk; ich bin spazierengegangen, I went for a walk

der **Spaziergang,** –(s), ⸚e, walk; einen — machen, to take a walk

die **Speise,** —, –n, food, dish

der **Spiegel,** –s, —, mirror

das **Spiegelteleskop,** –s, –e, reflecting telescope, reflector

das **Spiel,** –(e)s, –e, play, game

spielen, to play

die **Spitze,** —, –n, head; point; lace

spitzen, to sharpen

die **Sprache,** —, –n, language

sprechen, sprach, gesprochen, spricht, to speak, talk; — über (*w. acc.*) [*or* von (*w. dat.*)], to talk about

die **Spree,** —, Spree (River)

das **Sprichwort,** –(e)s, ⸚er, proverb

springen, sprang, ist gesprungen, to jump

spüren, to feel, notice

der **Staat,** –(e)s, –en, state

der **Stab,** –(e)s, ⸚e, staff, stick

die **Stadt,** —, ⸚e, city

der **Stall,** –(e)s, ⸚e, stable

der **Stand,** –(e)s, ⸚e, class; standing

stark, strong; — regnen, to rain hard

starr, fixed; stiff

statt (= anstatt) (*prep. w. gen.*), instead of

stattfinden, fand statt, stattgefunden, to take place

stattlich, stately

der **Staub,** –(e)s, –e, dust

stechen, stach, gestochen, sticht, to prick, sting

stecken, to stick; put; — Sie das in die Tasche!, put that in your pocket

stehen, stand, gestanden, to stand

stehlen, stahl, gestohlen, stiehlt, to steal; er hat mir die Uhr gestohlen, he stole my watch

steigen, stieg, ist gestiegen, to climb, mount, rise, ascend

steil, steep

der **Stein,** –(e)s, –e, stone

die **Stelle,** —, –n, spot, place; position

stellen, to place, put; eine Frage **an** eine Person (*acc.*) —, to ask a person a question

die **Stellung,** —, –en, position; rank

sterben, starb, ist gestorben, stirbt, to die

der **Stern,** –(e)s, –e, star

die **Sternwarte,** —, –n, observatory

stets, always

still, quiet, still

die **Stimme,** —, –n, voice

der **Stock,** –(e)s, ⸚e, cane, stick

der **Stoff,** –(e)s, –e, material; mat-ter

stolz, proud; — sein auf (*w. acc.*), to be proud of

stören, to disturb

stoßen, stieß, gestoßen, stößt, to push

strafen, to punish

strahlen, to shine, be radiant

der **Strand,** –(e)s, –e, shore

die **Straße,** —, –n, street

die **Straßenbahn,** —, –en, street car

die **Stratosphäre,** —, stratosphere

der **Streit,** –(e)s, –e (*or* —igkeiten), quarrel, fight, strife

streng, strict, severe

der **Strom,** –(e)s, ¨e, river, stream

die **Stube,** —, –n, room

das **Stück,** –(e)s, –e, piece

der **Student,** –en, –en, student; — auf einer Universität sein, to be a student **at** a university

studieren, to study

die **Stufe,** —, –n, step

der **Stuhl,** –(e)s, ¨e, chair

stumm, dumb, mute, silent

stumpf (*opp. of* spitz), blunt, without a point

die **Stunde,** —, –n, hour; ich nehme –n, I take lessons

der **Sturm,** –(e)s, ¨e, storm

stürmisch, stormy

stützen, to support; *refl. w.* auf *and acc.*, to lean on

suchen, to look for, seek

der **Süden,** –s, south

die **Summe,** —, –n, amount, sum

die **Suppe,** —, –n, soup

süß, sweet

die **Szene,** —, –n, scene

T

tadeln, to criticize, rebuke

die **Tafel,** —, –n, blackboard

der **Tag,** –(e)s, –e, day; — für —, day after day; einen — um den anderen, every other day; am —e, in the daytime; eines —es (*indef. time*), one day; heute über acht —e, a week from today; vor acht —en, a week ago

täglich, daily

das **Tal,** –(e)s, ¨er, valley

die **Tanne,** —, –n, fir (*or* pine) tree

die **Tante,** —, –n, aunt

der **Tanz,** –es, ¨e, dance

tanzen, to dance

tapfer, brave(ly)

die **Tapferkeit,** —, bravery

die **Tasche,** —, –n, pocket

das **Taschentuch,** –(e)s, ¨er, hand-kerchief

die **Taschenuhr,** —, –en, watch

die **Tasse,** —, –n, cup

die **Tat,** —, –en, deed; in der —, indeed, in fact

tätig, active

die **Tätigkeit,** —, –en, activity, action

tauchen, tauchte, ist getaucht, to dive

taugen, to be fit (good, useful)

tauschen, to exchange

täuschen, to deceive

tausend (*num. adj.*), thousand

das **Tausend,** –(e)s, –e, thousand

tausendmal, a thousand times

der **Techniker,** –s, —, technician

technisch, technical

der **Tee,** –s, –s, tea

der **Teil,** –(e)s, –e, part

die **Teilung,** —, –en, division

das **Telefon** (*or* **Telephon**), –s, –e (= der Fernsprecher), tele-phone

telefonieren (*or* **telephonie-ren**), to telephone

telefonisch (*or* **telephonisch**), telephonic, by phone; — erreichen, to reach by phone

telegrafieren (*or* telegraphieren), to telegraph
das Teleskop, –s, –e, telescope
der Teller, –s, —, plate
das Temperament, –s, –e, temperament
die Temperatur, —, –en, temperature
der Temperatureinfluß,...flusses,
...flüsse, influence of temperature
die Temperaturschwankung, —,
–en, temperature variation,
fluctuation in temperature
der Tenor, –s, ˮe (*or* –e), tenor
das Territorium, –s, ...ien, territory
teuer, dear; expensive
der Teufel, –s, —, devil
das Theater, –s, —, theater; ins —
gehen, to go to the theater
tief, deep
die Tiefe, —, –n, depth
das Tier, –(e)s, –e, animal
die Tinte, —, –n, ink
der Tisch, –es, –e, table; den —
decken, to set the table; nach
—, after dinner
das Tischtuch, –(e)s, ˮer, table-
cloth
die Tochter, —, ˮ, daughter
der Tod, –es, –esfälle, death
toll, mad, crazy; — vor
Schmerz, frantic (*or* mad)
with pain
der Ton, –(e)s, ˮe, tone, sound
das Tonbandgerät, –s, –e, tape
recorder
tot, dead
töten, to kill
tragen, trug, getragen, trägt, to
carry; wear
die Träne, —, –n, tear
der Trank,–(e)s,ˮe,drink, beverage
der Traum, –(e)s, ˮe, dream
träumen, to dream
traurig, sad

treffen, traf, getroffen,
trifft, to meet; hit
treiben, trieb, getrieben, to
drive; be engaged in, do
trennen, to separate
die Treppe, —, –n, stairs
treten, trat, ist getreten, tritt,
to step
treu, faithful(ly), true
trinken, trank, getrunken, to
drink
das Trinkgeld, –(e)s, –er, tip
trocken (*adj.*), dry
trocknen, to dry
trösten, to comfort, console
trotz (*prep. w. gen.*), in spite of
trotzdem, nevertheless, in spite
of it (*or* the fact that)
die (*or* das) Trübsal, — [*òr* –(e)s], –e,
affliction, trouble
der Trunk, –(e)s, ˮe, drink, draught
die Tschechoslowakei, —,
Czechoslovakia
das Tuch, –(e)s, ˮer, cloth
tüchtig, capable; strong; —
arbeiten (studieren), to work
(study) hard
tun, tat, getan, tut, to do; act,
pretend; er tut als ob ...,
he acts as if ...
die Tür, —, –en, door
die Türkei, —, Turkey
der Turm, –(e)s, ˮe, tower

U

üben, to practice
über (*prep. w. dat. or acc.*), over,
above
überall, everywhere
überhaupt, on the whole, alto-
gether; — nicht, not at all.
übermorgen, day after to-
morrow
überráschen, to surprise
der Überrock, –(e)s, ˮe, overcoat
überschwémmen, to flood

übersétzen, übersétzte, übersétzt, to translate

überwínden, überwánd, überwúnden, to overcome

die **Übung,** —, -en, exercise

das **Ufer,** -s, —, shore

die **Uhr,** —, -en, watch; clock; o'clock; um zwei —, at two o'clock; wieviel — ist es?, what time is it?

um (*prep. w. acc.*) around, about; — drei Uhr, at three o'clock; — . . . willen, for the sake of; — . . . zu (*w. pres. inf.*) in order to

umsonst, in vain

unbemannt, unmanned, pilotless

und, and

unehrlich, dishonest

ungefähr, about, approximately

das **Unglück,** -(e)s, -sfälle, misfortune

unglücklich, unhappy, unlucky

die **Universität,** —, -en, university; **auf** der —, **at** 'the university (*of a student*); **an** der —, **at** the university (*of a professor*)

unmöglich, impossible

unser, uns(e)re, unser (*poss. adj.*), our

uns(e)rer, uns(e)re, uns(e)res (*poss. pron.*) our

unten (*adv.*), below; downstairs

unter (*prep. w. dat. or acc.*), under, below, beneath; among

die **Untergrundbahn,** —, -en, subway

unterhalb (*prep. w. gen.*), below

unterhálten, unterhiélt, unterhálten, to entertain; (*refl.*) to converse

der **Unterschied,** -(e)s, -e, difference

unterscheíden, unterschíed, unterschíeden, to distinguish

untersúchen, untersúchte, untersúcht, to examine, test, investigate

die **Untersuchung,** —, -en, investigation, test

unzufrieden, dissatisfied

der **Urgroßvater,** -s, ¨, great-grandfather

die **Ursache,** —, -n, cause

urteilen, urteilte, geurteilt, to judge

V

der **Vater,** -s, ¨, father

das **Vaterland,** -(e)s, ¨er, fatherland, native land

die **Vaterstadt,** —, ¨e, native city

die **Venus,** —, Venus, the planet Venus

die **Venus-Oberfläche,** —, surface of (the planet) Venus

verändern, to change, alter, transform

verbergen, verbarg, verborgen, verbirgt, to hide, conceal

verbessern, to correct

sich **verbeugen** vor (*w. dat.*), to bow to (*or* before)

verbieten, verbot, verboten (*w. dat. of the pers.*), to forbid

verbinden, verband, verbunden, to unite

verbrennen, verbrannte, verbrannt (*tr.*) to burn up; (*intr. w.* sein) to burn up

verbringen, verbrachte, verbracht, to pass, spend (*the time*)

verdanken (*w. dat. of the pers.*), to owe

verdienen, to earn; deserve

der **Verein,** –(e)s, –e, club
die **Vereinigten Staaten,** —
(*pl.*), United States
die **Verfassung,** —, –en, constitution
verfolgen (*w. acc.*), to pursue
die **Vergangenheit,** —, –en, past
(time)
vergeben, vergab, vergeben,
vergibt (*w. dat. of the pers.*),
to forgive
vergebens, in vain
vergehen, verging, ist vergangen, to pass; elapse;
disappear
vergessen, vergaß, vergessen,
vergißt, to forget
vergleichen, verglich, verglichen, to compare
das **Vergnügen,** –s, —, pleasure
das **Verhältnis,** –ses, –se, relation
verkaufen, to sell
verlangen, to demand
verlassen, verließ, verlassen,
verläßt, to leave, forsake;
leave behind; sich — auf (*w.
acc.*), to depend (*or* rely)
on
verlegen, to misplace
sich **verlieben** in (*w. acc.*), to fall in
love with
verlieren, verlor, verloren,
to lose
sich **verloben** mit, to become engaged to
vermissen, to miss
das **Vermögen,** –s, —, fortune
verpassen (= versäumen), to
miss (*as a train*)
der **Verrat,** –(e)s, treason
sich **versammeln,** to gather, assemble
versäumen (= verpassen), to
miss
verschieden (*adj.*), different;
(*pl.*) several, various

verschlingen, verschlang, verschlungen, to devour
verschwenden, to squander
verschwinden, verschwand, ist
verschwunden, to disappear
die **Versicherungsgesellschaft,**
—, –en, insurance company
versprechen, versprach, versprochen, verspricht, to promise
verstehen, verstand, verstanden, to understand
versuchen, to try
das **Versuchstier,** –(e)s, –e, animal
used for experimental purposes
verteidigen, to defend
vertreten, vertrat, vertreten,
vertritt, to represent
verwandt (*adj.*), related
der **Verwandte,** –n, –n (*w. adj.
decl.*), relative; ein —r, a
relative; meine —n, my
relatives
verwenden, verwandte *or* verwendete, verwandt *or* verwendet, to use, utilize, employ, apply
die **Verwendung,** —, –en, utilization, use, application
verwöhnen, to spoil, pamper
verzeihen, verzieh, verziehen
(*w. dat.*), to pardon
der **Vetter,** –s, –n, (*male*) cousin
das **Vieh,** –(e)s, cattle
viel (mehr, meist), much, a
great deal; (*pl.*) many; —es,
many things
vielleicht, perhaps
vielmehr, rather
vier, four; auf allen —en, on
all fours
viert–, fourth
das **Viertel,** –s, —, quarter, onefourth
die **Viertelstunde,** —, –n, quarter
of an hour

der **Vogel**, –s, ⸚, bird
der **Vokal**, –s, –e, vowel
das **Volk**, –(e)s, ⸚er, people, nation
das **Volkslied**, –(e)s, –er, folksong
voll, full
vollständig, complete(ly)
von (*prep. w. dat.*), of, from
vor (*prep. w. dat. or acc.*), before, in front of; (*w. dat. only*), ago; — einem Monat, a month ago; ich bin außer mir — Freude, I am beside myself with joy; er brennt — Ungeduld, he burns with impatience
vorbei, past, over
vorbeifliegen, flog vorbei, ist vorbeigeflogen, to fly past (*w.* **an** *and dat.*)
vorbereiten, to prepare; (*refl. w.* **auf** *and acc.*), to prepare for
vorgehen, ging vor, ist vorgegangen, to precede; die Uhr geht vor, the watch (*or* clock) is fast
vorgestern, day before yesterday
vorig, last, previous; —e Nacht, last night
vorkommen, kam vor, ist vorgekommen, to happen; occur; appear
vorlesen, las vor, vorgelesen, liest vor, to read aloud to
vorletzt–, before (the) last; —es Jahr, year before last
der **Vormittag**, –(e)s, –e, forenoon
vorn (*adv.*), in front
die **Vorstadt**, —, ⸚e, suburb
die **Vorstellung**, —, –en, performance
vorwärts, forward

W

wach, awake; — sein, to be awake

wachsen, wuchs, ist gewachsen, wächst, to grow
die **Waffe**, —, –n, weapon
der **Wagen**, –s, —, wagon, carriage; car (*of a train*); car (*or* auto)
wagen, to dare
die **Wagneroper**, —, –n, Wagnerian opera, opera by Richard Wagner
die **Wahl**, —, –en, choice, selection; election
wählen, to choose; elect
wahr, true; nicht —? (= French "*n'est-ce pas?*"), isn't (*or* wasn't) it?, not so?, will he not?, etc. (*always implies an affirmative answer*)
während (*prep. w. gen.*), during; (*conj.*) while
die **Wahrheit**, —, –en, truth
wahrscheinlich, probable, probably
der **Wald**, –(e)s, ⸚er, forest
die **Walpurgisnacht**, —, Walpurgis Night (*falls between April 30 and May 1*)
die **Wand**, —, ⸚e, wall
wandern (*w.* sein), to walk, travel (*on foot*), go; wander
die **Wandkarte**, —, –n, wall map
die **Wange**, —, –n, cheek
wann (*inter. adv.*), when; seit —?, since when?
die **Ware**, —, –n, ware; (*pl.*) merchandise
warm, warm
warnen, to warn
warten, to wait; — auf (*w. acc.*), to wait for
warum, why
was (*inter. pron.*), what; (*rel. pron.*), what, that which; alles, — ich habe, all (that) I have; — für ein, what kind (*or* sort) of
waschen, wusch, gewaschen, wäscht, to wash; ich wasche

mir die Hände, I wash my hands; (*often used as dir. refl.*) ich wasche mich, I wash (myself)

das **Wasser,** –s, —, water

der **Wasserfall,** –(e)s, ⁔e, waterfall
weder ... noch, neither ... nor

der **Weg,** –(e)s, –e, way; gehe deines —es!, go your way!
wegen (*prep. w. gen.*), on account of; meinet—, on my account
weggehen, ging weg, ist weggegangen, to go away
weh tun, to hurt; es tut mir weh, it hurts me

das **Weib,** –(e)s, –er, woman (*usually contemptuous*)
weich, soft

die **Weihnachten,** — (*pl. w. sing. vb.*), Christmas
weil, because

der **Wein,** –(e)s, –e, wine
weinen, to weep

die **Weise,** —, –n, way, manner; auf diese —, in this manner
weise, wise

die **Weisheit,** —, –en, wisdom
weiß, white
weit, wide; far
welcher, welche, welches (*rel. & inter. adj. & pron.*), which (one), what (one), who; (*in excls.*) what; welch eine Stadt!, what a city!

die **Welle,** —, –n, wave

die **Welt,** —, –en, world
weltbekannt, known throughout the world

der **Weltmeister,** –s, —, world champion

der **Weltraum,** –(e)s, world space (interplanetary *or* interstellar space)

der **Weltraumfahrer,** –s, —, world space traveler

der **Weltraumflug,** –(e)s, ⁔e, world space flight, interplanetary flight

die **Weltraumrakete,** —, –n, interplanetary rocket

das **Weltraum-Recht,** –(e)s, –e, world-space law, law applying to rights in world space

das **Weltraumschiff,** –(e)s, –e, interstellar craft, astronautical craft

die **Weltraumstrahlung,** —, cosmic radiation, world space radiation
wenden, wandte, gewandt, to turn
wenig, little, not much
wenige (*pl.*), few
wenigstens, at least
wenn, if, whenever
wer (*inter. pron.*), who; (*indef. rel. pron.*) he who, whoever
werden, wurde, ist geworden, wird, to become; — aus, to become of
werfen, warf, geworfen, wirft, to throw

das **Werk,** –(e)s, –e, work, product of work

die **Werkstatt,** —, ⁔e, workshop
wert, worth; einen Dollar —, worth a dollar; der Mühe (*gen.*) —, worth the trouble; der Rede —, worth talking about

der **Wert,** –(e)s, –e, worth
wesentlich, essential, (materially) intrinsic
weshalb, why
wessen (*gen. of* wer), whose

der **Westen,** –s, west
wetten, to bet, wager

das **Wetter,** –s, —, weather
wichtig, important
wider (*prep. w. acc.*), against
widerspréchen, widersprách,

widerspróchen, widersprícht (*w. dat.*), to contradict

wie, how; as

wieder, again

wiederhólen, wiederhólte, wiederhólt, to repeat

das **Wiedersehen,** –s, meeting again; auf —!, goodbye

die **Wiege,** —, –n, cradle

die **Wiese,** —, –n, meadow

wieviel, how much

der (die *or* das) **wievielte,** which of a (*or* what) number (*lit.,* the how much); der — ist heute?, what is today's date?

willkommen (*adj.*), welcome

der **Wind,** –(e)s, –e, wind

windig, windy

winken, to wink, beckon; einem mit den Augen —, to wink to a person; mit der Hand —, to beckon, wave

der **Winter,** –s, —, winter

der **Wipfel,** –s, —, tree top

wirken, to be effective, make an impression

wirklich, real(ly)

die **Wirklichkeit,** —, –en, reality

der **Wirt,** –(e)s, –e, host, innkeeper

wissen, wußte, gewußt, weiß, to know (*a fact*)

das **Wissen,** –s, knowledge, learning; meines —s, as far as I know

die **Wissenschaft,** —,–en, science; knowledge

der **Wissenschaftler,** –s, —, scientist

wissenschaftlich, scientific; wissenschaftlicher Versuch, experiment

der **Witz,** –es, –e, joke

wo, where

die **Woche,** —, –n, week

wöchentlich, weekly

wofür, for what (*or* which)

woher, from where (*or* what place), whence; — wissen Sie das?, how do you know that?

wohin, whither, to what place

wohl, well; indeed; probably

wohnen, to live, dwell

die **Wohnung,** —, –en, residence

der **Wolf,** –(e)s, ¨-e, wolf

die **Wolke,** —, –n, cloud

wolkenerfüllt, cloud-filled

wollen, wollte, gewollt, will, to want, wish; er will morgen abfahren, he intends to leave tomorrow; er will eine reiche Tante haben, he professes to have a rich aunt; er will es getan haben, he claims to have done it; er wollte eben ausgehen, he was (just) on the point of going out

womit, with what (*or* which)

das **Wort,** –(e)s, –e (*in connected discourse*) [*or* ¨-er (*disconnected words*)], word; er hält —, he keeps his word

das **Wörterbuch,** –(e)s, ¨-er, dictionary

wörtlich, literally

das **Wunder,** –s, —, wonder, miracle

sich **wundern** über (*w. acc.*), to be surprised at

wunderschön, exceedingly beautiful

der **Wunsch,** –es, ¨-e, wish, desire

wünschen, to wish

die **Würde,** —, –n, dignity

würdig, worthy; (*w. gen.*) worthy of

die **Wurst,** —, ¨-e, sausage

die **Wut,** —, rage

wüten, to rage

wütend, raging, very angry

Z

die **Zahl,** —, –en, number
zahlen, to pay
zählen, to count
zahllos, countless, innumerable
zahlreich, numerous
zahm, tame
der **Zahn,** –(e)s, ̈-e, tooth
der **Zahnarzt,** –es, ̈-e, dentist
das **Zahnweh,** –(e)s, toothache; — (*no art.*) haben, to have a toothache
zart, tender, delicate
der **Zauber,** –s, —, charm, magic
der **Zaun,** –(e)s, Zäune, fence
zehn, ten
das **Zeichen,** –s, —, sign, signal
zeichnen, to draw
zeigen, to show
die **Zeile,** —, –n, line
die **Zeit,** —, –en, time; zur —, **als** (da *or* wo), at the time when
das **Zeitalter,** –s, —, age; era; das atomische Zeitalter, the Atomic Age
die **Zeitschrift,** —, –en, magazine
die **Zeitung,** —, –en, newspaper
zerbrechen, zerbrach, zerbrochen, zerbricht, to break (to pieces)
zerfleischen, to mangle
zerreißen, zerriß, zerrissen, to tear (to pieces)
der **Zeuge,** –n, –n, witness
die **Ziege,** —, –n, goat
ziehen, zog, gezogen, to draw, pull; (*intr. w.* sein), to go, move
das **Ziel,** –(e)s, –e, aim, goal
ziemlich, rather
das **Zimmer,** –s, —, room
der **Zimmermann,** –(e)s, Zimmerleute, carpenter
zittern, to tremble
zornig, angry
zu (*prep. w. dat.*), to; at; for;

(*adv.*) too; — Hause, at home; — Weihnachten, for (*or* at) Christmas
der **Zucker,** –s, sugar
zuerst, at first
zufällig, accidental(ly); er war — zu Hause, he happened to be at home
zufälligerweise (*adv.*), by chance; — war ich auch da, I happened to be there too.
zufrieden, satisfied
zufriedenstellend, satisfactory
der **Zug,** –(e)s, ̈-e, train; draught; feature
zugleich, at the same time
zuhören, hörte zu, zugehört (*w. dat.*), to listen to
die **Zukunft,** —, future
zuletzt, finally, at the end
zum (= zu dem), to (at *or* for) the; — Geburtstag, for one's birthday
zumachen, machte zu, zugemacht, to close
zunächst, first of all
die **Zunge,** —, –n, tongue
zur (= zu der), to (at *or* for) the; — Zeit **als** (da *or* wo), at the time when
zurückkehren, kehrte zurück, ist zurückgekehrt, to turn (*or* come) back, return
zusammen, together
zusammenbringen, brachte zusammen, zusammengebracht, to bring together; gather
die **Zusammensetzung,** —, –en, composition, *e.g.*, Luftzusammensetzung, composition of the air
der **Zustand,** –(e)s, ̈-e, condition
zuverlässig, reliable, dependable
zuvor, before

zuweilen, occasionally

zuwenden, wandte zu, zuge-
wandt, to turn to(ward);   er
wandte mir den Rücken zu,
he turned his back on me

zwanzig, twenty

zwanzigst–, twentieth

zwar, to be sure, I admit

der **Zweck,** –(e)s, –e, purpose

zweierlei, of two (different)
kinds (*or* sorts)

der **Zweifel,** –s, —, doubt

der **Zweig,** –(e)s, –e, twig

zweimal, twice

zweit–, second

der **Zwerg,** –(e)s, –e, dwarf

zwingen, zwang, gezwungen,
to force

zwischen (*prep. w. dat. or
acc.*), between

der **Zwischenraum,**   –(e)s,   ̈e,
space, gap, interval, range,
intervening (*or* interstitial)
space

English-German Vocabulary

A

a, ein, eine, ein; not —, kein, keine, kein

able: to be —, können, konnte, gekonnt, kann

about (= approximately), ungefähr; to talk —, sprechen von (*w. dat.*) [*or* über (*w. acc.*)]; to worry (*or* bother) —, sich kümmern um; what was it (all) —?, um was handelte es sich?; do you know what you are —?, sind Sie Ihrer Sache gewiß?; he was — to leave, er wollte eben abfahren (*or* er war im Begriff abzufahren)

above (*prep.*), über (*w. dat. or acc.*); oberhalb (*w. gen.*)

absent, abwesend; to be —, fehlen; he is —, er fehlt

accompany, begleiten

accomplishment, die Leistung, —, –en

according to (*prep.*), nach (*w. dat.*); — the alphabet (*or* alphabetically), nach dem Alphabet; — the legend, der Sage nach (*Note that* nach *may follow the noun it governs.*)

account: on — of (*prep.*), wegen (*w. gen.*); on — of the weather, wegen des Wetters (*or* des Wetters wegen); on my —, meinetwegen; on your —, Ihretwegen

accuse of, ánklagen *or* beschuldigen (*w. acc. of the pers. & gen. of the th.*)

accustomed: to become — to, sich gewöhnen an (*w. acc.*); I am

— to it, ich bin daran gewöhnt (*or* ich bin es gewohnt)

acquaintance, der Bekannte, –n, –n (*w. adj. decl.*); an —, ein Bekannter; I made his —, ich lernte ihn kennen (*or* ich machte seine Bekanntschaft)

acquainted: to be — with, kennen, kannte, gekannt

acquire: to — knowledge (*or* information), Kenntnisse erlangen

across (*prep.*), durch (*w. acc.*)

act (= pretend), tun, tat, getan, tut; he acts as if, er tut, als ob

actually (= really), wirklich; (= indeed) in der Tat

add, hinzufügen, fügte hinzu, hinzugefügt

address, die Adresse, —, –n

admire, bewundern

advance, der Fortschritt, –(e)s, –e; *esp. in plur. w. meaning of* **progress**

advice, der Rat, –(e)s, –schläge

advise, raten, riet, geraten, rät (*w. dat.*)

afford, sich (*dat.*) leisten

afraid: to be — of, sich fürchten vor (*w. dat.*); to be — that, fürchten, daß

after (*prep.*), nach (*w. dat.*); — dinner, nach Tisch; — school, nach der Schule

after (*conj.*), nachdem

afternoon, der Nachmittag, –(e)s, –e; this —, heute nachmittag; tomorrow —, morgen nachmittag; yesterday —, gestern nachmittag; the whole —, den ganzen Nachmittag (*duration of time*); one

—, eines Nachmittags (*indef. time*); in the —, am Nachmittag (des Nachmittags *or* nachmittags)

afterwards (*adv.*), nachher, darauf, danach

again, wieder, noch einmal

against (*prep.*), gegen (*w. acc.*); wider (*w. acc.*)

age, das Alter, –s, —; (= *period of time*) das Zeitalter, –s, —; Middle Ages, das Mittelalter, –s; *see* **atomic**

ago, vor (*w. dat.*), her; two years —, vor zwei Jahren; a week —, vor acht Tagen; that **was** a long time —, das **ist** schon lange her

agreeable, angenehm

air, die Luft, —, ¨e

air density, die Luftdichte, —

air layer, die Luftschicht, —, –en

airplane, das Flugzeug, –(e)s, –e

airship, das Luftschiff, –(e)s, –e

air traffic, der Luftverkehr, –s

air-traffic law, das Luftverkehrsgesetz, –es, –e

all, alle; ganz; — Europe, ganz Europa; for — I care, meinetwegen; it was — the same to me, es war mir ganz gleich; almost — week, fast die ganze Woche; — I have, alles, was ich habe; — good things, alles Gute; — else, alles andere; not at —, gar nicht; nothing at —, gar nichts

allow, erlauben (*w. dat.*)

allowed: to be —, dürfen, durfte, gedurft, darf

almost, fast, beinah(e)

alone, allein

along (*prep.*), entlang (*usually w. acc.*); he is going — the river, er geht den Fluß entlang

along (*adv.*), mit; to bring —, mítbringen; come —, kommen Sie mit!

aloud, laut; to read — to, vorlesen, las vor, vorgelesen, liest vor (*w. dat. of the pers.*)

alphabet, das Alphabet, –(e)s, –e

Alps, die Alpen, — (*pl.*)

already, schon

also, auch

although, obgleich

altitude, die Höhe, —, –n

altitude flight, der Höhenflug, –(e)s, ¨e

altitude-research rocket, die Höhenforschungsrakete, —, –n

always, immer, stets

America, (das) Amerika, –s

American (*adj.*), amerikanisch

among (*prep.*), unter (*w. dat. or acc.*); — other things, unter ander(e)m

an, *cf.* **a**

and, und; colder — colder, immer kälter

anger, der Zorn, –(e)s

angry, zornig, böse; — with, böse (*or* zornig) auf (*w. acc.*); he is — with me, er ist mir böse (*or* er ist böse auf mich)

animal, das Tier, –(e)s, –e

another (= an additional one), noch ein; (= a different one) ein anderer; one after —, einer nach dem anderen

answer (*noun*), die Antwort, —, –en; an — to, eine Antwort auf (*w. acc.*)

answer, antworten (*w. dat. of the pers.*); to — a question, auf eine Frage (*acc.*) antworten [*or* eine Frage (*dir. obj.*) beantworten]; I — him, ich antworte ihm

any, etwas (*indecl. w. sing. noun or alone as pron.*); irgend– (*in various combinations*); (irgend) welche (*w. a pl. noun*); not —, kein; I haven't — money, ich habe kein Geld; not — longer, nicht mehr; he doesn't live in this house — longer, er wohnt nicht mehr in diesem Haus

anybody, (irgend) jemand, –(e)s

anyhow (= somehow, by hook or crook), irgendwie, auf irgendeine Weise; (= in any case) jedenfalls

anyone, (irgend) jemand, –(e)s; — else, jemand anders, sonst jemand

any(thing), (irgend) etwas

appear, erscheinen, erschien, ist erschienen

appetite, der Appetit, –(e)s, –e

apple, der Apfel, –s, ⸚

apply for, sich bewerben um (*w. acc.*)

approach, sich nähern (*w. dat.*)

April, der April, –(e)s, –e

arm, der Arm, –(e)s, –e

army, das Heer, –(e)s, –e

around (*prep.*), um (*w. acc.*)

arrest, verhaften

arrive, ankommen, kam an, ist angekommen

art, die Kunst, —, ⸚e

article, der Artikel, –s, —

artificial, künstlich

artist, der Künstler, –s, —

artistic, künstlerisch, artistisch

as (*conj.*), wie; (*causal*) da; (*temp.*) indem; white — snow, weiß wie Schnee; he was famous — an orator, als Redner war er berühmt; — if (*conj.*), als ob; — far — (*prep.*), bis; — soon — (*conj.*), sobald; — long — (*conj.*), solange; — often — (*conj.*), sooft; — well —, so gut wie; just — . . . (*adj. or adv.*) —, ebenso . . . wie; — far — I know, soviel ich weiß (*or* meines Wissens)

ascend, steigen, stieg, ist gestiegen; aufsteigen

ashamed: to be —, sich schämen; to be — of, sich schämen (*w. gen. or* über *& acc.*)

ask (= to question), fragen; to — a person a question, eine Frage an eine Person (*acc.*) stellen; to — for (= to request) something, um etwas (*acc.*) bitten; to — about, fragen nach (*w. dat.*)

asleep: to fall —, einschlafen, schlief ein, ist eingeschlafen, schläft ein

assert, behaupten

associated: — with, verbunden mit

assume, annehmen, nahm an, angenommen, nimmt an

astonished, erstaunt; — at, erstaunt über (*w. acc.*)

astronaut, der Astronaut, –en, –en

astronautical: — craft, das Weltraumschiff, –(e)s, –e

astronomer, der Astronom, –en, –en; der Sternforscher, –s, —

at (*prep.*), an, auf, in, bei, zu (*w. dat.*); — eight o'clock, um acht Uhr; — the top of, oben auf; — his house, bei ihm; — home, zu Hause; — once, gleich, sogleich, sofort; — the time when, zur Zeit, **als** (da *or* wo); — the university (*of a student*), **auf** der Universität; — the university (*of a professor*), **an** der Universität; — night, in der Nacht; not — all, gar nicht; nothing — all, gar nichts

atmosphere, die Atmosphäre, —, –en

atmospheric, atmosphärisch

atomic, atomisch; the — Age, das atomische Zeitalter

attain, erreichen

attempt, versuchen

attend (*a school*), besuchen; (*various ceremonies, performances, etc.*), beiwohnen (*w. dat.*); (*a lecture*), einem Vortrag beiwohnen; eine Vorlesung hören (*or* besuchen)

attention, die Aufmerksamkeit, —, –en; to pay —, aufpassen, paßte auf, aufgepaßt; I paid no — to (*or* didn't bother about) it, ich kümmerte mich nicht darum

attentive, aufmerksam

August, der August, — [*or* –(e)s], –e
aunt, die Tante, —, –n; at my —'s, bei meiner Tante
auto, das Auto, –s, –s
autumn, der Herbst, –es, –e
avail oneself of, sich bedienen (*w. gen.*); von etwas (*dat.*) Gebrauch machen
average speed, die Durchschnittsgeschwindigkeit, —
aviator, der Flieger, –s, —
awake, wach; to be —, wach sein
awaken (*tr.*), aúfwecken; (*intr.*) aufwachen, wachte auf, ist aufgewacht
aware of: before I was — it, ehe ich es mir versah; not that I am —, nicht daß ich wüßte
away, fort, weg

B

back (*adv.*), zurück
back, der Rücken, –s, —
bad, schlecht, böse, übel; (= annoying, unpleasant, disquieting, serious) schlimm; — times, schlechte Zeiten; that is not a — idea, das ist kein übler Einfall; that is too —, schade!
bake, backen, buk, gebacken, bäckt
bakery, die Bäckerei, —, –en
ball, der Ball, –(e)s, ¨e
balloon, der Ballon, –s, –e *or* –s
bank (*of a river*), das Ufer, –s, —; (*for money*) die Bank, —, –en
barber, der Barbier, –s, –e
bark, bellen
bathe, baden
bathroom, das Badezimmer, –s, —
Bavaria, (das) Bayern, –s
be (= exist), sein, war, ist gewesen, ist; (= be situated) liegen, lag, hat gelegen; — it early or — it late, sei es früh, sei es spät; Cologne is (situated) on the Rhine, Köln liegt am Rhein; how are

you?, wie geht es Ihnen?; that is (*abbr.* i.e.), das heißt (*abbr.* d.h.); there is (was), es gibt (gab) (*w. acc.*); he is right, er hat recht; he is wrong, er hat unrecht; what am I to do?, was soll ich tun?
beach, der Strand, –(e)s, –e; to go to the —, an den Strand gehen
beard, der Bart, –(e)s, ¨e
beautiful, schön; most — of all, allerschönst–
because (*conj.*), weil; — of (*prep.*), wegen (*w. gen.*)
become, werden, wurde, ist geworden, wird; to — of, werden aus; to — engaged to, sich verloben mit; what will — of him?, was wird aus ihm werden?
bed, das Bett, –(e)s, –en; to go to —, zu Bett gehen; in —, **im** Bett
bedroom, das Schlafzimmer, –s, —
beer, das Bier, –(e)s, –e; dark (light) —, dunkles (helles) Bier
before (*prep.*), vor (*w. dat. or acc.*); day — yesterday, vorgestern; year — last, vorletztes Jahr
before (*conj.*), ehe, bevor
before (*adv.*), vorher, früher; the day —, den Tag vorher (*w. adv. force*)
begin, beginnen, begann, begonnen, beginnt; anfangen, fing an, angefangen, fängt an; — at the beginning, fangen Sie von vorn an!
beginning, der Anfang, –(e)s, ¨e
behave, sich betragen (*or* benehmen) (*str.*)
behind (*prep.*), hinter (*w. dat. or acc.*)
behind (*adv.*), hinten
believe, glauben (*w. dat. of the pers. & acc. of the th.*); to — in, glauben an (*w. acc.*); he believes me (it), er glaubt mir (es); he believes in me (in it), er glaubt an mich (daran); meinen (*to have an opinion*)

bell, die Glocke, —, –n; die Klingel, —, –n; the — rings, es klingelt

belong to, gehören (*w. dat. & no prep. if ownership is denoted*) [**Zu** *precedes the dative when* **gehören** *means* to be a part (*or* member) of.]

below (*prep.*), unter (*w. dat. or acc.*), unterhalb (*w. gen.*)

bench, die Bank, —, ̈e

beside (*prep.*), bei (*w. dat.*), neben (*w. dat. or acc.*); I am — myself with joy, ich bin außer mir vor Freude

best (*adj.*), best–; — of all, allerbest–; I like it —, es gefällt mir am besten [*or* ich habe es **am liebsten** (*superl. of* **gern**)]; the — I have, das Beste, was ich habe

betray, verraten, verriet, verraten, verrät

better, besser (*comp. of* **gut**)

between (*prep.*), zwischen (*w. dat. or acc.*)

Bible, die Bibel, —, –n

bicycle, das Fahrrad, –(e)s, ̈er; das Rad, –(e)s, ̈er

big, groß

biological, biologisch

biology, die Biologie, —; die Lebenslehre, —

bird, der Vogel, –s, ̈

birthday, der Geburtstag, –(e)s, –e; for one's —, zum Geburtstag

bite, beißen, biß, gebissen

black, schwarz; the Black Forest, der Schwarzwald, –(e)s

(black)board, die Tafel, —, –n

blame, die Schuld, —, –en; he is to — for that, er ist schuld daran

blind, blind; — in, blind auf (*w. dat.*)

blond, blond

blue, blau

board, das Brett, –(e)s, –er

board (= blackboard), die Tafel, —, –n; (*of a ship*) der Bord, –(e)s, –e; at the —, an der Tafel; to the —, an die Tafel; to write on the —, an die Tafel schreiben; on — a steamer, an Bord eines Dampfers

boast of, prahlen mit (*w. dat.*); sich rühmen (*w. gen.*)

body, der Körper, –s, —

bold, kühn; (= impudent) frech

book, das Buch, –(e)s, ̈er

bored: to be —, sich langweilen, langweilte, gelangweilt

born, geboren (*p.p. of* gebären); was —, (*of the dead*) **wurde** geboren; was —, (*of the living*) **ist** geboren; when were you —?, wann sind Sie geboren?

both, beide; — (= the two) brothers, beide (*or* die beiden) Brüder; — . . . and, sowohl . . . als auch

bother about, sich kümmern um (*w. acc.*)

bottle, die Flasche, —, –n

box, der Kasten, –s, —; die Kiste, —, –n

boy, der Junge, –n, –n; der Knabe, –n, –n

brave, tapfer

bread, das Brot, –(e)s, –e

break, brechen, brach, gebrochen, bricht; to — one's arm, sich (*dat.*) den Arm brechen; to — (to pieces), zerbrechen

breakfast, das Frühstück, –(e)s, –e; for —, zum Frühstück; after —, nach dem Frühstück; to eat —, frühstücken, frühstückte, gefrühstückt

breath, der Atem, –s, –züge; to take —, Atem holen

breathe, atmen

breathless, atemlos

bridge, die Brücke, —, –n

bright, hell

bring, bringen, brachte, gebracht; — along, mitbringen

broad, breit
brook, der Bach, –(e)s, ̈e
brother, der Bruder, –s, ̈
brown, braun
brush, (sich) bürsten; to — one's teeth, sich (*dat.*) die Zähne putzen
build, bauen
building, das Gebäude, –s, —
bundle, das (*or* der) Bündel, –s, —
burn, brennen, brannte, gebrannt; to — with (*fig.*), brennen vor
business, das Geschäft, –(e)s, –e; to go into —, ein Geschäft eröffnen (*or* gründen)
busy, beschäftigt
but, aber; sondern (*cf. Index for grammatical references as to use*)
butcher, der Fleischer, –s, —; der Metzger, –s, —
buy, kaufen
by (*prep.*), von (*pers. agent*), mit, bei (*all w. dat.*); durch (*means or instrument; w. acc.*); an, neben (*both w. dat. or acc.*); — heart, auswendig; — steamer, mit dem Dampfer; — rail, mit der Eisenbahn

C

cake, der Kuchen, –s, —
call, rufen, rief, gerufen; (= to name) nennen, nannte, genannt; (= to be called) heißen, hieß, geheißen; (= to call names) schimpfen (*wk.*), schelten, schalt, gescholten, schilt; to — on (= to visit), besuchen; to — on (*to recite*), aúfrufen; to — up (*on the phone*), ánrufen; to — for (= to go *or* come for), ábholen
can, können, konnte, gekonnt, kann
Canada, (das) Kanada, –s
canal, der Kanal, –s, . . . näle
candle, die Kerze, —, –n
cane, der Stock, –(e)s, ̈e
cap, die Mütze, —, –n
capable of, fähig (*w. gen.*)

capital, die Hauptstadt, —, ̈e
capitalize, großschreiben
capitalized, großgeschrieben
car (= auto), das Auto, –s, –s; der Wagen, –s, —; (*of a train*) der (Eisenbahn)wagen, –s, —; street —, die Straßenbahn, —, –en
care, die Sorge, —, –n; for all I —, meinetwegen; to take —, sich in acht nehmen; to take — of, sorgen für (*w. acc.*)
care for (= to like), mögen, gern haben
careful, sorgfältig; (= cautious) vorsichtig; to be —, sich in acht nehmen
Carl (*or* **Charles**), (der) Karl, –s
carpenter, der Zimmermann, –(e)s, Zimmerleute
carry, tragen, trug, getragen, trägt; to — away, fórttragen
carry out (*often ref. to sci. tests*), ausführen, führte aus, ausgeführt; durchführen, führte durch, durchgeführt
case (= circumstance *or* grammatical —), der Fall, –(e)s, ̈e; in — (*sub. conj.*), falls; in any —, jedenfalls
cash, das Bargeld, –(e)s
cask, das Faß, Fasses, Fässer
castle, das Schloß, Schlosses, Schlösser; die Burg, —, –en; — ruins, Schloßruinen (*pl. of* die Schloßruine)
cat, die Katze, —, –n
catch, fangen, fing, gefangen, fängt; to — (a) cold, sich erkälten; to — sight of, erblicken
cathedral, der Dom, –(e)s, –e
cause, die Ursache, —, –n; der Grund, –(e)s, ̈e
celebrate, feiern
celestial: — body, der Himmelskörper, –s, —; — chart, die Himmelskarte, —, –n; — navigation, astronomische Navigation

cellar, der Keller, –s, —
cent, der Cent, –(s), –(s);   twenty —s' worth of stamps, für zwanzig Cent Briefmarken
century, das Jahrhundert, –(e)s, –e
certain(ly), gewiß
chain, die Kette, —, –n
chair, der Stuhl, –(e)s, ̈e
chalk, die Kreide, —
chancellor, der Kanzler, –s, —
change (*noun*), die Abwechs(e)lung, —, -en;   for a —, zur Abwechs(e)-lung
change (= to alter), ändern;   (*for better or worse*) (sich) verändern; (= to exchange) wechseln;   to — money, Geld wechseln; to — cars, úmsteigen (*w.* sein); to — clothes, sich úmziehen (*or* úmkleiden); to — one's mind, sich anders [*or* eines anderen (*or* Besseren)] besinnen;   you have changed very much, Sie haben sich sehr verändert;   I have changed my place of residence, ich habe meine Wohnung gewechselt (*or* ich bin umgezogen)
Charlemagne, Karl der Große
Charles (*also* **Carl**), (der) Karl, –s
charm, bezaubern
charming, reizend
cheap, billig
cheek, die Wange, —, –n
cheese, der Käse, –s, —
chess, das Schach, –(e)s;   a game of —, eine Partie Schach
child, das Kind, –(e)s, –er
chimpanzee, der Schimpanse, –n, –n
choose, wählen
Christmas, (die) Weihnachten, — (*pl. form w. sing. vb.*);   for (*or* at) —, zu Weihnachten
church, die Kirche, —, –n
cigar, die Zigarre, —, –n
cigarette, die Zigarette, —, –n
circle, der Kreis, –es, –e

circumstance, der Umstand, –(e)s, ̈e
circus, der Zirkus, —, –se
citizen, der Bürger, –s, —
city, die Stadt, —, ̈e;   the — of Hamburg, die Stadt Hamburg
city hall, das Rathaus, –es, . . . häuser
claim (= assert *or* maintain), behaupten;   wollen, wollte, gewollt, will;   he claims to have done it, er will es getan haben
clap, klatschen;   to — one's hands, in die Hände klatschen
class, die Klasse, —, –n;   to travel second —, zweiter Klasse (*gen.*) fahren
classroom, das Klassenzimmer, –s, —
clean (*adj.*), rein
clean, reinigen;   to — up, aúfräumen
clear(ly) (= bright), hell;   klar; (= distinct) deutlich
cleft, die Spalte, —, –n
clever, klug
cliff, der Felsen, –s, —
climb (**up**), klettern (*w.* sein) auf (*w. acc.*)
clock, die (Wand)uhr, —, –en
close, zumachen, machte zu, zugemacht;   schließen, schloß, geschlossen
cloth, das Tuch, –(e)s, ̈er
clothes, Kleider (*pl. of* das Kleid)
club (a group of people), der Verein, –s, –e;   der Klub, –s, –s
coal, die Kohle, —, –n;   rich in —, reich an Kohlen
coast, die Küste, —, –n
coat, der Rock, –(e)s, ̈e
coat of ice, die Eisdecke, —, –n
coffee, der Kaffee, –s
coffee cup, die Kaffeetasse, —, –n
cold (*adj.*), kalt;   I am —, mir ist kalt
cold (*state of weather*), die Kälte, —;

(*as in the head*) die Erkältung, —, –en; to catch (a) —, sich erkälten; I caught a bad —, ich habe mich stark erkältet

collar, der Kragen, –s, —

collect, sammeln

Cologne, (das) Köln, –s

color, die Farbe, —, –n

comb (*noun*), der Kamm, –(e)s, ̈e

comb, kämmen

come, kommen, kam, ist gekommen; to — back, zurückkommen; to — up, heraúfkommen; to — in (= to enter), hereínkommen; to — in (*of money*), eínkommen (*cf.* § 70 **H**); to — late, zu spät kommen; he came running, er kam gelaufen

comfortable, bequem

command, befehlen, befahl, befohlen, befiehlt (*w. dat.*)

company (= social gathering), die Gesellschaft, —, –en; (= visitors) der Besuch, –(e)s, –e; we had —, wir hatten Besuch (*or* Gäste)

comparatively, verhältnismäßig

compare, vergleichen

compel, zwingen, zwang, gezwungen

complain about, klagen über (*w. acc.*)

complete (*adj.*), ganz, vollständig, fertig, vollendet

complete, vollenden

composition (= essay), der Aufsatz, –es, ̈e

composition of the air, die Luftzusammensetzung, —

confirm, bestätigen

congratulate, gratulieren (*w. dat.*); I — you on your great success, ich gratuliere Ihnen zu Ihrem großen Erfolg

conquer (*intr.*), siegen; (*tr.*) besiegen

conscious of, bewußt (*w. gen.*)

consequence, die Folge, —, –n; as a —, zur Folge; in — of that, infolgedessen

consequently, infolgedessen

conservation of energy, die Energieerhaltung, —

consist of, bestehen aus (*w. dat.*)

construct, konstruieren, bauen

contain, enthalten, enthielt, enthalten, enthält

continually, fortwährend

continue, fortfahren, fuhr fort, hat fortgefahren, fährt fort; — reading, lesen Sie weiter!; he continued reading, er hat fortgefahren zu lesen (Er **ist** fortgefahren *would mean* he has gone away.)

contradict, widerspréchen, widersprách, widerspróchen, widerspricht (*w. dat.*)

contrary to (*prep.*), gegen (*w. acc.*)

control: in — of, mächtig (*w. gen.*)

conversation, das Gespräch, –(e)s, –e

converse, sich unterhálten

convince, überzeúgen

cook, kochen

cool, kühl

copy, abschreiben, schrieb ab, abgeschrieben

corner, die Ecke, —, –n

correct (*adj.*), richtig

correct, verbessern, korrigieren

cosmic, kosmisch

cosmic radiation, die kosmische Strahlung, —; die Weltraumstrahlung, —

cosmic rays, kosmische Strahlen (*or* Ultrastrahlen), *m. pl.*; Höhenstrahlen, *m. pl.*

cost, kosten; it — me a dollar, es kostete mich (*or* mir) einen Dollar

could (= was able), konnte (*refers to a fact*); (= would be able) könnte (*contrary to fact*); he — have done it, er hätte es tun können

countless, zahllos

country, das Land, –(e)s, ⸚er; in the —, auf dem Lande; to the —, aufs Land

couple, das Paar, –(e)s, –e

course (*of a meal*), der Gang, –(e)s, ⸚e; (*of time*) der Lauf, –(e)s, ⸚e; in the — of time, im Laufe der Zeit

court, der Hof, –(e)s, ⸚e; (*of justice*) das Gericht, –(e)s, –e; at —, am Hofe

cousin (*male*), der Vetter, –s, –n; (*female*), die Cousine, —, –n

cover, bedecken

covered, bedeckt; — with ice, eisbedeckt (*or* mit Eis bedeckt)

cow, die Kuh, —, ⸚e

cowardly, feige

crazy, verrückt

crooked, krumm

crowd, die Menge, —, –n

cruel, grausam; — to, grausam gegen (*w. acc.*)

cup, die Tasse, —, –n

curious, neugierig

custom, die Sitte, —, –n

cut, schneiden, schnitt, geschnitten; to — class, schwänzen

Czechoslovakia, die Tschechoslowakei, —

D

dance (*noun*), der Tanz, –es, ⸚e

dance, tanzen

dangerous, gefährlich

Danube, die Donau, —

dare, wagen

dark, dunkel

darkness, die Finsternis, —, –se

date, das Datum, –s, Daten; what is today's —?, der wievielte ist (*or* den wievielten haben wir) heute?

daughter, die Tochter, —, ⸚

day, der Tag, –(e)s, –e; — before yesterday, vorgestern; — after tomorrow, übermorgen; one —

(*indef. time*), eines Tages; all — (*duration of time*), den ganzen Tag; — after —, Tag für Tag; every other —, einen Tag um den anderen; the — before, den Tag vorher (*w. adv. force*)

daytime: in the —, am Tage

dead, tot

deaf, taub

deal: a great — (of), viel

dear (= beloved), lieb, teuer; (= expensive) teuer

death, der Tod, –(e)s, –esfälle

debt, die Schuld, —, –en

December, der Dezember, –(s), —

decide, sich entschließen; I have decided upon a trip, ich habe mich **zur** Reise entschlossen; I have decided to work hard, ich habe mich entschlossen, schwer (*or* tüchtig) zu arbeiten

decorate, schmücken

deed, die Tat, —, –en

deep, tief; a foot —, einen Fuß tief

defend, verteidigen

deliver (*a speech*), halten, hielt, gehalten, hält; he delivered a long speech, er hat eine lange Rede gehalten

dentist, der Zahnarzt, –es, ⸚e

deny, leugnen; (= refuse) verweigern

depend, darauf ánkommen; that depends, es kommt darauf an; it all depends on the weather, alles hängt vom Wetter ab

dependent, abhängig

describe, beschreiben, beschrieb, beschrieben

desk, das Pult, –(e)s, –e

dessert, der Nachtisch, –es, –e; for —, zum Nachtisch

destroy, zerstören

devil, der Teufel, –s, —

dictionary, das Wörterbuch, –(e)s, ⸚er

die, sterben, starb, ist gestorben, stirbt; to — of, sterben an (*w. dat.*); he died of consumption, er ist an der Schwindsucht gestorben

difference, der Unterschied, –(e)s, –e; that makes no —, das macht nichts aus

different, ander–: verschieden

difficult, schwer

difficulty, die Schwierigkeit, —, –en; (*obstacle*), das Hindernis, –ses, –se

diligent(ly), fleißig; most — of all, allerfleißigst–

dining room, das Eßzimmer, –s, —

dinner, das Mittagessen, –s, —; is — ready?, ist das Mittagessen fertig?; after —, nach **dem** Mittagessen (*or* nach Tisch)

direct (*vb.*), richten; — toward (*aim at*), richten auf (*w. acc.*)

direction, die Richtung, —, –en; in all —s, nach allen Richtungen

dirty, schmutzig

disappear, verschwinden, verschwand, ist verschwunden

disappointed, enttäuscht

discharge, entlassen, entließ, entlassen, entläßt

discover, entdecken

discoverer, der Entdecker, –s, —; der Erfinder, –s, — (*inventor*)

discovery, die Entdeckung, —, –en; die Erfindung, —, –en (*invention*)

discuss, besprechen (*str.*)

dish, die Schüssel, —, –n; —es, das Geschirr, –(e)s; to wash (dry) —es, Geschirr ábwaschen (ábtrocknen)

dishonest, unehrlich

dissatisfied, unzufrieden

distance, die Ferne, —, –n; die Entfernung, —, –en; from a —, aus der Ferne; at a —, in der Ferne

disturb, stören

divide, teilen

dizzy, schwind(e)lig; she is —,

ihr ist schwind(e)lig (*or* ihr schwindelt)

do, tun, tat, getan, tut; machen; what are we to —?, was sollen wir tun?; he does me a favor, er tut mir einen Gefallen; he does his lessons, er macht seine Aufgaben

doctor, der Arzt, –es, ¨e; der Doktor, –s, –en

dog, der Hund, –(e)s, –e

doll, die Puppe, —, –n

dollar, der Dollar, –s –(s); a thousand —s, tausend Dollar; a —'s worth of sugar, für einen Dollar Zucker

domestic animal, das Haustier, –(e)s, –e

domesticated, zahm

door, die Tür, —, –en

doubt (*noun*), der Zweifel, –s, —

doubt, bezweifeln (*tr.*)

doubtless, wohl (*often w. fut.*); ohne Zweifel

down, nieder; hinab, hinunter; to lie —, sich níederlegen; to settle —, sich níederlassen; to go —, hinúntergehen; to go — (= to descend), hinábsteigen (*Verbs denoting motion toward the observer substitute* **her–** *for* **hin–**.)

downstairs, (nach) unten; to go —, nach unten gehen (*or* die Treppe hinúntergehen)

dozen, das Dutzend, –s, –e; half a —, ein halbes Dutzend

dragon, der Drache, –n, –n

drama, das Drama, –s, Dramen

draught, der Zug, –(e)s, ¨e

draw (= to pull), ziehen, zog, gezogen; (= to sketch) zeichnen

dream (*noun*), der Traum, –(e)s, ¨e

dream, träumen

dress (*noun*), das Kleid, –(e)s, –er

dress (oneself), sich ánziehen (*or* ánkleiden)

drink, trinken, trank, getrunken (*of*

people); saufen, soff, gesoffen, säuft (*of animals*)

drive, treiben, trieb, getrieben; (= to go driving) fahren, fuhr, ist gefahren, fährt; to — a car, (ein) Auto fahren (*tr.*)

drop (*noun*), der Tropfen, –s, —

drop, fallen lassen; she dropped her handkerchief, sie hat das Taschentuch fallen lassen

drown (*tr.*), ertränken (*wk.*)

drowned: to be —, ertrinken, ertrank, ist ertrunken

drugstore, die Apotheke, —, –n

dry (*adj.*), trocken

dry, trocknen

duke, der Herzog, –(e)s, –e (*or* ‥e)

during (*prep.*), während (*w. gen.*)

dusty, staubig

duty, die Pflicht, —, –en

dwarf, der Zwerg, –(e)s, –e

E

each, jeder, jede, jedes; — other, einander (*or* sich)

ear, das Ohr, –(e)s, –en

early, früh; — in the morning, frühmorgens

earn, verdienen

earth, die Erde, —

earth satellite, der Erdsatellit, –en, –en

easily, leicht

east, der Osten, –s; — of, östlich von (*w. dat.*)

Easter, Ostern (*pl. form w. sing. vb.*)

easy, leicht

eat, essen, aß, gegessen, ißt (*of people*); fressen, fraß, gefressen, frißt (*of animals*); what does he — for breakfast?, was ißt er zum Frühstück?

eclipse: — of the moon, die Mondfinsternis, —, –se; — of the sun, die Sonnenfinsternis, —, –se

educated, gebildet

egg, das Ei, –(e)s, –er

eight (*adj.*), acht

eight (*figure*), die Acht, —

eighteen, achtzehn

eighty, achtzig

either (*adj. & pron.*), (= both) beide; [= each (*of two or more*)] jeder, jede, jedes; on — side, auf jeder Seite (*or* beiden Seiten); I did not see — of them, ich habe keinen von ihnen gesehen

either (*conj.*), entweder; — . . . or, entweder . . . oder; (*adv.*) nor I —, ich auch nicht

elderly, älter–

eldest, ältest–

elect, wählen

election, die Wahl, —, –en

electric, elektrisch

elevated railroad, die Hochbahn, —, –en

eleven, elf

else (= otherwise), sonst; ander–; no one —, niemand anders (*or* sonst niemand); someone (*or* anyone) —, jemand anders (*or* sonst jemand)

embarrassed, verlegen

emperor, der Kaiser, –s, —

empire, das Reich, –(e)s, –e

empty, leer

end (*noun*), das Ende, –s, –n; at the —, am Ende

end, enden

enemy, der Feind, –(e)s, –e

engaged, verlobt; to become — to, sich verloben mit

England, (das) England, –s

English (*adj.*), englisch

English (*language*), Englisch; he is learning —, er lernt Englisch; in —, auf englisch

English-German (*adj.*), englisch-deutsch; an — dictionary, ein englisch-deutsches Wörterbuch

enjoy, genießen, genoß, genossen;

froh werden (*w. gen.*); she does not — life (= she leads an unhappy life), sie wird ihres Lebens nicht froh

enough, genug

enter, eíntreten (gehen *or* kommen) in (*w. acc.*) (*These verbs often have the separable prefixes* **herein** *and* **hinein:** hereínkommen, hineíngehen, *etc.*)

entire, ganz

entrance, der Eingang, –(e)s, ¨e

especially, besonders

Europe, (das) Europa, –s

even (*adj.*), eben, gerade

even (*adv.*), sogar, selbst; — a physician, selbst ein Arzt; — if, wenn . . . auch; — if he were here, **wenn** er **auch** hier wäre

evening, der Abend, –s, –e; this —, heute **a**bend; tomorrow —, morgen **a**bend; yesterday —, gestern **a**bend; one — (*indef. time*), eines Abends; all — (*duration of time*), den ganzen Abend; in the —, am Abend (abends *or* des Abends); good —, guten Abend!

ever (= at all times *or* always), immer; (= at any time), je(mals)

every, jeder, jede, jedes

everybody, jedermann, –s

everything, alles; — he had, alles, was er hatte; — possible, alles mögliche; — else, alles andere; — good, alles Gute

everywhere, überall

evil, übel

exact(ly), genau

examination, die Prüfung, —, –en; das Examen, –s, Examina; to take an —, eine Prüfung machen; to pass an —, eine Prüfung bestehen; to fail in an —, bei einer Prüfung dúrchfallen (*w. sein*)

example, das Beispiel, –(e)s, –e;

for — (*abbr.* e.g.), zum Beispiel (*abbr.* z.B.)

excited, aufgeregt

exercise (*noun*), die Aufgabe, —, –n; die Übung, —, –en

exercise, üben (*often refl.*)

expect, erwarten

expensive, teuer

experience (*noun*), das Erlebnis, –ses, –se; die Erfahrung, —, –en

experience, erleben; erfahren (*str.*)

explain, erklären

expose, aussetzen, setzte aus, ausgesetzt (*often in sci. sense, e.g., ref. to variations of temperature*)

express, aúsdrücken

expression, der Ausdruck, –(e)s, ¨e

express train, der Schnellzug, –(e)s, ¨e

extremely, höchst; äußerst

eye, das Auge, –s, –n

F

face, das Gesicht, –(e)s, –er

fact, die Tatsache, —, –n; in —, in der Tat

fail (*in an examination*), (bei einer Prüfung) dúrchfallen, fiel durch, ist durchgefallen, fällt durch

fair, die Messe, —, –n

fairy tale, das Märchen, –s, —

faithful, treu (*w. dat.*)

fall (*season*), der Herbst, –es, –e

fall, fallen, fiel, ist gefallen, fällt; to — asleep, einschlafen, schlief ein, ist eingeschlafen, schläft ein; to — in love with, sich verlieben in (*w. acc.*)

family, die Familie, —, –n

famous, berühmt; — for, berühmt durch (*w. acc.*) [*or* wegen (*w. gen.*)]

far, weit; — and wide, weit und breit; as — as I know, soviel ich

weiß (*or* meines Wissens); as
— as (*prep.*), bis
fare, der Fahrpreis, –es, –e
farewell, leben Sie wohl!
farmer, der Bauer, –s (*or* –n), –n
fast, schnell; my watch is —, meine
Uhr geht vor
father, der Vater, –s, ̈
fault, die Schuld, —, –en; it is not
his —, er kann nichts dafür
favor, der Gefallen, –s, —; he does
me a —, er tut mir einen Gefallen
favorable, günstig
fear (*noun*), die Furcht, —
fear, fürchten; (= to be afraid of)
sich fürchten vor (*w. dat.*); to —
that, fürchten, daß
February, (der) Februar, –(s), –e
Federal Republic of Germany, die
Bundesrepublik Deutschland
feed, füttern
feel, fühlen; sich fühlen (*or* befinden); how do you — (= how
are you)?, wie geht es Ihnen?
fell (= cut down), fällen
fellow, der Kerl, –(e)s, –e
fence, der Zaun, –(e)s, ̈e
few, wenige; a —, ein paar
(*indecl.*)
field, das Feld, –(e)s, –er; in the —,
auf dem Feld
fifteen, fünfzehn
fifty, fünfzig
fight (*noun*), der Kampf, –(e)s, ̈e
fight, kämpfen; (= to come to
blows) sich prügeln
fill, füllen
finally, endlich, schließlich, zuletzt
find, finden, fand, gefunden
fine, fein; that is all very — (*sarcas-
tic*), but . . . , das ist alles sehr
schön, aber . . .
finger, der Finger, –s, —
finish, vollenden
fire, das Feuer, –s, —
firm (*adj.*), fest
firm, die Firma, —, Firmen

first, erst–; in the — place, erstens;
at —, zuerst
fish, der Fisch, –es, –e
fishing: to go —, fischen gehen; I
went —, ich bin fischen gegangen
fist, die Faust, —, ̈e
five, fünf; — times, fünfmal
flag, die Fahne, —, –n
flame, die Flamme, —, –n
flat, flach
flatter, schmeicheln (*w. dat.; often
refl.*); you — yourself, du
schmeichelst dir
flee, fliehen, floh, ist geflohen
floor, der Boden, –s, ̈ (*or* —); (=
ground floor), das Erdgeschoß,
. . . geschosses, . . . geschosse; first
— (up), das erste Stockwerk (*or*
der erste Stock); the top —, der
oberste Stock
flour, das Mehl, –(e)s, –e (*or* –arten)
flow, fließen, floß, ist geflossen
flower, die Blume, —, –n
fluent(ly), fließend
fly, fliegen, flog, ist geflogen; (*of
time*) vergehen, verging, ist vergangen; how time flies!, wie
schnell die Zeit vergeht!
flyer, der Flieger, –s, —
folksong, das Volkslied, –(e)s, –er
follow, folgen, folgte, ist gefolgt (*w.
dat.*)
fool, der Narr, –en, –en; der Tor,
–en, –en
foolish, närrisch, töricht
foot, der Fuß, –es, ̈e; on —, zu
Fuß
for (*prep.*), für (*w. acc.*); — what
reason?, **aus** welchem Grunde?;
— Christmas, **zu** Weihnachten;
— one's birthday, **zum** Geburtstag; — example (*abbr.* e.g.),
zum Beispiel (*abbr.* z.B.); —
heaven's sake!, **um** Himmels
willen!; — all I care, meinetwegen; — two years, zwei Jahre
lang; he is going to the country

— a month, er geht **auf** einen Monat aufs Land; I have been here — a month, ich bin **seit** einem Monat hier; to ask —, bitten **um** (*w. acc.*); to long —, sich sehnen **nach**

for (*causal conj.*), denn

force, die Gewalt, —, –en

foreign, fremd

foreign language, die Fremdsprache, —, –n

forenoon, der Vormittag, –(e)s, –e (*cf.* **afternoon** *for similar idioms and phrases with* **forenoon**)

forest, der Wald, –(e)s, ¨er

forget, vergessen, vergaß, vergessen, vergißt

fork, die Gabel, —, –n

form, die Form, —, –en; — of government, die Regierungsform

former, jener (*esp. when used with* dieser *in specific contrast*); vorher erwähnt (previously mentioned)

formerly, früher

fortunately, glücklicherweise

fortune (= good luck), das Glück, –(e)s; (= wealth), das Vermögen, –s, —

fountain, der Brunnen, –s, —

fountain pen, die Füllfeder, —, –n

four, vier; — times, viermal; — kinds of, viererlei

fourfold, vierfach

fourteenth, vierzehnt–

fourth (*adj.*), viert–

fourth (= quarter), das Viertel, –s, —

fox, der Fuchs, –es, Füchse

France, (das) Frankreich, –s

frantic, toll; — with pain, toll vor Schmerz

free, frei

free balloon, der Freiballon, –s, –e *or* –s

freedom, die Freiheit, —

freeze, frieren, fror, gefroren; it froze hard, es hat stark gefroren

French (*adj.*), französisch

French (*language*), Französisch; do you speak —?, sprechen Sie Französisch?

Frenchman, der Franzose, –n, –n

fresh, frisch

Friday, der Freitag, –(e)s, –e

friend (*male*), der Freund, –(e)s, –e; (*female*) die Freundin, —, –nen; a — of mine, ein Freund von mir

friendly, freundlich; he is — to me, er ist mir freundlich (*or* er ist freundlich gegen mich)

friendship, die Freundschaft, —, –en

frighten (*tr.*), erschrecken (*wk.*)

frightened: to be — (*intr.*), erschrecken, erschrak, ist erschrocken, erschrickt

from (*prep.*), von, aus (*both w. dat.*)

front: in — of (*prep.*), vor (*w. dat. or acc.*)

front door, die Haustür, —, –en

fruit, die Frucht, —, ¨e; das Obst, –es

full, voll

fun, der Spaß, –es, ¨e

funny, komisch

furious, wütend

further, weiter

future (*adj.*), (zu)künftig

future, die Zukunft, —; — plans, Zukunftspläne (*pl. of* der Zukunftsplan)

G

game, das Spiel, –(e)s, –e; football —, das Fußballspiel; to play a — of chess, eine Partie Schach spielen

garden, der Garten, –s, ¨

gas, das Gas, –es, –e

gay, fröhlich, lustig, heiter

generally, gewöhnlich, in der Regel

gentleman, der Herr, –n, –en

German, (*adj.*), deutsch; in —, auf deutsch

German (*language*), Deutsch; are you studying —?, lernen Sie Deutsch?; (*native of Germany*) der Deutsche, –n, –n (*w. adj. decl.*); a —, ein Deutscher

Germany, (das) Deutschland, –s

get (= to receive), erhalten, erhielt, erhalten, erhält; bekommen, bekam, bekommen; to — in, einsteigen, stieg ein, ist eingestiegen; to — to be (= to become), werden, wurde, ist geworden, wird; to — up, aufstehen, stand auf, ist aufgestanden; to — used to, sich gewöhnen an (*w. acc.*)

giant, der Riese, –n, –n

giant (*adj.*) *or* gigantic, riesig

gift, das Geschenk, –(e)s, –e

girl, das Mädchen, –s, —

give, geben, gab, gegeben, gibt; it gives me pleasure, es macht mir Freude

glad, froh; I am — of it; ich freue mich darüber (*or* es freut mich)

glass, das Glas, –es, Gläser; a — of beer, ein Glas Bier

glasses (= spectacles), die Brille, —, –n

glee club, der Gesangverein, –(e)s, –e

glove, der Handschuh, –(e)s, –e; a pair of —s, ein Paar Handschuhe

go, gehen, ging, ist gegangen; (= to travel) fahren, fuhr, ist gefahren, fährt; reisen, reiste, ist gereist; to — home, nach Hause gehen; to — to bed, zu Bett gehen; to — walking, spazierengehen (*or* einen Spaziergang machen); to — to school, in die (*or* zur) Schule gehen; to — to the theater (to the opera), ins Theater (in die Oper) gehen; to — away, fórtgehen; to — along mítgehen; to — out, (hin)aúsgehen (*cf.* § 70 H); to — down, hinúntergehen; to — to sleep, einschlafen, schlief ein, ist eingeschlafen, schläft ein; to — out of the door, zur Tür hinaúsgehen; he goes (= travels) second class, er fährt zweiter Klasse; the fire is going out, das Feuer geht aus

God, der Gott, –es, ⸚er

gold, das Gold, –(e)s

golden, golden

good, gut; to have a — time, sich amüsieren

goodbye, auf Wiederseh(e)n!

goods (= wares, commodities), die Waren (*pl. of* die Ware)

gorgeous, prächtig

govern, regieren

grade (= school mark), die Zensur, —, –en; die Note, —, –n

gradually, allmählich, nach und nach

grammar, die Grammatik, —, –en

grandfather, der Großvater, –s, ⸚

grandmother, die Großmutter, —, ⸚

grandparents, die Großeltern, — (*pl.*)

grandson, der Enkel, –s, —

grape, die Traube, —, –n

grass, das Gras, –es, Gräser

grateful, dankbar (*w. dat.*)

grave, das Grab, –(e)s, ⸚er

gray, grau

great, groß

green, grün

greet, grüßen

groan, stöhnen

ground, der Boden, –s, ⸚ (*or* –); der Grund, –(e)s, ⸚e

group, die Gruppe, —, –n

grow, wachsen, wuchs, ist gewachsen, wächst

guard, bewachen

guess (= to succeed in guessing *or* solve), erraten, erriet, erraten, errät; to — at, raten, riet, geraten, rät

guest, der Gast, –es, ⸚e

guilty, schuldig

gymnasium, die Turnhalle, —, –n; (= *the German school that prepares students for the* Universität) das Gymnasium, –s, ... ien

gymnastic, gymnastisch

H

hail, hageln

hair, das Haar, –(e)s, –e; I had my — cut, ich habe mir das Haar schneiden lassen; **my** — stood on end, mir standen die Haare zu Berge

half (*adj.*), halb; one and a —, anderthalb; at — past nine, um halb zehn; — a pound, ein halbes Pfund

half, die Hälfte, —, –n; the other —, die andere Hälfte

hall, der Saal, –(e)s, Säle

halt, halten, hielt, gehalten, hält; ánhalten

hammer, der Hammer, –s, ⸚

hand, die Hand, —, ⸚e; on the other —, dagegen

handful, die Handvoll, —, —

handkerchief, das Taschentuch, –(e)s, ⸚er

happen, geschehen, geschah, ist geschehen, geschieht; vorkommen, kam vor, ist vorgekommen; passieren (*w.* sein); he happened to be at home, er war zufällig (*or* zufälligerweise war er) zu Hause

happiness, das Glück, –(e)s

happy, glücklich, fröhlich; I am — about it, ich freue mich darüber (*or* es freut mich)

harbor, der Hafen, –s, ⸚

hard, hart; schwer; to study

(work) —, fleißig (tüchtig *or* schwer) studieren (arbeiten); to rain —, stark regnen

hardly, kaum

harmful, schädlich (*w. dat.*)

hat, der Hut, –(e)s, ⸚e

hate, hassen

hatred, der Haß, Hasses

have, haben, hatte, gehabt, hat; to — a good time, sich amüsieren; to — something done, etwas tun lassen; to — to, müssen, mußte, gemußt, muß; I — to go, ich muß gehen; you don't — (*i.e.,* **need**) **to** do that, das **brauchen** Sie nicht **zu** tun; I had a new suit made, ich habe mir einen neuen Anzug machen lassen

he, er

head, der Kopf, –(e)s, ⸚e; das Haupt, –(e)s, ⸚er

headache, das Kopfweh, –(e)s; I have a —, ich habe Kopfweh (*or* Kopfschmerzen) (*no art.*)

health, die Gesundheit, —, –en

healthy, gesund

heap, der Haufe(n), –ns, –n

hear, hören; I heard him sing, ich habe ihn singen hören

heart, das Herz, –ens, –en; by —, auswendig

hearty, herzlich

heat, die Hitze, —

heaven, der Himmel, –s, —; for —'s sake!, um Himmels (*or* Gottes) willen!

heavy, schwer

height, die Höhe, —, –n

helium, das Helium, –s

helium gas, das Heliumgas, –es

help, helfen, half, geholfen, hilft (*w. dat.*); I couldn't — it, ich konnte nichts dafür; I couldn't — telling him the truth, ich konnte nicht umhin, ihm die Wahrheit zu sagen; to help out, aushelfen

help, die Hilfe, —, –n; with the —

of such satellites, mit Hilfe solcher
Satelliten
Henry, (der) Heinrich, –s
her (*pers. pron.*), ihr (*dat.*); sie
(*acc.*)
her (*poss. adj.*), ihr, ihre, ihr
here, hier; spring is —, der
Frühling ist gekommen; come
—!, kommen Sie her!
hero, der Held, –en, –en
hers (*poss. pron.*), ihrer, ihre, ihres;
der (die *or* das) ihre (*or* ihrige)
herself (*refl. pron.*), sich; (*intens.*)
selbst; she —, sie selbst (*or*
selber)
hesitate, zögern
high, hoch; a foot —, einen Fuß
hoch
hill, der Hügel, –s, —
him (*pers. pron.*), ihm (*dat.*); ihn
(*acc.*)
himself (*refl. pron.*), sich; (*intens.*)
selbst; he —, er selbst (*or* selber)
his (*poss. adj.*), sein, seine, sein
his (*poss. pron.*), seiner, seine,
seines; der (die *or* das) seine (*or*
seinige)
historic, historisch
history, die Geschichte, —, –n
hit, treffen, traf, getroffen, trifft;
schlagen, schlug, geschlagen,
schlägt
hold, halten, hielt, gehalten, hält;
fassen; to — together, zusám-
menhalten
holidays, die Ferien, — (*pl.*)
holy, heilig
home, das Heim, –(e)s, –e; (=
dwelling) das Haus, —es,
Häuser; (= native place) die
Heimat, —, –en; at —, zu Hause
(*or* daheim); make yourself at —,
machen Sie es sich (*dat.*) bequem!
homeland, die Heimat, —, –en
homeward, heim(wärts), nach
Hause
honest, ehrlich

honesty, die Ehrlichkeit, —; —
personified, die Ehrlichkeit selbst
honor, die Ehre, —, –n
hope, hoffen; to — for, hoffen auf
(*w. acc.*)
hope, die Hoffnung, —, –en
horse, das Pferd, –(e)s, –e
horseback: on —, zu Pferde
hostile, feindlich (gesinnt) (*w. dat.*)
hot, heiß
hotel, das Gasthaus, –es, . . . häuser;
das Hotel, –s, –s
hotelkeeper, der Wirt, –(e)s, –e
hour, die Stunde, —, –n; half an
—, eine halbe Stunde; an — and
a half, anderthalb Stunden; zero
—, die Angriffszeit, —, die Nullzeit, —
house, das Haus, –es, Häuser; at
his —, bei ihm; at whose —?,
bei wem?
how, wie; — much?, wieviel?; —
many?, wie viele?; — long (a
time)?, wie lange?; — are you?,
wie geht es Ihnen?; — do you
know that?, woher wissen Sie das?;
— much does it cost?, was kostet
es?
however, aber; doch
huge, ungeheuer; riesig (*gigantic,
immense*)
humor (= mood), die Laune, —,
–n; he is in a good —, er ist
guter Laune (*gen.*)
hundred (*num. adj.*): a —, hundert
(*no art.*)
hundred, das Hundert, –(e)s, –e
hungry, hungrig; I am —, ich bin
hungrig (*or* ich habe Hunger)
hunt (*noun*), die Jagd, —, –en
hunt, jagen; to — (= to go hunting), auf die Jagd gehen
hunter, der Jäger, –s, —
hurry, eilen (*w.* sein); sich beeilen
hurt, schaden (*w. dat.*); to — oneself, sich (*dat.*) weh tun [*or* sich
(*acc.*) verletzen]; that will —

your health, das wird Ihrer Gesundheit schaden; it hurts me, es tut mir weh

husband, der Gatte, –n, –n; der Mann, –(e)s, ¨–er

hydrogen, der Wasserstoff, –(e)s

I

I, ich; nor —, ich auch nicht

idea, der Einfall, –(e)s, ¨–e; die Idee, —, –n; that is not a bad —, das ist kein übler Einfall

idiomatic, idiomatisch

if, wenn, falls; ob (*in indir. ques.*); as —, als ob

ill, krank

imagine, sich (*dat.*) denken (eínbilden *or* vórstellen)

immediately, sogleich, gleich, sofort

impatience, die Ungeduld, —; he is burning with —, er brennt vor Ungeduld

impatient, ungeduldig

implore, bitten, bat, gebeten, bittet

importance, die Wichtigkeit, —; die Bedeutung, — (*significance*)

important, wichtig; bedeutend (*significant*)

impossible, unmöglich

impression, der Eindruck, –(e)s, ¨–e; it made a deep — on me, es hat einen tiefen Eindruck auf mich gemacht

in (*prep.*), in (*w. dat. or acc.*); — 1934, **im** Jahre 1934; — German, auf deutsch; to believe —, glauben an (*w. acc.*); to take part —, teílnehmen an (*w. dat.*)

inch, der Zoll, –(e)s, —

incombustible, unverbrennbar; — matter, unverbrennbarer Stoff

income, das Einkommen, –s, —

indeed, wirklich, in der Tat; they would be stupid —!, sie wären schön dumm!

independent, unabhängig

Indian, der Indianer, –s, —

individual, (*adj.*), einzeln

individual, das Individuum, –s, Individuen

industrious, fleißig

industry (= diligence), der Fleiß, –es

inevitable, unvermeidlich

information, die Nachricht, —, –en; die Auskunft, —, ¨–e

inhabit, bewohnen

inhabitant, der Einwohner, –s, —

injustice, das Unrecht, –(e)s

ink, die Tinte, —, –n

inn, das Gasthaus, –es, . . . häuser

in order to (*conj.*), damit

in order to (*prep.*), um . . . zu; — learn, um zu lernen

inquire about, sich erkundigen nach

insist (up)on, bestehen auf (*usually w. dat.; occasionally w. acc.*)

in spite of (*prep.*), trotz (*w. gen.*)

instance, das Beispiel, –(e)s, –e; for — (*abbr. e.g.*), zum Beispiel (*abbr.* z.B.)

instead of (*prep.*), (an)statt (*w. gen.*); — working, anstatt **zu** arbeiten

intend, beabsichtigen; vórhaben; wollen, wollte, gewollt, will; he intends to leave tomorrow, er will morgen abfahren

intentionally, absichtlich

interest, das Interesse, –s, –n; to bear — (on money), Zinsen tragen; to take an — in, sich interessieren für (*w. acc.*)

interested: to be — in (= to take an interest in), sich interessieren für (*w. acc.*)

interesting, interessant

interplanetary aviation, die Weltraumschiffahrt, — (see entries under **world space**)

interrupt, unterbréchen

into (*prep.*), in (*w. acc.*)
introduce, vórstellen; he introduced him to me, er hat ihn mir vorgestellt
in vain, vergebens, umsonst
invention, die Erfindung, —, –en
investigate, untersúchen
investigation, die Forschung, —, –en; die Untersuchung, —, –en; die Prüfung, —, –en
investigator, der Forscher, –s, —; der Untersucher, –s, —
invite, einladen, lud ein, eingeladen, ladet (*or* lädt) ein; he invited me for supper, er hat mich zum Abendessen eingeladen
iron, das Eisen, –s
island, die Insel, —, –n
it, es (*nom. & acc.*); ihm (*dat.*); is — he?, ist er es?; — is he, er ist es (*When referring to* **things** *after prepositions governing the dative and accusative,* **es** *and* **ihm** *are usually replaced by* **da**-*forms:* with —, damit; on —, darauf; *etc.*)
Italian, italienisch
Italy, (das) Italien, –s
its, sein (*refers to masc. & neut. nouns*); ihr (*refers to fem. nouns*)

J

January, der Januar, –(s), –e
jet (aircraft), das Strahlflugzeug, –(e)s, –e
John, (der) Johann, –s
joke (*noun*), der Scherz, –es, –e; der Spaß, es, ̈–e
joke, scherzen
joy, die Freude, —, –n
judge, der Richter, –s, —
July, der Juli, –(s), –s
jump, springen, sprang, ist gesprungen; to — (in) through the window, zum Fenster hereínspringen (*or* hineínspringen) (*cf.* § 70 **H**)
June, der Juni, –(s), –s

just (*adj.*), gerecht
just (*adv.*), gerade; eben; — try it, versuchen Sie es nur!; — as . . . as, ebenso . . . wie; she is — as industrious as he, sie ist ebenso fleißig wie er
justice, die Gerechtigkeit, —, –en

K

keep, behalten, behielt, behalten, behält; he keeps his word, er hält Wort
key, der Schlüssel, –s, —
kill, töten; (= to murder) ermorden
kilometer, das Kilometer, –s, —
kind (*adj.*), gütig
kind, die Art, —, –en; what — of, was für ein (*pl.* was für)
king, der König, –(e)s, –e
kitchen, die Küche, —, –n
knee, das Knie, –s, —
knife, das Messer, –s, —
knight, der Ritter, –s, —
knighthood, das Rittertum, –s
knock at, klopfen an (*w. acc.*)
know (= to know a fact), wissen, wußte, gewußt, weiß; (= to be acquainted with) kennen, kannte, gekannt; (= to have knowledge acquired by study) können, konnte, gekonnt, kann; how do you — that?, woher wissen Sie das?; do you — what you are about?, sind Sie Ihrer Sache gewiß?; he knows German, er kann Deutsch
knowledge, die Kenntnis, —, –se; (= science) die Wissenschaft, —, –en
known (= well-known), bekannt

L

labor, die Arbeit, —, –en
lady, die Dame, —, –n
lamp, die Lampe, —, –n

land, das Land, –(e)s, ˵er; native
—, das Vaterland
land, landen, landete, ist gelandet;
to — on, landen auf (*w. dat.*)
landscape, die Landschaft, —, –en
language, die Sprache, —, –n
lap, der Schoß, –es, ˵e
large, groß
last (*adj.*), letzt–; before (the) —,
vorletzt–
last, dauern
late, spät; to come —, zu spät
kommen
later on, späterhin
latter, der (die, das) letztere;
dieser (*esp. when used with* jener
in specific contrast)
laugh, lachen; to — at, aúslachen
(*tr.*), lachen über (*w. acc.*)
laughter, das Lachen, –s; there
was much —, es wurde viel
gelacht
law, das Gesetz, –es, –e: — of the
conservation of energy, das Ener-
gieerhaltungsgesetz, –es; das
Gesetz von der Erhaltung der
Energie (*or* Kraft)
lawyer, der Advokat, –en, –en
lay, legen
layer of air, die Luftschicht, —, –en
laziness, die Faulheit, —
lazy, faul
lead (*noun*), das Blei, –(e)s, –e
lead, führen, leiten
leader, der Führer, –s, —
leaf, das Blatt, –(e)s, ˵er
leap, spring, sprang, ist gesprungen
leap, der Sprung, –(e)s, ˵e
learn, lernen; erfahren (*experience,
esp. discover knowledge*); to —
about, erfahren über (*w. acc.*)
least (*adv.*): at —, wenigstens; —
of all, am allerwenigsten
leather, das Leder, –s, —
leave, lassen, ließ, gelassen, läßt;
(= to bequeath) hinterlássen; (=
to depart) abfahren, fuhr ab, ist

abgefahren, fährt ab; to —
behind (= to forsake), verlassen,
verließ, verlassen, verläßt; to
take —, sich empfehlen, empfahl,
empfohlen, empfiehlt
lecture, die Vorlesung, —, –en;
der Vortrag, –(e)s, ˵e
left (*adj.*), link–
left (*adv.*), links; on the —, links;
to the —, nach links
left over, übrig; I have only three
bottles —, ich habe nur drei
Flaschen übrig
leg, das Bein, –(e)s, –e
legend, die Sage, —, –n; according
to the —, der Sage nach
lend, leihen, lieh, geliehen
less, weniger
lesson, die Lektion, —, –en; die
Aufgabe, —, –n; to take —s,
Stunden nehmen
let, lassen, ließ, gelassen, läßt
let know, wissen lassen; let me
know, lassen Sie mich wissen
letter, der Brief, –(e)s, –e
library, die Bibliothek, —, –en; to
take books out of (= borrow
books from) the —, Bücher aus
der Bibliothek entnehmen
lie (= falsehood), die Lüge, —, –n
lie (= to be prostrate *or* situated),
liegen, lag, gelegen; (= to tell a
lie) lügen, log, gelogen; to —
down, sich (hín)legen
life, das Leben, –s, —; to lead a
simple —, ein einfaches Leben
führen
lift, heben, hob, gehoben; aúfheben
light (*adj.*) (= bright), hell; (= of
small weight) leicht
light (*noun*), das Licht, –(e)s, –er
light, ánzünden
like (*adj.*), gleich (*w. dat.*); ähnlich
(*w. dat.*)
like, gern haben; gefallen (*w. dat.*);
mögen; to be — (= to resemble),
gleichen (*w. dat.*), ähnlich sein (*w.*

dat.); I — it, ich habe es gern (es gefällt mir *or* ich mag es); I — to read, ich lese gern; I — best to read, ich lese am liebsten; he would — to go along, er möchte mitgehen

line, die Zeile, —, –n (a printed or written line); die Linie, —, –n, *e.g.* eine gerade Linie, a straight line

lion, der Löwe, –n, –n

lip, die Lippe, —, –n

listen to, zúhören (*w. dat.*); (*tr.*) ánhören

little (*as to size*), klein; (*as to quantity*) wenig; a —, ein wenig (*or* bißchen)

live, leben; (= dwell) wohnen; to — in (*tr.*), bewohnen

long (*adj.*), lang; a foot —, einen Fuß lang

long (*adv.*) (= for a long time), lange; how — (a time)?, wie lange?

longer, länger; no — (*temp.*), nicht mehr

long for, sich sehnen nach

look, aussehen, sah aus, ausgesehen, sieht aus; to — at, ánsehen; to — for, suchen; to — forward with pleasure to, sich freuen auf (*w. acc.*); to — out of the window, zum Fenster hinaússehen; he looks as if he were ill, er sieht aus, als ob er krank wäre; I am looking for it, ich suche es; she is looking out of the window, sie sieht zum Fenster hinaus

Lord, der Herr, –n

lose, verlieren, verlor, verloren; to — one's way, sich verirren

loss, der Verlust, –es, –e

loud, laut

love, lieben; to fall in — with, sich verlieben in (*w. acc.*)

love, die Liebe, —, –n

luck: good —, das Glück, –(e)s

lunch, der Imbiß, Imbisses, Imbisse

M

magazine, die Zeitschrift, —, –en

maiden, die Jungfrau, —, –en

mail (*noun*), die Post, —, –en

mail, auf die Post bringen; he mailed the letter, er hat den Brief auf die Post gebracht

maintain (= to assert), behaupten

make, machen; to — up (*work, lessons, etc.*), náchholen; to — up one's mind, sich entschließen; to — money, Geld verdienen; to — a speech, eine Rede halten; that makes no difference, das macht nichts aus; he was made king, man machte ihn zum König; I made his acquaintance, ich lernte ihn kennen

man, der Mann, –(e)s, ¨er; (= human being) der Mensch, –en, –en

manner, die Weise, —, –n; in this —, auf diese Weise

many, viele; — a, mancher; — things, vieles; — beautiful things, viel Schönes; how —?, wie viele?

March, der März, –(es), –e

mark (*German coin*), die Mark, —; school — (= grade), die Zensur, —, –en; die Note, —, –n

market, der Markt, –(e)s, ¨e

married, verheiratet

marry, heiraten; sich verheiraten

master, der Herr, –n, –en

mathematics, die Mathematik, —

matter, die Sache, —, –n; die Angelegenheit, —, –en; what is the — with him?, was fehlt ihm?; what is the —?, was ist los?; that is a — of course, das versteht sich (von selbst)

May, der Mai, –(e)s, –e

may (= to be permitted), dürfen, durfte, gedurft, darf; mögen, mochte, gemocht, mag; that —

be, das mag (*or* kann) sein; whoever she — be, wer sie auch sein
mag; however that — be, wie
das auch sein mag (*or* wie dem
auch sei)

mayor, der Bürgermeister, –s, —

me, mir (*dat.*); mich (*acc.*)

meadow, die Wiese, —, –n

meal, das Essen, –s, —; die
Mahlzeit, —, –en

mean, meinen (*of people*); bedeuten (*of things*); what (in the world)
do you —?, was fällt Ihnen denn
ein?

means: by no —, keineswegs,
durchaus nicht

means (= expedient, contrivance),
das Mittel, –s, — (*pl. often* = re-
sources)

meantime: in the —, inzwischen,
währenddessen

meanwhile, *cf.* **meantime**

meat, das Fleisch, –es

medicine, die Medizin, —, –en

medieval, mittelalterlich

meet, begegnen, begegnete, ist
begegnet (*w. dat.*); treffen, traf,
getroffen, trifft (*w. acc.*)

melt, schmelzen, schmolz, ist geschmolzen, schmilzt

member, das Mitglied, –(e)s,
–er

mention, erwähnen

merchant, der Kaufmann, –(e)s,
Kaufleute

merry, fröhlich, lustig, munter

meter, das Meter, –s, — (39.37 U.S.
inches)

middle, die Mitte, —; in the — of
the forest, mitten (*adv.*) im
Walde

midnight, die Mitternacht, —

might (*noun*), die Macht, —, ¨e;
die Gewalt, —, –en

might, dürfte, könnte; — I ask
you for the book?, dürfte ich Sie
um das Buch bitten?; that —

(possibly) be, das könnte (*or* dürfte)
sein

mighty, mächtig, gewaltig

mile, die Meile, —, –n

milk, die Milch, —

miller, der Müller, –s, —

million, die Million, —, –en

millionaire, der Millionär, –s, –e

mind (= memory), das Gedächtnis,
–ses, –se; der Sinn, –(e)s, –e;
to make up one's —, sich
entschließen

mine (*poss. pron.*), meiner, meine,
meines; der (die *or* das) meine (*or*
meinige); a friend of —, ein
Freund von mir

minute, die Minute, —, –n

mirror, der Spiegel, –s, —

misfortune, das Unglück, –(e)s,
–sfälle

misplace, verlegen

miss (*friends*), vermissen; (*a train*)
versäumen, verpassen

mistake, der Fehler, –s, —

mistaken, to be —, sich irren

misunderstand, mißverstehen,
mißverstand, mißverstanden

model, das Muster, –s, — (*pattern,
sample*)

model airplane, das Musterflug-
zeug, –s, –e; das Flugzeug-
modell, –s, –e

modern, modern

modest, bescheiden

moment, der Augenblick, –(e)s, –e;
wait a —, warten Sie einen
Augenblick!

monarchy, die Monarchie, —, –n

money, das Geld, –(e)s, –er; to
make —, Geld verdienen; to
save (spend, squander) —, Geld
sparen (aúsgeben, verschwenden)

month, der Monat, –(e)s, –e; what
day of the — is it?, der wievielte
ist (*or* den wievielten haben wir)
heute?; for months, monatelang

monthly, monatlich

moon, der Mond, –(e)s, –e

more, mehr; — and —, immer, mehr; — beautiful, schöner; the — I read Goethe, the — I admire him, **je mehr** ich Goethe lese, **desto mehr** bewundere ich ihn

morning, der Morgen, –s, —; good —, guten Morgen!; tomorrow —, morgen früh; early in the —, frühmorgens; all — (*duration of time*), den ganzen Morgen (*Cf.* **afternoon** *for similar idioms and phrases with* **morning.**)

mortal, sterblich

most (*adj.*), meist–; — people, die meisten Leute (*Note that* meist– must *be preceded by the definite article.*)

most (*adv.*), am meisten; — (= highly) interesting, höchst interessant

mostly, meistens, meistenteils

mother, die Mutter, —, ̈

mother-in-law, die Schwiegermutter, —, ̈

mountain, der Berg, –(e)s, –e; we are going to the —s, wir gehen in die Berge (*or* ins Gebirge)

mouse, die Maus, —, Mäuse

mouth (*of a pers.*), der Mund, –(e)s, Münder (rarely Munde and Münde); (*of an animal*) das Maul, –(e)s, ̈er; (*of a river*) die Mündung, —, –en

move (*tr.*), bewegen; (*intr.*) ziehen, zog, ist gezogen; (*refl.*) sich bewegen (*or* rühren); (= to change one's place of residence) sich úmziehen; don't — from the spot!, rühren Sie sich nicht von der Stelle!; I have moved, ich bin umgezogen

movie, der Film, –s, –e; is there a good movie playing tonight?, gibt's heute abend einen guten Film?

movies, das Kino, –s, –s; we rarely go to the movies, wir gehen selten ins Kino.

Mr., Herr; — Wagner's overcoat, Herrn Wagners Mantel

Mrs., Frau; — Wagner's gloves, Frau Wagners Handschuhe

much (*quantity*), viel; (*degree*) sehr; how —?, wieviel?; how — does it cost?, was kostet es?; twice as —, zweimal soviel; he suffers —, er leidet sehr

Munich, (das) München, –s; of — (*adj.*), Münch(e)ner (*indecl.*)

museum, das Museum, –s, Museen

music, die Musik, —

must, müssen; you — **not** do that, das **dürfen** Sie **nicht** tun

my (*poss. adj.*), mein, meine, mein; for — sake, um meinetwillen

myself (*refl. pron.*), mich (*acc.*); mir (*dat.*); I — (*intens.*), ich selbst (*or* selber); I seat — (*or* sit down), ich setze **mich**; I hurt —, ich habe **mir** weh getan

N

nail, der Nagel, –s, ̈

naked, nackt; with the — eye, mit bloßem Auge

name (*noun*), der Name, –ns, –n; his — is, er heißt

name, nennen, nannte, genannt; to be named (*or* called), heißen, hieß, geheißen

narrow, eng

nation, das Volk, –(e)s, ̈er; die Nation, —, –en

native land, das Vaterland, –(e)s, ̈er

natural(ly), natürlich

nature, die Natur, —, –en

near, nah(e) (*w. dat.*); — them, in ihrer Nähe (*or* ihnen nahe)

necessary, nötig

neck, der Hals, –es, Hälse

need, brauchen, nötig haben, bedürfen (*w. gen.*)

need, die Not, —, ̈e; in — of repair (*adj.*), ausbesserungsbedürftig

neighbor, (*male*) der Nachbar, –s (*or* –n), –n; (*female*) die Nachbarin, —, –nen

neither (*conj.*), weder; — ... nor, weder ... noch; — the father nor the mother, weder der Vater noch die Mutter

nest, das Nest, –es, –er

Netherlands, die Niederlande, — (*pl.*)

network, das Netz, –es, –e; das Netzwerk, –(e)s, –e; — communication, der Netzverkehr, –s

never, nie(mals)

nevertheless, trotzdem, dessenungeachtet

new, neu; the — year, das neue Jahr

news, die Nachricht, —, –en; die Neuigkeit, —, –en; what's the —?, was gibt's Neues?

newspaper, die Zeitung, —, –en

New Year('s Day), das Neujahr, –(e)s, –e

next, nächst–; the — (= adjoining) room, das Nebenzimmer

night, die Nacht, —, ̈e; at —, in der Nacht; last —, gestern nacht (*or* abend), vorige Nacht; one — (*indef. time*), eines Nachts

nine (*num. adj.*), neun

nine (*figure*), die Neun, —, –en

ninth, neunt–

no (*adj.*), kein, keine, kein; — one, keiner; niemand, –(e)s; — one else, niemand anders, sonst niemand; — such, kein solch

no (*adv.*), nein; — more, nicht mehr

nobility, der Adel, –s

noble, edel; vornehm

nobody, niemand, –(e)s

none (*pron.*), keiner, keine, keines

nonsense, der Unsinn, –(e)s

nor, noch; neither ... —, weder ... noch; — I, ich auch nicht

north, der Norden, –s; — of, nördlich von (*w. dat.*)

northeast (*adj.*), nordöstlich

northeast, der Nordosten, –s

northwest (*adj.*), nordwestlich

northwest, der Nordwesten, –s

nose, die Nase, —, –n

not, nicht; — a, kein; — at all, gar nicht; — yet, noch nicht; — even, nicht einmal; — only ... but also, nicht nur ... sondern auch; — until seven o'clock, erst um sieben Uhr; is it (was it, will he, *etc.*) —?, nicht wahr? (= French "*n'est-ce pas*"?; *always implies an affirmative answer*)

notebook, das Heft, –(e)s, –e

nothing, nichts; — at all, gar nichts; — (that) he has, nichts, was er hat; — new, nichts Neues; — will come of it, nichts wird daraus werden

notice, bemerken

November, der November, –(s), —

now, jetzt

nowadays, heutzutage

nowhere, nirgendwo, nirgends

number, die Nummer, —, –n (*cipher, size; — of a work*); die Zahl, —, –en (*e.g.*, die geraden Zahlen, the even numbers)

numerous, zahlreich

nurse (*noun*), die Krankenschwester, —, –n

nurse, pflegen

O

obey, gehorchen (*w. dat.*)

objection: I have no — to that, ich habe nichts dagegen

observe (= to look at), betrachten; bemerken; beobachten (*notice, e.g.*, phenomena)

obstacle, das Hindernis, –ses, –se

occasionally, dann und wann, gelegentlich

occupy (= to live in), bewohnen (*w. dir. obj.*), wohnen in (*w. dat.*); (= to busy oneself) sich beschäftigen; take possession of, okkupieren, besetzen

occur to, einfallen, fiel ein, ist eingefallen, fällt ein (*w. dat.*); that never occurred to me, das ist mir nie eingefallen

ocean, der Ozean, –s, –e; — of ice, der Eis-Ozean

o'clock: what — is it?, wieviel Uhr ist es?; at two —, um zwei Uhr

of (*prep.*), von (*w. dat.*); — course, natürlich, selbstverständlich, das versteht sich (von selbst); I think — him, ich denke an ihn; full —, voll(er); the square is full — people, der Platz ist voll(er) Menschen; (*German often omits of*: the city — Munich, die Stadt München; a pound — butter, ein Pfund Butter.)

offer, bieten, bot, geboten; ánbieten

office (= post), das Amt, –(e)s, ̈–er; (= place of business) das Bureau (*or* Büro), –s, –s

official, der Beamte, –n, –n (*w. adj. decl.*); an —, ein Beamter

official (*adj.*), offiziell, amtlich

official record, der offizielle Rekord, –s

often, oft

old, alt; — age, das Alter, –s

on (*prep.*), auf, an (*w. dat. or acc.*); — Monday, am Montag (*or* Montags); — my account, meinetwegen; — the condition that, unter der Bedingung, daß

once, einmal; at —, sogleich, gleich, sofort; — upon a time there was, es war einmal; — more, noch einmal

one (*num. adj.*), ein; (= single) einzig; — and a half, anderthalb

one (*indef. art.*), ein, eine, ein

one (*pron.*), einer, eine, ein(e)s; man (*indef.*); which —?, welcher?; — of the pupils, einer von den Schülern; — does it, **man** tut es; it hurts —, es tut **einem** weh (*Note that* **man** *occurs only in the nominative;* **eines, einem,** *and* **einen** *are used for the other cases.*)

only (*adj.*), einzig

only (*adv.*), nur, bloß; (= not yet more than) erst; not — . . . but also, nicht nur . . . sondern auch; the boy is — four years old, der Knabe ist erst vier Jahre alt; it is — two o'clock, es ist erst zwei Uhr

open (*adj.*), offen

open, öffen, aúfmachen

opinion, die Meinung, —, –en

opportunity, die Gelegenheit, —, –en

opposite (*prep.*), gegenüber (*w. dat.*); we live — the park, wir wohnen dem Park gegenüber

or, oder; either . . . —, entweder . . . oder

oral, mündlich

orange, die Orange, —, –n, die Apfelsine, —, –n

orator, der Redner, –s, —

order (*noun*) (= command), der Befehl, –(e)s, –e; (= arrangement) die Ordnung, —, –en; to give an — for, bestellen; to put something in —, etwas in Ordnung bringen; it might perhaps be in —, es wäre wohl an der Zeit; in — to (*conj.*), damit; (*prep.*) um . . . zu (*w. inf.*)

order, befehlen, befahl, befohlen, befiehlt (*w. dat.*); (= to give an order for) bestellen; to — a taxi, ein Taxi bestellen (Taxi *is usually neut. in modern German*)

order take-off (*or* **launch**), der Startbefehl, –s, –e

originally, ursprünglich

originate, entstehen, entspringen (*both str. & w.* sein)

other (*adj.*), ander–

other (*pron.*), der (die *or* das) andere, (*pl.*) die anderen; they love each —, sie lieben einander (*or* sich)

otherwise (= else), sonst; anders, auf andere Weise

ought (= should), sollte (*imperf. subj. of* **sollen**); I — to work, ich sollte arbeiten

our (*poss. adj.*), unser, unsere, unser

ours (*poss. pron.*), uns(e)rer, uns(e)re, uns(e)res; der (die *or* das) unsrige [*or* uns(e)re)]

ourselves (*refl.*), **uns** (*dat. & acc.*); (*intens.*) we —, wir **selbst** (*or* **selber**)

out (*w. vbs. of motion*), hinaus, heraus; (= outside) draußen; (= not at home) nicht zu Hause, ausgegangen

out of (*prep.*), aus (*w. dat.*); — what?, woraus?; — it, daraus

outside, draußen; — of (*prep.*), außerhalb (*w. gen.*)

over (*prep.*), über (*w. dat. or acc.*)

over (*adv.*), vorüber; (*to this side*) herüber; (*to that side*) hinüber; (*on the other side*) drüben; (= in excess) übrig; (= past) vorüber; I have only ten marks left —, ich habe nur zehn Mark übrig; winter is —, der Winter ist vorüber

overcoat, der Überrock, –(e)s, ̈e; der Mantel, –s, ̈

overcome, überwínden, überwánd, überwúnden

own (*adj.*), eigen

own, besitzen, besaß, besessen

P

page, die Seite, —, –n

pain, der Schmerz, –es, –en; frantic with —, toll vor Schmerz

paint, malen; anstreichen, strich an, angestrichen (*as a house*)

painter, der Maler, –s, —

painting, das Gemälde, –s, —

pair, das Paar, –(e)s, –e; a — of gloves, ein Paar Handschuhe

palace, der Palast, –(e)s, ̈e

pale, blaß

paper, das Papier, –s, –e; (= newspaper) die Zeitung, —, –en

pardon (*noun*), die Verzeihung, —; I beg your —, (ich bitte um) Verzeihung!

pardon, entschuldigen (*wk. w. acc.*); verzeihen, verzieh, verziehen (*w. dat.*)

parents, die Eltern, — (*pl.*)

park, der Park, –(e)s, –e

part (*noun*), der Teil, –(e)s, –e; for the most —, meistens, meistenteils

part (= to take leave), Abschied nehmen, sich verabschieden

party (= social gathering), die Gesellschaft, —, –en; (= picnic) die Landpartie, —, –n; (= political party) die Partei, —, –en

pass (= to elapse), vergehen, verging, ist vergangen; [= to spend (*time*)] verbringen, verbrachte, verbracht; to — by, vorübergehen, ging vorüber, ist vorübergegangen (*w. an & dat.*); vorbeigehen (*w. sein, an & dat.*); to — an examination, eine Prüfung (*or* ein Examen) bestehen (*str.*); how do you — (= spend) your leisure hours?, wie verbringen Sie Ihre Mußestunden?; time passes, die Zeit vergeht

passenger, der Passagier, –s, –e

past (*adv.*), vorüber; summer is —, der Sommer ist vorüber; half — twelve, halb eins

past, die Vergangenheit, —

path, der Pfad, –(e)s, –e

patience, die Geduld, —

patient, geduldig

pay, bezahlen; — attention, aufpassen, paßte auf, aufgepaßt

pea, die Erbse, —, –n

peace, der Friede(n), –ns

peasant, der Bauer, –s (*or* –n), –n

peculiar, sonderbar

pen, die Feder, —, –n; fountain —, die Füllfeder, —, –n

pencil, der Bleistift, –(e)s, –e

people, die Leute, — (*pl.*); die Menschen, — (*pl. of* der Mensch); (= nation) das Volk, –(e)s, ̈–er; man (*indef. pron. w. sing. vb.*)

pepper, der Pfeffer, –s, —

perceive, gewahr werden (*w. gen.*)

perhaps, vielleicht; that might — be in order, das wäre wohl an der Zeit

permission, die Erlaubnis, —, –se

permit, erlauben (*w. dat.*)

permitted, erlaubt; to be —, dürfen, durfte, gedurft, darf

personified: kindness —, die Güte selbst

persuade, überréden, überrédete, überrédet (*w. acc. of the pers.*)

physician, der Arzt, –es, ̈–e

physicist, der Physiker, –s, —; der Naturforscher, –s, —

physics, die Physik, —; die Naturlehre, —

piano, das Klavier, –s, –e; to play the —, Klavier (*no art.*) spielen

pick, pflücken; to — up, aúfheben

pick up (*fig., ref. to radio messages, etc.*), aufnehmen, nahm auf, aufgenommen, nimmt auf

picture, das Bild, –(e)s, –er; to take —s of, Aufnahmen machen von (*w. dat.*)

picturesque, malerisch

piece, das Stück, –(e)s, –e; to tear to —s, zerreißen, zerriß, zerrissen

pipe, die Pfeife, —, –n

pity (*noun*), das Mitleid, –(e)s; that

would be a —, das wäre schade!; what a —!, schade!; for —'s sake!, um Gottes (*or* Himmels) willen!

pity, sich erbarmen (*w. gen. or* über *& acc.*); Mitleid haben mit (*w. dat.*)

place (*noun*), der Platz, –es, ̈–e; die Stelle, —, –n; (= locality) der Ort, –(e)s, –e (*or rarely* ̈–er); I would do it if I were in your —, ich täte es an Ihrer Stelle

place, (*in a horizontal position*) legen; (*in an upright position*) stellen; (= to set) setzen

plan (*noun*), der Plan, –(e)s, ̈–e; to carry out a —, einen Plan aúsführen

plan, planen

planet, der Planet, –en, –en

planetary, planetarisch

plant (*noun*), die Pflanze, —, –n

plant, pflanzen

plate, der Teller, –s, —

play, spielen; to — the piano, Klavier (*no art.*) spielen; to — ball, Ball spielen

pleasant, angenehm

please, gefallen, gefiel, gefallen, gefällt (*w. dat.*); (if you) —, bitte; it pleases me (= I like it), es gefällt mir

pleasure, die Freude, —, –n; das Vergnügen, –s, —; to look forward with —, sich freuen auf (*w. acc.*); I look forward with — to the vacation, ich freue mich auf die Ferien; I take — in it, ich finde meine Freude daran; it gives me —, es **macht** mir Freude

plum, die Pflaume, —, –n

pocket, die Tasche, —, –n

poem, das Gedicht, –(e)s, –e; a — by Goethe, ein Gedicht von Goethe

poet, der Dichter, –s, —

poetic, poetisch

point (*noun*), der Punkt, –(e)s, –e; he was on the — of going out, er wollte eben ausgehen (*or* er war im Begriff auszugehen)

point, zeigen

police, die Polizei, —

policeman, der Polizist, –en, –en; der Schutzmann, –(e)s, ⸚er (*or* Schutzleute); der Schupo, –s, –s (*abbr. for* der Schutzpolizist)

polite, höflich; — to, höflich gegen

poor (*adj.*), arm; — in, arm an (*w. dat.*)

poor person, der (*or* die) Arme, (*pl.*) die Armen

popular, beliebt

population, die Bevölkerung, —, –en

porter, der Gepäckträger, –s, —

position, die Stellung, —, –en; die Stelle, —, –n (*usually denotes a more menial position; may also mean* place)

possess, besitzen, besaß, besessen

possession, der Besitz, –es; to take — of, etwas (*acc.*) in Besitz nehmen

possessor, der Besitzer, –s, —

possible, möglich [*The idea of possibility is often brought out by the subjunctive (cf. § 79 C).*]

post office, das Postamt, –(e)s, ⸚er; die Post, —, –en

postpone, aufschieben, schob auf, aufgeschoben; — to, verschieben auf (*w. acc.*)

potato, die Kartoffel, —, –n

pound, das Pfund, –(e)s, –e; half a —, ein halbes Pfund; a — and a half, anderthalb Pfund; two marks a —, zwei Mark das Pfund

pour, gießen, goß, gegossen

powder (*for the face*), der Puder, –s, —

power, die Macht, —, ⸚e; die Gewalt, —, –en

powerful, mächtig, gewaltig

practice, üben (*often refl.*); he practices fencing (swimming), er übt sich im Fechten (Schwimmen)

praise (*noun*), das Lob, –(e)s

praise, loben

pray, beten

prayer, das Gebet, –(e)s, –e

prefer, vorziehen, zog vor, vorgezogen; lieber haben; I — it, ich habe es lieber; I — to do it, ich tue es lieber

prepare, bereiten; vórbereiten, often *refl.,* to — for, sich vórbereiten auf (*w. acc.*); I was preparing for the examination, ich bereitete mich auf die Prüfung vor

prepared, bereit; vorbereitet; he is — for the worst, er ist auf das Schlimmste gefaßt

present (*adj.*) (*in attendance*), anwesend; (= at present) gegenwärtig

present (= gift), das Geschenk, –(e)s, –e; (*time*) die Gegenwart, —; for the — (= time being), vorläufig (*adv.*)

presént (*as a gift*), schenken

preserve, erhalten, erhielt, erhalten, erhält

president, der Präsident, –en, –en

press (*clothes*), bügeln

pretty, hübsch, schön

pride, der Stolz, –es

prince, der Fürst, –en, –en; der Prinz, –en, –en

princess, die Prinzessin, —, –nen

print, drucken

prison, das Gefängnis, –ses, –se

prisoner, der Gefangene (*w. adj. decl.*); a —, ein Gefangen**er**

prize, der Preis, –es, –e

probability, die Wahrscheinlichkeit, —, –en

probably, wahrscheinlich; wohl

(*often w. fut. tenses*); he was —
twenty years old, er mochte wohl
zwanzig Jahre alt sein

procession, der Zug, –(e)s, ¨e

profess, wollen, wollte, gewollt,
will; he professes to have a rich
uncle, er will einen reichen Onkel
haben

professor, der Professor, –s, –en;
he is a professor **at** the university,
er ist Professor **an** der Universität

prominent, hervorragend

promise (*noun*), das Versprechen,
–s, —

promise, versprechen, versprach,
versprochen, verspricht

pronounce, aússprechen; he always
pronounces the word wrong, er
spricht das Wort immer falsch aus

proof, der Beweis, –es, –e

property, das Eigentum, –(e)s, ¨er

protect, (be)schützen

proud, stolz; — of, stolz auf (*w.
acc.*)

prove, beweisen, bewies, bewiesen

proverb, das Sprichwort, –(e)s,
¨er

provoked: to be — at, sich ärgern
über (*w. acc.*)

Prussia, (das) Preußen, –s

public(ly), öffentlich; — library,
die Volksbibliothek, —, –en

punctual(ly), pünktlich

punish, strafen, bestrafen

pupil, (*male*) der Schüler, –s, —;
(*female*) die Schülerin, —, –nen

pure, rein

pursue, verfolgen (*w. acc.*)

put (*in a horizontal position*) legen;
(*in an upright position*) stellen;
(= to set) setzen; híntun; to — a
question, eine Frage stellen; — it
there, tun Sie es hin!

put on (*as clothes, shoes*) [sich (*dat.*)
w. dir. obj.] anziehen, zog an,
angezogen; (*as hat, glasses*) aufsetzen, setzte auf, aufgesetzt

Q

quarrel (*noun*), der (Wort)streit,
–(e)s, –e (*or* Streitigkeiten)

quarrel, streiten, stritt, gestritten

quarter, das Viertel, –s, —; a — to
nine, ein Viertel vor neun; a —
after three, ein Viertel nach drei;
a — of an hour, eine Viertelstunde;
a — of a dollar (*or* twenty-five
cents), ein Vierteldollar (*masc.*)

queen, die Königin, —, –nen

quench, löschen

question, die Frage, —, –n; to ask
a —, eine Frage stellen; to answer a —, eine Frage beantworten
(*or* auf eine Frage antworten)

quick(ly), schnell

quiet(ly), ruhig

quiet, die Ruhe, —

quite, ganz

R

rabbit, das Kaninchen, –s, —

radiation, die Strahlung, —; cosmic —, die kosmische Strahlung,
die Weltraumstrahlung

radio, das Radio, –s, –s; to listen
to (turn on, turn off) the —, das
Radio ánhören (ánstellen, ábstellen); — set, der Radioapparat,
–(e)s, –e

radioactivity, die Radioaktivität, —

radio message, die Funkmeldung,
—, –en

radio-relay satellite, der Funk-
Relais-Satellit, –en, –en

rage, die Wut, —

railway, die Eisenbahn, —, –en;
by —, mit der Eisenbahn; —
station, der Bahnhof, –(e)s, ¨e;
elevated —, die Hochbahn, —,
–en

rain (*noun*), der Regen, –s, –fälle (*or*
Niederschläge)

rain, regnen; to — hard, stark
regnen

raincoat, der Regenmantel, –s, ⸚
raise, heben, hob, gehoben, hebt; aúfheben
rapid(ly), schnell
rare, selten
rat, die Ratte, —, –n
rather, ziemlich
reach, reichen; erreichen (*attain*); he cannot be reached by phone, er ist telefonisch nicht zu erreichen
read, lesen, las, gelesen, liest; to — aloud to, vórlesen (*w. dat. of the pers.*); to — through, zu Ende lesen
reading, das Lesen, –s
ready (= finished), fertig; (= prepared) bereit; he is — **for** everything, er ist **zu** allem bereit
real(ly), wirklich
realize, einsehen, sah ein, eingesehen, sieht ein; sich (*dat.*) etwas vórstellen
rear (= to bring up), erziehen, erzog, erzogen
reason, der Grund, –(e)s, ⸚e; for what —?, aus welchem Grunde?
receive, erhalten, erhielt, erhalten, erhält; bekommen, bekam, bekommen; (= to welcome), (freundlich) empfangen, empfing, empfangen, empfängt; (= to pick up *or* intercept, *e.g., ref.* to radio messages, *etc.*), aufnehmen, nahm auf, aufgenommen, nimmt auf
recently, neulich, kürzlich, vor kurzem
recognize, erkennen, erkannte, erkannt
recommend, empfehlen, empfahl, empfohlen, empfiehlt
reconnaissance: — satellite, der Aufklärungssatellit, –en, –en
recover (= recuperate) **from,** sich erholen von (*w. dat.*)
red, rot
reference: with — to (*w. regard to, as to*), in bezug (*or* Bezug) auf (*w. acc.*)

refuse, verweigern (*w. dat. of the pers. & acc. of the th.*)
regard: with — to, hinsichtlich (*w. gen.*)
regards, der Gruß, –es, ⸚e; best — to your father, besten Gruß an Ihren Vater
region, die Gegend, —, –en
regret, bedauern
regulate, regulieren
rejoice at, sich freuen über (*w. acc.*)
relate, erzählen
relatively, relativ; in a — short time, in relativ kurzer Zeit
reliable, zuverlässig
religion, die Religion, —, –en
rely on, sich verlassen auf (*w. acc.*)
remain, bleiben, blieb, ist geblieben; verbleiben (*esp.* to remain in a certain position)
remark (*noun*), die Bemerkung, —, –en
remark, bemerken
remarkable, merkwürdig
remember, sich erinnern [*w. gen. or* an & *acc.* (*latter customary in modern German*)], gedenken (*w. gen.*)
remind, erinnern; — me **of** that, erinnern Sie mich dar**an!**
remove (*as hat, glasses*), abnehmen, nahm ab, abgenommen, nimmt ab; (*as clothes, shoes*) ausziehen, zog aus, ausgezogen
rent (*noun*), die Miete, —, –n
rent (*from a pers.*), mieten; (*to a pers.*) vermieten
repair, ausbessern, besserte aus, ausgebessert; reparieren
repeat, wiederhólen, wiederhólte, wiederhólt
reply, antworten (*w. dat. of the pers.*) erwidern
reply, die Antwort, —, –en
report (*noun*), der Bericht, –(e)s, –e
report, berichten

represent, vertreten, vertrat, vertreten, vertritt
representative, der Vertreter, –s, —

republic, die Republik, —, –en
request (*noun*), die Bitte, —, –n
require, verlangen, fordern
research, die Forschung, —, –en
research rocket, die Forschungsrakete, —, –n
researcher (*esp. sci.* —), der Forscher, –s, —
resemble, gleichen (*w. dat.*), ähnlich sein (*w. dat.*)
reside, wohnen
respect, die Hinsicht, —, –en; in this —, in dieser Hinsicht
responsible, verantwortlich; — for, verantwortlich für
rest (*noun*), die Ruhe, —
rest, sich aúsruhen
restaurant, das Restaurant, –s, –s
result, die Folge, —, –n; as a —, zur Folge; as a — of that, infolgedessen
return (= to go back), zurückkehren, kehrte zurück, ist zurückgekehrt; (= to give back) zurückgeben, gab zurück, zurückgegeben
revolution, die Revolution, —, –en
Rhine, der Rhein, –(e)s
ribbon, das Band, –(e)s, ‒er
rich, reich; — in, reich an (*w. dat.*)
riches, der Reichtum, –(e)s, ‒er
rid of, los; he is — it, er ist es los
riddle, das Rätsel, –s, —
ride (*noun*) (= journey), die Fahrt, —, –en
ride (*on horseback*), reiten, ritt, ist geritten; (= to travel) fahren, fuhr, ist gefahren, fährt
rider, der Reiter, –s, —
right, recht; he is —, er hat recht; it serves him —, es geschieht ihm recht; to the —, nach rechts; on the —, rechts; I shall be there — **away,** ich bin **gleich** da

ring (*noun*), der Ring, –(e)s, –e
ring, läuten; klingeln; the bell is ringing, es klingelt
ripe, reif
rise (*of persons*), aufstehen, stand auf, ist aufgestanden; (*of the sun and moon*) aufgehen, ging auf, ist aufgegangen; (*of a river*) entspringen, entsprang, ist entsprungen; steigen, stieg, ist gestiegen *or* aufsteigen (*esp.* of a rocket)
river, der Fluß, Flusses, Flüsse
road, der Weg, –(e)s, –e
roar (*as of a lion*), brüllen
roast, braten, briet, gebraten, brät
rob, rauben (*w. dat. of the pers. & acc. of the th.*), berauben (*w. acc. of the pers. & gen. of the th.*); they robbed him of everything, man hat ihm alles geraubt; they robbed him of all his money, man hat ihn seines ganzen Geldes beraubt
robber, der Räuber, –s, —
rock, der Felsen, –s, —
rocket, die Rakete, —, –n
rocket research, die Raketenforschung, —, –en
roof, das Dach, –(e)s, ‒er
room, das Zimmer, –s, —; die Stube, —, –n; (= hall) der Saal, –(e)s, Säle; (= space) der Raum, –(e)s, ‒e
rope, der Strick, –(e)s, –e
rose, die Rose, —, –n
rouge, die Schminke, —, –n
round, rund
row (*noun*), die Reihe, —, –n
row, rudern
royal, königlich
ruin, die Ruine, —, –n; castle –s, Schloßruinen
rule, die Regel, —, –n; (= rulership) die Herrschaft, —, –en; as a —, in **der** Regel
run, laufen, lief, ist gelaufen, läuft; rennen, rannte, ist gerannt

S

sad, traurig

safe, sicher

said, gesagt; to be —, sollen; he is — to be rich, er soll reich sein

sake: for the — of . . ., um . . . willen; for my —, um meinetwillen; for heaven's —, um Himmels (*or* Gottes) willen!

same: the —, derselbe, dieselbe, dasselbe; it is all the — to me, es ist mir ganz gleich (*or* einerlei)

satellite, der Satellit, –en, –en

Saturday, der Samstag, -(e)s, –e; der Sonnabend, –s, –e; on —(s), am Samstag (*or* Samstags)

save (*by economizing*), sparen; (= to rescue), retten; — me the trouble, ersparen Sie mir die Mühe!

say, sagen

saying, der Spruch, –(e)s, ⸚e

scarcely, kaum

school, die Schule, —, –n; in —, in der Schule; to —, in die (*or* zur) Schule; after —, nach der Schule

schoolmate, der Schulkamerad, –en, –en

science, die Wissenschaft, —, –en

scientific, wissenschaftlich

scientist, der Wissenschaftler, –s, —; der Forscher, –s, —

scold, schelten, schalt, gescholten, schilt

scratch, kratzen

sea, die See, —, –n; das Meer, –(e)s, –e

seasick, seekrank

seasickness, die Seekrankheit, —, –en

season, die Jahreszeit, —, –en

seat, der Sitz, –es, –e; der Platz, –es, ⸚e

seated: be —, setzen Sie sich (*or* nehmen Sie Platz)!

second (*adj.*), zweit–; in the — place, zweitens

second, die Sekunde, —, –n

secret, das Geheimnis, –ses, –se

secretly, heimlich

see, sehen, sah, gesehen, sieht; — to it, sorgen Sie dafür; have you seen him **working?,** haben Sie ihn **arbeiten** sehen?

seek, suchen

seem, scheinen, schien, geschienen

seize (= to grasp), fassen; (= to take possession of) sich bemächtigen (*w. gen.*)

seldom, selten

self, selbst, selber (*For forms of the reflexive pronoun, cf.* **myself, herself, himself,** *etc.*)

sell, verkaufen

semester, das Semester, –s, —

send, senden, sandte, gesandt; schicken; to — by mail, mit der Post schicken; to — for, holen (*or* kommen) lassen; did you — for the doctor?, haben Sie den Arzt holen (*or* kommen) lassen?

sense, der Sinn, –(e)s, –e; there is no — in doing such a thing, es hat keinen Sinn, so etwas zu tun; he is not in his —s, er ist nicht bei Sinnen

sentence, der Satz, –es, ⸚e

separate, trennen

September, der September, –(s), —

serious, ernst(haft)

servant, der Diener, –s, —; — girl, das Dienstmädchen, –s, —

serve, dienen (*w. dat.*); that serves him right, das geschieht ihm recht

set (= to place, put), setzen; (*of the sun and moon*) untergehen, ging unter, ist untergegangen; to — the table, den Tisch decken

seven (*adj.*), sieben

seven (*figure*), die Sieben, —

seventeen, siebzehn

seventeenth, siebzehnt–
seventh, sieb(en)t–
several, mehrere, ein paar (*indecl.*)
severe (*as sickness*), schwer; (= strict) streng
shade, der Schatten, –s, —
shadow, *cf.* shade
shady, schattig
shall (*aux. of fut. tenses*), werden; (*to denote moral obligation*) sollen; I — go, ich werde gehen; — I (= am I to) do it?, soll ich es tun?
shape, die Gestalt, —, –en; die Form, —, –en
sharp, scharf; we left at ten o'clock —, **Punkt** zehn Uhr sind wir abgefahren
sharpen (*as a pencil*), spitzen
shave oneself, sich rasieren
shaved: to get —, sich rasieren lassen
she, sie
shine, scheinen, schien, geschienen
ship, das Schiff, –(e)s, –e
shirt, das Hemd, –(e)s, –en
shoe, der Schuh, –(e)s, –e (*cf. also* put on *and* take off)
shoot, schießen, schoß, geschossen
shore, das Ufer, –s, —
short, kurz
shot, der Schuß, Schusses, Schüsse
should (= ought), sollte (*imperf. subj. of* sollen); he — go, er sollte gehen; he — have gone, er hätte gehen sollen; I — like to travel, ich möchte (*imperf. subj. of* mögen) (gern) reisen
shout, schreien, schrie, geschrie(e)n
show, zeigen; to — honor to, Ehre erweisen (*w. dat.*)
shudder, grauen (*impers.*); I —, mir graut
sick, krank
side, die Seite, —, –n; on this — of (*prep.*), diesseits (*w. gen.*); on that — of (*prep.*), jenseits (*w. gen.*)
sight (= something worth seeing)

die Sehenswürdigkeit, —, –en; (= aspect) der Anblick, –(e)s, –e
sign (*noun*), das Zeichen, –s, —
sign, unterschreíben, unterschrieb, unterschríeben; unterzeíchnen
signature, die Unterschrift, —, –en
significance, die Bedeutung, — (*esp. of a sci. test*); die Wichtigkeit, — (*importance*)
silent (*adj.*), still, schweigsam; to be —, schweigen, schwieg, geschwiegen
silk (*adj.*), seiden
silk, die Seide, —, –n
silver (*adj.*), silbern
silver, das Silber, –s
similar, ähnlich (*w. dat.*)
simple, einfach
simply, *cf.* simple
since (*prep.*), seit (*w. dat.*); — when?, seit wann?
since (*conj.*), seitdem (*temp.*); da (*causal*)
since (*adv.*), seitdem; — then, seitdem
sincere(ly), aufrichtig; —ly yours, Ihr (ganz) ergebener
sing, singen, sang, gesungen
singer (*male*), der Sänger, –s, —; (*female*) die Sängerin, —, –nen
single (= only *or* sole), einzig; (= individual) einzeln; (= unmarried) ledig
sink (*intr.*), sinken, sank, ist gesunken (*w.* sein); versinken (*w.* sein); (*tr.*) versenken (*wk.*)
sister, die Schwester, —, –n
sit, sitzen, saß, gesessen; to — down, sich setzen
situated: to be — on, liegen (*str.*) an (*w. dat.*)
six, sechs
sixteen, sechzehn
sixteenth, sechzehnt–
sixth, sechst–
sixty, sechzig
size, die Größe, —, –n

skate (*noun*), der Schlittschuh, –(e)s, –e

skate, Schlittschuh laufen; I went skating, ich bin Schlittschuh gelaufen

skip, überspríngen, überspráng, übersprúngen; he skipped a grade, er hat eine Klasse übersprúngen

slave, der Sklave, –n, –n

sleep, schlafen, schlief, geschlafen, schläft; to go to — (= to fall asleep), eínschlafen (*w.* sein)

sleepy, schläfrig

sleeve, der Ärmel, –s, —

slide (= slip), gleiten, glitt, ist geglitten

slip, *cf.* **slide**

slow(ly), langsam

small, klein

smell, riechen, roch, gerochen; to — of, riechen nach (*w. dat.*)

smoke (*noun*), der Rauch, –(e)s

smoke, rauchen

smoking, das Rauchen, –s; — is forbidden, das Rauchen ist verboten

snore, schnarchen

snow (*noun*), der Schnee, –s

snow, schneien

so (*adv.*), so; and — forth (*abbr.* etc.), und so weiter (*abbr.* usw.)

sob, schluchzen

so-called, sogenannt

sofa, das Sofa, –s, –s

soft(ly) (*opp. of* firm & hard), weich; (*opp. of* loud) leise

soldier, der Soldat, –en, –en

solve, lösen; to — a puzzle, ein Rätsel lösen

some, etwas (*indecl.; w. sing. noun*); einige (*w. pl. noun*); — . . . or other (*adj.*), irgendein

somebody, *cf.* **someone**

someone, jemand, –(e)s; irgend jemand; — else, jemand anders (*or* sonst jemand)

something, etwas (*indecl.*); — he likes, etwas, was er gern hat; — good, etwas Gutes; — else (*or* different), etwas anderes

sometimes, dann und wann, zuweilen, gelegentlich, manchmal

somewhat, etwas; — sour, etwas sauer

somewhere, irgendwo(hin)

son, der Sohn, –(e)s, ̈e

song, das Lied, –(e)s, –er

soon, bald; as — as, sobald

sooner (= earlier), früher; (= rather) lieber

sorry: to be —, leid tun; I am — for him, er tut mir leid (*or* es tut mir leid um ihn)

sort, die Art, —, –en; what — of (a), was für ein; what — of (*pl.*), was für; all —s of, allerlei (*indecl.*)

so that, damit; (= in order to), um . . . zu (*w. pres. inf.*)

soul, die Seele, —, –n

sound (*adj.*) (= well), gesund; (= stout *or* strong), stark; (= firm) fest

sound, der Laut, –(e)s, –e

soup, die Suppe, —, –n

sour, sauer

source, die Quelle, —, –n

south, der Süden, –s; — of, südlich von (*w. dat.*)

southeast (*adj.*), südöstlich

southeast, der Südosten, –s

southwest (*adj.*), südwestlich

southwest, der Südwesten, –s

space, der Raum, –(e)s, ̈e (*see also* entries under **world space**)

space flight, der Raumflug, –(e)s, ̈e

space-flight experiment, das Raumflugexperiment, –s, –e

space-research rocket, die Raumforschungsrakete, —, –n

space ship, das Raumschiff, –(e)s, –e

space traveler, der Raumfahrer, –s, —

space wave, die Raumwelle, —,
–n; die Höhenwelle, —, –n
Spain, (das) Spanien, –s
Spanish, spanisch
spare (= unoccupied), frei; —
(= leisure) hours, die Mußestunden
speak, sprechen, sprach, gesprochen,
spricht; to — about, sprechen
über (*w. acc.*) [*or* von (*w. dat.*)]
speech, die Rede, —, –n; to make
(*or* deliver) a —, eine Rede halten
spend (*time*), verbringen, verbrachte,
verbracht; (*money*) ausgeben, gab
aus, ausgegeben, gibt aus
spit, speien, spie, gespie(e)n
spite: in — of (*prep.*), trotz (*w.
gen.*); in — of that, trotzdem,
dessenungeachtet
spoil (= pamper), verwöhnen
spring (*of water*), die Quelle, —,
–n; (*the season*) der Frühling, –s,
–e; in —, im Frühling; — is here,
der Frühling ist gekommen
squander, verschwenden, vergeuden
stamp, die Briefmarke, —, –n; two
five-cent —s, zwei Briefmarken zu
fünf Cent
stand, stehen, stand, gestanden
star, der Stern, –(e)s, –e
start (= to begin), ánfangen (*str.*),
beginnen (*str.*); (*on a journey*)
ábreisen (*wk. intr. w.* sein), sich
auf den Weg machen; (*esp. in mod.
sci.* German) starten (to take off)
starve, verhungern, verhungerte,
ist verhungert
state, der Staat, –(e)s, –en
station (= rank), der Stand, –es,
–e; (= situation) die Stelle, —,
–n; (= position) die Stellung, —,
–en; (= railroad depot) der
Bahnhof, –(e)s, –e; (= stopping
place) die Station, —, –en; die
Haltestelle, —, –n; at the —, auf
dem Bahnhof; to call for (*or* get)

someone at the —, jemand vom
Bahnhof abholen; radio (broadcasting) —, die Funkenstation, —,
–en; die Sendestation, —, –en;
der Sender, –s, —
stay, bleiben, blieb, ist geblieben;
to — at home, zu Hause bleiben
steamer, der Dampfer, –s, —; by
—, mit dem Dampfer
steel, der Stahl, –(e)s, ⁼e (*or less
common,* Stahle)
stem, der Stamm, –(e)s, ⁼e; der
Stengel, –s, —
step (*noun*), der Schritt, –(e)s, –e;
to keep —, Schritt halten
step, treten, trat, ist getreten, tritt
stick, stecken
stiff, steif
still (*adj.*), still, ruhig
still (= yet), noch, immer noch (*or*
noch immer) (*emphasizes continued
action*); (= nevertheless), doch
stingy, geizig
stocking, der Strumpf, –(e)s, ⁼e
stomach, der Magen, –s, —
stone, der Stein, –(e)s, –e
stop, halten, hielt, gehalten, hält;
ánhalten (*w.* haben); it has
stopped snowing, es hat aufgehört
zu schneien; suddenly he stopped,
plötzlich blieb er stehen; my
watch has stopped, meine Uhr
ist stehengeblieben
store, der Laden, –s, ⁼
stork, der Storch, –(e)s, ⁼e
storm, das Gewitter, –s, —
story, die Geschichte, —, –n; (*of a
house*) das Stockwerk, –(e)s, –e
(*cf.* **floor**)
stove, der Ofen, –s, ⁼
straight: a — line, eine gerade
Linie; — ahead, geradeaus (*adv.*)
straighten (**oneself**) **up,** sich áuf-
richten
strange, fremd (*w. dat.*)
stranger, der Fremde, –n, –n (*w.
adj. decl.*); a —, ein Fremd**er**; he

is a — to me, er ist mir fremd

stratosphere, die Stratosphäre, —

stratosphere flight, der Stratosphärenflug, –(e)s, ̈-e

stratosphere plane, das Stratosphärenflugzeug, –(e)s, –e

stream, der Strom, –(e)s, ̈-e

street, die Straße, —, –n; in (or on) the —, auf der Straße

street car, die Straßenbahn, —, –en; by —, mit der Straßenbahn

strict, streng

strike, schlagen, schlug, geschlagen, schlägt

strive for, streben nach (w. dat.)

strong, stark

student, der Student, –en, –en; to be a — at a university, **auf** einer Universität Student sein

study (noun), das Studium, –s, Studien; (= subject in school) das Fach, –(e)s, ̈-er

study (of students), studieren; (of pupils) lernen; to — hard, fleißig (schwer, tüchtig) studieren (or lernen)

stumble, stolpern

stupid, dumm; that would be — indeed, das wäre schön dumm!

stupidity, die Dummheit, —, –en

style, die Mode, —, –n; it is in — (or fashion), es ist (in der) Mode

subject (in school), das Fach, –(e)s, ̈-er

suburb, die Vorstadt, —, ̈-e

subway, die Untergrundbahn, —, –en

succeed, gelingen, gelang, ist gelungen (impers. w. dat.); I have not succeeded in deciphering your handwriting, es ist mir nicht gelungen, Ihre Handschrift zu entziffern

success, der Erfolg, –(e)s, –e

successful, erfolgreich

such, solcher, solche, solches; — a

storm, solch ein (or ein solches) Gewitter; he is no — fool, er ist kein solcher Narr

suddenly, plötzlich, auf einmal

suffer, leiden, litt, gelitten

sugar, der Zucker, –s

suit (of clothes), der Anzug, –(e)s, ̈-e

suit, passen (w. dat.)

suitcase, der Handkoffer, –s, —

summer, der Sommer, –s, —; in —, im Sommer

sun, die Sonne, —, –n; the — rises, die Sonne geht auf; the — sets, die Sonne geht unter

sunburnt, sonnverbrannt

Sunday, der Sonntag, –(e)s, –e

sunny, sonnig

sunrise, der Sonnenaufgang, –(e)s, ̈-e

sunset, der Sonnenuntergang, –(e)s, ̈-e

sunshine, der Sonnenschein, –(e)s

supper, das Abendessen, –s, —; after —, nach dem Abendessen; for —, zum Abendessen

sure, sicher, — of, sicher (w. gen.)

surface, die Oberfläche, —, –n; — of the earth, die Erdoberfläche

surprise (noun), die Überraschung, —, –en

surprise, überraschen, überraschte, überrascht

sweetheart, der Schatz, –es, ̈-e

swim, schwimmen, schwamm, ist geschwommen

Switzerland, die Schweiz, —

sword, das Schwert, –(e)s, –er

sympathetic(ally), mitleidsvoll

sympathy, das Mitleid, –(e)s

system, das System, –s, –e

T

table, der Tisch, –es, –e; to sit at (the) —, am Tisch(e) sitzen; to sit down at (the) —, sich an den Tisch setzen

tachometer, der Geschwindigkeitsmesser, −s, —
tail, der Schwanz, −es, ̈e
tailor, der Schneider, −s, —
take, nehmen, nahm, genommen,
nimmt; to — a walk (a trip, an
examination), einen Spaziergang
(eine Reise, eine Prüfung) machen;
to — off (as clothes, shoes), [sich
(dat.)w.dir.obj.]aúsziehen; (ashat,
glasses), ábnehmen; to — part in,
teílnehmen an (w. dat.); to —
leave, sich empfehlen, empfahl,
empfohlen, empfiehlt; will you —
tea or coffee?, wollen Sie Tee oder
Kaffee?
talk, sprechen, sprach, gesprochen,
spricht; to — about, sprechen
über (w. acc.) [or von (w. dat.)];
to — to oneself, vor sich (acc.)
hínsprechen; he talks to himself,
er spricht vor sich hin
tall, hoch; von hoher Gestalt;
groß; lang
tape recorder, das Tonbandgerät,
−s, −e
taste (noun), der Geschmack, −(e)s,
̈e
taste, schmecken; to — of,
schmecken nach (w. dat.); it
tastes of sour milk, es schmeckt
nach saurer Milch
tax, die Steuer, —, −n
tea, der Tee, −s, −s
teach, lehren (w. two accs.); she
taught him the song, sie lehrte **ihn
das Lied**
teacher (male), der Lehrer, −s, —;
(female) die Lehrerin, —, −nen
team (in a game), die Mannschaft,
—, −en
tear, reißen, riß, gerissen; — to
pieces, zerreißen
technical, technisch; — dictionary,
das Fachwörterbuch, −(e)s, ̈er;
— term (or expression), der
Fachausdruck, −(e)s, ̈e

technician, der Techniker, −s, —;
der Facharbeiter, −s, —
telegraph, telegrafieren (or telegraphieren)
(tele)phone, telefonieren (or telephonieren) he cannot be reached
by —, er ist telefonisch (adv.)
nicht zu erreichen
telescope, das Teleskop, −s, −e;
das Fernrohr, −s, −e
telescopic, teleskopisch
tell, erzählen, sagen
temperature, die Temperatur, —,
−en; influence of —, der Temperatureinfluß,...flusses,...flüsse;
— variation, die Temperaturschwankung, —, −en
temptation, die Versuchung, —,
−en
ten, zehn; — times, zehnmal
tennis, das Tennis, —
tenor, der Tenor, −s, ̈e (or rarely −e)
tent, das Zelt, −(e)s, −e
tenth, zehnt−
terrible, schrecklich
test (noun), die Prüfung, —, −en;
der Versuch, −(e)s, −e
test, prüfen
than, als
thank, danken; to — for, danken
(w. dat. of the pers.) für (w. acc.);
to — a person for something,
sich **bei** einer Person **für** etwas
bedanken
thankful, dankbar (w. dat.)
that (conj.), daß; so (= in order) —
(conj.), damit; so — (= in order
to), um . . . zu (w. pres. inf.)
that (one) (dem. adj. & pron.), jener,
jene, jenes; der, die, das; — is
not a bad idea, das ist kein übler
Einfall; on — side of (prep.),
jenseits (w. gen.)
that (rel. pron. = which), der, die,
das; welcher, welche, welches
thaw, tauen
the, der, die, das

theater, das Theater, –s, —; to go to the —, ins Theater gehen

theft, der Diebstahl, –s, ‑̈e

their (*poss. adj.*), ihr, ihre, ihr

theirs (*poss. pron.*), ihrer, ihre, ihres

them, ihnen (*dat.*); sie (*acc.*)

themselves (*refl. pron.*), sich (*dat. & acc.*); (*intens.*) selbst (*or* selber); they —, sie selbst (*or* selber)

then, dann; da; why — did he do it?, warum hat er es denn getan? [**Dann** *and* **da** *are conjunctive adverbs of time requiring the inverted word order;* **denn** *in the sense of* then *is an adverb which usually refers to some well-known fact or to some statement just expressed, and must not be confused with the causal conjunction* **denn** (for) *which requires the normal word order.*]

there, da, dort; — is (*or* are), es gibt (*w. acc.*), es ist (*or* sind) (*w. nom.*)

thereafter, danach, nachher

therefore, darum, deshalb, deswegen, daher, also (*These are all conjunctive adverbs requiring inverted word order.*)

thereupon, darauf

the . . . the (*correl.*), je . . . desto; — oftener I read the book, — better I like it, je öfter ich das Buch lese, desto besser gefällt es mir

they, sie

thick, dick; a foot —, einen Fuß dick

thief, der Dieb, –(e)s, –e

thin, dünn

thing, die Sache, —, –n; das Ding, –(e)s, –e; the main —, die Hauptsache, —, –n; the most beautiful —, das Schönste (*adj. used as a noun*); such a —, so etwas (*indecl.*); such —s, dergleichen (*indecl.*); all good —s,

alles Gute; among other —s, unter ander(e)m; many —s, vieles

think, denken, dachte, gedacht; to — of, denken an (*w. acc.*); he has **thought out** a good plan, er hat **sich** einen guten Plan **ausgedacht**

third, (*adj.*), dritt–

third, das Drittel, –s, —

thirst, der Durst, –es

thirsty, durstig

thirteenth, dreizehnt–

thirtieth, dreißigst–

thirty, dreißig

this, dieser, diese, dieses; — morning, heute **m**orgen; — evening, heute **a**bend; — afternoon, heute **n**achmittag; on — side of (*prep.*), diesseits (*w. gen.*)

thorough(ly), gründlich

thought, der Gedanke, –ns, –n

thousand (*adj.*), tausend

thousand, das Tausend, –(e)s, –e; two —, zweitausend; many —s, viele Tausende

threaten, drohen (*w. dat.*)

three, drei; — times, dreimal; of — kinds (*adj.*), dreierlei (*invar.*)

threefold, dreifach

three-legged, dreibeinig

three-stage, dreistufig; — rocket, die dreistufige Rakete; — amplifier, der Dreifachverstärker, –s, —

through (*prep.*), durch (*w. acc.*); the whole year —, das ganze Jahr hindurch

through (*adj.*) (= finished), fertig

throw, werfen, warf, geworfen, wirft

thumb, der Daumen, –s, —

thunder (*noun*), der Donner, –s, —

thunder, donnern

Thursday, der Donnerstag, –(e)s, –e

thus, so; auf diese Weise

ticket, die Fahrkarte, —, –n; — of admission, die Eintrittskarte, —, –n

tie (= cravat), die Krawatte, —, –n; der Schlips, –es, –e; die Halsbinde, —, –n

tie, binden, band, gebunden

tiger, der Tiger, –s, —

time, die Zeit, —, –en; (= occasion) das Mal, –(e)s, –e; at what —?, um wieviel Uhr?; what — is it?, wieviel Uhr ist es?; to have a good —, sich amüsieren; at the — when, zur Zeit, als (da *or* wo); for the first —, zum ersten Male (*or* zum erstenmal); for the last —, zum letzten Male (*or* zum letztenmal); (for) a long —, lange; how long a —?, wie lange?; ten —s, zehnmal; old(en) —s, die alten Zeiten

tip, das Trinkgeld, –(e)s, –er

tired, müde; he is — of life, er ist des Lebens müde; he is — of it, er ist es müde

title, der Titel, –s, —

to (*prep.*), zu, nach (*both w. dat.*); auf, in, bis (*all w. acc.*); — my brother's (house), zu meinem Bruder; (up) — the window, bis an das Fenster; to go — the theater, ins Theater gehen; to go — the country, aufs Land gehen; to go — school, in die (*or* zur) Schule gehen; (in order) —, um ... zu (*w. pres. inf.*) [*or* damit (*sub. conj.*)] (**Bis** *is often followed by another preposition which determines the case of the following noun.*)

tobacco, der Tabak, –(e)s

today, heute; a week from —, heute über acht Tage; what is —'s date?, der wievielte ist (*or* den wievielten haben wir) heute?

together, zusammen

tomato, die Tomate, —, –n

tomorrow (*adv.*), morgen; — morning, morgen früh; — afternoon, morgen nachmittag; day after —, übermorgen

tongue, die Zunge, —, –n

tonight, heute abend (*or* nacht)

too, zu; (= in addition *or* also) auch

tooth, der Zahn, –(e)s, –̈e

toothache, das Zahnweh, –(e)s; I have a —, ich habe Zahnweh (*no art.*)

top, die Spitze, —, –n; (= mountain top) der Gipfel, –s, —; at the — of, oben auf; on the — floor, im obersten Stock(werk)

toward (*prep.*), gegen (*w. acc.*)

tower, der Turm, –(e)s, –̈e

town, die Stadt, —, –̈e; in —, in der Stadt; to —, in die Stadt

toys, die Spielsachen, — (*pl.*)

train, der Zug, –(e)s, –̈e

translate, übersétzen, übersétzte, übersétzt; — into English, ins Englische übersetzen

translation, die Übersetzung, —, –en

transmission, die Übertragung, —, –en; radio (*or* broadcast) transmission, die Rundfunkübertragung

transmit, übertrágen, übertrúg, übertrágen

transparent, durchsichtig

travel, reisen, reiste, ist gereist; fahren, fuhr, ist gefahren, fährt; he travels second class, er fährt zweiter Klasse

traveler, der Reisende, –n, –n (*w. adj. decl.*); a —, ein Reisender

treason, der Verrat, –(e)s

treasure, der Schatz, –es, –̈e

treat, behandeln

tree, der Baum, –(e)s, –̈e

tremble, zittern

trick (= prank), der Streich, –(e)s, –e

trip, die Reise, —, –n; to take a —, eine Reise machen

trouble, die Mühe, —, –n; it is not worth the —, es ist nicht der Mühe wert

trouble oneself about, sich kümmern um (*w. acc.*)

true, wahr; (= faithful) treu

trunk, der Koffer, –s, —

truth, die Wahrheit, —, –en

try, versuchen

Tuesday, der Dienstag, –(e)s, –e

tune, die Melodie, —, –n (*pl. w. four syllables*)

tunnel, der Tunnel, –s, –s (*or* —)

turkey (*bird*), der Truthahn, –(e)s, ̈–e; der Puter, –s, —

Turkey, die Türkei, —

turn (*noun*), die Reihe, —, –n; it is my —, ich bin an der Reihe (*or* die Reihe ist an mir); his — has come, er ist an die Reihe gekommen

turn, kehren; wenden, wandte, gewandt; (= to become) werden; to — on (*light, gas, water*), ándrehen, (*radio*) ánstellen; to — off (*light, gas, water*), ábdrehen, (*radio*) ábstellen; to — one's back on someone, jemand (*dat.*) den Rücken zúwenden; he turned pale with (*or* from) fright, vor Schreck ist er blaß geworden

twelve, zwölf

twentieth, zwanzigst–

twenty, zwanzig

twenty-second, zweiundzwanzigst–

twice, zweimal; — as much, zweimal soviel

two, zwei; beide (*or* die beiden); his — (*or* both his) sons, seine beiden Söhne

two hundred, zweihundert

U

umbrella, der Regenschirm, –(e)s, –e

unable: to be —, nicht können; he is — to go, er kann nicht gehen

uncle, der Onkel, –s, —

under (*prep.*), unter (*w. dat. or acc.*)

understand, verstehen, verstand, verstanden; that is understood, das versteht sich (von selbst) (*or* selbstverständlich)

undertake, unternéhmen, unternáhm, unternómmen, unternímmt

undress (**oneself**), sich aúsziehen (*str.*)

unemployed (*adj.*), arbeitslos

unemployed, der Arbeitslose, –n, –n

unexpected, unerwartet

unfinished, unvollendet

unfortunately, leider

unhappy, unglücklich

unite, vereinigen

United States, die Vereinigten Staaten, — (*pl.*)

university, die Universität, —, –en; to be a student **at** the —, **auf** der Universität Student sein; to be a professor **at** the —, **an** der Universität Professor sein

unjust, ungerecht

unknown, unbekannt

unless, wenn ... nicht; (*after a neg. statement*) es sei denn, daß ...

until (*prep.*), bis (*w. acc.; often followed by another prep., which determines the case of the following noun*); not —, erst; not — seven o'clock, erst um sieben Uhr

unusual, ungewöhnlich

up, auf; — and down, auf und ab

upset, úmstürzen (*wk. tr. w.* haben; *intr. w.* sein)

upstairs, oben; he goes —, er geht nach oben (*or* die Treppe hinauf)

urge, treiben, trieb, getrieben

us, uns (*dat. and acc.*)

use (*noun*), der Gebrauch, –(e)s, ̈–e; of what — is that to you?, was nützt Ihnen das?

use, gebrauchen; to make — of, sich bedienen (*w. gen.*); Gebrauch von etwas (*dat.*) machen; verwenden, verwandte (*or* verwendete), verwandt (*or* verwendet)

used to, gewohnt (*w. acc. & no prep.*); he is — it, er ist es gewohnt (*or* **daran** gewöhnt); to become —, sich gewöhnen an (*w. acc.*); he — smoke, er pflegte zu rauchen, früher rauchte er

useful, nützlich (*w. dat.*)

usual(ly), gewöhnlich

V

vacation, die Ferien, — (*pl.*)

vain: in —, vergebens, umsonst

valuable, wertvoll

value, der Wert, –(e)s, –e

various (*adj.*), verschieden

vast, riesig; unermesslich (immeasurable)

velocity, die Geschwindigkeit, —; — of sound, die Schallgeschwindigkeit, —

velvet, der Samt, –(e)s, –e

verb, das Zeitwort, –(e)s, ˜er; das Verb(um), –s, Verben

verse, der Vers, –es, –e

very, sehr

vest, die Weste, —, –n

vicinity, die Nähe, —, –n

victim, das Opfer, –s, —

Vienna, (das) Wien, –s

view (*noun*), die Aussicht, —, –en

view, betrachten

village, das Dorf, –(e)s, ˜er

vinegar, der Essig, –s, –e

violent, heftig

virtue, die Tugend, —, –en

visit (*noun*), der Besuch, –(e)s, –e

visit, besuchen

voice, die Stimme, —, –n

volume, der Band, –(e)s, ˜e

vote (*noun*), die Stimme, —, –n

vote for, stimmen für (*w. acc.*)

W

wait, warten; to — for, warten auf (*w. acc.*)

waiter, der Kellner, –s, —

wake, aúfwecken (*tr.*); aúfwachen (*intr. w.* sein)

walk (*noun*), der Spaziergang, –(e)s, ˜e; to take a —, einen Spaziergang machen

walk, gehen, ging, ist gegangen; zu Fuß gehen

walking: to go —, spazierengehen; he went —, er ist spazierengegangen

wall, die Wand, —, ˜e; (*outside*) die Mauer, —, –n

wander, wandern (*w.* sein)

want (*noun*) (= need), die Not, —, ˜

want, wollen, wollte, gewollt, will

war, der Krieg, –(e)s, –e

ware, die Ware, —, –n

warm, warm

warn, warnen

wash, waschen, wusch, gewaschen, wäscht; to — dishes, Geschirr (*neut. sing.*) ábwaschen; I — my hands, ich wasche mi˙ die Hände; (*dir. refl.*) I — (myself), ich wasche mich

waste (= squander), verschwenden

wastepaper basket, der Papierkorb, –(e)s, ˜e

watch (*noun*), die (Taschen)uhr, —, –en

watch, bewachen

water, das Wasser, –s, —

wave, die Welle, —, –n

way, der Weg, –(e)s, –e; go your —, gehe (*or* ziehe) deines Weges!

we, wir

weak, schwach

wear, tragen, trug, getragen, trägt

wear out, abnutzen, nutzte ab, abgenutzt

wearability, die Abnutzbarkeit, —

weather, das Wetter, –s, —; — forecast, die Wettervoraussage, —, –n; — information, die Wetternachrichten (*plur.*)

wedding, die Hochzeit, —, –en
Wednesday, der Mittwoch, –(e)s, –e
week, die Woche, —, –n; once (five times) a —, einmal (fünfmal) die Woche; a — ago, vor acht Tagen; a — from today, heute über acht Tage; he is going to the country **for** a —, er geht **auf** eine Woche aufs Land
weekly, wöchentlich
weep, weinen
welcome, begrüßen, freundlich empfangen (*str.*)
welfare (= prosperity), der Wohlstand, –(e)s
well, gut; wohl (*occurs only in a few set phrases as adv. of* well); I am very —, es geht mir sehr gut; did you sleep —?, haben Sie gut geschlafen?; fare you — (*or* farewell), leben Sie wohl!; sleep —, schlafen Sie wohl!
well-known, bekannt
well-meant, wohlgemeint
well off, wohlhabend
west, der Westen, –s; — of, westlich (*adj.*) von (*w. dat.*)
wet, naß
what (*inter.*), was; — is today's date?, der wievielte ist heute (*or* den wievielten haben wir heute)?; out of —?, woraus?; with —?, womit?; (*inter. adj.*) welcher, welche, welches; (*adj. in excls.*) welch; — a man!, welch ein Mann!; — time is it?, wieviel Uhr ist es?; — kind of, was für ein, (*pl.*) was für
whatever, was; was ... auch; — he says, was er auch sagt
wheel, das Rad, –(e)s, ̈er; (= bicycle) das (Fahr)rad
when, wann (*in both dir. & indir. ques.*); (= whenever) wenn; (*relating to one def. past action*) als; since —?, seit wann?

whenever, wenn
where, wo (*w. vb. of rest*); wohin (*w. vb. of motion*)
whether, ob
which, der, die, das; welcher, welche, welches; — one?, welcher?, welche?, welches?
while (*conj.*), während; indem
while (*noun*), die Weile, —; for a —, eine Zeitlang; a little — ago, vor kurzer Zeit (*or* vor kurzem)
whisper, flüstern
whistle, pfeifen, pfiff, gepfiffen
white, weiß
who (*inter.*), wer
whoever, wer; wer ... auch; — she may be, wer sie auch sein mag
whole, ganz
whom (*inter.*), wem (*dat.*), wen (*acc.*); (*rel.*) dem, der, dem, (*pl.*) denen (*dat.*); den, die, das, (*pl.*) die (*acc.*); (*or proper forms of* welcher)
whose (*inter.*), wessen; at — house?, bei wem?
whose (*rel.*), dessen, deren, dessen, (*pl.*) deren
why, warum
wide, weit; breit; a foot —, ein**en** Fuß breit
wife, die Frau, —, –en; die Gattin, —, –nen
wild, wild
will (*to form fut. tenses*), werden; (= to wish *or* be willing) wollen, wollte, gewollt, will
will, der Wille, –ns, –n
William, (der) Wilhelm, –s
win, siegen
wind, der Wind, –(e)s, –e
wind (*a watch*), aúfziehen (*str.*)
window, das Fenster, –s, —; to the —, ans Fenster; at the —, am Fenster; to look out of the —, zum Fenster hinaússehen
windy, windig
wine, der Wein, –(e)s, –e
wing, der Flügel, –s, —

winter, der Winter, –s, —; in —, im Winter

wise, weise, klug

wish (*noun*), der Wunsch, –es, ‑‑e

wish, wollen, wollte, gewollt, will; wünschen (*w. zu & dep. inf.*); (= to long for) sich sehnen nach

with (*prep.*), mit, bei (*both w. dat.*); to fall in love —, sich verlieben in (*w. acc.*); have you any money — you?, haben Sie etwas Geld bei sich?; — what?, womit?; — it, damit

within (*prep.*), innerhalb (*w. gen.*); — a short time, in kurzer Zeit

without (*prep.*), ohne (*w. acc.*)

witness, der Zeuge, –n, –n

wolf, der Wolf, –(e)s, ‑‑e

woman, die Frau, —, –en

wonderful, wunderbar

wood, das Holz, –es, ‑‑er

wooden, hölzern

word, das Wort, –(e)s, ‑‑er (*disconnected*) [*or* –e (*in connected discourse*)]; he keeps his —, er hält Wort

work (*noun*), die Arbeit, —, –en; das Werk, –(e)s, –e; Schiller's —s, Schillers Werke

work, arbeiten; to — hard, schwer (fleißig *or* tüchtig) arbeiten; to go to —, an die Arbeit gehen

world, die Welt, —, –en

world space (interplanetary *or* interstellar space), der Weltraum, –(e)s; — flight, der Weltraumflug, –(e)s, ‑‑e; — law, das Weltraum-Recht, –(e)s, –e; — radiation (*or* cosmic radiation), die Weltraumstrahlung, —; — traveler, der Weltraumfahrer, –s, —

worry about (= be anxious), sich (*dat.*) Sorgen machen um; (= to bother about) sich (*acc.*) kümmern um

worth (*adj.*), wert; it is — a dollar, es ist einen Dollar (*acc.*) wert; it

is not — while (*or* the trouble), es ist nicht der Mühe (*gen.*) wert; five marks' — of sugar, für fünf Mark Zucker

worth, der Wert, –(e)s, –e

worthy of, würdig (*w. gen.*)

would: — like, möchte (gern) (*w. inf.*); he — like to go to the theater, er möchte (gern) ins Theater gehen. (*English* would *is translated by the imperfect indicative if it refers to a customary past action.*)

wrap up, einwickeln; wrap it up in clean paper, wickeln Sie es in sauberes Papier ein!

write, schreiben, schrieb, geschrieben; to — on the (black)board, an die Tafel schreiben; to — to a person, schreiben (*w. dat. & no prep.*) [*or* schreiben an (*w. acc.*)]; I wrote my friend a letter, ich habe meinem Freund einen Brief geschrieben (*or* ich habe einen Brief an meinen Freund geschrieben)

writing (*noun*), das Schreiben, –s; — is difficult for him, das Schreiben ist (*or* fällt) ihm schwer

written (*adj.*), schriftlich

wrong: he is —, er hat unrecht

Y

yard (*court or space around a house*), der Hof, –(e)s, ‑‑e; (*measure*) das (*or* der) Meter, –s, — (= *39.37 inches*); die Elle, —, –n (*obs.*) (= $\frac{7}{10}$ *of an English yard*). (*Since it has no exact equivalent in modern German, English* yard *is sometimes translated by* eine englische Elle.)

year, das Jahr, –(e)s, –e; leap —, das Schaltjahr; the child is five —s old, das Kind ist fünf Jahre alt

yell, schreien, schrie, geschrie(e)n

yellow, gelb

yes, ja; — indeed, jawohl

yesterday, gestern; — evening, gestern abend; — morning, gestern **m**orgen; day before —, vorgestern

yet (*temp.*), noch; not —, noch nicht; (= nevertheless) doch

you, du, ihr, Sie (*nom.*); dir, euch, Ihnen (*dat.*); dich, euch, Sie (*acc.*)

young, jung

your (*poss. adj.*), dein, deine, dein (*sing. fam.*); euer, eu(e)re, euer (*pl. fam.*); Ihr, Ihre, Ihr (*formal*)

yours (*poss. pron.*), deiner, deine, deines; eurer, eure, eures; Ihrer, Ihre, Ihres (*cf.* **your**)

yourself (*refl. pron.*), dich, euch, sich (*all acc.*); dir, euch, sich (*all dat.*); (*intens.*) du, ihr, Sie selbst (*or* selber); you seat — (*or* sit down), du setzt dich, ihr setzt euch, Sie setzen sich; you flatter —, du schmeichelst dir, ihr schmeichelt euch, Sie schmeicheln sich

youth, die Jugend, —

Z

zeal, der Eifer, –s

zealous, eifrig

zero, die Null, —, –en

zero hour, die Angriffszeit, —; die Nullzeit, —

zoölogical, zoologisch; — garden, der Tiergarten, –s, ⸚; der zoologische Garten

zoölogy, die Zoologie, —; die Tierkunde, —

Index